RCAHMS

SOUTH-EAST
PERTH
an archaeological landscape

SOUTH-EAST PERTH

an archaeological landscape

ROYAL COMMISSION
ON THE ANCIENT
AND HISTORICAL
MONUMENTS
OF SCOTLAND
1994

CONTENTS

The Royal Commission on the Ancient and Historical Monuments of Scotland

PREFACE

The publication of *South-east Perth* completes the archaeological recording-programme whose object, when commenced in October 1986, was to survey the entire eastern portion of Perth and Kinross District, Tayside Region, and provides a companion volume to *North-east Perth: an archaeological landscape* (RCAHMS 1990). That volume marked a significant departure from many of the practices that have characterised Commission surveys over the last eighty years, and its preface drew attention to a number of fundamental changes in the approach to survey and publication. The most significant of these is the designation of the archives of the National Monuments Record of Scotland as the 'Inventory of Ancient and Historical Monuments and Constructions' whose compilation was entrusted by Royal Warrant to the Commissioners. Thus, the emphasis of the work in North-east and South-east Perth, and all future projects, lies in the enhancement of the Record, where all survey information is made available for public inspection.

North-east Perth presented a distillation of the descriptive material recorded in the course of the survey, organised within a framework similar to that of the old county Inventories, but viewing the archaeology as an element of the landscape. Internal review of that publication, and the difficulties of dealing with the cropmark evidence of this volume in terms of traditional archaeological categories, have led to a radical reappraisal of the Commission's approach to the contents of survey-publications. While the brief of survey remains the same — to identify, accurately map, describe, interpret and selectively illustrate the archaeological monuments of an area — the objectives of the publication have been refocussed, so as to characterise and interpret the archaeology. In this sense, the changes initiated by *North-east Perth* have been taken a stage further, and no attempt has been made in this volume to provide a detailed description of each site within the area of South-east Perth; that is the role of the Record-entries in the National Monuments Record of Scotland (which are available to the public for personal inspection, as well as by print-out or photocopy on application by post and telephone). The recorded evidence is discussed under major thematic headings and sub-headings, with additional sections setting the material in a wider context. Locational information and references for each of the known archaeological sites and monuments in the survey-area are provided in a brief gazetteer at the end of the volume.

The survey has been mainly concerned with archaeological evidence, and items included range from flint scatters of Mesolithic date to farmsteads abandoned in the last century. All sites and monuments that can be shown to date from before 1600 have been recorded, but thereafter the emphasis of the work has lain in the identification of the farmsteads and buildings of the pre-Improvement rural landscape. With the small numbers of staff available for the project, it has not been possible to quarter the ground exhaustively, or to walk arable fields in search of artefact scatters. Nevertheless, all the areas of the hills that have escaped modern cultivation have been examined by teams of two, and other likely areas of survival in the lowlands have been briefly inspected. For similar reasons, it has not been practical to record all the old trackways and the fragments of rig-systems that survive in the Sidlaws, although such remains have been noted in passing where they lie adjacent to other categories of recorded site, or have been revealed by oblique aerial photography. All structures shown roofed on the first edition of the OS 6-inch map (1860s) have been omitted, and no account has been taken of any remains of more recent date.

The bulk of the fieldwork took place in 1989, between March and November, but some additional site-visits were carried out in the summer of 1992. All the results of oblique aerial photography prior to April 1992 have been been examined in the course of the survey. The 1992 flying programme has produced remarkable results from many parts of Scotland, but, with the exception of the probable mortuary enclosures at Upper Gothens and Carsie Mains, it has not proved possible to incorporate the new material from South-east Perth into either the gazetteer or the distribution maps; for information about the latter, the reader is referred to forthcoming Catalogues of Aerial Photographs.

Fieldwork for the survey has been carried out by J Borland, BA, MAAIS, M M Brown, BA, DipArch, P Corser, BEd, DipArch, A J Leith, I G Parker, S P Halliday, BSc, G S Maxwell, MA, FSA, FRSA, J N G Ritchie, MA, PhD, FSA, S Scott, J R Sherriff, BA, AIFA, I M Smith, BA, PhD, J B Stevenson, BA, FSA, MIFA, J N Stevenson, NDD, and A R Wardell, MA. Aerial reconnaissance has been conducted by M M Brown and G S Maxwell, the majority of the photography falling to A G Lamb and A P Martin. The text has been written by P Corser, S P Halliday, G S Maxwell, J N G Ritchie, J R Sherriff, I M Smith and A R Wardell, with considerable word-processing assistance from C Allan and C C Buglass, and edited by G S Maxwell and S P Halliday, with the assistance of I Fisher, MA, FSA. The index has been prepared by E Gilfeather, Dip IntDes and S P Halliday. The drawings and other illustrative work have been undertaken by J Borland, H Graham, BA, A J Leith, K H J Macleod, BSc, MSc, HNC, S Scott and J N Stevenson. Ground photographs were taken by J Keggie and G B Quick. The layout of the volume has been prepared by E Gilfeather and J N Stevenson. The results of the survey have been incorporated into the National Monuments Record of Scotland by D Easton, BA, M M McDonald, MA, MSocSci, and R J Mowat, MA, DipSciArch.

The Commission wishes to acknowledge the assistance given by all the owners of the archaeological monuments, who have allowed access for study and survey. Particular thanks are also due to the following for assistance and information: G J Barclay Esq, Major P O Carmichael, M Cassels Esq, G Cox Esq, R R K Dalziel Esq, W Drummond-Moray Esq, Mrs E Easton (Meigle Museum), J B Farquhar Esq, M King Esq, Lord and Lady Kinnaird, Dr W Kinnear, the Marquis of Lansdowne, the Earl of Mansfield, Lady Robert Mercer Nairne, the Earl of Perth, Mrs Irvine Robertson, Lieutenant Commander A R Robinson and Lady Strange. We are indebted to the staffs of Aberdeen Anthropological Museum, Marischal College, Dundee Museum and Art Gallery, Glasgow Art Gallery and Museum, Historic Scotland, the National Museums of Scotland and Perth Museum for their much valued co-operation in the course of this survey.

Figure 26B is reproduced with the permission of Cambridge University Collection of Aerial Photographs; figure 114B, the Trustees of the National Library of Scotland; figures 115A and 116, the Keeper of the Records of Scotland, with the agreement of the Controller of Her Majesty's Stationery Office; figure 124, Historic Scotland; figures 22A & B, 23 and 133A, Perth Museum; and figure 139C, Perth and Kinross District Library.

EDITORIAL NOTES

The contents and layout of this volume are significantly different from those of previous archaeological survey-publications. The volume is divided into three main sections: the first discusses factors that have had a direct bearing on the state of the archaeological record in the area; the second deals with the recorded archaeology in thematic sections and sub-sections, each describing a different type of monument and supported by detailed distribution maps; and the third lists all the recorded sites.

The Text
Site-names: where these are highlighted by bold print in the text, a site-entry will be found in the appropriate section of the Gazetteer. Where a name is repeated in the volume, it is only highlighted if other names occur in the intervening text. All the site-names appear in the Index.

Radiocarbon Dates: these are quoted in uncorrected form (bc/ad).

Bibliographical References: Harvard-style short titles are used throughout the text and are expanded in the full bibliography at the end of the volume. The main body of the text contains only those references that are relevant to the specific points under discussion; general references for all the sites in South-east Perth can be found in the appropriate sections of the Gazetteer.

Margin References: the majority of these are to illustrations (see below), but a small number, prefixed by *p.* or *pp.*, provide cross-references to other sections of text.

The Gazetteer
The Gazetteer is a key component of the volume for the reader who wishes to discover further information about any of the sites or stray finds known from South-east Perth. Its organisation reflects the main headings under which the sites are dealt with in the text. With the exception of linear cropmarks, and the cropmarks of natural features, all the sites of South-east Perth recorded in the National Monuments Record of Scotland, together with the find-spots of artefacts dating from before the medieval period, will be found in the Gazetteer. A description of each of the sites will be found in the archive of the National Monuments Record of Scotland, where it can be identified by the unique record number (*e.g.* NO 14 SE 11) cited in the list. In the case of stray finds, museum accession numbers have also been included. An individual site may be identified in the Gazetteer by reference to the heading under which it is discussed, and then by alphabetical order of site-name; in some sections of the Gazetteer, particularly those dealing with artefacts, the entries have also been grouped by type. The reader is referred to the introduction to the Gazetteer (p.149) for further information concerning the structure of each entry.

The Index
This relates to both the main body of the text and the Gazetteer, allowing reference by site-classification, artefact-type or site-name.

Illustrations
All illustrations are classed as figures and are cited in the margins by the number of the page on which they appear, together with a letter suffix, where appropriate for further identification.

Figure-captions: each of these contains the name of the site and its National Grid Reference. Where a negative or original illustrative material is held by the National Monuments Record of Scotland, the appropriate number of the photograph or drawing in the archive is included (*e.g.* NMRS PT 1405). For drawings, the scale of reproduction is quoted as a representative fraction.

Distribution Maps: the distribution of each type of monument appears on a map of South-east Perth at a standard scale. While it has not proved possible to mark each of the sites mentioned in the text with a letter or number on the map, these may be identified from National Grid References provided in the appropriate section of the Gazetteer. Most of the visible sites and monuments have been plotted on a map at the beginning of the Gazetteer; the majority are in private ownership, and the visitor must seek permission for access locally.

Plans: these are derived from two sources: surviving earthworks have been surveyed in the field by plane table and self-reducing micropic alidade, whereas cropmark sites have been transcribed from oblique aerial photographs using computer-aided rectification techniques. While every effort has been made to ensure that the features of the latter are plotted at their correct positions, the metrical accuracy of the plots is dependent on the character of the control-points common to both the photographs and the Ordnance Survey maps, the accuracy of the map detail and local variations in the topography.

Copyright
Unless otherwise specified, the contents of this volume are Crown Copyright; copies of Commission photographs and drawings (individually identifiable by reference to the figure-caption; see above) can be purchased on application to:

The Secretary
The Royal Commission on the Ancient and
    Historical Monuments of Scotland
John Sinclair House
16 Bernard Terrace
Edinburgh EH8 9NX

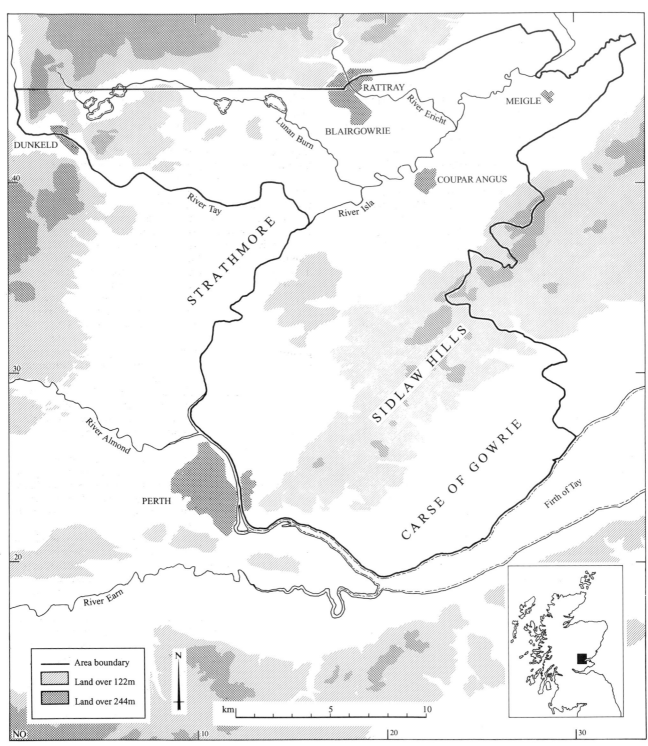

South-east Perth (NMRS DC 25009)

INTRODUCTION

The city of Perth occupies a commanding position in both the history and the geography of Scotland. Today, road and rail links tend to draw travellers past the ancient burgh, unaware of its key position on the banks of the River Tay. It may no longer be the lowest bridging point across the river, a role now assumed by Dundee, but, in the past, this stretch of the Tay was a vital crossing. The burgh itself lies at the highest navigable point on the river, an essential position for a town whose prosperity was to be founded on trade. In earlier times, the important fords, and possibly an earlier navigable limit too, may have lain a little further to the north, close to the confluence of the Tay and the Almond. This probably accounts for the position of the Roman fort of Bertha at the confluence of the two rivers. Indeed, the chain of Roman forts along the face of the Highlands, flanking, as it were, the legionary fortress at Inchtuthil some 12km to the north of Bertha, provides an apt parallel to the key strategic position occupied by Perth. Similar considerations may have underlain the selection of Scone as the place of assembly for the inauguration of Scottish kings.

Set at the south-western end of Strathmore, with the estuary of the Tay slicing deeply into the coast on the east, and the mountains rising up to the north and west, Perth commands the major routeways across Scotland to the north of the Forth and, like Stirling or Dumbarton, stands sentinel between the Highlands and the Lowlands. Strathmore may represent the widest natural corridor opening from Perth, but the others, though more restricted, are of equal significance: a narrow gap to the south-east between the Sidlaws and the Tay affords access to the Carse of Gowrie and the eastern coastal plain; the Tay and its tributaries give passage to Deeside on the north, to the Spey *via* the Drumochter Pass on the north-west and westward, by ridge-route and river-valley to Rannoch and Loch Fyne. Today, it is difficult to grasp the problems that beset early travellers in Scotland. The hills, bogs and rivers that were such obstacles in the past, exercise less restraint on modern transport-planners. Nevertheless, the topography of Scotland still dictates the basic outline of the transport-system and key strategic locations, such as Perth, retain their significance in the pattern of human geography.

While the strategic importance of Perth and its environs may not be so obvious today, for most people the area has strong literary or traditional associations. Who has not heard of the Stone of Scone, Macbeth and Dunsinane, or the Fair Maid of Perth? The mental image may spring from the writings of Scott or Shakespeare, or even folk-tale, but beneath all lies a stratum of reality; the element common to each is a statement about past political or social structures. In the pages of this survey will be found, as it survives, the archaeological record of these remote events and personages. Sometimes, as at Scone, the evidence is tenuous. Occasionally, as on Dunsinane Hill, the imagination has more to work on. Who could stand within the ramparts of this hilltop fort and not be struck by a sense of the past? Looking north-westward to Birnam and its long-vanished wood, 16km distant across the valley of the Tay, the view embraces some of the fairest and richest agricultural land in Scotland, a landscape of fields and woods interspersed with farms and villages.

It is this agricultural wealth that sets the seal on the importance of Perth's strategic position. Modern agricultural statistics (Coppock 1976) show that the soils around Perth will sustain a wide range of crops, and there is every reason to believe that this has always been the case. The landscape that has come down to us today, of course, has a long history of modification. The Improvements of the eighteenth and early nineteenth centuries saw a complete reorganisation, which created the pattern of fields, woods and rough pasture that is visible today. The extent of this reorganisation can only be gauged by comparing modern maps with General Roy's survey of the mid-eighteenth century (1747-55, sheets 17.2-3, 18.2-3). Despite the stylisation of his depiction, the map clearly shows that the pattern of arable fields sweeping unbroken across Strathmore is a relatively modern creation. Before the Improvements, the arable land was concentrated into discrete areas and these were separated by swathes of what was presumably rough pasture, moorland and bog. The Improvers drained the bogs and cleared the land, and little trace of these wastes now survives outside the areas of higher ground. The earlier pattern of concentrated farming activity interspersed with rough grazing and forest had probably been a characteristic of the landscape for several millennia. Roy's map thus provides a useful clue to the core areas of agricultural land, not only in the Medieval period, but probably in earlier periods too. If this land was able to support a substantial population in the eighteenth century, it would be reasonable to suppose that this was always the case. The very presence of a Roman garrison in strength in Strathmore between about AD 79 and 87, is itself an eloquent demonstration of a considerable prehistoric population living in the vicinity. This was a farming population who had already been exploiting the soils around Perth for some four thousand years.

Given the wealth of the landscape around Perth, the survey of its archaeology provides exciting possibilities for prehistorian and historian alike. It is an area that has sustained prosperous communities for at least six millennia, and numerous traces of their activities are preserved in the archaeological record. The present volume deals with an area of about 430 square kilometres to the east of Perth, and completes the campaign of survey work that was initiated in Glen Shee and Strathardle in 1986 and published in *North-east Perth: an archaeological landscape* (RCAHMS 1990). Bounded by the Tay to the south and west, and the district boundaries of Angus and the City of Dundee to the east, South-east Perth provides the perfect foil to the glens and heather-clad moors to the north. Where heather gives way to grass and crops, roughly along a line coinciding with the escarpment on the north-west side of Strathmore, the character of the archaeology appears to change dramatically. The distribution of hut-circles and clearance heaps that characterise the archaeology of the moors ends abruptly at the edge of the heather, and the same is apparently true of the upland farmsteads and fermtouns. A major objective of this survey has been to examine this boundary, to determine whether it is real or apparent.

The topography of South-east Perth provides a stark contrast to that of North-east Perth. In the latter, the geology is dominated by the hard metamorphic rocks that have given rise to the Grampian Highlands. The south-eastern boundary of these rocks is formed by the great Highland Boundary Fault, a major fault-line extending from Stonehaven in the north-east to Rothesay on the Isle of Bute in the south-west. In eastern Perth the line of the Highland Boundary Fault runs from Alyth to Stenton, about 5km to the east of Dunkeld, and is marked by the escarpment that forms the north-western side of Strathmore. To the south-east of the fault-line the rocks are predominately of Old Red Sandstone Age. The majority are relatively soft sediments, but they also include harder lavas and tuffs. The major axis of folding of the underlying tectonic structures lies parallel to the Highland Boundary Fault and is ultimately responsible for the marked grain of the country running from north-east to south-west across the area. Differential erosion across the strata that have been thrown up in these structures has created three topographical zones within the area surveyed: Strathmore on the north-west; the Sidlaw Hills in the centre; and the Carse of Gowrie along the northern shore of the Firth of Tay on the south-east.

Strathmore

The underlying geology of Strathmore mainly consists of soft sandstones. These have been heavily eroded by fluvio-glacial action to create the broad, open valley that extends from the River Tay to the Mearns. This part of Strathmore is drained south-westwards by the River Isla, whose main tributary, the River Ericht, drains much of the area surveyed to the north, cutting through the line of the Highland Boundary Fault in a deep gorge to the north of Blairgowrie and then meandering eastwards to join the Isla at Coupar Grange. The Lunan Burn follows a similar pattern, flowing through a string of small lochs to the west of Blairgowrie.

The floor of the valley undulates gently, much of it lying between 40m and 100m OD, but the ground rises into a series of low, rounded hills towards the south-west. The underlying rocks are largely masked by fluvio-glacial deposits, whose composition varies from sands and gravels to heavy clays. These have given rise to a range of soil types with different characteristics and have been described extensively by the Soil Survey of Scotland (1982). The soils derived from the sands and gravels are freely draining, whereas those developed on clays tend to retain water and are more difficult to work agriculturally. By and large, the principal freely-draining soil types lie between the middle of Strathmore and the line of the Highland Boundary Fault, the less freely-draining soils lying to the south-east and rising up to the lower slopes of the Sidlaws. The latter soils, however, have been extensively improved since the beginning of the nineteenth century and now make up about three-quarters of the Class 2 agricultural land in this part of Strathmore. Land in this category, which is capable of sustaining a wide range of crops and high yields, forms a broad band running along the axis of the valley. The soils with a clay component are less susceptible to drought and are more able to retain plant nutrients. Intensive cultivation is by no means restricted to the Class 2 land, however, and adjacent areas of Class 3 land, notably to the west of Blairgowrie, are also regularly cropped.

The Sidlaw Hills

The Sidlaws are composed of hard lavas and tuffs, which form the south-eastern bulwark of Strathmore and extend south-westwards through the Ochil Hills to Stirling. The River Tay has broken through this rocky barrier immediately south of Perth, forcing its way to the sea through a fairly narrow cleft, the northern side of which swings north-eastwards to form the Sidlaw escarpment overlooking the Carse of Gowrie; the hills here climb steeply from the Carse, attaining heights in excess of 100m OD within the space of no more than 500m. On their north-west flank, the Sidlaws shelve more gradually from heather-clad moors on the higher ridges to the arable fields of Strathmore. Few of the hills rise above 250m OD, however, the highest being King's Seat above Collace at 377m OD. The glaciation of the hard strata has created a fairly broken landscape with a range of topographical features embracing rounded hills and high crags, but it has also produced a series of passes which traverse the hills from east to west. Many of the hills are covered with shallow, stony drift derived from the hard parent material, and this has given rise to freely-draining soils throughout much of the area. Consequently, only the highest of the hills have escaped modern pasture improvement, and many of the lower slopes are under intensive cultivation.

The Carse of Gowrie

The Carse of Gowrie has long been known as the Garden of Scotland, but its older character is perhaps best expressed by its place-names, many of which contain some watery connotation. Names like Bogmiln and Waterybutts imply a fairly damp environment, although those with the prefix or suffix 'inch' (= island) suggest the presence of some more favourable locations. The Carse is essentially an area of low-lying clays, above which rise the 'inches', slightly elevated banks and ridges of sand and gravel. Both types of deposit owe their origin to the complex inter-relationships between glacial erosion and the relative levels of land and sea in the post-Glacial Period. The underlying rocks of the Upper Old Red Sandstone were gouged out by glaciation to create a deep trough, which, in common with other low-lying areas along the eastern seaboard of Scotland, was submerged from about 7000 BC by a marine transgression. With the rise in sea level, the area of the Carse developed an estuarine environment. Much of the hollow was gradually infilled with silts and clays brought down by the River Tay, but substantial beach deposits of sands and gravels were also laid down, and these came to form the 'inches'. By about 3500 BC the sea was in retreat and, relieved of the immense burden of the ice sheets, the isostatic recovery of land levels gradually raised the Carse above the high watermark. Nevertheless, the clays would have remained wet and liable to flooding for a considerable period of time, and the pattern of intense agricultural exploitation that is evident today has only come about through extensive drainage. Even now the clays are difficult to work. It is a matter of some interest when these soils were first brought under cultivation, but, despite the evidence of intensive settlement of all periods around the edges of the Carse and on the 'inches', little has been recovered from the clays. The problems of recovering archaeological evidence from such areas is discussed further in another section. Nevertheless, it is likely that the first extensive drainage schemes were initiated by the Cistercians from Coupar Angus, who had several holdings around Grange, and by the eighteenth century most of the area was already under plough (Roy 1747-55). Suffice it to say, that the place-names hint at a locally unattractive environment for agricultural settlement persisting until quite recently, although it may have provided quite adequate support for a more mixed economy, geared to exploiting the natural resources that coastal wetlands would have offered in abundance. With the exception of a crannog (an artificial island) at Kinfauns, however, and log-boats found at Errol, the archaeological record has little to say about this possibility.

Hallyards (NO 2790 4642), the flood-waters around the moated site showing the low-lying character of parts of Strathmore (NMRS A 72327)

THE NATURE OF THE EVIDENCE

This section attempts to review the sources of information that are available for South-east Perth. It examines the antiquarian traditions in the area and discusses the relationship of modern land-use to patterns of monument survival and destruction, considering how the application of different recording techniques is reflected in the results of the survey. Inevitably, in an area of rich agricultural land, the problems and constraints of aerial photographic evidence are an important aspect of the discussion.

THE ANTIQUARIAN TRADITION

The traditions of archaeological survey work in South-east Perth are themselves now of considerable antiquity. The earthworks of the Roman fortress at **Inchtuthil** were known to Hector Boece in the sixteenth century (1526, iv, 14), even if then identified as a Pictish town, and the footsteps of a series of later antiquaries can be traced to and fro across the county. The main incentive for their labours, especially in the early days, was undoubtedly provided by the Roman occupation and, more particularly, by the account of Agricola's conquest of northern Britain written by Tacitus. The detailed descriptions of Agicola's campaigns, culminating in his victory over the Caledonians at Mons Graupius in AD 84, have excited the imagination for centuries and the quest for the battlefield continues to this day (Maxwell 1990). The kindling of antiquarian interest in the structures and artefacts of the prehistoric period was to come later, and its gradual growth in South-east Perth parallels that observed with reference to Scotland as a whole (Graham 1973; Maxwell 1993).

These antiquarian studies cast little light on the archaeology of South-east Perth until the middle of the eighteenth century. Alexander Gordon, for instance, whose description of Roman remains in Scotland represented such a significant step forward in Roman studies in the early eighteenth century (Maxwell 1989, 7), passed through the survey-area with few comments. 90A-B. 94B-D. 98-102. He was content to place Mons Graupius in Strathearn and, pausing briefly at the carved stones in **Meigle** (1726, 162), continued north-eastwards on his journey. It was left to Robert Melville and William Roy to pursue the Roman armies up Strathmore some thirty years later. The occasion for this leap forward was provided by the military survey of Scotland in the wake of the 1745 rebellion. Although familiarly known as Roy's map, this massive undertaking was born of the initiative of Lieutenant-Colonel David Watson, an engineer officer faced with a programme of road- and fort-construction and a dearth of adequate maps (Seymour 1980, 4-5). Roy was an Assistant Quartermaster to Watson and was given the task of preparing the map. His interest in antiquities was first aroused in 1752, but it was not until 1755, left in charge by Watson, that he embarked on a detailed survey of any of the Roman earthworks. In that year, Roy not only directed his survey teams to prepare a detailed plan of the Antonine Wall and its stations, but he also spent part of the summer in Strathmore. The inspiration for this work appears to stem from Melville, then a captain in the 25th Foot, who had discovered the remains of four Roman temporary camps the year before. The camps at Kirkbuddo, 3A. Keithock and Oathlaw lie in Angus but the fourth, at **Lintrose**, falls within the bounds of South-east Perth. These discoveries were the result of a classic piece of archaeological detective work: dissatisfied with Gordon's placing of the defeat of the Caledonian army in Strathearn, Melville set off up Strathmore to 'make enquiries and searches, especially in heaths and uncultivated places' (Stuart 1870a, 29-30) along what he considered to be the most likely line of advance.

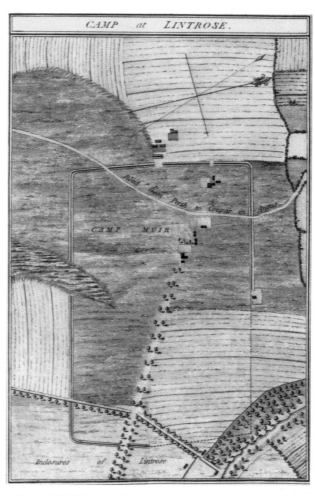

*A. **Lintrose** (NO 2200 3760), plan of the Roman temporary camp by Roy (1793, pl.xiv)*

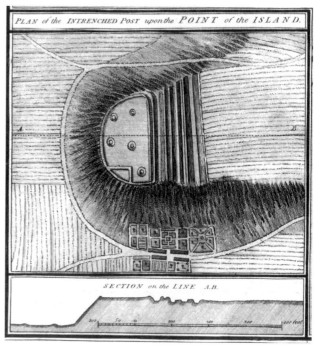

*B. **Inchtuthil** (NO 1150 3928), plan of the native fort by Roy (1793, pl.xviii)*

Roy's archaeological work was not published until after his
death, but the illustrations of **Lintrose** and **Inchtuthil** in his
Military Antiquities (1793, plates xiv, xviii) date from the 1755
survey campaign. They provide the first detailed records of
earthworks in South-east Perth and their surrounding landscape.
The survey of Inchtuthil also includes a detail of the native fort
that lies to the west of the legionary fortress. Once fired, Roy's
interest was to last the rest of his life and he carried out further
surveys in Scotland in 1764, 1769 and 1771. On the last of
these trips he searched for a temporary camp at the crossing of
the Tay opposite Bertha and was rewarded with the discovery
of **Grassy Walls**, on the east bank of the river, within South-
east Perth. In both Melville and Roy we find military minds
applied to military problems, but we can also detect the kindred
spirit of a field archaeologist. Melville's emphasis on heaths
and uncultivated places is immediately familiar and is echoed
by Roy's pessimism at the chances of locating a camp in the
vicinity of **Coupar Angus**: 'The country hereabouts is too
much cultivated to suffer us to expect any remains of
intrenchments so very temporary in their nature' (Roy 1793,
85).

It is unfortunate that the standards of observation and
recording set by Roy were not matched until the preparation of
the first edition of the large-scale Ordnance Survey maps in the
second half of the nineteenth century. By then the landscape
portrayed by Roy's plans had largely vanished and traces of
numerous sites far slighter than the temporary camps had
probably been swept away. The earthworks of some early
settlements must have survived on the moors in the middle of
Strathmore up until the agricultural improvements of the late
eighteenth century but hardly any record of their existence
survives. Exceptionally, however, an account of the parish of
Alyth dating from 1727 mentions the 'vestiges of an old Pictish
toun about a quarter of a mile in length which appears from the
ruines of their buildings' (Macfarlane 1906, 114); unfortunately
nothing of this site can now be seen.

This is not to say that knowledge of archaeological sites did
not exist locally. It is noticeable, for instance, that of the four
Roman camps found by Melville, three are commemorated in
local place-names — Battledykes at Keithock and Oathlaw, and
Camp Muir at **Lintrose**; Roy's discovery at **Grassy Walls** may
be another example. Other sites must have been known, but in
the days before the Ordnance Survey there was no uniform
mechanism for graphically or toponymically conveying their
location. For South-east Perth a certain amount of information
can be gleaned from the pages of Thomas Pennant's tour of
1772, but only for the more obvious and imposing monuments.
The cairns and standing stone to the south of Meigle at
Belmont Castle caught his attention, along with the **Meigle**
carved stones; he provides an early description of the fort on
Dunsinane Hill and, perhaps inevitably, a plan of **Inchtuthil**
(Pennant 1776, 67-70, 175-80).

The first opportunity for comment on the antiquities in the
country at large only comes with the preparation of the
Statistical Account at the end of the eighteenth century. By then
the Improvements were in full swing and it is possible to sense
the changes that were being wrought upon the landscape. The
account for Scone mentions that 'From those rough grounds
and moorlands, which within a few years have been converted
into beautiful and fertile corn-fields' and observes later that 'a
great part of the parish is inclosed; and, on some farms, young
hedges of hawthorn are raising' *(Stat. Acct.*, 18 [1796], 73, 75).
As one might expect, the more imposing monuments stood a
better chance of survival, and it is hardly surprising that these
are the sites that are mentioned in the parish descriptions. The
contents of the accounts, however, depended on the interests of
the author, who was usually the minister, but in one instance in
South-east Perth, the entry for Collace, simply 'A friend to
Statistical Inquiries'. The entries for four of the parishes in the
Carse of Gowrie contain no archaeological information at all
and two others only mention the ruins of castles. In Strathmore,
however, the situation is rather different, and most of the

ministers appear to have had a much greater awareness of their
heritage. In part this may be the legacy of the survey work of
Roy and the travels of Pennant, but it must also reflect the
influence of James Playfair, later to become the principal of St
Andrews University but then described by a fellow minister as
'the ingenious antiquary' (*Stat. Acct.,* 9 [1793], 259).

Playfair wrote the accounts for both Meigle and Bendochy
but his presence can be detected much further afield. He is
recorded as excavating in the fort on Dunsinane Hill in Collace,
and also in the Haer Cairns near Middle Mause on the hills to
the north (RCAHMS 1990, 18, no.23). His abiding passion,
however, was provided by Mons Graupius, which he believed
had been fought in the vicinity of Stormont to the south-west of
Blairgowrie. The Buzzart Dykes, a medieval deer park on
Middleton Muir (RCAHMS 1990, 93-4, no.216), was the
Caledonian camp, and the dead were buried in the cairns that
litter the surrounding moors (see Maxwell 1990, 76-7 for a
fuller account). He had a first-hand knowledge of the
description of Agricola's campaigns and was well acquainted
with the opinions of later historians on the site of the battle. He
set out his views in a long footnote to the account of Bendochy
(*Stat. Acct.,* 19 [1797], 367-71) and was clearly the moving
influence behind a similar footnote appended to the account of
William M'Ritchie for Clunie (*Stat. Acct.,* 9 [1793], 259-64).
Of more direct interest are Playfair's detailed description of
several souterrains discovered at **Mudhall** to the north of
Coupar Angus (*Stat. Acct.,* 19 [1797], 359-60) and some of the
other references to cairns, standing stones and stone circles that
are to be found in the accounts for other parishes. His
neighbour John Ritchie, who wrote the accounts for both
Coupar Angus and Kettins, mentions two cairns near **Pitcur**,
one estimated as being 1000 cart loads of stones in size and
containing a cist, and the other covering an urn (*Stat. Acct.,* 17
[1796], 17); neither site can be located now. But Ritchie also
tells us that there are no 'Roman ways or Druidical circles' in
either parish, clearly indicating some knowledge of the
antiquities to be found elsewhere in Strathmore. What was then
supposed to be a Roman road running north-eastwards from
Grassy Walls is referred to in the accounts of Scone, St
Martins and Cargill.

The *Statistical Account* is a vitally important document,
providing almost the sole source of information for sites that
were being destroyed in the course of the Improvements. Its
references to the discovery of cists and burials found in cairns
signal the removal of these monuments, either to provide stone
for the new enclosures or simply to clear obstructions from the
new fields. Some survived long enough to appear on the early
OS maps, but others have been lost for ever. Following on from
the *Statistical Account* there are few contemporary descriptions
of local discoveries until the preparation of the *New Statistical
Account*. With the exception of one written in 1833 and later
revised, all these later parish accounts for South-east Perth date
from the period 1837-43. They draw heavily on the earlier
parish descriptions but every single one contains some
information about local antiquities. They constitute particularly
important records of the discovery of cists and burials and
provide a major source for the inclusion of this material in the
first edition of the OS 6-inch maps, which for South-east Perth
date from the 1860s. The lists of names prepared by the
surveyors for each parish, the Original Name Books, also
contain details of archaeological discoveries, whose
cartographic presentation was now, for the first time, set within
an accurate topographic framework at a uniform scale.

This was a period of considerable development for
antiquarian studies generally, although the sudden access of
cartographic information is not matched by any increase in
private antiquarian activity in the landscape of South-east
Perth. At about this time, Daniel Wilson coined the term
prehistory (1851; 1863), bringing reasoned order to Scottish
archaeological collections, and the inauguration of the
Proceedings of the Society of Antiquaries of Scotland in 1851
provided a channel for publication and communication. It is

St Madoes *(NO 1966 2119), Pictish cross-slab (NMRS B 1443)*

student of these carvings today. Of greater importance for the recording of field monuments are David Christison and Fred Coles, whose work helped to precipitate the establishment of the Royal Commission on the Ancient and Historical Monuments of Scotland. Christison first embarked on a study of forts and earthworks in Peeblesshire in 1885-6 and progressively extended his survey over much of Scotland during the next twenty years, publishing descriptions for the examples in South-east Perth in 1900. Coles systematically examined the sites of stone circles over a similar period, but concentrated his efforts in southern and eastern Scotland; he published his accounts of the stone circles of South-east Perth in 1909. It is interesting to note that in both cases the surveys are written commentaries on the monuments shown on Ordnance Survey maps; indeed, the maps played a crucial role in the preparation of Christison's plans (1894, vi-viii).

In the field of Roman studies a rather different step forward was being taken, and the 1890s were to see Roman archaeology come of age, with programmes of excavation along the Antonine Wall and in the forts to both the north and the south. The stimulus for this step came from developments on Hadrian's Wall and the frontier in Germany (Maxwell 1989, 12-13). First in the field were the Glasgow Archaeological Society, but they were shortly followed by the Society of Antiquaries of Scotland, whose campaign of excavations tackled a series of the key structures. One of these was **Inchtuthil** in 1901, where Lord Abercromby not only directed the excavation of the legionary fortress but also examined the native fort to the west. These campaigns of excavation put the study of Roman archaeology on to an entirely new footing, a footing furthermore which has continued to develop throughout the present century. The ramifications of this work were considerably wider, however, for by then it was evident that excavation was the only way forward for prehistoric archaeology. Christison, for instance, writing the annual report for the Society of Antiquaries of Scotland in 1899, commented "I could almost regret that the Society have undertaken the excavation of Roman 'Camps' in preference to our own Native Forts. The secrets that lie beneath the ruins of the Caterthuns, Dunsinnan, and hundreds of other native fortresses, are no less worthy of being brought to light than the relics left behind by the Romans" (*Proc Soc Antiq Scot,* 34 [1900], 12). Having just completed his survey of the forts of Perthshire (1900), the discovery by earlier excavators of buried structures at **Dunsinane Hill** was perhaps uppermost in his mind.

With the completion of Coles' survey of the stone circles of the area the archaeological work in South-east Perth is reduced to brief reports on the chance discoveries of cists and burials and the occasional foray of Roman archaeologists. In 1939 Sir Ian Richmond cut trenches across the **Cleaven Dyke**, a massive linear earthwork which had been known since the eighteenth century to the east of **Inchtuthil**, and, together with James McIntyre, excavated the Roman watch-tower on **Black Hill** a little further to the south-east (Richmond 1940). However, the opportunities for discovering upstanding archaeological sites in South-east Perth were severely restricted by patterns of arable land-use in the area, and until different methods of detection became available there was little that could be done in the area by fieldwork. Fortunately techniques of aerial prospection for buried archaeological sites were being developed. It would be no exaggeration to say that aerial photography since the 1920s has revolutionised the archaeology of Lowland Britain, and it has certainly made a major contribution to the present survey of South-east Perth. The first aerial photographic sorties flown in Scotland were by OGS Crawford and, at about the same time, Wing-Commander Insall (Maxwell 1990, 93). It was not until June 1939, however, when Crawford made a second flight in the course of his duties for the Ordnance Survey, that any significant discoveries were made (Crawford 1939, 280-92). A brief trip up Strathmore revealed the Roman fort at Cardean just across the Perthshire border into Angus. Shortly afterwards, in 1941, Eric Bradley, a Royal Air Force instructor,

also a period which sees the emergence of the first parish and county histories, many of which are still important sources of historical information today. Andrew Jervise's *Memorials of Angus and the Mearns* (1861) is one of the best examples, together with the slightly later *Angus or Forfarshire* by Alexander Warden (1880-5). Both these, however, deal with the neighbouring county of Angus and there is little else covering the parishes of South-east Perth until a considerably later date. Nevertheless, John Stuart is to be found recording Pictish monuments at **Dunkeld**, **Keillor**, **Kettins**, **Meigle**, **Rossie** and **St Madoes** at about this time (1867), and James Simpson some of the cupmarked stones of the area (1868). Cists and other incidental discoveries are also reported at irregular intervals, but it is not until the end of the century that any of the field monuments were subjected to systematic study.

These systematic studies stemmed from two sources. The first was from a trend towards catalogues of archaeological material, which was spilling over from museum collections into the field at the end of the nineteenth century, and the second was from developments in Roman archaeology. Again Pictish stones figure in these studies, the survey conducted by Romilly Allen in the 1890s producing a classic work of reference (Allen and Anderson 1903) which is still essential reading for the

5. 95-103.

78. 52A.
91A.

56. 73B.

26B. 27.

85C.

made the first aerial discoveries in South-east Perth. He
recorded part of the temporary camp at **Grassy Walls**, the
camp enclosing the curious earthworks known as **Steeds Stalls**
on the Hill of Gourdie and the forts at **Cargill** (Crawford 1949,
66, 76, 79-80). These were by no means the first cropmarks
identified in South-east Perth, however, for Graham Callander
had identified the line of the ditch on the eastern side of the
camp at **Grassy Walls** in a field of wheat in August 1917
(Callander 1919b).

    The Roman frontier in Scotland has always exerted a
powerful attraction and it should come as no surprise that
Crawford's initial flights were directed along Roman roads.
After the end of the Second World War in 1945, archaeological
flying in Britain rapidly expanded, leading to the establishment
of a curator in aerial photography at the University of
Cambridge in 1948 and the appointment of a Committee for
Aerial Photography in the following year. Given the distance of
Cambridge from Scotland, it is perhaps fortunate that the newly
appointed curator, JKS St Joseph, was so interested in the
exploration of the frontier of Rome's northernmost province.
His dedication to this task led him across **Inchtuthil** and up
Strathmore in virtually every year from 1945 to 1980 (Pitts and
St Joseph 1985, 49), revealing stunning detail of the interior
of the fortress and of a series of adjacent temporary camps. His
flying, however, is of greater significance than simply
recording the sites of Roman earthworks that had been erased
by centuries of ploughing. For the first time, traces of
prehistoric settlements began to emerge from the arable fields
of South-east Perth.

    The photographs taken of Inchtuthil in 1949, which revealed
traces of the bedding trenches of timber buildings within the
interior, paved the way for a project conceived as early as 1937.
Sir Ian Richmond, fresh from his campaign of excavations at
Fendoch at the mouth of the Sma' Glen, recognised that
Inchtuthil offered an opportunity that was unique in Britain.
Here was a legionary fortress, occupied only briefly, whose
entire plan could be recovered by a judicious campaign of
exploratory trenching. Fourteen seasons of excavation were
carried out from 1952 to 1965 under the direction of Richmond
and St Joseph (St Joseph and Pitts 1985, 49-50). Although
principally aimed at delineating the Roman features, the
excavation also revealed several prehistoric structures,
including a rectangular enclosure now known to be Neolithic in
date (Barclay and Maxwell 1992). The project also had the
effect of placing Inchtuthil on any archaeological flight path
into the north-east of Scotland, and this is partly responsible for
the cluster of cropmark sites known in the vicinity.

    The pioneering work of St Joseph in Scotland pointed to the
immense potential of areas like South-east Perth, but this
potential could not be fully realised from a base in the south of
England. In 1975 aerial reconnaissance became a regular part
of the work of the Royal Commission on the Ancient and
Historical Monuments of Scotland and has led to a mass of new
data. In South-east Perth the vast bulk of the archaeological
sites for which we have evidence of surviving remains, whether
they be visible or invisible on the ground, have been recorded
by aerial photography. On the one hand they include familiar
types of site such as the ditches of ploughed-down forts, but on
the other there are structures which bear little comparison to
sites surviving on the Sidlaws or the hills to the north.

    However, fieldwork since the war has by no means been
limited to aerial photography. Indeed, the post-war archaeology
of Perthshire was dominated by Margaret Stewart, who settled
in Perth after her marriage and for thirty years acted as an
unofficial 'county archaeologist'. Over the years she carried out
numerous surveys and rescue excavations, several of them in
South-east Perth. She was also active behind the scenes
encouraging others to undertake work in the county and, for a
time, was one of the most vigorous Local Correspondents for
the Ordnance Survey, adding innumerable sites and comments
to the 6-inch maps provided by the OS. Thematic survey in the
tradition of Christison and Coles, was continued by FT

Wainwright, who published *The Souterrains of Southern
Pictland* in 1963, but, as a whole, the few surviving sites of
South-east Perth did not lend themselves to extensive field
campaigns. This situation is only now beginning to change as a
result of the stimulus provided by aerial photography. The large
numbers of cropmark sites have transformed a somewhat
lacklustre archaeological picture into one of Scotland's more
exciting prehistoric and medieval landscapes.

PATTERNS OF LAND-USE

The role of land-use, principally agriculture, in the survival,
destruction and discovery of archaeological sites will already
have become evident from the review of the history of
fieldwork in South-east Perth. As we have seen, both Melville
and Roy realized in the eighteenth century that they must look
in the gaps between the fields if they were to discover the
earthworks of Roman camps in Strathmore. Conversely, most
of the earlier discoveries of other types of site were made by
destructive disturbance of the landscape. Many cists and burials
or souterrains, for instance, have only come to light through
ploughing in fields, or digging in cairns and natural features for
stones, sand and gravel. Here, in a nutshell, are the reasons why
patterns of land-use in an area, both at the present day and over
the relatively recent past, should be examined in some detail.
The pattern of land-use which creates the opportunity for
discovery of one type of site may be removing the opportunity
for another.

    The modern patterns of land-use in South-east Perth present
a complete contrast to those of North-east Perth. The major
form of land-use is arable agriculture, with large areas of
Strathmore and the Carse of Gowrie regularly under crop. The
greater part of the area is made up of land identified by the Soil
Survey of Scotland (1982) as Classes 2 and 3.1, and is capable
of sustaining high yields in a variety of crops. For the purposes
of the survey, the difference between the two is only the greater
flexibility of the Class 2 land, allowing the regular cultivation
of a wider range of crops. Land of these two classes is by no
means limited to the lower ground of Strathmore and the Carse
of Gowrie, and the Class 3.1 land sweeps up on to the Sidlaws.
Indeed, there is little ground on the Sidlaws that does not fall
into a category capable of reclamation and improvement.
Consequently, only the summits of the highest hills have
escaped the plough since the initiation of the agricultural
Improvements at the end of the eighteenth century.

    It is, of course, the Improvements that have set the physical
framework within which modern land-use is practised. This
was a period of immense change in the landscape, which saw
the old order almost entirely swept away. The whole landscape
was taken in hand: the bogs and wastes were drained and
broken into cultivation; enclosures spread their net across the
countryside; and the new fields were interwoven with
decorative plantations and more practical shelter-belts.

    Patterns of land-use before the Improvements are more
difficult to gauge. The only visual record of the landscape is
provided by Roy's map (1747-55), which provides an
impression of the pre-Improvement farms and fermtouns sitting
amongst their unenclosed fields. Around Errol and Megginch in
the Carse of Gowrie some extensive areas of enclosures had
already been laid out across the earlier pattern of unenclosed
rigs, and a few plantations of woodland are in evidence across
the area as a whole. Although the detail of the original map
cannot be directly overlaid on to the modern map, the extent of
agricultural land has been roughly transcribed. It shows that at
this date the main weight of cultivation lay on the Carse of
Gowrie and between Blairgowrie and Coupar Angus.
Elsewhere, there is a more broken pattern, the blocks of fields
interspersed with areas of rough grazing. The approximate
nature of the transcription does not allow direct comparisons
with the site distributions that have been recovered in the

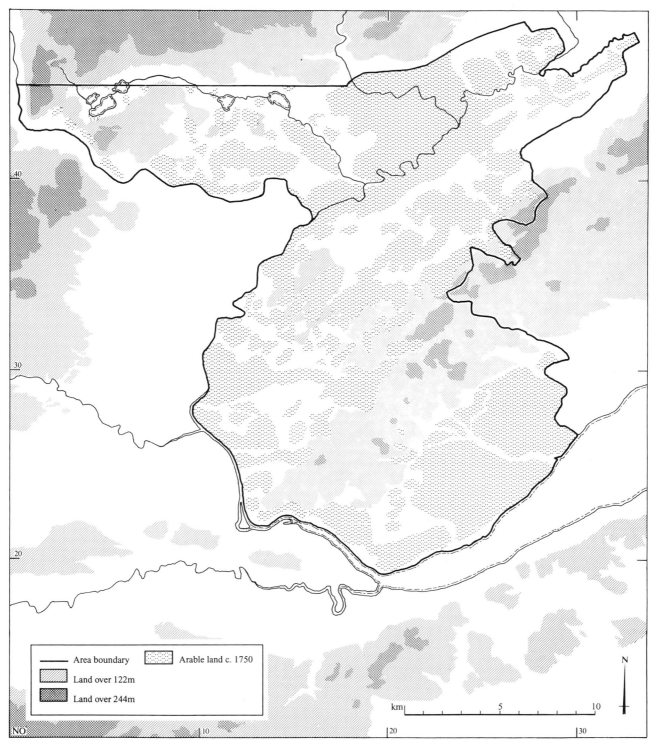

Legend:
- Area boundary
- Land over 122m
- Land over 244m
- Arable land c. 1750

N

km | 5 | 10

NO | 10 | 20 | 30

Distribution map of arable land c. 1750 (NMRS DC 25010)

8. 9.   course of the survey. Nevertheless, the map provides an
important reference point when the patterns of survival and
destruction are considered for sites that were almost all
discovered long after the Improvements had begun.

    To a certain extent the pattern presented by Roy must reflect
a much earlier organisation of the landscape. By his time most
of the better-drained soils were under plough and these
probably represent core areas of medieval cultivation.
Nevertheless, considerable changes must have taken place since
the medieval period, and the evidence of extensive rig

122.   cultivation on the hills strongly suggests at least one major
phase of expansion — and subsequent contraction — of
settlement and agricultural land. The Carse too, must have been
an area of change, the pattern of cultivation in the mid-
eighteenth century being the culmination of a process of

improvement initiated by the monks of Coupar Angus in the
twelfth century.

SURVIVAL, DESTRUCTION AND DISCOVERY

Modern field survey can only discover sites and monuments in
so far as the history of land-use has allowed them to survive.
The gaps between the blocks of fields depicted on Roy's map
certainly suggest that there was considerable potential for
upstanding monuments to have survived in many parts of the
lowlands right up to the Improvements. It would be too

7

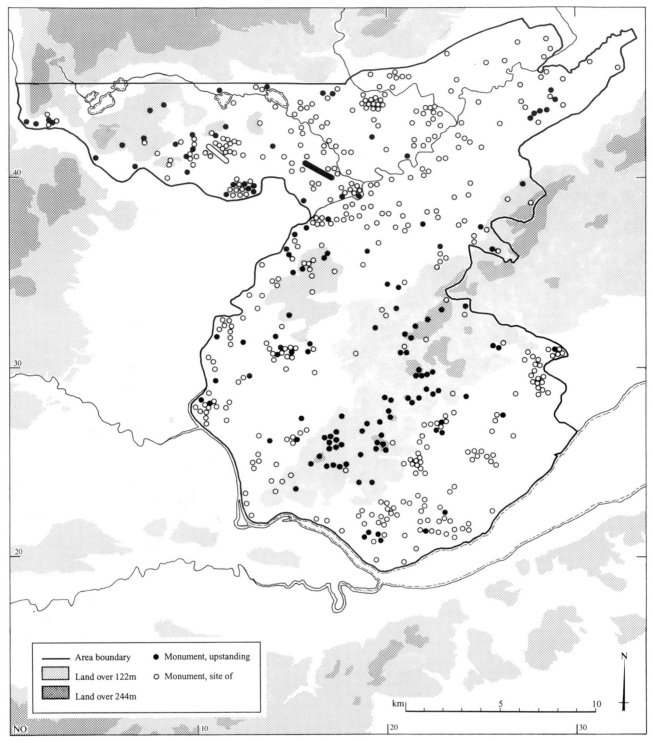

Distribution map of recorded archaeological monuments (NMRS DC 25011)

simplistic, however, to assert that the changes in agricultural practices and organisation at the end of the eighteenth century are entirely to blame for the comparative dearth of field monuments in South-east Perth today. As will emerge, more complex patterns are detectable in the discovery of different categories of site. That said, modern land-use regimes in South-east Perth have left very little scope for the terrestrial surveyor to discover upstanding remains of any period, either on the Sidlaws or in the adjacent lowlands. By comparison with the hills of North-east Perth, the Sidlaws are virtually empty.

8. The overall pattern of survival and destruction can be shown by mapping the sites in terms of those that survive as upstanding monuments and those that are invisible on the ground. Sites of all periods are included on the map, but castles and churches, which were exclusively built in the lowlands,

have been omitted in the interests of clarity. The category of invisible sites is largely made up of cropmarks, cist discoveries, and upstanding monuments that are known to have been removed, but it also includes four collections of stone tools which have been picked up from the surfaces of arable fields. The most striking aspect of the map is the distribution of invisible sites, which are concentrated on land below 122m OD, with a thin scatter extending up on to the hills. These invisible sites are in effect an index of the intensity of agricultural exploitation in the lowlands. The cropmarks included in the category are of course a direct reflection of regular cultivation, but many of the other invisible sites were also found or destroyed through agricultural activity over the past 200 years. Despite the broad correlation between the intensity of arable agriculture in the lowlands and levelled

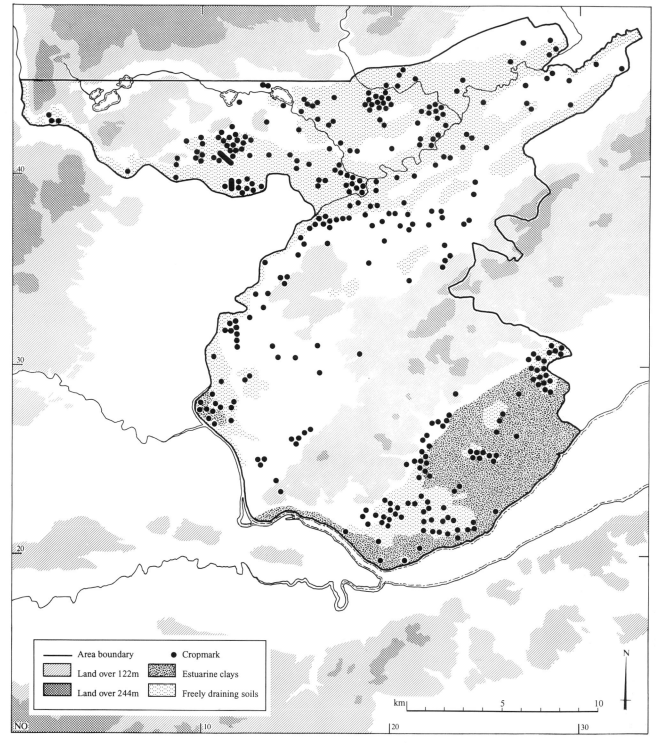

Distribution map of cropmarkings and selected soil-types (NMRS DC 25012)

archaeological sites, there is still a substantial scatter of
upstanding monuments across Strathmore. The majority of
these monuments are large burial cairns, or standing stones and
stone circles, which have been incorporated into the margins of
the fields and plantations in the Improved landscape.

Above 122m OD on the hills of the Sidlaws, the bulk of the
sites that have been recorded are upstanding monuments. In
contrast to those of the lowlands, they represent a much wider
variety of types, ranging from prehistoric forts and settlements
to the footings of old farmsteads, the latter otherwise unknown
as upstanding features across the rest of South-east Perth. The
survival of these sites, coupled with the complete absence of
cropmarks, reflects much less intense arable production, but the
sparseness of the distribution is itself an indicator of the degree
of agricultural improvement that has taken place here. These

improvements were by no means limited to the last two
centuries, and some of the extensive swathes of rig-cultivation
that survive on the hills must be the result of earlier episodes of
ploughing from the medieval period onwards. Ironically, few of
the farmsteads that accompanied these episodes of cultivation
have survived, and the clusters of hut-circles that characterise
hills of a similar altitude in North-east Perth have long since
disappeared. A scatter of six hut-circles on **Law Hill,
Arnbathie**, however, and single examples at three other
locations, demonstrate that it is probably differences in later
land-use that create this apparent contrast between the Sidlaws
and the hills to the north of Strathmore.

The corollary of the destruction that has been wrought upon
South-east Perth, however, is the potential offered to the aerial
surveyor, a potential that barely existed in North-east Perth. A

122.

120-3.

45.

general discussion of the principles of cropmark formation can be found in text books on aerial photograph interpretation (e.g. Wilson 1982, 53-69). The majority of cropmarks form over features that have been cut into the subsoil, but there are also numerous examples of marks that have formed over ploughed mounds and banks that are still visible on the surface of the ground. In general terms, cropmarks form most readily in shallow soils on crops whose roots penetrate from 0.3m to 0.6m into the ground; they are caused by a combination of factors, such as the depth, texture and stoniness of the soil, the supply of plant nutrients, and the availability of moisture in the soil (see Jones and Evans 1975 for a detailed discussion). Thus, the potential for cropmarks differs from soil to soil and crop to crop, and even when all the conditions favourable to cropmark formation are apparently met, markings may still not appear. There is also a considerable element of luck as to whether aerial survey will effect a successful identification.

Distributions of cropmark material must be examined with these problems in mind. The first point to make about the cropmarks of South-east Perth is that the majority have been recorded in wheat and barley crops. Since these two crops are mainly grown in the lowlands, it follows that the distribution of cropmarks will also tend to be limited to the lowlands. Any traces that survive below the ground from the hut-circle groups that may once have existed on the Sidlaws are unlikely to be recovered as cropmarks. Conversely, types of settlement that are only known as cropmarks in the lowlands may well extend up on to the hills but will probably remain invisible to the aerial camera. Under severe drought conditions parchmarks may form in grass crops and rough pasture, but none have been recorded in the Sidlaws to date.

Within the zone where wheat and barley are grown, the characteristics of the soils are the most important factors governing the distribution of the cropmarks. The occurrence of freely-draining soils, principally fluvio-glacial sands and gravels, broadly hold the key to where the cropmarks are most likely to form. These soils dry out quicker than clays, and thus the crops growing on them respond quicker to hot weather and low rainfall. The distribution of the main freely-draining soil types in South-east Perth can be identified from the work of the Soil Survey of Scotland (1982). Those that are mainly under intensive cultivation today have been mapped against the distribution of cropmarks. Other freely-draining soils exist, but they are either largely under pasture or their extent cannot be distinguished. Care must be exercised in the interpretation of the map, since it compares fixed points in the landscape, that is the locations of the cropmarks, with estimated positions of the boundaries between the soil types. Nevertheless, there is a broad correlation between the better-drained soils and the cropmarks over the area as a whole.

9.

A more detailed examination of the Carse of Gowrie demonstrates the problems of using cropmark data. Here, two soil types have been mapped: those developed on raised beach deposits; and those on the estuarine clays. By far the majority of the cropmarks occur on the freely-draining raised beach deposits and also on other freely-draining soils along the foot of the Sidlaw escarpment. Of the small number apparently on the clays, at least half are so close to the raised beaches as to suggest that the mapped soil boundary is in error, and there is also the possibility that the remaining six are on small unmapped beach deposits. Some of the sites that are being revealed by the cropmarks are of a type that is almost certainly restricted to the raised beaches; for instance, souterrains (subterranean passages lined with drystone masonry) would simply fill with water if they were cut into a clay soil. Other types, however, particularly settlements and enclosures dating from the medieval period, when areas of the carse were being drained and reclaimed, may well extend down on to the clays. Of these very little evidence has been recovered, and the characteristics of the clays are such that it is exceptionally unlikely that they will be revealed by cropmarks.

Elsewhere in South-east Perth, the distinctions are not so clear cut. The majority of the soils along the south-east side of Strathmore have developed on till, giving rise to soil types with a mixture of well-drained and imperfectly drained soils according to the local characteristics of the underlying parent material. The differences between the two are not distinguished on the soil maps, but pockets of better-drained soil must account for the scatter of cropmarks that have been photographed in this part of the area. Nevertheless, aerial investigators have noted that finding sites on this side of Strathmore is much more time-consuming than on the freely-draining soils to the north, and the cropmarks that have been recorded here rarely have the sharp definition of some of those on the gravels.

Apart from the problems of differential cropmark formation, there are other factors, such as the pattern of reconnaissance, that affect the distribution of cropmarks. To a certain extent, it is inevitable that the areas of prolific cropmarkings are self-intensifying. Clusters of sites on responsive soils not only provide the aerial investigator with an indication of rewarding hunting grounds, but also provide a series of pre-set targets for the sortie, allowing the pilot a rough idea of where he is going. As we have seen, the first targets for aerial sorties into Scotland were provided by Roman sites, and there can be little doubt that these have played their part in creating concentrations of photographs, if not of actual cropmarks. The clusters of sites to the north of **Inchtuthil** are clearly the result of repeated reconnaissance, while flight-lines up Strathmore from here will naturally carry the aircraft over the better-drained soils around Blairgowrie. In reality, however, the pattern that has been recorded to date would probably have been much the same if the initial targets had been parish churches rather than Roman earthworks. The flight-paths between the churches would have rapidly led to the identification of the same rewarding areas where the combinations of soils and crops are most favourable for cropmark formation. In their turn, these would have immediately provided a second series of targets. Indeed, this pattern of target flying is implicit in the patterns of repeat photography of cropmark sites. Over the past fifteen years, a more structured application of aerial reconnaissance has developed, built upon the early successes, but consciously seeking to sample both areas of known cropmark susceptibility and apparently less productive areas. Recognition of cropmark sites, of course, involves a more complex pattern of cognitive enquiry than merely covering the right ground.

Although the Improvements and the reorganisation of the landscape at the end of the eighteenth century have been presented as crucial factors in determining the contents of the archaeological record, this presents a simplistic view of some of the patterns of survival and discovery that may be detected. For instance, the general distribution of the cropmarks in South-east Perth is remarkably similar to the pattern of agriculture depicted on Roy's map. Most of these sites have been under plough since long before the Improvements, a statement that is hardly surprising in view of the ubiquitous traces of rig and furrow across so many of the cropmark sites. A similar coincidence exists between the areas shown under cultivation by Roy and the distributions of cists and burials, while the patterns of standing stones, stone circles, cupmarked stones and burial cairns appear to relate to the areas where the blocks of fields were more fragmented. The major swathes of fields shown by Roy between Blairgowrie and Coupar Angus are virtually devoid of cairns and stone circles. It is difficult not to conclude that a pattern of destruction had already been stamped on these types of monument by centuries of medieval cultivation.

A more complex pattern can be demonstrated in relationship to the cists and burials of the area. The pattern of discovery through time has been charted by plotting the number of discoveries that have been made in each decade, where known, since the middle of the eighteenth century. Because of the

7. 9.

11.

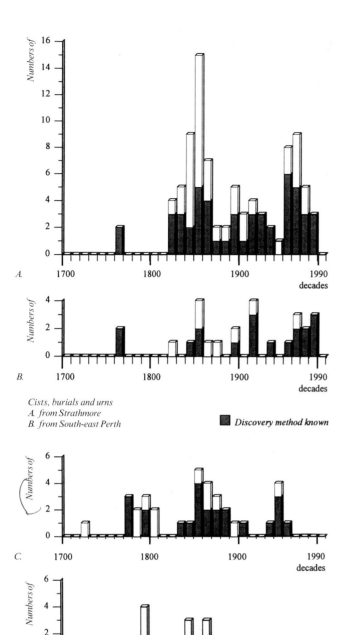

Cists, burials and urns
A. from Strathmore
B. from South-east Perth

■ *Discovery method known*

Souterrains from eastern Scotland
C. discovery date known
D. discovery date unknown

■ *Discovery method known*

Graphs showing the discoveries of cists, burials and souterrains since the eighteenth century

relatively small number of discoveries in South-east Perth, a larger sample has been collected for discoveries in Strathmore to the north-east. These provide an overall pattern which is reflected in the discoveries in South-east Perth, but would not have emerged so clearly with the small numbers involved. Perhaps the most striking aspect of the chart is that the period of change at the end of the eighteenth century is not matched by any discoveries. Indeed, an analysis of the references in the *Statistical Accounts* shows that the only burials discovered during this period were found in cairns or barrows. It is not until the 1820s that there is a spate of burials found across Strathmore, which continues until the 1860s. The figures for South-east Perth are not so emphatic, although a further ten undated discoveries referred to in the Name Books are likely to

belong in this period. In Strathmore as a whole there is no clear pattern to the methods by which the cists were found; ploughing, digging, quarrying and building work all figure in the descriptions of the various discoveries. In all, they imply a period of intense activity in the landscape, but not one related to the initiation of the Improvements. The implications of some of the other peaks in the rate of discovery are not clear. Nevertheless, from 1900 onwards the bulk of the cists are coming to light in the course of ploughing and, to a lesser extent, quarrying. Particularly noticeable is the increase in discoveries since 1950, which presumably matches the development of more powerful tractors and deeper ploughs.

Although the detailed study of the cists does not support the role of the Improvements in their discovery, there can be little doubt that the reorganisation of the landscape at the end of the eighteenth century has played a major part in shaping the archaeological record. The discoveries of the burials in cairns that were referred to above, reflecting the removal of the cairns, is one aspect of the impact of these changes, the discovery of souterrains in some numbers is another. It is particularly interesting to compare the pattern of souterrain discoveries in eastern Scotland with that of the cists of Strathmore. The souterrains follow roughly the same pattern in the middle of the nineteenth century, with the bulk of the discoveries falling between 1830 and 1910, but there is also a cluster of discoveries between 1770 and 1810, a cluster which is the more impressive if the six undated discoveries published at this time are taken into account. The method of discovery is only known for five of the late eighteenth-century cluster, and these were all found by ploughing and earth-moving. Of those recorded later in the nineteenth century, building work and roads figure much more frequently, again reflecting the same intense activity that brought so many of the cists to light.

11.

INTERPRETATION AND CLASSIFICATION OF CROPMARKS

The problems posed by cropmarks are not restricted to the patterns that have been discussed in the previous section on survival and discovery. There are at least two other areas which pose considerable difficulties for the archaeologist. The first of these concerns the interpretation of a cropmark in relation to the physical features that it represents beneath the surface of the ground, and the second to the overall interpretation of those features in terms of the different categories of archaeological site to which they may belong.

By their very nature, cropmarks are simply a response of particular crops to local anomalies in the plough-soil or the subsoil, anomalies that may be natural or artificial, ancient or modern. The first level of interpretation must be to distinguish cropmarks that have formed over artificial features from those of natural origin. Again guidance on this aspect of interpretation can be found in text books on the subject and will not be dealt with in detail here. Nevertheless, particular attention should be drawn to the obscuring effects of cropmarks produced by post-glacial geomorphology, whether in the form of old watercourses, frost-wedges, or areas of deeper alluvium. In South-east Perth, as elsewhere, such features may conceal the existence, or mask the extent, of untold numbers of archaeological sites.

The vast majority of what are considered to be artificial features that have been recorded as cropmarks in South-east Perth appear to be pits, ditches, or other features cut into the subsoil. The exceptions to this rule — 'negative' cropmarks forming above walls, cobbles or other stone-built structures — are comparatively rare and do not present significant problems of interpretation. Thus, the cropmarks can be divided into four basic categories. The first of these, and probably the most common across the area as a whole, are what can be described as 'solid' cropmarks or maculae (dark spots or stains); the second are the cropmarks of ditches defining enclosures; the third are what appear to be pits, either scattered indiscriminately or arranged in orderly settings; and the fourth are linear cropmarks of one form or another.

12. Solid cropmarks or maculae: these are of relatively small area, discs and crescents being amongst the commonest curvilinear forms, but in many instances these descriptions give only an impression of a mark which may be very diffuse around its edges. Indeed, there are a substantial number of marks which can only be described as amorphous, whose interpretation as artificial features rests on an occasional hard edge or their proximity to other well-defined discs and crescents. In addition, there is also a series of curvilinear or banana-shaped marks, which come in a wide range of sizes and occur singly, in clusters and among groups of other solid marks. Of particular note amongst the solid marks, however, are a small number of markedly rectangular features; other examples may lie hidden, awaiting the resolution of future interpretation or reconnaissance sorties.

At the outset, it should be said that there is very little information to be gleaned from the hills surrounding South-east Perth to aid the interpretation of the solid cropmarks in structural terms. Nevertheless, data gathered from a wide range of sites, both upstanding and cropmark, across southern and eastern Scotland, allows the discs and crescents to be interpreted as elements of the sunken floors of circular buildings (Maxwell 1983, 33-9). The majority appear to be unenclosed by any ditches or palisade trenches, both here in South-east Perth and across the whole of eastern Scotland to the north of the Forth, and, in this sense at least, the pattern of recorded archaeology in the Perth lowlands mirrors the dense concentrations of unenclosed hut-circles that have been recorded on the hills to the north. The banana-shaped marks can also be interpreted as a facet of this pattern of unenclosed settlement and have been convincingly demonstrated as the remains of souterrains (Maxwell 1987, 36-42). The rectangular marks pose more of a problem, since their date is quite unknown, but they are likely to indicate the positions of unenclosed rectangular buildings (RCAHMS 1992, 3). Many of the settlements that have been recorded as cropmarks are of types that have never been seen before and their interpretation is discussed under various sub-headings in a section on settlement.

Enclosures: the second group of cropmarks, the sites with enclosing ditches, exhibit as wide a range of forms as the solid cropmarks. A basic distinction can be made between those that are rectilinear and those that are circular or oval, but whether there is any real significance in this observation is quite unknown. The rectilinear enclosures exhibit a wide range of size and little can be said about the majority of them. Amongst them, however, there are a series of small square enclosures, often with central pits, which frequently occur in clusters with small circular enclosures, or ring-ditches, and have been identified as the remains of barrow cemeteries. Other small rectilinear enclosures appear to be the remains of rectangular buildings; these have been taken into account under the same sub-heading as the solid rectangular markings in the section on settlement, but there is a possibility that some at least are early prehistoric ritual or ceremonial enclosures, and these are discussed further in that section. The Roman earthworks are theoretically a subset of the rectilinear enclosures, although, in reality, the major examples can usually be distinguished without any great difficulty. Nevertheless, the diversification of the category of minor Roman structures over recent years raises the possibility that other examples may be lurking amongst the mass of cropmark enclosures. There is also good reason to believe that some of the cropmarks represent the buried remains of granges or secular earthworks of medieval date, or even of the policies of long-vanished houses, and these are dealt with under the appropriate headings of the medieval sections. The rest of the rectilinear enclosures are discussed briefly under the sub-heading of enclosures in the settlement section.

The circular and oval enclosures cover a more diverse range of sizes and clearly represent a wide variety of different types of structure. The smaller examples are traditionally identified as ring-ditches, but there are usually considerable difficulties in defining the size range that constitutes this group of sites. So often there is a grey area where the two categories merge into each other, but in South-east Perth the distinction between the two is quite clear-cut. This can be shown on a graph displaying the diameters of all the circular enclosures, irrespective of their size. The diameters have been divided into 2m bands to even out slight variations which undoubtedly exist in the measurements estimated from different aerial photographs. The break occurs at about 24m and is particularly clear on account of the different types that can be distinguished amongst both the enclosures and the ring-ditches. For instance, four of the enclosures that are larger than 24m are defined by narrow ditches which are almost certainly palisade trenches. Another four are enclosures containing a large centrally placed crescent; a single example of one of these at 20m, however, suggests that this particular type may have a wider size range. These enclosed crescents form a sub-heading of the settlement section, as do the palisaded enclosures.

Examination of the ring-ditches less than 24m in diameter shows that these can also be sub-divided into different types, at least one of which again serves to accentuate the division

Middle Gourdie (*NO 1181 4186*), *probable round-houses and souterrain* (*NMRS B 22688*)

between ring-ditches and enclosures. In this particular type, perhaps best called interrupted ring-ditches, the ditch is usually broken by at least two causeways, through one of which a narrow banana-shaped mark extends. These fall between 12m and 24m in internal diameter and make up a substantial proportion of those at the upper end of the size range of ring-ditches. In this part of the range there are also a few C-shaped cropmarks, which are probably a related category. The characteristics of the interrupted ring-ditches, and their disposition both singly and in clusters, leaves little doubt that they are a facet of settlement across the area, and they are dealt with under a sub-heading of that name in the settlement section.

Another type of site that can be distinguished amongst the ring-ditches comprises those which appear to enclose a central pit. These are likely to be the remains of levelled barrows, many of them occurring in the clusters of square barrows, and

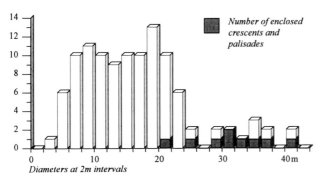

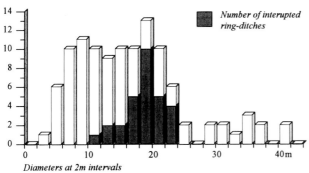

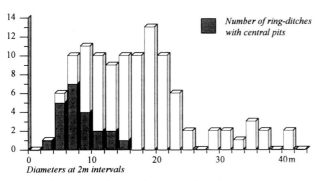

A. Graphs showing sizes of ring-ditches and circular enclosures
in South-east Perth

B. Over Durdie (NO 2096 2492), cropmark fort (NMRS A 64756)

are dealt with in the relevant section. Two others are possibly the remains of the prehistoric ceremonial enclosures known as henges. However, this still leaves a substantial number of ring-ditches of unknown function, not all of which need be of ancient origin, the construction of roundels for small clumps of trees providing at least one possible source of confusion. Thus, the sites classified simply as ring-ditches, and for that matter enclosures too, should be viewed as the subjects of ongoing assessment, be it survey or excavation. Nevertheless, there are reasonable grounds for suggesting that the majority of such ring-ditches in South-east Perth, many of which are poorly-defined cropmarks, represent the remains of the various types of small circular settlement structures that can be identified, and, therefore, they are discussed briefly under the sub-heading of unenclosed circular buildings.

The larger curvilinear enclosures must also represent a wide range of different types of site. The group of palisaded sites that can be distinguished has already been referred to, and there are
13B.
also four enclosures with multiple ditches, which can be conveniently identified as forts. The latter, together with two other broad-ditched enclosures, are discussed in a section dealing with all the prehistoric and Early Historic fortifications in the area. All the other enclosures are defined by relatively narrow, single ditches and have very few distinguishing characteristics. Again, many of these are probably the remains of settlements, and, along with the rectilinear enclosures, they are described in that section.

Pits: these appear on virtually all photographs of cropmarks. In some cases a crop may appear to be entirely speckled with

small punctuate marks and it is by no means certain that these indicate the positions of pits below. In others, however, the marks are well-defined and occur on photographs from several seasons of flying. While the latter can be identified as pits with some confidence, this does not bring a closer understanding of their date or purpose. More formal arrangements of pits can also be detected, with examples of four-pit and six-pit settings, and of small circular and rectangular enclosures defined by pits. Two parallel rows of pits extending over some distance have been identified at one site and there are several examples of single pit-alignments. The latter are usually irregular straggles of large unevenly-spaced pits, whose date and purpose are unknown. None of the pitted cropmarks in South-east Perth has been excavated, but evidence from elsewhere suggests that many of these types of site are early prehistoric ritual and ceremonial monuments. Whether the single pit-alignments should also be seen in this light is debatable, but for convenience they have also been included in the same category. Similar uncertainties extend to the smaller pit-circles, one of which lies adjacent to a probable souterrain in an enclosure and may be reasonably identified as the post-ring of a circular timber building.

Linear Cropmarks: the cropmark record of every area includes photographs that simply show single ditches running across a field. South-east Perth is no exception and may even have more than its due proportion. Roman temporary camps are born of such cropmarks and the coincidence of interests and opportunities in the skies above Strathmore has led to an extensive record of a wide variety of linear features. The majority of these marks are of unknown significance and will not be discussed in the descriptive sections of this survey. Drains and old field-boundaries figure prominently amongst them, reflecting the indiscriminate nature of cropmark formation. Some, however, may be of considerable antiquity and it should be borne in mind that the Neolithic cursus at **Blairhall** and the levelled portion of the **Cleaven Dyke**, both
26A-B.
27.
described under the heading of ceremonial and ritual monuments, are characterised by little more than parallel pairs of linear cropmarks.

By and large, however, there is relatively little evidence for boundaries of any date in South-east Perth, despite medieval records that imply their existence. Similarly no direct parallels for the types of earlier boundary known elsewhere in Scotland have been found in eastern Perthshire, either in the uplands of North-east Perth or the lowlands of South-east Perth. The pit-alignments of South-east Perth, for instance, are of rather different character to the pitted boundary works of East Lothian and it is far from certain that they fulfilled similar functions.

Perhaps the more interesting of the linear marks are those that indicate the course of old roads. The Roman road at **Wester Drumatherty** was an engineered road, and parts of it can still be seen as a low mound running across the field. As such, it is a relatively unusual feature, the majority of later roads being unmetalled tracks. Traffic along such roads has often worn a hollow in the ground, the depth of the hollow reflecting the hardness of the underlying rock or till. Where they survive on the hills, these trackways tend to be intermittent features and often braid into numerous hollows on the most difficult stretches of terrain. These characteristics allow trackways to be distinguished relatively easily from other linear cropmarks, and several examples can be identified in South-east Perth. The cropmark of a trackway hollow has been photographed to the south-west of Berryhill on the line of what was traditionally identified as a Roman road (Crawford 1949, 67-9). The Roman origin of this road is not supported by trustworthy evidence but it must be a routeway of considerable antiquity. Other cropmarks of this sort have been recorded running down to a ford on the Isla below the Roman fort at **Cargill**, on the slope adjacent to the probable pitted mortuary enclosure at **Littleour** (see Ceremonial and Ritual Monuments), on the slope to the north-east of Hallhole, and running across a field at Kemphill.

14B.

14A.

A. **Littleour** *(NO 1734 4024), cropmarks of old trackways dropping down the slope adjacent to a probable pit-defined mortuary enclosure (NMRS B 22397)*

B. **Cargill** *(NO 168 364), cropmarks of a trackway hollow to the south-west of Berryhill (NMRS PT 14724)*

14

FUNERARY MONUMENTS

The most conspicuous prehistoric funerary monuments of South-east Perth are mainly large burial mounds, comprising both earthen barrows and stone-built cairns, which are often set in dramatic positions that dominate wide stretches of the landscape. The impression of the generality of early funerary practices that such monuments create is misleading and is not reflected in the mass of other evidence that has been recorded over the last two hundred years. Relatively few people in ancient communities can have been of a status that justified the construction of tombs on this scale. Indeed, even in numerical terms, the burial sites recorded below can only represent a minor fraction of the population that farmed the area from the Neolithic onwards.

The section has been divided into two parts, the first dealing with the barrows and cairns and, the second, the cists, urns and other apparently unmarked burials. The processes that control the survival of the barrows and cairns, and the discovery of the cists and urns, have been discussed in the introductory sections. Broadly speaking, those that have been involved in the destruction of barrows and cairns are also responsible for the discovery of cists and urns. The maps that have been prepared for the two sections reveal that the distributions of these two

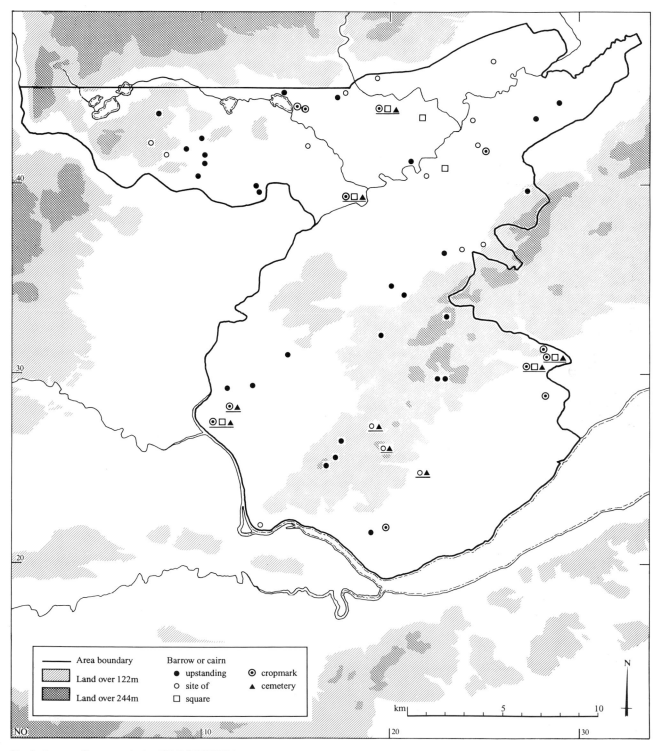

Distribution map of barrows and cairns (NMRS DC 25013)

pp.7-11

15

types of burial-site are complementary and the presence or absence of a covering mound should not be overstressed. Some of the burial mounds clearly became the focus for a cluster of flat graves, while others may have been raised over earlier cemeteries. Furthermore, there can be little doubt that some of the discoveries of cists represent the sites of barrows and cairns long since swept away.

The addition of aerial photography to the prospective techniques of the archaeologist has added an exciting new dimension to the burial record of eastern Scotland. For the first time it is possible to identify a series of cemeteries of relatively late date, each of them distinguished by the presence of square ditched barrows, complementing the discoveries made in two round barrows at **Inchtuthil** earlier this century. Other burials of this date may be represented in the antiquarian record of cists from the area, but there is no way of identifying them.

15. **Barrows and cairns**

About forty-five barrows and cairns have been identified from historical records or fieldwork in South-east Perth. In addition, at least twenty-two of the ring-ditches recorded as cropmarks enclose what are probably central grave-pits and may be interpreted as the remains of levelled barrows. About three-quarters of the ring-ditches that fall into this category are distributed between four small cemeteries, three of them including both circular and square barrows. From a total in excess of sixty-five, however, only twenty-nine of the cairns and barrows survive as upstanding monuments, and of these only ten appear to be undisturbed. Another twelve display evidence of having been 'explored' and seven have been heavily robbed. With this level of disturbance, it is almost impossible to be certain of the original form of the majority of the cairns, but at least one of those identified in the course of the survey is probably a ring-cairn.

Barrows and cairns are distributed widely throughout South-east Perth, but the majority are situated on the lower-lying ground. A few cairns occupy hilltop positions along the Sidlaws, and these include some of the most impressive examples in the area. The only group appears to be that lying to the north of the River Tay at Caputh, where there are the remains of, or records for, at least eight large mounds; it is perhaps worth noting that the same area contains evidence for four cupmarked stones and three stone-settings. The gaps in the distribution, which are partly occupied by cists and burials, may be more apparent than real, for it should be borne in mind that the latter category may include examples originally covered by cairns or barrows. The only areas which appear to be totally devoid of any burial monuments are those where there has been a history of very poor drainage, such as the Carse of Gowrie, where all the burials that have been recorded, whether represented by cists, cairns or cropmarks, are restricted to the better-drained soils around the edges of the low-lying clays. The distribution of square-barrow cemeteries within the survey area is too thin to be informative, but it is consistent with the distribution of this type of site on raised beaches and fluvio-glacial deposits throughout the eastern part of central Scotland (Maxwell 1987 34-5, fig. 3), a pattern that may have more to do with the nature of cropmarks than favoured locations for cemeteries.

The majority of the surviving barrows and cairns are relatively featureless, tree or shrub-covered mounds. Indeed, many of them owe their survival to the creation of decorative roundels in the Improved landscape. In at least one case, this reflects the foresight of a landowner. In November 1791, William MacDonald, first laird of St Martins, 'settled with George Reoch to drive stones to Tomteethy Clump, at ffifteen shillings in all, during the winter'(Scott 1911, 35) in order that a protective wall be built around the cairn now known as **Tammieteeth**. Today it survives as a relatively undisturbed tree-covered mound, measuring about 12m in diameter and 1m in height. This cairn is one of the smaller ones to survive in South-east Perth, the rest ranging in size from 7m to a little over 32m in diameter. There is some doubt concerning the classification of the largest of the surviving mounds that may fall into this category. Known as **Macbeth's Law**, it stands within the garden of Lawton House, near Kinrossie in Strathmore, and has previously been identified as a possible motte. Flat-topped, the mound stands 5m high, and its base is partially surrounded by a low terrace. Whether this is a prehistoric burial mound, or medieval motte, or even a more recent landscape feature, can only be determined by excavation. Nevertheless, this is not the only large mound in the area. There are three other cairns over 30m in diameter and two of these, **Shien Hill** and **Kinloch**, are 4m and 2.5m in height respectively. The third, **Cairn Muir**, near Caputh, once stood to a height of 4.2m, but was heavily robbed in the nineteenth

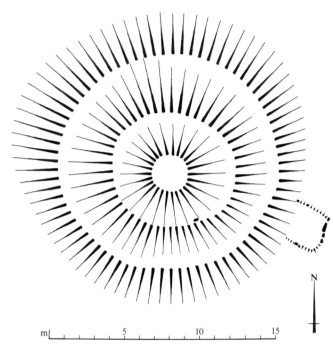

Pole Hill (NO 1955 2606), cairn, 1:250 (NMRS DC 25015)

century and now survives as a low amorphous mass of rubble.

Several of the other mounds in South-east Perth are also of considerable size. At **Peattie**, for instance, there is one measuring 25m in diameter by 3.5m in height, while the example on **Pole Hill** measures 19.5m by 2.2m. Pole Hill is of particular interest because it is one of two hilltop cairns in the Sidlaws which exhibit evidence of composite construction. In this case, the stepped profile of the mound shows three clear stages of construction, and there are also the remains of a small boulder-edged platform on the south-east. At **Shien Hill**, the other example, there is a clear distinction between the top and the bottom of the mound. The lower part is much sandier in composition than the relatively stony upper part.

The smaller cairns and barrows were more easily removed than these big mounds, and it is not surprising that the majority of those less than 10m in diameter have been identified from cropmarks. A small cairn measuring 7.5m in diameter and 0.4m in height survives within the fort on the summit of **Law Hill, Arnbathie**, and another of similar size is known to have been destroyed at **Dalreichmoor**, on the Sidlaws, shortly before 1819 (Melville 1939, 124); it covered a cist containing only a 'little fine mould'. A number of other, smaller cairns in the vicinity were also removed, and these contained 'large quantities of ashes and numbers of human bones, half-burnt'.

Only two of the cairns that have been recorded have visible kerbs, the more impressive being at **Ninewells** to the east of Dunkeld. This cairn measures 10m in diameter and 0.75m in height and has a near-complete kerb of large contiguous boulders and slabs set on edge. The kerb is graded so that the largest, though not the tallest, stones are situated in the south-

16. *(margin)*

53. *(margin)*

17A. *(margin)*

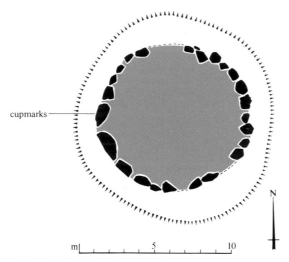

A. Ninewells (NO 0757 4360), cairn, 1:250 (NMRS DC 25017)

western quadrant, and one of the stones on the west bears four cupmarks. Today the cairn material is roughly level with the top of the kerbstones, but there is no evidence to suggest that it has been heavily robbed and it was probably never much higher. Concentric with the kerb there is an external platform about 0.2m high. This type of feature is more usually associated with Clava ring-cairns and passage graves around Inverness, which are believed to be of Late Neolithic date, but, despite the disturbance of the centre of the Ninewells cairn, there is no evidence of stones defining an internal court. The kerbed cairn at **Culfargie**, however, may safely be assigned to the ring-cairn category. Situated in an unimposing topographic position, like

17B.

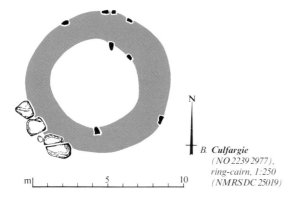

B. Culfargie (NO 2239 2977), ring-cairn, 1:250 (NMRS DC 25019)

so many other ring-cairns, it measures about 10m in overall diameter, with a central court 5.5m across. The largest surviving kerb-stones are situated on the south-west, and it is reasonable to assume that they only survive because they were the biggest stones of a graded kerb. Some 60m to the south-west there is another heavily-robbed cairn about 9.6m in diameter.

It has already been noted that the majority of the smaller burial mounds can only be identified from cropmarks. There are, however, considerable difficulties in the identification of levelled barrows from cropmarks, if only because it is impossible to demonstrate the character of the relationship between the main diagnostic features — ring-ditch and central grave-pit — and the presence of a barrow (far less its height and composition) cannot be deduced from cropmark evidence alone. Some observations may, however, be significant. For example, a common characteristic of the ring-ditches with central pits is that the ditches are relatively narrow and cannot have provided enough upcast material for a large mound. This contrasts with other annular ring-ditches where there is a well-defined broad ditch but no trace of a central pit. An example of the latter category, which occurs within 130m of elements of the square-barrow cemetery at **Rossie**, should almost certainly

be identified as a levelled barrow rather than the remains of a circular house. The practical problems of covering a burial with a barrow suggest that there may be a direct relationship between the height of a barrow as reflected in the breadth of the enclosing ditch and the presence or absence of a grave-pit, particularly if the funerary remains were to be deposited in a cist. If this is the case, it is probable that the majority of barrows identified from cropmarks, whose key characteristic is the presence of a central pit, will have narrow ditches. The argument should not be pushed too far, for evidence recovered from the excavation of the barrows at **Inchtuthil** in 1901 (see below) shows that some of these smaller mounds may be of composite construction, not only incorporating soil dug from a surrounding ditch, but also materials brought in from elsewhere. Nor should it be forgotten that a broad-ditched annular cropmark may occasionally represent the superimposition of successive penannular structures with differently aligned entrances. Nevertheless, a series of other barrows is probably lost amongst the ring-ditches and circular enclosures, the only feature pointing to their identity being an unbroken circuit of ditch. The ring-ditch 20m in diameter at **Wester Denhead** is a possible example, but others may be considerably larger. Although all warrant serious consideration as the remains of barrows, only the example at **Rossie** has been plotted on the distribution map of the barrows and cairns.

78. p. 19

It is also noticeable that most of the cropmark barrows that have been identified in South-east Perth occur in cemeteries. Single examples certainly exist, but they are by no means common. The largest of these, at **Glencarse**, is 15m in diameter, and appears to be in isolation, although there are other faint cropmarks in the vicinity, and a pit-alignment, possibly defining an enclosure, not far away. More often than not, traces of other ring-ditches will be found close by apparent singletons. Thus, the clearly-defined example, 10m in diameter, at **Hallhole** has a second ring-ditch within 50m. At **Leys of Marlee** too, there are at least two barrows, 7m and 8m in diameter respectively, set about 250m apart to the west of the stone circle, and there is possibly a third smaller one near the western example. At **Blairhall** there are at least seven barrows ranging in size from 6m to 8m in diameter, five of them set in a line and the other two on opposite sides of the cursus that occurs in the same field. The ditches of the latter two barrows and the cursus intersect, but the relationship between them is uncertain.

18B.

17C. 26A.

At least three of the other cemeteries that have been identified in South-east Perth contain both round and square barrows. They are at **Rossie** at the east end of the Carse of Gowrie, at **Sherifftown** on the east bank of the Tay to the north

18A.

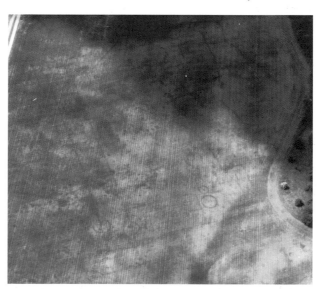

C. Blairhall (NO 116 281), cemetery of round barrows with traces of a cursus monument on the left (NMRS PT 10724)

of Perth, and at **The Welton** immediately south-east of Blairgowrie. To these should probably be added the **Hallhole** site mentioned above. The composition and size of these cemeteries varies enormously: at **Sherifftown** there is a compact group with two circular and at least four square barrows, three of them set in a contiguous row, but at **The Welton** the barrows are spread over a distance of about 100m with only one certain square example and no fewer than seven round ones, their diameters ranging from 4m to 12m. At The Welton they are also scattered amongst settlement remains, and one is intersected by the ditch of a fort. The barrows at **Rossie** occur at two locations. The westerly group is little more than a miscellaneous straggle of small enclosures, some with central pits, but none markedly round or square. The easterly group is of rather more interest, but again few of the barrows are clearly defined. The broad-ditched barrow that has already been described lies about 300m south-south-west of the standing stone known as the Falcon Stone (which lies immediately outside the survey area). Between the two there is a pair of clearly-defined barrows, one circular the other square, while to the north-east of the Falcon Stone there is possibly a block of contiguous square barrows. The most recent photographs of the area also show that the Falcon Stone itself stands roughly at the centre of a ring-ditch about 13m in internal diameter.

The remains at **Hallhole** are of a rather different character. Some 50m to the north of the probable round barrow revealed by the cropmarks, there is a small, roughly square earthwork, surviving unploughed in what has been a small plantation. It comprises a low central mound some 10m across and up to 0.5m high, enclosed by twin ditches with low external banks, and is notable for the clearly defined gaps in the perimeter that occur at three of the angles. Partial excavation of the site in 1903 (Abercromby 1904, 87-96) failed to establish its function, only recovering a few artefacts of relatively recent date and several fragments of burnt bone. The causeways at the corners of the earthwork, however, are very distinctive features, not only characterising numerous examples of square barrows recorded as cropmarks, but also several of those that have survived as upstanding monuments, including examples where no internal mound is visible (Stevenson 1984).

Square barrows are not usually of this size, most of those in South-east Perth ranging from 4m to 8m across within narrow ditches, but the most recent photographs of a double-ditched cropmark enclosure at **Wester Denhead**, near Coupar Angus, have revealed that the inner element, which measures about 15m square, has the same distinctive gaps at each of its angles. Almost certainly, this is either a square barrow or some kind of related funerary enclosure, although it should, perhaps, be mentioned that no evidence of funerary activity was found during trial-trenching of the perimeter of this enclosure in 1978, when a fragment of Roman amphora was found in the upper fill of the outer ditch, and a shallow palisade trench detected immediately within the inner. Neither of these two sites may be claimed as typical square barrows, but they may well indicate the existence of a series of more complex ceremonial or funerary enclosures within such barrow cemeteries, and open up the possibility for a similar interpretation for other square enclosures of this size, such as one recorded close to the square-barrow cemetery at Forteviot, in Strathearn.

Although the evidence for the existence of cemeteries in South-east Perth is largely drawn from cropmarks on the gravels, other possible examples may have been destroyed on the Sidlaws. The removal of the small cairns at **Dalreichmoor**, for instance, which has already been referred to, apparently revealed evidence of burials, while the cairns containing cists found near **Evelick** some time before 1845 (*NSA*, 10, Perth, 1164) might equally well have represented a small cemetery. Such possibilities may appear remote, but what appears to be a small cemetery of four cairns survives on the north edge of the Sidlaws at Nether Handwick in Angus District (RCAHMS 1983, 12, nos.63-4). Here, all four cairns, which measure 4m,

18A.

48B.
54A.

67A.

18B.

58.

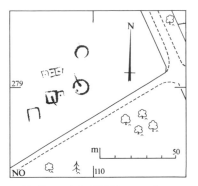

A. *Sherifftown (NO 109 279), square-barrow cemetery, 1:2500 (NMRS DC 25022)*

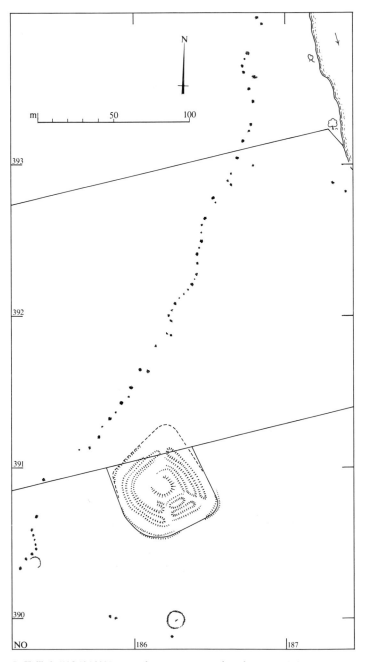

B. *Hallhole (NO 186 390), square-barrow cemetery and pit-alignment, 1:2500 (NMRS DC 25023)*

5m, 14m and 27m in diameter respectively, have been heavily robbed, but one of the smaller cairns still contains the remains of a central cist. Upstanding remains of cemeteries in the lowlands are more difficult to find, but the two surviving barrows at **Inchtuthil** may be one such example. Pennant (1776, 67-70) refers to low, circular 'Tumuli' with ditches, which were 'very frequent over the face of this [Inchtuthil] plain', and also records that many bones 'neither lodged in stone chests nor deposited in urns' had been found in some of the barrows. There may have been some confusion, however, for Roy's account only mentions five additional 'tumuli', and his plan of 1755 shows them within the interior of the native fort (Roy 1793, 76 and plate 18). The same features are also depicted on Pennant's plan. To date, aerial photography has revealed only one ring-ditch within the fortress (Pitts and St. Joseph, 1985, 261), and, given the spectacular level of detail that has been recorded over large areas of the plateau, it is unlikely that many more await discovery.

It is unfortunate that the site at Inchtuthil cannot be certainly identified as a barrow cemetery, because partial excavation of both of the round barrows by Abercromby in 1901 provided some remarkable results (Abercromby, Ross and Anderson 1902, 197-201). The largest, The Women's Knowe, had been examined towards the end of the eighteenth century (*Stat. Acct.*, 9 [1793], 505-6), but no structural features or artefacts were recorded then. Abercromby drove a trench four feet (1.2m) wide across the mound and located a central long cist which had been dug into the natural gravel. Crudely built of thin stone slabs, it was aligned from east to west and measured about 2.25m in length; it contained the remains of an extended inhumation and fragments of decayed wood. The grave was covered by a mound of clayey loam measuring up to 15.5m in diameter by 2.7m in height, and it was surrounded by a ditch. At a later date, after the primary mound material had begun to weather into the ditch, a capping of stone up to 0.6m in thickness was laid over both the mound and the ditch. The capping included quarried Gourdie stone, which had presumably been robbed from the fortress rampart, and also some fragments of Roman brick or tile and possibly glass. The second barrow, which measures about 10m in diameter by 0.7m in height within a narrow ditch, actually overlies the defences of the fortress, and is clearly post-Roman in date. Again, the excavation revealed a central grave-pit, measuring about 2.1m in length, but in this case it contained only fragments of decayed wood. The grave-pit was covered by a circular mound of earth, which had been capped by a layer of gravel and then boulders.

Much of what is known about the rest of the barrows and cairns in South-east Perth is derived from various antiquarian sources, recording both deliberate excavation and chance discoveries. Often, however, the only evidence of an earlier excavation is the trench visible on the surface of the mound. The earliest recorded discoveries were made in two cairns to the south-east of Coupar Angus, near **Pitcur** (*Stat. Acct.*, 17 [1796], 17). The first cairn, which was composed of '1000 cartloads' of stone, covered a cist containing an inhumation, and the second, a much smaller cairn, yielded an 'urn' (now lost) containing 'ashes'. Slightly later, in about 1800, cists were found in a cairn at **Rannaleroch** to the south of Alyth; the stones of the cists were used for building purposes. Another, fruitless, search of the cairn was undertaken just before 1865, by which time the mound had been nearly levelled (Name Book, Perth, No.5, p. 101), and nothing remains today. Another 'artificial mound of earth' was levelled in 1818 at **Stobcross**, between Coupar Angus and Meigle, revealing a Late Bronze Age hoard; a single spearhead survives (NMS DG 1; Name Book, Perth, No.18, p.9). Two years later, a cist containing an inhumation was found when a cottage on the west side of **Blairgowrie** was built on the remains of a cairn (*NSA*, 10, Perth, p. 914). In 1839 two cists were found in a cairn at **Innerbuist** on the east bank of the River Tay (Name Book, Perth, No.75, p. 96); in this case the cairn is still visible as a

low swelling some 20m in diameter and 0.3m in height. One of the few artefacts to be recorded from a burial in a cairn is a 'dagger', found in a cist containing ashes in the **Haer Cairn** at Rattray; it was found when the cairn was removed some time before 1864 (Name Book, Perth, No.70, p. 37).

The majority of the discoveries catalogued above were made as the cairns were swept away in land-improvement before the middle of the nineteenth century. Thereafter, the pace of destruction slowed, but chance discoveries, such as the cist ploughed up at **West Buttergask** in 1920, continued to be made. From the same time, archaeological excavation also began to make its contribution. For example, Andrew Jervise, a well-known antiquarian, reported the excavation of a cairn measuring 15m in diameter and 1.8m in height, which lies within the grounds of **Belmont Castle** on the south side of Meigle (Jervise 1859, 246). An apparently empty cist was found two feet (0.6m) down, its position now marked by a hollow in the summit of the grass-grown mound. Apart from the two barrows at **Inchtuthil**, Abercromby himself also excavated a barrow in the grounds of **Glendelvine House** (1902, 202-3). The mound appears to have been somewhat higher in 1901, but today it measures about 17m in diameter by 1.5m in height, and there is a small standing stone 1.8m high on its east side. Abercromby drove a narrow trench from east to west across the mound, revealing that it was composed of sandy soil. At about the centre, some 1.7m below the top, a pit containing 'ashes but no burnt bones' was located on the east side of an area of burnt soil and charcoal. A second pit was discovered cut into the natural gravel a further 0.3m below; measuring 0.7m in diameter and 0.38m in depth, it was 'full of charcoal, discoloured earth, and a very few fragments of human bone', and was covered with 'puddled clay'. A layer of bright red soil mixed with charcoal, both elements probably indicating an episode of burning on the old ground-surface, was also observed. There can be little doubt that Abercromby had dug through a complex monument which must have had at least two periods of use and construction.

To the early excavations may be added the partial examination of a previously disturbed mound at **Hillpark**, in Barnhill on the south-east edge of Perth, by Thomas McLaren in 1923. To his credit, McLaren produced a scale plan of the cairn and also discovered a hammerstone and a flint knife (PMAG 2388 & 2389 respectively). The cairn, which measured 25m in diameter by 3m in height, was removed by bulldozer in about 1972, but no further structural features or artefacts were recovered.

The only modern excavation of a cairn in South-east Perth took place in 1989, prior to redevelopment at **Beech Hill House** (Stevenson 1989). The results of the excavation provide a glimpse of the complex nature of these burial mounds, which is otherwise largely unattested in the antiquarian accounts. The Beech Hill cairn had probably been a focus of activity over a long period of time. Two cists had been built before the cairn was raised, but one of these cut an earlier pit and this may have been a grave too. Both these cists, and the pit, lay within the area enclosed by what may be conveniently described as a ring-ditch some 8.5m in internal diameter. The fill of the ring-ditch, however, suggested that it had never been an open feature and may have held upright timbers. The ring-ditch had been dug through an earlier pit on the south-east, but was itself cut by a third cist on the east. This cist, and two further cists on the west, lay outside the edge of the cairn, which measured 8.5m in diameter over a boulder kerb. The cairn was set concentrically within the ring-ditch, but the relationship between the two could not be proved stratigraphically. For various reasons, the radiocarbon dates for three of the cists and the ring-ditch cannot be relied upon to clarify the sequence of events on the site, but grave-goods accompanying the burials show that this cemetery was certainly in use at the beginning of the 2nd millennium BC. The grave-goods include Food Vessels, a bronze pin and two bone artefacts, one a pommel and the other a toggle. Some of the artefacts found beneath the cairn, which include sherds of

Grooved Ware of Late Neolithic date, are thought to derive from manure spread in the course of earlier agricultural activity on the site.

The recent excavations at Beech Hill House, and also at Sketewan, a cairn outside South-east Perth in Strathtay (Mercer 1988), have served to show how apparently nondescript barrows and cairns can mask evidence of a long and complex history. It is probably fair to assume that the majority of the round barrows and cairns date from the Early Bronze Age, a period of about 1000 years beginning in the middle of 3rd millennium BC. Nevertheless, excavations at Pitnacree in Strathtay (Coles and Simpson 1965) have shown that large circular mounds can be considerably earlier, in that case dating from early in the Neolithic; on the other hand, as noted above, the two excavated examples at **Inchtuthil** are post-Roman. The size and shape of the larger cairns and barrows thus provide little clue as to their date, but the presumption that low-lying circular barrows are probably of Neolithic date (Megaw and Simpson 1988, 107) should be avoided. It should not be forgotten that the large cairn at Strathallan, which was 40m in diameter and 5.5m in height, was constructed during the second half of the third millennium BC (Barclay 1984).

The apparent absence of Neolithic cairns and barrows in eastern Perth does present a problem. The ring-cairn at **Culfargie**, which adds to the small group recorded in North-east Perth (RCAHMS 1990) and Angus, may be of Late Neolithic date, and the possible parallels between features of the **Ninewells** cairn and the Clava group to the north has already been mentioned. There is very little evidence, however, for earlier Neolithic cairns, the long mound reported on Herald Hill (NO 1867 3961) apparently being a natural feature. The only barrow or cairn in South-east Perth for which such an early date might be suggested is the barrow excavated by Abercromby at **Glendelvine House**. It is unfortunate that no pottery was recovered, but the evidence of burning over a wide area of what was probably the old land surface, the presence of cremated human bone, and the central pit, are reminiscent of features discovered below a mound at Boghead in Moray, which has been firmly dated to the beginning of the fourth millennium BC (Burl 1985). The practice of burning a mortuary enclosure and the deposition of pyre material at this period is attested elsewhere (Kinnes 1979), and it has also been argued that markers such as the standing stone adjacent to the Glendelvine barrow may be a feature of Neolithic graves (Burl 1985, 55). It is interesting to note that none of the other large mounds in the vicinity of Glendelvine has produced any recorded cists or finds, despite the fact that three have been virtually or completely destroyed and another two have been dug into. This absence of internal structures may well be an indicator of a Neolithic context for some of these cairns, particularly in view of the regular occurrence of what appear to be Early Bronze Age cists within cairns elsewhere in Strathmore and the surrounding hills.

The dating of the ditched barrows is even more difficult. The cropmark examples are indistinguishable from either the ring-ditch discovered beneath the **Beech Hill** cairn, on the one hand, or the post-Roman barrows at **Inchtuthil** on the other. There is nothing inherently dateable in the design of a round barrow with an enclosing ditch. Square barrows are a slightly different matter, however, and there is a general consensus that they are probably of relatively late date. None has been precisely dated but the grave-pit of a square barrow excavated at Boysack Mills, in Angus (*DES 1977*, 5; Murray 1991), produced an iron pin probably datable to the early centuries of the first millennium AD (Close-Brooks 1984, 94). Considerably more evidence, some of it admittedly circumstantial, has been recovered for the dating of small square and rectangular cairns. Fragments of Class I Pictish symbol stones have been recovered from a round cairn in a mixed group of round and square mounds at Garbeg, Inverness, (Wedderburn and Grime 1984; Stevenson 1984), and also from a rectangular cairn at Dunrobin, Sutherland (Close-Brooks 1981). Closer to South-

east Perth, part of a cemetery of round and rectangular cairns has been excavated in the sand-dunes at Lundin Links, in Fife. Radiocarbon dates for burials from beneath two of the round cairns suggest a date in the middle of the first millennium AD. Such a date would fit the evidence from the barrows excavated at **Inchtuthil**, but it is by no means clear whether it should be extended to cemeteries such as **Blairhall**, where no square barrows have been recorded, or possibly to some of the other round cairns in South-east Perth.

Burials and cists

In addition to the round barrows and cairns, burials in cists and cinerary urns have been found at thirty-nine sites where there is no evidence of a covering mound. In all, at least sixty-five cists have been discovered, as many as forty-three of them in cemeteries, at least thirteen of which are known in the area, each comprising from two to eight burials. Indeed, it is quite likely that some of the single cists also belong to cemeteries, and the same probability exists for at least two of the five locations where cinerary urns have been found. Needless to say, there are considerable difficulties in establishing the nature and extent of all these funerary sites, partly on account of the ways in which they have been found, but also because of the often meagre references to their discovery. The antiquarian accounts rarely distinguish between prehistoric cists and long cists of relatively late date, and it is only quite recently that it has become standard excavation-practice to examine the area surrounding a cist to establish whether it was a single grave or part of a cemetery, and to learn if it was originally set within some form of enclosure or covered by a mound. In contrast with stone-built cists, the rate of discovery of urn burials has diminished significantly with the mechanisation of farming, quarrying and building work, for, while the slabs of a cist will resist all but the heaviest machinery, the destruction of an urn or an inhumation in a pit is likely to pass unnoticed; even when examples of the latter have been discovered, it is seldom possible to assign them a definite date (see below).

The distribution of cists and burials across South-east Perth is patchy and it may be presumed that dozens have been destroyed without record, while many more remain to be discovered. The majority of the known examples occur on well-drained sites, and a number are situated on knolls and natural rises, an association which perhaps reflects the same desire for conspicuity that inspired the construction of some of the cairns and barrows. However, the dynamics of soil erosion are such, that cists placed on the crests of knolls are more likely to be discovered by ploughing than those situated on flat ground or in hollows. Their overall distribution complements that of the cairns and barrows, with the majority lying on gravel terraces beside the main rivers of the area. None occurs within the cluster of cairns and barrows to the north-west of Inchtuthil, for instance, but dense concentrations of cists have been recorded on the south side of the River Isla between Coupar Angus and Little Keithick, and at Williamston near St Martins. The distribution of urns within South-east Perth is particularly thin and the small number of sites contrasts with the patterns of discovery in the adjoining areas of Angus, Dundee and Fife, suggesting a real gap in the distribution of urn-burials in the southern part of Strathmore and the Carse of Gowrie.

The earliest reference to the discovery of a cist or burial in South-east Perth describes 'some half consumed human bones' found in 'an excavation in the solid rock' at **Bully Quarry** on the east flank of the Hill of Dores in about 1768 (*Stat. Acct.*, 17 [1796], 18). The details of these early discoveries are usually too vague to be of much use and the standards of reporting do not improve until the second half of the nineteenth century. The difficulties of assessing the funerary record from such sources are further compounded by the poor quality of the surviving grave-goods from cists in South-east Perth, which again contrast with the relatively rich grave-goods accompanying burials in surrounding areas (see Coutts 1971). At least seven 'urns' are known to have been lost in the nineteenth century,

17B.

17A.

17C. 26A.

21.

p. 23

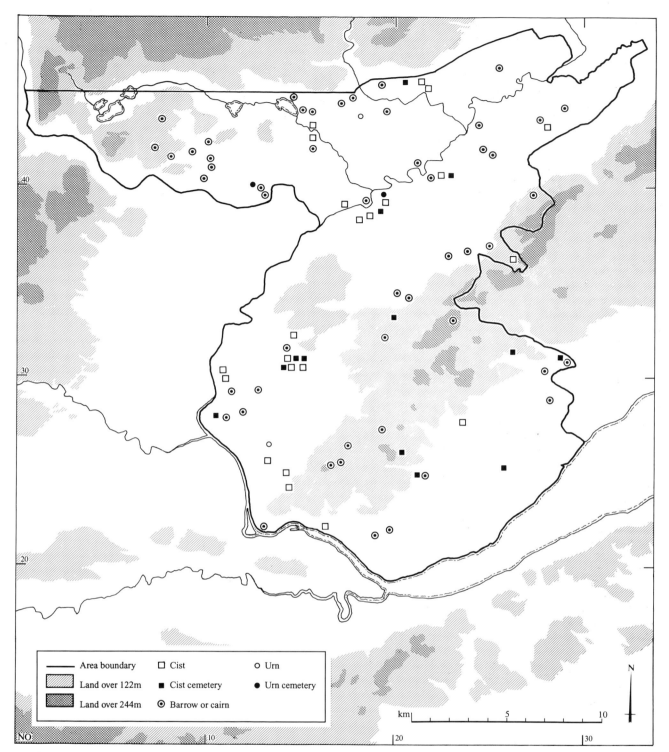

Distribution map of cist- and urn-burials (NMRS DC 25026)

and these may have helped to redress the balance.

In addition to the gap in the distribution of cinerary urns, there is also a dearth of Beakers from funerary contexts in South-east Perth. A fine Beaker (PMAG 1984-641) accompanying an inhumation in a cist was found at **Upper**
22A. **Muirhall** in 1984 (Reid, Shepherd and Lunt 1987), but the circumstances surrounding the discovery of another Beaker from the **Fingask Estate** are unknown; found intact, however, the latter was almost certainly also from a burial. A small sherd from a Beaker was recovered from a rabbit scrape at **Fingask** in the course of the present survey.

Six Food Vessels have been recovered from cists, however, accompanying burial deposits which range from single and double cremations to single adult inhumations. Three further Food Vessels (PMAG 214, 216-7), possibly associated with a

cremation burial, were found in 1917 at **Sherifftown**; they were probably placed upright in a line, and each appears to have had a small stone covering its mouth (Callander 1918). A cupmarked stone was also found nearby and a probable cist lay only 21m to the south-south-east; in 1990, aerial photography revealed a small ring-ditch in the immediate vicinity. Of the Food Vessels associated with cists, the example found at **Easter Essendy** accompanied a cremation with the only recorded jet necklace (DUNMG 1974-561-2) from the survey area; there was also a second cremation deposit in the cist (Thoms 1980). A second cist, found some 150m away to the north-north-west, also contained a Food Vessel (DUNMG 1980-270.1), but in this case it accompanied an inhumation; the underside of the coverstone bore four small cupmarks (Thoms 1980).

22B.

21

A

B

C

D

E

F

G

Prehistoric pottery. all approximately 1:2
*A. **Upper Muirhall** (NO 1454 2405), Beaker (PMAG; NMRS B 14974)*
*B. **Sherifftown** (NO 1049 2801), Food Vessel (PMAG; NMRS B 14977)*
*C. **Moor of Blairgowrie** (NO c.182 437), Accessory Vessel (NMS; NMRS B 39030)*
*D. **Law Hill, Arnbathie** (NO 1696 2580), pottery vessel (NMS; NMRS B 39028)*
*E. **Law Hill, Arnbathie** (NO 1696 2580), tuyere (NMS; NMRS B 39026)*
*F. **Belmont Castle** (NO c.28 43), Food Vessel (NMS; NMRS B 39015)*
*G. **Flawcraig** (NO c.236 276), Food Vessel (NMS; NMRS B 39018)*

Apart from the 'dagger' from the **Haer Cairn**, Rattray, the only recorded discovery of metalwork accompanying a burial in South-east Perth is a bronze armlet (PMAG 1473), found with an inhumation at **Williamston** in 1918 (Callander 1919a). Other 'human remains' were discovered a few metres to the south-west before 1863 (Name Book, Perthshire, No. 74, pp.17-18), possibly indicating that the cist belonged to a cemetery. A small cupmarked stone (now lost), which was also found in 1918, may have broken off a larger cup-and-ring marked slab (NMS IA 20) found close to in 1888 (Hutcheson 1889). The practice of placing funerary offerings of meat in a cist has been recorded only at **Muirhall**, near Perth, where the body of a young adult was accompanied by a flint knife (PMAG 1977.2622) and pig bones (*DES 1970*, 36).

Apart from the urns found during the excavation of the Roman legionary fortress at **Inchtuthil** in 1955 (Pitts & St Joseph 1985, 313) and that of the stone circle at **New Scone** in 1961 (Stewart 1966), three urn-burial sites from South-east Perth were recorded in the late-nineteenth century. The first to be discovered, in 1878, was a cinerary urn containing a cremation and an undecorated accessory vessel (NMS EC 5) from the **Moor of Blairgowrie** (Fraser 1878). The urn, which had been covered with a stone slab, was broken on removal, and only one fragment now survives (NMS EC 6). Slightly later, in 1894, a group of four vessels was discovered at **Little Keithick**, in an area on the south bank of the River Isla which has produced several cists (Name Book, Perth, No.15, p.3). One of these urns contained an accessory vessel, but this was lost soon after its discovery, and only fragments of the other urns now survive (PMAG 218-9, 221). The two urns from **Inchtuthil** probably also belonged to a cemetery; both were inverted and their bases had been destroyed in the Roman period (Pitts & St Joseph 1985, 252). Another cinerary urn which may be from South-east Perth is preserved in Perth Museum; it is labelled as having been found at the New Scone stone circle, but no mention is made of it in the excavation report (Stewart 1966).

Several of the vessels that have been found with burials in South-east Perth are not readily classifiable into the major groups of prehistoric pottery. A crudely-made vessel from **Bridge Farm**, Meikleour, falls into this category; it was found, with part of a flint blade (PMAG 215 & 215a) and the remains of an adult female inhumation, in a cist in 1933 (Ritchie 1935). The vessel, of which only the top part survives, measures about 125mm in overall diameter at the rim and is decorated with incised triangles within an upper border of three incised horizontal lines and a lower border of at least two lines. Although not parallelled exactly, aspects of this design may be seen in Beaker, Food Vessel and cinerary urn decoration (Clarke 1970, nos. 704, 737-8; Longworth 1984, no. 2102), and it is possible that the vessel is some form of hybrid. Another vessel (NMS EQ 564) of uncertain type or date was found in an unrecorded context at **Law Hill,** Arnbathie, in the late 1940s. Conceivably, it accompanied a prehistoric burial, but a tuyere (nozzle for bellows inserted into a furnace) was found at the same time and the vessel may have had a domestic or industrial function.

Most of the burials in cists have no accompanying grave-goods and, like the barrows and cairns, they may be of widely differing dates. One, described as being long and narrow, which was found at **Cairnbeddie** (Callander 1919a, 16), was possibly a long cist of Early Historic date. Other burials that have come to light may be more recent still. These include the remains of possible plague burials that were ploughed up about 1.6km north of Inchture in about 1760 (Melville, 1939, 86). Other human bones were discovered close to **Hangie's Well**, a natural spring near Newbigging, some time before 1845 (Name Book, Perthshire, No. 15, p. 17), while in 1981 human ribs and a clavicle were found in a load of gravel from a quarry at **Cleaves** to the south-west of Blairgowrie (*DES 1981*, 48-9).

The majority of the cists and urns probably belong to the Early Bronze Age, a period extending from about 2500 BC to 1500 BC. No radiocarbon dates are available for any of the Beaker or Food Vessel burials that have been described in this section, but some of them can be roughly dated by comparing their grave goods with material from elsewhere. For instance, radiocarbon dates for Beaker associations in Scotland indicate that this type of pottery was in use between about 2500 BC and 1600 BC. The style of the **Fingask** Beaker suggests a relatively early date in this period, while that of the **Upper Muirhall** example appears to be later, probably the first half of the second millennium BC. Radiocarbon dates for Food Vessels from Fife and Angus, ranging from the end of the third millennium BC to about the thirteenth or fourteenth century BC, overlap with those of the Beakers. As in Angus (Coutts 1971), most of the Food Vessels from South-east Perth are of Yorkshire Vase or Northern types; the Food Vessels from **Flawcraig** (Coates 1919, 149-50) and **Easter Essendy 1** (Thoms 1980), for instance, are typical Yorkshire Vases. Most of the cinerary urns from South-east Perth, and indeed from eastern Scotland, are Collared Urns, another type of vessel which was current throughout the first half of the second millennium BC. The only radiocarbon date available for a South-east Perth cinerary urn, however, is for a bucket-shaped vessel found at the centre of the stone circle at **Sandy Road,** New Scone. The cremation in the urn returned a single date of 1200 bc±150 (GaK-787) (Stewart 1966).

Sandy Road, New Scone (NO 1327 2646),
cinerary urn from the central burial, 1:4
(PMAG; NMRS B 14980)

CEREMONIAL AND RITUAL MONUMENTS

The early prehistoric ceremonial and ritual monuments of South-east Perth include remarkably diverse categories of sites; indeed, over recent years, their diversity has grown with virtually every season of aerial photography. These monuments are by no means limited to cropmarks, however, and there is an important group of standing stones and stone circles in the area. To these may be added the cupmarked stones, which so often turn up in ritual and ceremonial contexts, and also the **Cleaven Dyke**, a massive linear earthwork once believed to be Roman, but now thought to be related to cursus monuments of the Neolithic. The cropmark evidence includes a ditched cursus, and also what is probably a pit-defined example, together with a number of other pit-defined structures ranging from circles to square and rectangular settings, not all of which may be of ritual or ceremonial character. For convenience the small number of pit-alignments have also been dealt with alongside the other pit-defined features. Apart from these various structures, at least two of the cropmark ring-ditches may be Class I henges, a type of early prehistoric ceremonial enclosure. To these may be added the Neolithic mortuary enclosure excavated at **Inchtuthil** (Barclay and Maxwell 1992), and at least one other probable example amongst the cropmarks.

It is in their overall distribution that our knowledge of the ceremonial monuments has been most significantly enhanced.

26B. 27.

28A. 82.

24.

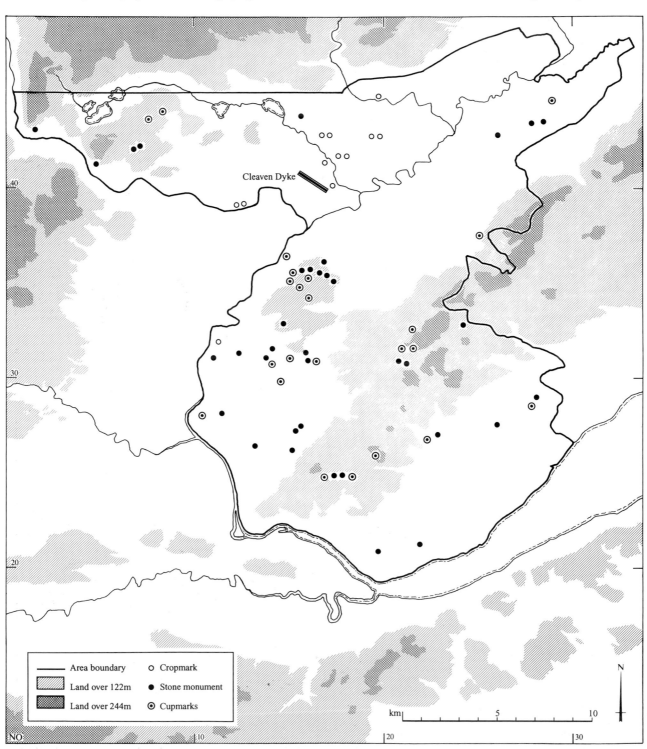

Distribution map of ritual and ceremonial monuments (NMRS DC 25027)

Whereas the standing stones, stone alignments and stone circles tend to be concentrated at the south-western end of the area, the majority of the cropmarks that fall into this category have been recorded on the gravels between Blairgowrie and the confluence of the Rivers Tay and Isla to the south of Meikleour. This is the area where maximum damage has been inflicted by centuries of agricultural exploitation and only one stone monument survives, but the area is also notable for the **Cleaven Dyke**. The date of the Cleaven Dyke is still not beyond doubt, but, if eventually proved to be of Neolithic origin, it would confirm the importance of the area as a centre of Neolithic ceremonial activity.

Some of the cropmarks, particularly the circles of pits and four-pit settings, could theoretically be interpreted as structural traces of now vanished settings of stones, but others are of a completely different character. Whilst the apparent concentration of these types of cropmark around the Cleaven Dyke might be used to enhance the ceremonial significance of the area, their distribution should be treated with some caution. In the first place, it should be borne in mind that some of the pit-settings and other monuments assigned to the ceremonial or ritual category may in fact have been domestic structures and *vice versa*; those that fall within recognised settlement complexes have been excluded from the overall map of ceremonial monuments, but can be found on a map showing all the pit-defined structures. There is, furthermore, the problem of differential cropmark formation. Most of these structures consist of relatively slight, interrupted features that, even on freely-draining soils, may be difficult to detect as cropmarks. Their absence from other parts of South-east Perth, where the

26B. 27.

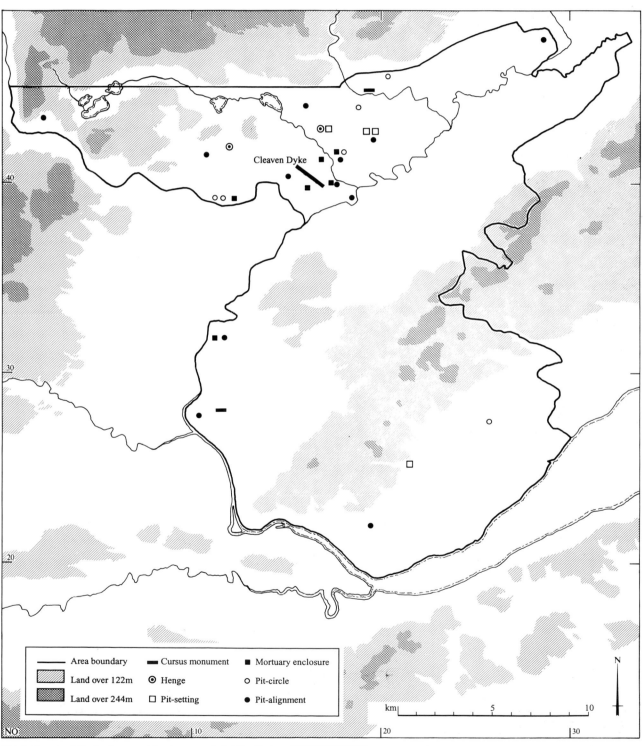

Distribution map of ritual and ceremonial enclosures, and pit-defined features (NMRS DC 25028)

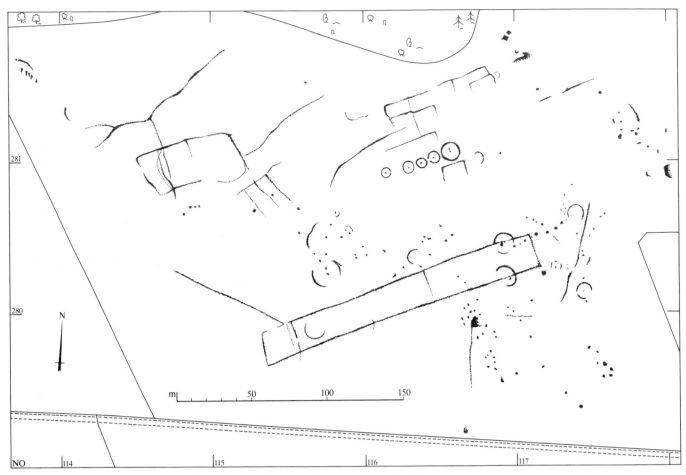

A. *Blairhall (NO 1160 2800), cursus monument, barrow cemetery and cropmarks, 1:2500 (NMRS DC 25029)*

soils are not so responsive to cropmarks, may be more apparent than real.

25. Cursus monuments

These curious monuments have long been recognised as components of early ceremonial complexes in southern England, but it is only more recently that their distribution has been extended northward into Scotland. Traditionally thought of as ceremonial avenues, perhaps linking locations of funerary and ritual significance in the landscape, most of the English examples are characterised by a pair of parallel ditches, sometimes accompanied by banks and extending over considerable distances. Their discovery in some numbers in Scotland has been a direct result of the programmes of aerial reconnaissance, but, in contrast to the situation in England, the majority of Scottish cursus monuments are defined by rows of pits. In South-east Perth, however, there is one of each type, in addition to the **Cleaven Dyke**.

17C.
26A.
    A ditched cursus has been recorded at **Blairhall**, a site which is also notable for its cemetery of small barrows (see Barrows and Cairns). The cursus measures about 190m in length by 24m in average breadth, and several transverse linear cropmarks cut across it, at least one of which, some 75m from the east-north-east end, appears to be an original feature. The easternmost portion thus defined is set at a slight angle to the rest and is also appreciably wider. Other Scottish cursus monuments display these transverse features, and it is not clear whether they are subdivisions of the interior or indicate the extension of an existing monument. In this case, the change of width and alignment suggests the latter, although there is no evidence as to which end might be the earlier. Another interesting feature of this particular cursus is its intersection with two probable barrows close to the eastern end, and also the existence of a possible ring-ditch near the western end of the interior. There is no direct evidence for their relationship to the cursus.

B. *The Cleaven Dyke (NO 1754 3976), the ploughed-out south-eastern terminal (CUCAP CDB-54)*

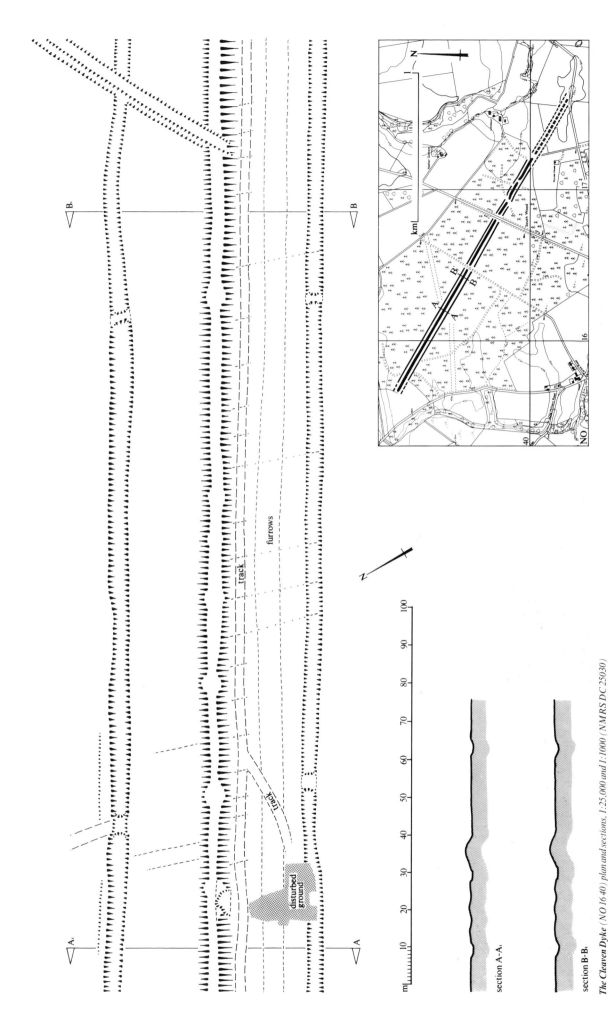

track

furrows

track

disturbed
ground

N

ml 10 20 30 40 50 60 70 80 90 100

section A-A₁

section B-B₁

The Cleaven Dyke (NO 16 40) plan and sections. 1:25,000 and 1:1000 (NMRS DC 25030)

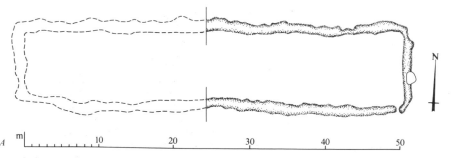

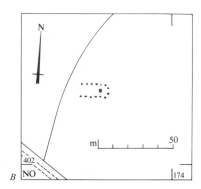

A. **Inchtuthil** (*NO 1254 3956*), *mortuary enclosure, its western end plotted from aerial photographs, 1:500*
(*NMRS DC 25032*)

B. **Littleour** (*NO 1734 4024*), *probable mortuary enclosure, 1:2500*
(*NMRS DC 25033*)

The cursus that has been discovered at **Milton of Rattray**, on the north bank of the River Ericht, appears to comprise two parallel rows of pits set about 18m apart. The pits are spaced at intervals of about 4m and have been traced over a distance of 120m, but neither terminal has so far been recorded.

The sites at **Blairhall** and **Milton of Rattray** can be assigned to the category of cursus with a reasonable level of confidence, but there is considerable doubt concerning the precise date and classification of the the **Cleaven Dyke**. The earthwork has a long history in antiquarian studies; it was traditionally associated with the Roman fortress at **Inchtuthil**, being latterly identified as a formal boundary of the military *territorium*, and it is only more recently that this interpretation has been questioned (Maxwell 1983; Pitts and St Joseph 1985, 257-60). Despite these uncertainties, there can be no doubting the monumental character of the earthwork. With only minor deviations in alignment, it extends across the country to the north of Meikleour for a distance of 2.3km, and the altitudinal variation along its entire length is little more than about 6m. For much of its length, the bank is about 8m to 10m in thickness, but towards the west end it increases to about 16m and is at least 1.8m in height. Again, its monumental character is reflected in the topographical position of the western end, from which the ground falls gently away to the north-west. A similar case can be made out at the ploughed-out eastern end, which, despite the antiquarian accounts, almost certainly rested on a knoll beside the public road to the north-west of the farm of Hallhole.

Viewed in detail, however, the earthwork is not absolutely straight, or totally regular, displaying small changes in alignment at several places along its course. At least one original gap may be identified in the portion that lies in the trees to the east of the A93, and the road itself may run through another. The bank is flanked by two ditches and there is slight evidence to suggest that these were dug in short segments. Sections cut across the earthwork have shown that the bank consists of a core of sand and gravel revetted with turf cheeks (Abercromby, Ross and Anderson 1902, 234; Richmond 1940, 41; Adamson and Gallagher 1986, 63). The broad berms, or platforms, to either side of the bank give the monument a breadth of between 45m and 50m within its ditches, and there is no evidence that the ditches return around the terminals. These features set it apart from the generality of cropmark cursus monuments in eastern Scotland, which are all considerably narrower, display square or variously rounded terminals and lack any evidence of a central bank.

25. **Mortuary enclosures**

The cursus monuments described above are probably structurally related to the class of small Neolithic ceremonial sites known as mortuary enclosures (Loveday 1985). Although embracing a wide diversity of structures, these sites are linked by their apparent role in Neolithic funerary and ritual practices, a function which it is difficult to demonstrate without excavation. Their recognition in South-east Perth as a group of oblong ditched or pit-defined enclosures rests largely on the interpretation of cropmarks on aerial photographs, although one has now been confirmed by excavation.

The excavated example lies within the Roman fortress at **Inchtuthil**. It was first revealed by cropmarks and was also partly excavated in 1961 (Pitts and St Joseph 1985, 248-51), but more recently the whole of the eastern half was examined in greater detail (Barclay and Maxwell 1992). The enclosure measures 54m by up to 10m within a ditch about 1.5m in breadth and 0.9m in depth. The ditch had been dug in linked segments and provided evidence of having served, on two separate occasions, as the bedding-trench for a line of posts probably supporting a fence. In the secondary phase, when the ditch was half full, the oak supports and fencing had been burnt *in situ*, and the ditch back-filled with sand and gravel while the timbers were still burning. The only artefacts recovered related to the Roman occupation of the site, but radiocarbon assay of charcoal derived from the fence produced a date in the late fourth or early third millennium BC.

The identification of other examples amongst the cropmarks poses considerable difficulties. Several other long rectangular enclosures have been identified as the probable remains of rectangular buildings (see the section on settlement), but the interpretation cannot be regarded as secure in every case. One particular site which should be considered here, comprises two structures identified at **Berryhill**. The first measures 38m by 8m within a ditch up to 1.5m in breadth; its ends are rounded, there are two pits placed symmetrically on its axis within either end, and two entrances in its south side. There are also traces of a similar, but slightly smaller, structure about 30m to the east. The Berryhill enclosures differ in various details from the mortuary enclosure at **Inchtuthil**, but the larger of the two certainly shares features in common with what is probably a pit-defined mortuary site at **Littleour**. Here, a setting of pits measures at least 25m in length by 8m in breadth; within the rounded east end there is a centrally positioned pit, and it is possible that the west end, which is lost in the hedgerow at the edge of the field, was of a similar appearance.

The most recent aerial sorties into South-east Perth in 1992 have recorded two further examples of this type of pit-defined enclosure. The first, at **Upper Gothens**, measures about 21m by 9m and it comprises eight pits, six of them in opposed pairs along the sides and one centrally-placed at each end. The second lies adjacent to a pit-circle near **Carsie Mains** and is rather smaller, measuring about 15m by 6m; its plan is not so clearly defined as the others, but at least one rounded end can be distinguished.

It must be admitted, however, that there is very little evidence to link these sites together, the only feature common to all of them being a roughly east to west alignment. Nevertheless, some kind of ceremonial or funerary context in early prehistory is the most probable interpretation for them, the more so, since there is a certain amount of evidence to suggest that such structures are often but one element of larger ceremonial complexes, which, in South-east Perth, are slowly being pieced together through the aerial reconnaissance programme, and elsewhere in Scotland also by excavation.

26B. 27.

28A. 82.

30B. 69C.

14A. 28B.

25. Pit-settings and pit-circles

In addition to the pit-defined mortuary enclosures described above, a number of other settings of pits have been identified from cropmark evidence. These range in shape from circular to roughly square, but, in the absence of excavation, their interpretation is far from clear. Nevertheless, there are good reasons for describing them in this section; examples of rings of pits, which once held upright timbers, are known from several Neolithic ceremonial contexts in Perthshire (e.g. Barclay 1984; Stewart 1987), and recent excavation of a small circular enclosure at Balneaves Cottage in the Lunan valley, Angus, has provided convincing evidence for the stone-holes of a four-poster setting (Russell-White 1988). This said, however, settings of posts were used to support circular and rectangular buildings throughout much of prehistory, as at Douglasmuir in Angus (Kendrick 1982).

To date, three roughly square, four-pit settings have been identified in South-east Perth. One about 2.5m square lies in the settlement complex at **Pitroddie** and its identity must, therefore, remain ambiguous. The other two, however, appear to be relatively isolated features, at **Whiteloch** lying about 70m to the south-west of a penannular ring-ditch identified as a possible henge (see below), and at **Ardmuir** some 150m to the east of a larger six-pit setting. The maximum dimensions of these two settings are about 4m and 2m square respectively, although the **Whiteloch** example appears to be trapezoidal rather than square. The pits of the larger setting at **Ardmuir** are arranged in three opposed pairs. The rows of pits forming the sides, which measure about 15m in length, are not exactly parallel, and splay from 14m apart at the east end to 16m on the west.

At least five pit-circles have also been recorded as cropmarks in South-east Perth. Like the square settings, however, some lie amongst settlement remains, and these are

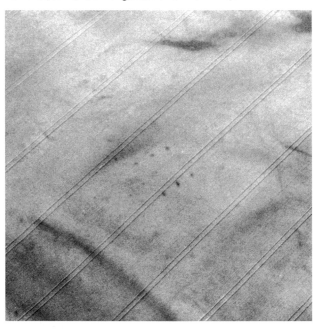

Ardmuir (NO 1947 4311), pit-setting (NMRS B 22414)

likely to be the pits that held the post-rings of circular buildings (Maxwell 1983, 33-4). A rough circle of pits at **Middlebank** in the Carse of Gowrie falls into this category, as does a pit-circle adjacent to a souterrain in an enclosure at **Old Mains of Rattray**. Less certain is the pit-circle 12m in diameter at **The Welton**, which lies close to two palisaded enclosures and several probable circular timber buildings.

Several of the other pit-circles, however, are perhaps more likely to belong to small ceremonial complexes. The pit-circle adjacent to the probable pit-defined mortuary structure at **Carsie Mains**, for instance, has already been mentioned, and a

similar interpretation may be put forward for two at **Inchtuthil**. The **Carsie Mains** example measures about 10m in diameter and consists of fifteen close-set pits, while those at **Inchtuthil** are 6m and 18m in diameter, comprising thirteen small pits and at least seven large pits respectively. The presence of the mortuary enclosure indicates ceremonial or ritual activity nearby and it may well be that some of the other pits that are scattered across the Inchtuthil plateau, both inside and outside the perimeter of the labour camp, are the result of more extensive ceremonial and funerary activity in the area. It is also worth observing, however, that the excavation of the fortress not only produced two inurned cremations, but also what was interpreted as a sacrificial pit of Roman date in the middle of the *principia* (Pitts and St Joseph 1985, 59).

Pit-alignments

In addition to the pit-defined cursus at **Milton of Rattray**, there are at least eight sites where apparent alignments of pits have been recorded. Any thoughts that these single alignments of pits may be hiding further examples of cursus monuments should be immediately dispelled, although one at **Glencarse** may form a rectilinear enclosure. Most of them conform to a simple pattern, with relatively large pits up to 2m in diameter formed into irregular straggles which may change direction at short intervals.

It is rarely possible to be certain that alignments of this type are complete, but in one instance in South-east Perth what may be the greater portion of an alignment has been recorded. This is at **Hallhole**, where a line of pits extends over a distance of about 400m, cutting across a sweeping bend of the River Isla and disappearing on the edge of the terrace above the haughland at its southern end. The purpose of the pits is far from clear; the irregular pattern of pit-size and interval, is not generally found in the pitted land-boundaries of Lothian and the Borders, and the line does not apparently form an enclosure comparable with early prehistoric pit-defined ceremonial sites known elsewhere in Scotland. Nor is there any reason to suppose that the juxtaposition of the alignment with the probable square-barrow cemetery at Hallhole is significant.

There are, however, obvious similarities between the Hallhole pit-alignment and some of the other examples of this type of cropmark that have been identified not only in South-east Perth, but also across a wider area of eastern Scotland. At **Berryhill**, for instance, in the same field as the possible mortuary enclosures, there is the same pattern of relatively large pits set at irregular intervals, wriggling along the edge of what appears to be an area of deeper alluvial soils. At **Ardmuir**, too, a little way to the south of the settings that have been described above, this same irregular pattern has been recorded. The apparent topographical relationship between the pit-alignment and the edge of deeper alluvium or a terrace at **Berryhill** is also detectable in the short sectors of alignments that have been photographed at **Millbank** and **Balendoch**. A similar physical relationship between pit-alignments and cropmarks indicating the edge of deeper alluvium has been observed widely in eastern Scotland north of the Forth.

Large ceremonial enclosures, defined by what can be fairly irregular perimeters of pits, have been recorded in the adjacent parts of both Perthshire and Angus, but no certain examples have come to light in South-east Perth. There is, however, the possible example of a smaller rectilinear enclosure at **Glencarse**. Here, the south end of a curving row of close-set pits, which cuts across the axis of a low ridge to the south-west of a probable rectangular building and ditched barrow, appears to turn eastwards at right-angles, and there are also traces of what may be a third side; together they define an area about 30m wide and at least 45m in length. Further aerial reconnaissance may yet reveal that some of the other pit-alignments are elements of large enclosures, the most likely candidates including: one in the shallow saddle to the west of **Dunkeld Park**, where a standing stone some 200m to the west possibly provides a clue to its character; another at the west end

A. Ardmuir (NO 196 428), pit-alignment (NMRS B 22406)

of the gravel plateau north of **Spittalfield**; and a third amongst the complex at **Tay Farm**.

25.

Henges

The ceremonial enclosures known as henges appear, at first sight, to be totally absent from South-east Perth. Circular or oval on plan, with either one or two entrances and a broad ditch flanked by an external bank, henges, often of some size, form a significant element in many of the country's larger ceremonial complexes. With the emergence of so much evidence for ceremonial activity in the neighbourhood of the **Cleaven Dyke**, it is therefore surprising that no major example of this type of earthwork has come to light in the course of the survey. Nevertheless, there are two reasons for suggesting that this absence is more apparent than real: firstly, there is the possibility that some of the cropmark ring-ditches may in fact be small henges; and secondly, other examples may conceivably be revealed by the excavation of stone circles.

It is important to appreciate that the term ring-ditch has no functional connotation, being applied generally to cropmark traces of small circular enclosures of unknown date and purpose. There are, however, two sites classified in this survey as ring-ditches for which a ceremonial interpretation is the more than plausible. The first of these is the penannular ring-ditch at **Mains of Gourdie**, which measures 14m in diameter within a ditch 5m in breadth, and the second is the smaller penannular example, some 7m in internal diameter, at **Whiteloch**. The scale of the ditch in proportion to the size of the interior at **Mains of Gourdie**, is a strong indication of the enclosure's character, although the width of the cropmark could theoretically have been produced by the coincidence of successive ring-ditches with different diameters. The interpretation of the **Whiteloch** ring-ditch rests, even more tentatively, on its superficial resemblance to the small henge identified by excavation beneath a stone circle at Moncreiffe House, not far distant in Strathearn (Stewart 1987).

30C.

Stone circles and settings

31.

Standing stones and stone settings probably arouse more curiosity than any other feature surviving from the prehistoric landscape, their lack of any obvious utilitarian function providing a tenuous contact with the ritual beliefs from a

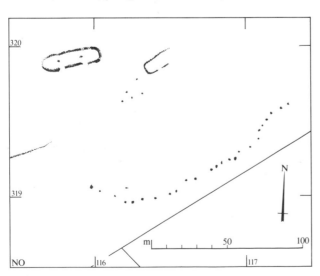

B. Berryhill (NO 116 319), rectangular structures and pit-alignment, 1:2500 (NMRS DC 25034)

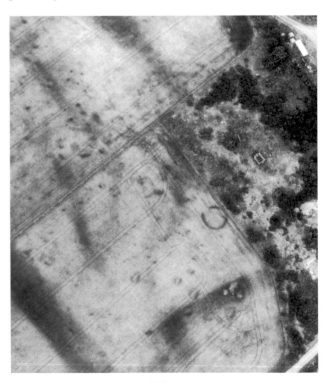

C. Whiteloch (NO 1676 4284), possible henge (NMRS PT 5428)

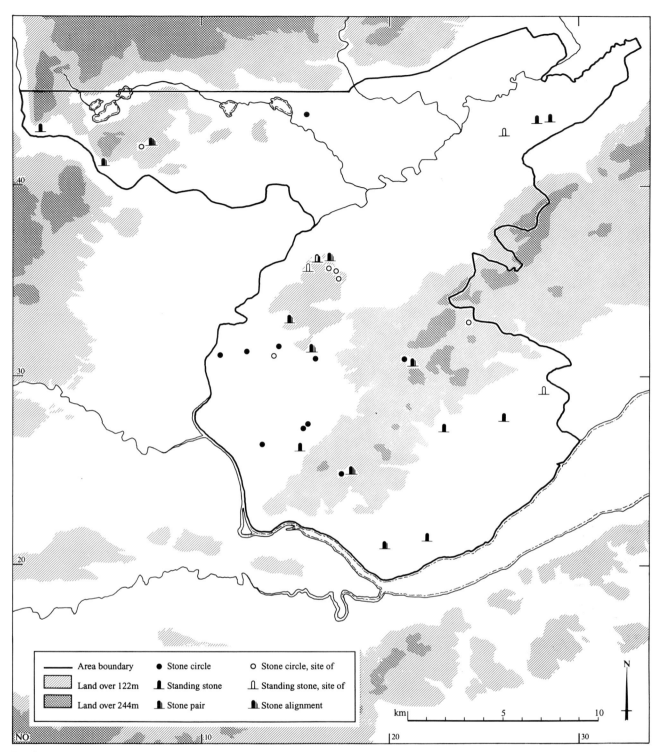

Distribution map of standing stones and stone circles (NMRS DC 25035)

remote past. Detailed survey has not only shown that some
have been set up on important astronomical alignments, but has
also revealed that many of the stone circles hide a complex
geometrical layout, their plans ranging from simple circles,
some with a flattened side, to elliptical or ovate shapes.

A total of fifteen stone circles and at least one setting are
known to have existed in South-east Perth, but the remains of
only ten of these structures have survived. The others were
destroyed in the course of agricultural improvements in the first
half of the nineteenth century. Of these ten sites, eight are small
and roughly circular, forming an apparently homogeneous
group in the south-western part of the survey area. The
character of the ninth, at **Leys of Marlee**, is not entirely clear,
while the tenth is a four-poster setting at **Commonbank**. The
remarkable distribution of small circles in the area immediately

32.

north-east of Perth — thirteen in an area of 76 square
kilometres — is one of the densest concentrations that can be
found in Britain.

The imperfect preservation of the circles makes it impossible
to base their classification on any factor apart from size,
although certain details of their architecture hint at a more
complex grouping. They range from 6m to 8.8m in internal
diameter and, depending on their size, the number of stones
varies from seven to eleven. The two destroyed circles near the
'Roman' road at **Gallowhill**, and a third at **Stockmuir**, had
nine stones and may also have belonged to this group, as may
the 'small circle' at **East Cult**.

The stones composing at least five of the surviving circles,
namely **Bandirran, Druids' Seat Wood, Colen, Blackfaulds**
and **Sandy Road,** New Scone, were probably arranged in

32.

31

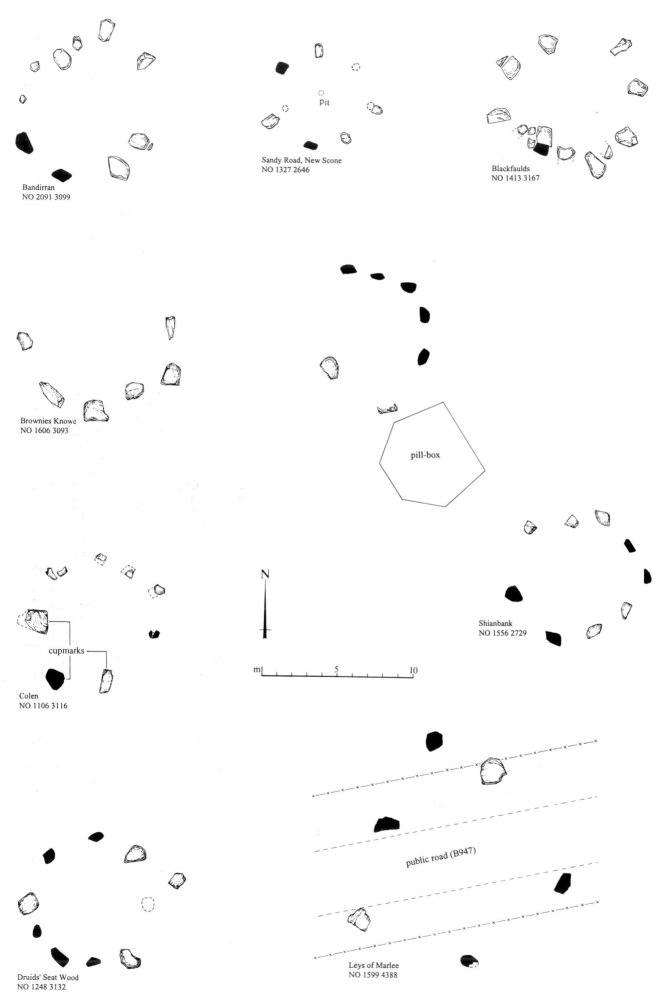

Bandirran
NO 2091 3099

Sandy Road, New Scone
NO 1327 2646

Pit

Blackfaulds
NO 1413 3167

Brownies Knowe
NO 1606 3093

pill-box

Shianbank
NO 1556 2729

cupmarks

Colen
NO 1106 3116

N

m⊢   5   10

Druids' Seat Wood
NO 1248 3132

public road (B947)

Leys of Marlee
NO 1599 4388

Comparative plans of stone circles in South-east Perth, 1:250 (NMRS DC 25063)

Bandirran (NO 2091 3099), drawing of the stone circle by Skene in 1832, (NMRS PTD 320/1)

accordance with their size, with the largest, but not necessarily the tallest, stones located on the south-west. Close examination of these circles, shows that the patterns of size-grading can be quite complex. At least four of the stones at **Bandirran** must have stood about 1.5m high, but of these, the two massive boulders standing on the south-west, are significantly larger than the others, both of which have fallen. An early plan of the circle also shows a central stone (Skene 1832; NMRS SAS 464), but no trace of this unusual feature survives. The circle in **Druids' Seat Wood** comprises nine stones and again the more massive boulders are on the south-west. Here, however, it is clear that tall stones up to 1.4m high, were alternated with smaller stones, the latter no more than 0.8m high; it is likely that a pair of tall stones stood side by side on the north-east, although one of these is now broken and the evidence is ambiguous. It must also be significant that the two shortest stones (0.6m high) are situated directly opposite each other on the north and south respectively. Another complex pattern may be detected at **Blackfaulds**, where the lengths of the fallen stones vary from 0.7m to 1.8m; again, the largest, now broken into at least four fragments, was on the south-west, but it was flanked by the two smallest stones, and while the rest of the stones around the north-west half of the circle are all of a similar size (1.4m to 1.5m in length), the three around the south-east are apparently graded (1.2m to 1.8m in length), with what would have been the tallest on the south.

Even where the stones of a circle are all quite small, similar relationships can be detected. For example, at **Colen**, despite its poor state of preservation, it is clear that the largest stones, although only about 1m high, stood on the south-west; indeed, three of them also bear cup-markings. At **Shianbank**, too, the spacing of the stones of the south-eastern of this remarkable pair of circles suggests the concern of the builders with the south-western arc.

The cup-markings at **Colen** are not the only examples of this type of carving that have been recorded at a stone circle in South-east Perth. A cupmarked boulder lies 17.5m south-west of the ring at **Brownies Knowe** and one of the stones of the destroyed circle at **Stockmuir** may also have been decorated in this way.

There is an appreciable difference in scale between these small rings and the larger setting of imposing stones at **Leys of Marlee**, which straddles the minor road leading from Blairgowrie to Essendy and was recently the subject of an exploratory excavation (Gibson 1988). Several of the stones have been knocked down and re-erected, but today there are six, forming an oval or elliptical shape measuring about 16m by 11.5m internally. Excavation established that four of the stones were probably in their original positions, but the socket of the southernmost, which had previously been concreted into its present position, could not be examined, and the original stone-hole of the re-erected stone on the north-east was not located either. Although usually classed as a circle, the three stones forming the western arc stand almost in a straight line, and it is possible that the stones belong to some kind of rectilinear setting, perhaps comparable with the large pit-setting recorded as a cropmark at **Ardmuir**. Like the smaller graded circles, however, the axis of the plan lies from north-east to south-west.

Last to be considered is a small four-post setting at **Commonbank**. The site is peripheral to the main concentration of four-posters in central Perthshire and on the Perthshire/Angus border, but the emergence of comparable pit-settings amongst the cropmarks (see above) will almost certainly redraw the boundaries of this distribution. Like most other four-posters, the Commonbank setting occupies a slighly elevated position. All four stones have fallen, but it probably measured about 3m across, and the north-west stone bears at least three cupmarks. Adjacent to the four-poster there is a probable alignment of three boulders, one of which bears a single cupmark, but nothing now survives of another setting, also including one cupmarked stone, which was previously recorded about 250m to the east (*DES 1964*, 44; *1973*, 44).

Very little dating evidence is available for any of the stone circles in South-east Perth, although a token cremation-deposit interred in a coarse urn at the centre of the circle at **Sandy Road**, New Scone, has been dated to 1200 bc ± 150 (Gak-787). This circle, one of the cluster of small rings described above, originally comprised seven stones, with the largest probably on the south-west, but whether the burial of the urn coincided with the erection of the stones, or merely represents the reuse of the site, is not known. Similar problems are encountered with the dating of four-posters, the nearest excavated example being at Lundin Farm in Strathtay. The outward simplicity of that setting belied a complex history (Stewart 1966), but, although an abraded sherd of a Beaker was recovered, neither the precise sequence of events, nor their chronology was established.

33

31. Stone pairs and alignments

The prehistoric stone monuments of Perthshire are also notable for the presence of pairs of standing stones and three-stone alignments. South-east Perth is no exception, with four surviving examples of each class. To these should probably be added two upright stones near **Newbigging**, which were deliberately thrown over and buried at the end of the eighteenth century. One of these stones, however, was apparently decorated with a 'moon and seven stars' (*Stat. Acct.*, 13 [1794], 536-7; Simpson 1868, 59-60), a description more reminiscent of the crescent symbol of Pictish carvings than prehistoric cup-markings.

The stones forming pairs are rarely more than a few metres apart and are usually at least 1.5m in height. At **Loanhead**, for instance, they are about 1.5m in height and stand 5.5m apart, while at **Newtyle** they are 2.7m apart, the more north-westerly rising to a height of 2.1m and the other to 1.6m. The position of the latter is slightly unusual in that the stones are set at the back of a terrace overlooking the River Tay, with the ground rising sharply immediately behind them.

Little excavation has been undertaken on this class of monument, but the **Pitfour** stones were examined prior to modern development (*DES 1967*, 44-5) and now form the centre-piece for a flowerbed in front of St Madoes Primary School. The group currently comprises three stones, but there is no evidence that the southernmost ever stood upright. The other two are pointed blocks about 1.5m high, and the more northerly is heavily decorated with cupmarks. The excavation showed that the site had been extensively disturbed, but neither upright appears to have been set up in a prepared socket, and no dating evidence was recovered.

No more is known of the three-stone alignments than of the pairs. The four surviving examples in South-East Perth range from 8m to 25m in length, and there appears to be little uniformity in their orientation. The **East Cult** alignment, once allegedly accompanied by a small circle close by (*Stat. Acct.*, 9 [1793], 504), is undoubtedly the most impressive today. Extending for a distance of 25m along the crest of a broad ridge to the west of the farmhouse, it comprises three stones, the central one being about 2.1m high and the westernmost 1.8m; the easternmost, which is now fallen, is heavily cupmarked. Examples of cup-markings have also been recorded on a single stone from each of the fallen alignments at **Gallowhill Wood** and **Commonbank**.

The only dated alignment in Scotland is the four-stone example excavated at Duntreath, in Strath Blane at the west end of the Campsie Fells (NS 532 807), where a radiocarbon date of 2860 ± 270 bc (GX-2781) was obtained, suggesting that the stones were erected in the Neolithic period (MacKie 1973).

31. Standing stones

Of the ten single standing stones recorded in South-east Perth, only six survive, most being undressed erratic boulders or slabs over 1.4m in height. The exceptional size of **Macbeth's Stone** at Belmont Castle may, therefore, have corresponded to the significance attached to it. Rectangular in cross-section, the stone tapers to a point some 3.6m above the ground; each of its sides is decorated with cupmarks, as many as forty occurring on the east face and twenty-four on the west.

Apart from the example 600m east-north-east of Macbeth's Stone, none of the standing stones of South-east Perth have been examined by excavation, and even here the results were uninformative (Jervise 1859, 246; Wise 1859, 94). Nevertheless, it would be reasonable to presume that the majority of these curious and enigmatic monuments are of prehistoric date, probably forming but one aspect of the Neolithic ceremonial and ritual complexes that are beginning to emerge from the landscape of South-east Perth. It is worth bearing in mind that timber equivalents of the single standing stones may also have been a component of these complexes, but the cropmark traces of the massive pits that would have held them have yet to be recognised.

Macbeth's Stone (NO 2799 4346), cupmarked standing stone (NMRS B 39012)

Cup-and-ring markings

A total of thirty-nine cupmarked stones are now known in South-east Perth, several of them recorded for the first time in the course of the present survey. At least eleven of them are stones which have been set upright, either as single standing stones or as components of stone circles and other types of setting. All but one of the rest of the carvings appear on stray boulders, the exception, at **Commonbank**, being pecked into living rock.

The composition of the carvings varies immensely. One of the stones of the **Colen** circle bears a single cupmark, while the easternmost stone of the **East Cult** alignment displays at least 130 cups on one face alone. The latter, however, is clearly an exception, and well over half the stones are decorated with fewer than fifteen cupmarks. Twelve of the stones have in excess of twenty cupmarks and some of these carvings are quite impressive in their appearance. This is particularly the case with **Macbeth's Stone**, the standing stone which has already been described, and the northern upright of the **Pitfour** stones. The small slab at **Rait** is also a strikingly handsome stone, with no fewer than seventy cupmarks on its upper surface; one of the large cups on this stone is surrounded by a ring of six equally-spaced smaller ones in a rosette pattern.

Ten of the stones have more complex designs involving rings, while several others are embellished with dumbbell markings and channels. In South-east Perth, the addition of ringmarks is a regular feature of the stones that bear between ten and forty cupmarks, the one exception being a small boulder from **Newbigging** (Simpson 1868, 60), now set up beside the lawn at Balholmie House. This stone bears only eight cups, but five of these are surrounded by three concentric rings, and one also has a radial channel. Another of the four cupmarked stones from Newbigging which has been decorated in this manner was examined when it was moved to its present location at the corner of the field to the west of the farm

35.

32.

34.

35B.

35C.

34

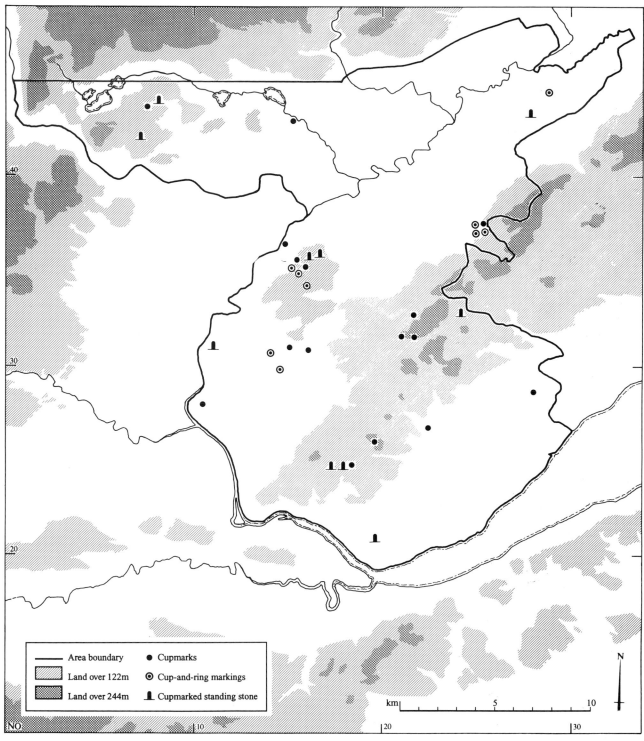

A. Distribution map of cup-and-ring marked stones (NMRS DC 25064)

B. **Rait** *(NO 2275 2677), cupmarked stone*
(NMRS B 14698)

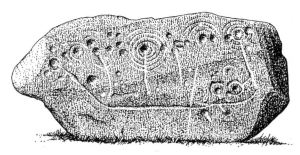

C. **Newbigging** *(NO 1558 3521), cup-and-ring marked stone, 1:25*
(NMRS DC 25269)

(Barclay, Brooks and Rideout 1983). Measuring 1.8m in length by 0.95m in breadth and 0.65m in thickness, the stone bears at least thirty-seven cupmarks, five of which have single or double ringmarks and a further three up to five. Several of the cupmarks have radial grooves and there are also other lengths of channel in the design. Although the stone has been set upright on at least two occasions since its initial discovery (Simpson 1868, 60), the position of the carvings suggests that they were executed when the boulder was recumbent.

Dumbbell markings occur on three stones, and two of these, at **East Cult** and **Pitcur**, are heavily cupmarked. The third stone is a small slab bearing eight cups, which was found close to a cist at **Williamston** in 1918 (Callander 1919a, 22-3); this stone is now lost, but it was possibly a fragment of a stone with twenty-one cupmarks, two of them ringed, which was found close to the same spot in 1888 (Hutcheson 1889, 142-3; NMS IA 20). Channels have been recorded on at least seven of the stones, and on four of these they have been set radially to cupmarks. One of these stones, now lost, was alleged to have come from a stone circle near **West Whitefield** (Hutcheson 1884, 315); it bore at least twenty cups, and had no fewer than four channels radiating from the only one that was ringed.

The most impressive collection of cupmarked stones that can be seen in South-east Perth today is undoubtedly at **Pitcur**, where no fewer than four have been incorporated into a souterrain. Two of the stones have been used as basal stones for the walls of the passage, while the other two are displaced capstones. Between them, these four stones illustrate most of the elements of designs that have been recorded in South-east Perth. One, a capstone that has fallen into the passage, bears at least seventeen plain cupmarks, but the others display ringmarks, dumbbells and channels, most of the latter set radially to both plain cupmarks and cup-and-ring marks.

The dating of these decorated stones is far from certain, and there is little evidence to be gathered from their contexts, many of them having been moved or even deliberately buried in the course of agricultural improvements. Recently it has been argued that the *floruit* of cup-and-ring carvings lay in the Late Neolithic and that there is no evidence to show that this form of decoration was practised after about 2000 BC (Burgess 1990). The decorated stones that turn up in Early Bronze Age contexts, and in contexts that are often assumed to be of that date, are usually in re-use, a practice that is generally accepted for the stones built into souterrains such as **Pitcur**, but not so readily agreed for those incorporated into Early Bronze Age cists, such as the example that formed the coverstone of a cist at **Easter Essendy**. The discovery of a small cupmarked stone in the mortuary structure beneath the long barrow at Dalladies, Kincardineshire (Piggott 1974), shows that some of these carvings may date from considerably earlier in the Neolithic period. Furthermore, the radiocarbon date from the stone alignment at Duntreath, Stirlingshire (see above), suggests that some of the stone settings upon which these carvings are found may be of Neolithic date anyway.

The precise significance of these decorated stones is unknown, but they almost certainly played some part in the ceremonial and ritual activities of the Neolithic. The appearance of such impressive cup-markings on the alignment at **East Cult** or the pair at **Pitfour** suggests much more than aesthetic appreciation of the decoration at a later date. There is a clear implication of contemporary significance, which is also borne out by the position of the carvings on **Macbeth's Stone**, where it is hard to escape the conclusion that the decoration was intended to be seen with the stone upright and not recumbent. Most of the cupmarked stones, however, are decorated on only one face, and, although none is in its original position, these have probably always lain flat on the surface of the ground.

Chronology and context

The chronology of the various types of ritual and ceremonial monuments that have been discussed in this section is far from clear. While some of the stone circles may date from relatively late in the second millennium BC, the radiocarbon dates of 3210 ± 70 bc (GU-2760) and 3120 ± 50 bc (GU-2761) from **Inchtuthil** clearly show that some of the other types of site are considerably earlier, in that particular case dating from early in the Neolithic period. The importance of these monuments cannot be overstressed, for they are almost the sole source of evidence for specific locations that were in use at this time, (see also the settlement section). In this respect, the pattern of archaeological monuments recorded in this survey reflects a much wider area of eastern Scotland than simply South-east Perth. The apparent absence of Neolithic funerary monuments (chambered tombs, and long barrows and cairns), for instance, is repeated throughout lowland Angus, but there, as in South-east Perth, there is a steadily growing body of cropmark evidence for ceremonial and ritual activity.

28A. 82.

pp. 41-3

The problems that attend the identification of Neolithic settlements in South-east Perth are familiar elsewhere, although it may be argued that the difficulties arise from our ignorance rather than absence of evidence. Little is known of the characteristics of Neolithic domestic structures in Scotland, with the result that some sites may not be identified by current survey techniques, while the classification of others may be wrongly attributed. The massive timber structure excavated at Balbridie, Kincardine (Ralston 1982), is a case in point; originally interpreted from aerial photographs as an Early Historic timber hall, it proved to be Neolithic. Nearly twice as wide as any other excavated Neolithic building in Europe, however, there is considerable doubt as to its identification as a roofed structure, and, until more examples are excavated, it will not be known whether such structures are typical components of Neolithic settlements or simply an extension of the known range of ceremonial monuments.

A similar problem is encountered with the miscellaneous enclosures that have been located by the Commission's aerial survey programme the length and breadth of eastern Scotland. The assumption that these are all of Iron Age date is unfounded, as has been demonstrated at Kinloch Farm, Fife, where a cropmark comprising two concentric ditches was partially excavated in advance of construction work (Barber 1983). By its very nature, the salvage excavation that took

A *Williamston (NO 1416 3074), cup-and-ring marked stone (NMS; NMRS B 39022)*

B. *Gallowhill (NO c.167 359), cup-and-ring marked stone (NMS; NMRS B 39021)*

A   *B*

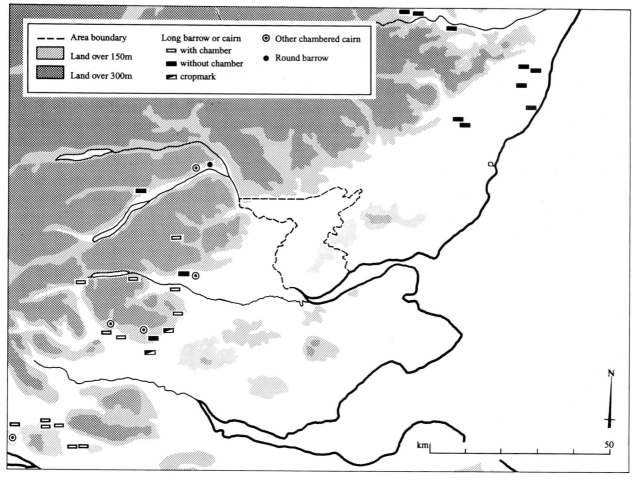

A. Distribution map of Neolithic funerary monuments in eastern Scotland (NMRS DC 25065)

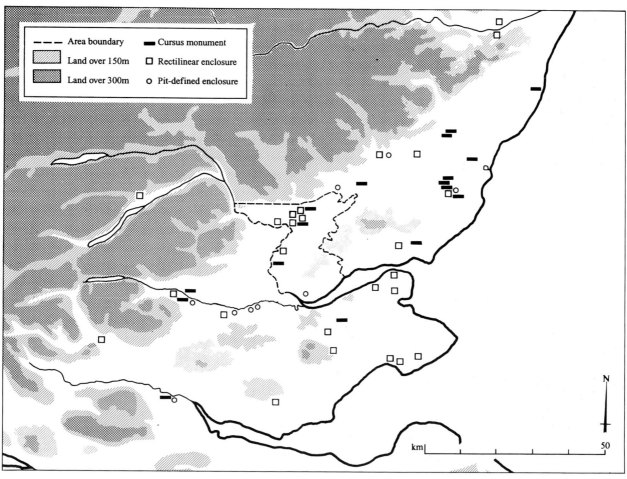

B. Distribution map of cursus monuments, rectilinear enclosures (possible mortuary enclosures) and pit-defined enclosures in eastern Scotland (NMRS DC 25068)

place could not answer many of the broader questions concerning the chronology and relationships of the various features recorded, but a radiocarbon date of 2775±70 bc (GU-1375) from the fill of the inner ditch clearly indicates a phase of occupation relatively early in the Neolithic period. An assemblage of Late Neolithic or Early Bronze Age pottery was also recovered from two pits within the interior.

The impact of Neolithic communities in eastern Scotland is well-attested in the environmental record and in the distribution of artefacts, such as stone axes, but a vast gap is apparent in the pattern of recorded funerary monuments in the area running from the hills west of Perth to the River North Esk (Kinnes 1987). To a certain extent, the pattern may be one of survival and destruction, or possibly differing intensities of fieldwork, but, in so far as it is possible, the gap has been tested by the surveys of North-east and South-east Perth (RCAHMS 1990). Despite the tracts of ancient landscape surviving in Glen Shee and Strathardle in North-east Perth, no chambered tombs or long cairns were recognized, and the only possible example of a long barrow in South-east Perth, on Herald Hill, is more likely to be a natural feature. By contrast a survey of Kincardine led to the identification of two new long cairns in the southern part of the district (RCAHMS 1982, 7, nos.1-2), while more recent fieldwork in the hills to the west of Strathearn suggests a remarkable concentration there of Neolithic funerary monuments. The discovery of the long cairns at Edinchip (Davidson and Henshall 1984) and Auchenlaich (Foster and Stevenson forthcoming) pointed to the potential of this area, and a survey of the Braes of Doune by the Commission's Afforestable Land Survey in 1992 has led to the identification of no fewer than four additional monuments. The concentration here is also accentuated by two possible examples of levelled long barrows amongst the cropmarks, both represented by a pair of roughly parallel ditches. In both cases, the ditches are of minor proportions, but they correspond closely with the token ditches that flanked the Dalladies long barrow in Kincardine (Piggott 1974). What is of more significance is that, as yet, pairs of ditches of this sort are unknown amongst the cropmarks of South-east Perth and Angus.

That contemporary Neolithic communities exploited what is now some of Scotland's richest farmland in the gap between the two concentrations of funerary monuments can hardly be doubted. A sparse distribution of pottery has been recovered by excavation (Kinnes 1987, 47; Cowie 1992), but, more importantly, stone axes have a remarkably dense distribution throughout the area. Factors of survival are clearly at play, and the long-term arable use of these fertile lowlands, which has levelled any upstanding monuments, has maintained the rate of discovery of stray finds. Of these, stone axes, and perhaps leaf-shaped arrowheads, are the most durable and readily recognisable parts of the Neolithic tool-kit. In addition to the evidence of the artefacts, aerial survey, as has been shown in South-east Perth, has revealed a series of structures which appear to belong to well-known categories of Neolithic ceremonial monuments. Furthermore, the excavation of the mortuary enclosure at **Inchtuthil**, and what may be a short pit-defined cursus monument at Douglasmuir, Angus (Kendrick 1980), have confirmed that some, at least, are of Neolithic date.

In effect, it is possible to detect a pattern of regionality emerging from the distributions of Neolithic monuments in eastern Scotland, the most striking elements being the clusters of funerary structures at either end of Strathmore. To the north-east these are all non-megalithic long cairns and barrows, while to the south-west megalithic tombs predominate, but possibly with as many as four non-megalithic long cairns and barrows. The apparent integrity of these distributions, however, suggests that the gap between them, which embraces the whole of South-east Perth, is perhaps some kind of region in its own right; its archaeology is certainly not characterised by the principal types of known funerary monuments. There are, however, other types of, nominally later, funerary monument in this area. In particular, there are numerous large round barrows,

some of which, as was demonstrated by excavation at Pitnacree in Strathtay (Coles and Simpson 1965), may well be of Neolithic date. The temptation to assume that many of the large lowland round barrows are of Neolithic date has been resisted in the section of this volume describing the barrows and cairns of South-east Perth; this, however, might provide an explanation for the apparent absence of Neolithic funerary monuments across so much of eastern Scotland.

The cropmark evidence, however, has made a tremendous impact in this lowland zone and, while evidence of funerary monuments may be wanting, several types of ceremonial and ritual monuments can be identified. Principally, these are cursus monuments and mortuary enclosures, which, as in South-east Perth, may be defined by either ditches or pits, but they also include larger pit-defined enclosures of the type excavated at Meldon Bridge, Peeblesshire (Burgess 1976).

While there is considerable room for debate over the character of possible mortuary enclosures from cropmark evidence, the cursus monuments can be identified with some confidence, particularly those defined by rows of pits. Fortunately, two of the pitted examples, Douglasmuir in the Lunan Valley (Kendrick 1980), and Bannockburn near Stirling (Tavener 1987), have been excavated, revealing in both instances that the pits had held upright timbers. The identification of the Douglasmuir example is perhaps less secure than some of the others that have been recorded, since it only measures about 60m in overall length, but the transverse

Balneaves Cottage, Angus, (NO 606 496), terminal and transverse division of a pit-defined cursus (NMRS AN 5514)

division at its mid-point is a feature that has been noted elsewhere, and has already been discussed in connection with **Blairhall** in South-east Perth. No such division has been identified at Bannockburn, where the excavation not only uncovered the squared eastern terminal of the cursus, but also part of a large, pit-defined enclosure, lying immediately to the east; sections cut across the pits defining the enclosure revealed a complex history of use, in which at least three phases of activity could be recognised, and, at some stage, the pits appear to have been left open.

Unfortunately the full extent of the Bannockburn site is not yet known, but the results of aerial survey suggest that the

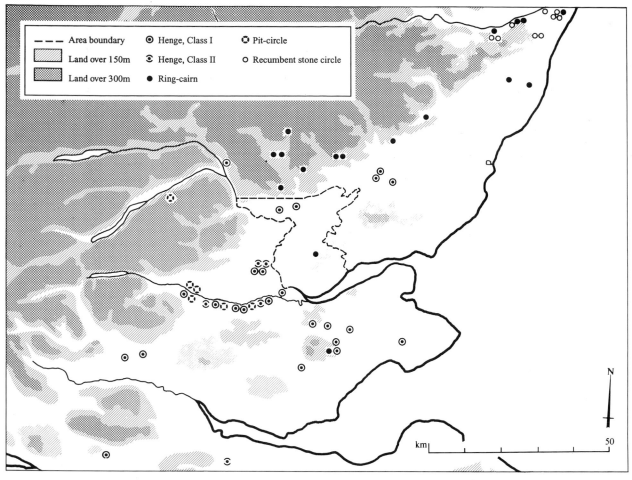

A. *Distribution map of henges, ring-cairns, pit-circles and recumbent stone circles in eastern Scotland (NMRS DC 25066)*

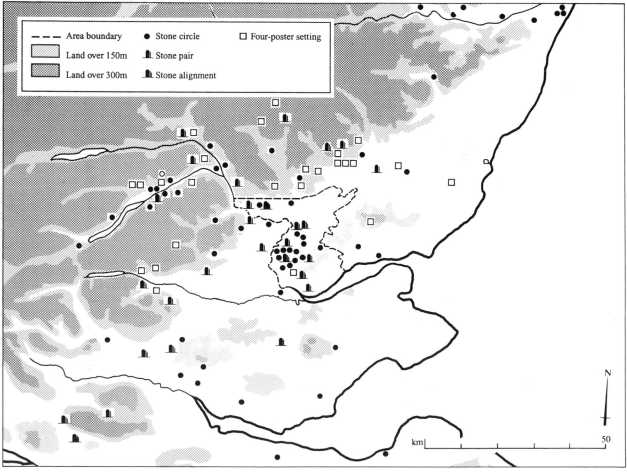

B. *Distribution map of stone settings in eastern Scotland (NMRS DC 25067)*

juxtaposition of ceremonial monuments of various types is perhaps the rule rather than the exception, even if they should prove to be of widely differing dates. This is certainly the impression created by the distribution of monuments around the *24.* **Cleaven Dyke** in South-east Perth, and it is a pattern that can be repeated at sites such as Forteviot (St Joseph 1978) and Leadketty, both in Strathearn, where large pit-defined enclosures approached by short avenues lie at the core of a cluster of ring-ditches and enclosures. The plans of these particular pit-defined structures would suggest a parallel with the Meldon Bridge enclosure, where the pits had held massive upright timbers, possibly signifying an entirely separate category of structure to that at Bannockburn. However, the important point here, is that potentially Neolithic monuments appear to cluster together. Even at Douglasmuir, there are several much longer cursus monuments at no great distance, together with at least two other pit-defined structures, one almost certainly a mortuary enclosure, and the other a square enclosure containing a small rectangular structure, in a *40.* neighbouring field. In this context, it is worth noting that there is even a possible causewayed enclosure close to the complex of structures recorded at Leadketty.

Whatever the difficulties of identifying mortuary enclosures from cropmark evidence, there can be little doubt that they are also components of these kinds of complexes. Both pit-defined and ditched examples are a feature of the area around the Cleaven Dyke, and also of the ceremonial complex uncovered by aerial survey and excavation at Balfarg, Fife (Barclay and Russell-White forthcoming). The distribution presented here, however, should be treated with extreme caution, for reasons that have already been explored in relation to the examples in South-east Perth. While it may be possible to distinguish between the cropmark evidence of the ditched enclosure at *28A. 82.* **Inchtuthil** and the bedding-trenches of the timber structure at Balbridie, regardless of whether the latter was indeed a roofed building, there are a mass of less well-defined structures that cannot be categorised in this way. Accordingly, all the cropmark sites that conform in size and shape to these structures have been included on the map as rectilinear enclosures. Some, such as the pit-defined example at Boysack, near Douglasmuir, or the long and narrow ditched enclosure at Kilmany, Fife, are almost certainly mortuary enclosures, but the lesson of Balbridie should not be forgotten, and such structures may turn out to have a wide range of dates and functions.

It cannot be denied that there are many problems of interpretation of the evidence discussed above, but it is equally clear that the gap in the distribution of Neolithic funerary mounds is more than filled by what appear to be structures which, on the available evidence, are of broadly similar date. The distribution of these structures may, of course, extend up on to the hills, where they are less likely to be identified as cropmarkings, but, taken at face value, the ceremonial structures appear to occupy the core areas of the best agricultural land, while the funerary mounds lie on the peripheries, a pattern that has also been observed in the relative distributions of stone axes and long cairns in Grampian (Shepherd 1987, 121-3). Quite what this patterning might mean in human terms will require considerably more research, but such an interpretation allows a better understanding of the coincidence of the megalithic and non-megalithic tombs in the hills of western Perthshire. Here, it might reasonably be inferred, is a peripheral zone which lies between two core areas, one centred on the Forth valley, the other on the Tay (a similar disposition may be detected in Dumbarton).

Whatever the underlying pattern of organisation and land-use, it does not appear to have survived to the end of the *39A.* Neolithic, as the distribution of the different types of ceremonial monuments that are usually regarded as of Late Neolithic date shows. Again the map should be treated with caution, particularly with regard to the henges and the pit-circles. The latter category is here taken to comprise only rings

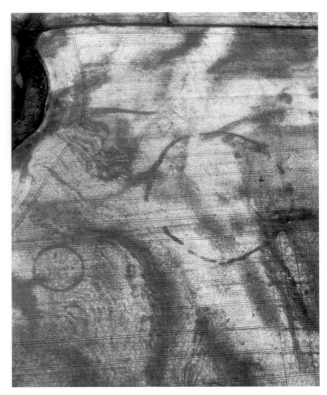

Leadketty, Perth and Kinross (NO 021 161), large enclosure with numerous causeways across its ditch, with adjacent ring-ditch possibly marking the site of a barrow (NMRS PT 15085)

of elongated pits, which should be distinguished from the rings of smaller pits that are more likely to have held the posts of later timber houses. Class II henges can also be identified with a reasonable degree of confidence, but the probable Class I examples may well reflect a wider range of structures; in short, the majority may be characterised as broad-ditched ring-ditches with a single well-defined entrance causeway. Even with such a generous interpretation of Class I henges, it is remarkable how the majority of the Late Neolithic cropmark monuments are concentrated towards the south, notably along Strathearn. In contrast, ring-cairns, here interpreted as a broad ring of cairn material, usually with a graded kerb and a relatively small inner court, clearly extend down through the hills to either side of Strathmore from the related group of structures that are found within recumbent stone circles in Grampian. By this time, South-east Perth appears to lie on the boundary between two different style-zones of ceremonial monuments.

It is, therefore, of some interest to compare this map with that of the distribution of various types of stone settings — *39B.* circles, pairs, alignments and four-posters. Clearly these are of widely differing dates, some, such as the alignments, perhaps contemporary with the funerary mounds, but the concentration on the Tay and its tributaries, is truly remarkable. It may be reasonably concluded that the social and political divisions attested in later prehistory, which may perhaps be detected in the distributions of structures such as souterrains, are firmly rooted in the Neolithic.

SETTLEMENT

With the advent of aerial photography, South-east Perth has been recognised as one of several intensely rich areas of settlement archaeology that can now be identified on the eastern seaboard of Scotland. The coincidence of soils responsive to cropmark formation and a key strategic position in the geography of Scotland, has given the area a significance that has not previously been recognised. The lowlands of South-east Perth contain some of the richest agricultural land of eastern Scotland, and there can be little doubt that they have provided one of the core areas of Scottish settlement throughout both prehistory and history. While the evidence recovered from

the hills of North-east Perth (RCAHMS 1990) revealed a fringe of settlement that had expanded and contracted on numerous occasions, occupation of the adjacent lowlands of Strathmore must have been nearly continuous for at least six millennia. This is not to say that it is possible to identify evidence for unbroken settlement on any one site in South-east Perth, and habitation sites belonging to the earlier part of prehistory are still few and far between.

The evidence for settlement in South-east Perth can be derived from several sources. Firstly, there are stray finds, which, together with the funerary and ceremonial monuments

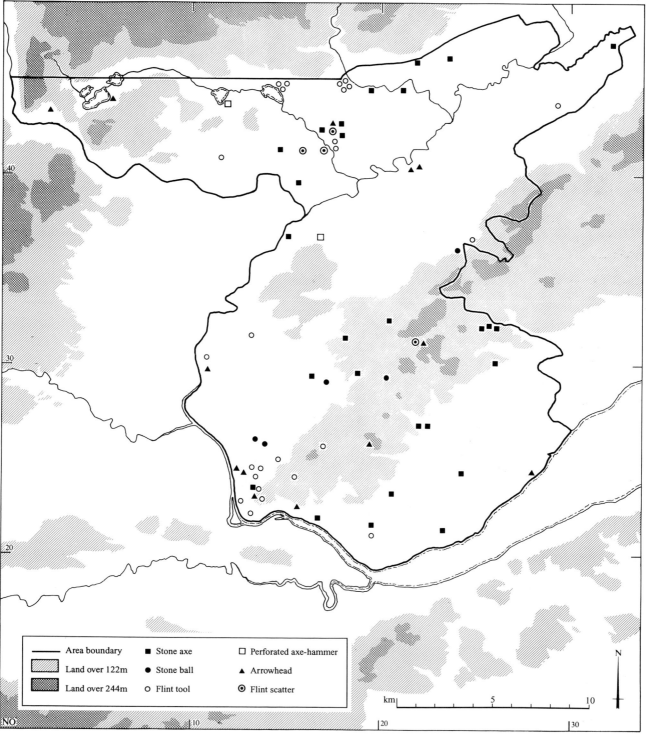

Distribution map of stone tools (NMRS DC 25069)

41

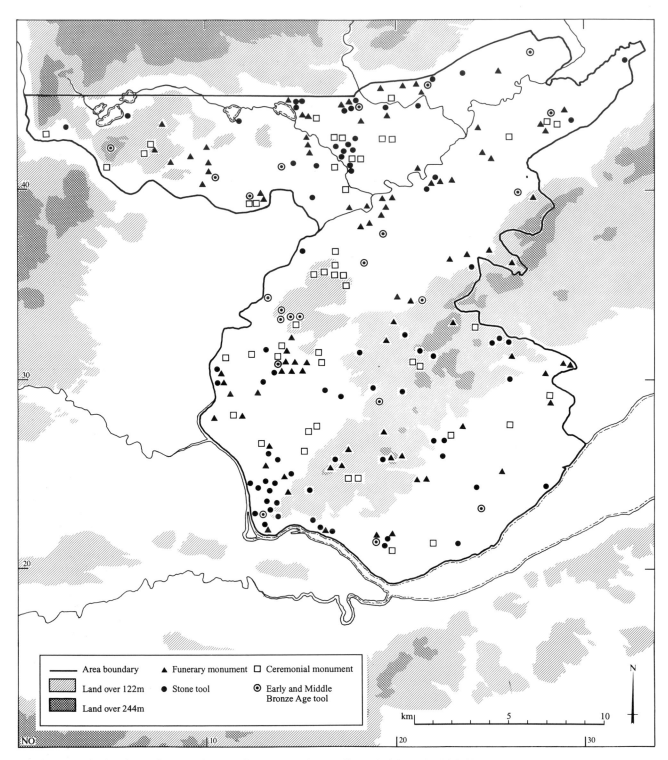

Distribution map of early prehistoric funerary and ceremonial monuments, and stone and bronze tools (NMRS DC 25070)

described above, constitute the major source of our information about early prehistory; secondly, there are a handful of surviving hut-circles and forts, and the documentary records of a few souterrains; and thirdly, there are the cropmarks. In the present state of knowledge, we can only presume that the majority of these belong to the later part of the prehistoric and Early Historic periods, but in the absence of excavation it is impossible to be certain. The bulk of the cropmarks appear to be of clusters of unenclosed circular timber buildings, but several rectangular buildings have also been recorded. A few of the circular buildings appear to have been enclosed by a concentric palisade trench or ditch, the latter usually with several gaps in its circuit. These two types have been called enclosed crescents and interrupted ring-ditches, terms that broadly describe the appearance of the cropmarks. There are

also a number of palisaded and ditched enclosures with no trace of any internal structures, and many of these are also probably the remains of settlements.

The range of evidence for settlement included in this section is discussed under the following headings: early prehistoric settlement; unenclosed circular buildings (including ring-ditches); enclosed crescents; palisades; fortifications; enclosures; interrupted ring-ditches; souterrains; rectangular buildings; and chronology and context.

Early prehistoric settlement

41.

The pattern of early prehistoric settlement is notoriously difficult to establish, much of the evidence being represented by little more than alterations to the natural succession in the paleo-environmental record. Four scatters of flints have been recorded in South-east Perth, all including material likely to be of Mesolithic date. Three of these are from the gravel terraces along the Lunan Burn to the south of Blairgowrie, but the fourth is from the Sidlaws, marking an interesting departure from the normal riparian distribution. Evidence from Morton in north-east Fife (Coles 1971b) indicates that Mesolithic groups of hunter-gathering people had probably reached Tayside by at least the sixth millennium BC. Early shell middens and associated flint implements have been found on the north side of the Tay at Stannergate, Dundee (Mathewson 1879) and Broughty Ferry (Hutcheson 1886), but no middens have yet been identified in South-east Perth. Furthermore, since prospection for surface scatters of artefacts in arable fields has not fallen within the scope of this survey, it is not possible to confirm or deny the existence of coastal communities in the Carse of Gowrie at this time. The apparent absence of Mesolithic sites in the Carse of Gowrie may also be accounted for by the evolution of the Carse, which was briefly described in the topographical introduction. It seems likely that a number of Mesolithic encampments would have existed along the old shoreline that fringes the Carse, but evidence of activity may well have been buried beneath estuarine deposits. The log-boat found in the nineteenth century in a clay-pit at the Friarton brickworks to the south of Perth appears to have come from such deposits (Mowat forthcoming).

The arrival of the first farming communities in many areas of Scotland is signalled by disturbances in the pollen record preserved in peat bogs. Traditionally, the transition from hunting and gathering to farming has been identified with the apparent reduction in the amount of elm represented in pollen diagrams, an event known as the Elm Decline. More recently, the significance of the Elm Decline has been called into question, largely because of the occurrence of cereal pollens at earlier levels within a series of peat deposits across the British Isles (Edwards and Ralston 1985, 20-22) and of pathogenic factors. Evidence of the Elm Decline is not available for the area of South-east Perth, although it has been recorded at Stormont Loch, to the south of Blairgowrie, and in two pollen diagrams from the area of North-east Perth (Caseldine 1979).

pp. 24-40
Apart from the Neolithic ceremonial monuments described above, the only tangible evidence for early farming
41.
communities in South-east Perth is provided by the discovery of stone tools. The principal survivor of the Neolithic tool-kit is the stone axe, and examples have turned up over wide areas of Strathmore, the Sidlaws and the Carse of Gowrie. In reality, however, stone axes, together with other types of stone implements, almost certainly remained in use from the fifth until at least the second millennium BC, and they are unlikely to have been supplanted by bronze equivalents until well on into what is traditionally known as the Bronze Age.

The problem of locating habitation sites dating from before the late second millennium BC in the lowlands cannot be solved without intensive field-walking and invasive sampling techniques. Nevertheless, the areas that were in use during this period may be identified by reference to the distribution of contemporary tools; due weight should also be given to the evidence from elsewhere in the lowlands, which shows that funerary and ceremonial monuments were often closely associated with the farmed landscape. Pollen samples from the fill of the ditch of the henge at Moncreiffe House, to the south-west of Perth, produced very high levels of cereal-type pollen (Caseldine 1983, 44-5), while at North Mains, in Strathearn, another henge was constructed on ground that had already been cultivated, and a nearby barrow had been raised on the surface of a ridged field (Barclay 1984, 180; 1990). From within the survey area, the only evidence of this sort that has been recovered comes from beneath the cairn at **Beech Hill House**, Coupar Angus; here, a scatter of artefacts, which included Grooved Ware of Late Neolithic date, has been interpreted as midden spread on an earlier field.

When the monuments and finds dating from before the end
42.
of the second millennium BC are plotted together on one map,
they provide a remarkably comprehensive pattern of distribution, each element complementing the others. Given the lengthy period spanned by the material, the distributions may, on the one hand, provide a clue to changing patterns of land utilisation and, on the other, indicate a more complex pattern of organisation in the contemporary landscape. What is readily apparent, however, is that some areas of the landscape were consistently unattractive throughout this period. In Strathmore, for instance, there is a swathe of country from Burrelton north-eastwards to Ardler which is apparently barren of both monuments and artefacts — a state of desolation that evidently continued until the draining and land improvements of the nineteenth century.

Unenclosed circular buildings
44.
As has already been indicated, aerial photography has revealed a mass of evidence of the remains of unenclosed circular buildings in South-east Perth. Before discussing this evidence further, it is important to consider to what extent the structural characteristics displayed by the handful of upstanding examples in the Sidlaws might be represented by cropmark traces, if the relevant sites were brought under cultivation. What, for instance, could the aerial investigator expect to see of a hut-circle, once its wall had been ploughed away?

The apparent contrast between the archaeology of the Sidlaws and that of the hill country surveyed in North-east Perth has already been discussed. Prior to the present survey, the only major hut-circle group known in South-east Perth was on **Law Hill**, Arnbathie, but at least two, and possibly three,
45.
additional hut-circles had also been identified at **Whitemyre**. Two other small circular enclosures at Northlees appear to be of much more recent date (*DES 1964*, 43-4). Five of the hut-circles on **Law Hill** are scattered across the gentler slopes to the north-east of the fort that crowns the summit, and a sixth lies downslope from the ramparts on the south-east. The latter is the only one where any structural details are visible, and it appears to display evidence of two successive external wall-faces on its south-west side. The rest have been heavily damaged by the later cultivation that has swept over most of this part of the hill. The hut-circles range from 8.5m to 12.8m in internal diameter, and the largest, which lies in the saddle some 150m north of the fort, was partially excavated in 1950; this revealed that its centre was roughly paved and that a cremation deposit in a small setting of stones had been inserted into the entrance (Stewart 1950, 11; NMRS, MS/591/1). The **Whitemyre** hut-circles measure 7m, 10m and 15m in internal diameter respectively, and the interiors of the two larger ones have been levelled into the slope.

In addition to these hut-circles, the stances of two circular timber buildings defined by no more than shallow annular depressions have been located on the Sidlaws in the course of the survey. One lies on the west side of **Dunsinane Hill**, some 270m west of the fort, and the other is at the foot of **Pole Hill**, on a low knoll 150m north of **Evelick** fort. Buildings of this type, in which the annular depression is an intentional feature, representing the sunken portion of a house-floor, are known as ring-ditch houses, but they should not be confused with the cropmarks that are classified as ring-ditches, whose interpretation is discussed below. The two examples recorded in South-east Perth measure about 12.5m in overall diameter, but comparable structures in the Border hills are sometimes of the order of 17m in diameter, while one recorded on the Hill of Alyth, on the north side of Strathmore, is 14.5m in diameter (RCAHMS 1990, 52, no.129.2). Internal ring-ditches are also a feature of at least forty of the hut-circles which are defined by stone walls or banks in North-east Perth (RCAHMS 1990, 4).

It will have become evident, from the description of these widely differing types of upstanding building, that they are all remarkably vulnerable to changes in land-use. Unless some element of the structure is deeply cut or hollowed into the old ground surface, there is little chance of any traces surviving prolonged cultivation or being recovered as cropmarks.

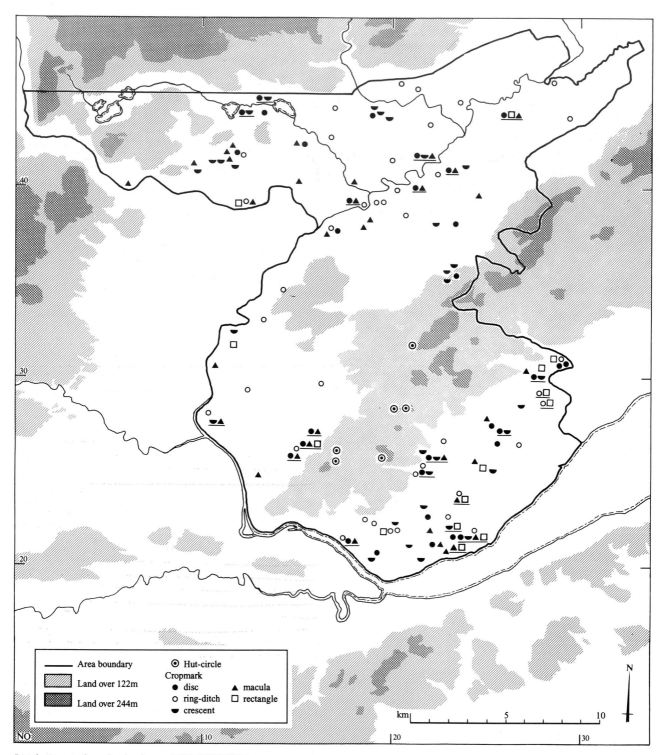

Distribution map of unenclosed settlements (NMRS DC 25071)

Excavation of a hut-circle at Drumcarrow in Fife showed, for example, that the only features to penetrate the subsoil were a single post-hole and seven stake-holes at the entrance (Maxwell 1969). The cropmark traces of a palisaded enclosure near Callander include a pair of pits which probably mark the entrance to a round-house, but this sort of evidence is remarkably difficult to detect; what are presumed to be rings of internal post-holes are also rare in the entire cropmark record of eastern Scotland (Maxwell 1983, 33-4; Tolan 1990), and such evidence has only been recorded under exceptional circumstances, on the most responsive soils. It is no exaggeration to suggest that hut-circles such as those on **Law Hill**, or indeed, many of the examples recorded in North-east Perth, would be virtually irrecoverable as cropmarks, and many

would even be undetectable by excavation after a relatively short period of cultivation.

Where the interior of a hut-circle has been levelled into the slope, however, as in the two recorded at **Whitemyre**, there is, theoretically, a much better chance of elements of the floor both surviving, and being identified, as a substantial feature buried below the plough-soil. In terms of a cropmark, it would not be unreasonable to anticipate that its ground-plan would appear as a solid mark, with a well-defined arc around the upslope side. If the whole floor had been sunk into the ground, on the other hand, a characteristic that was noted in several hut-circles on the hills to the north (*e.g.* RCAHMS 1990, 61, no.141.2), then the cropmark-form expected would probably be a solid disc.

Law Hill, Arnbathie (*NO 171 262*), *hut-circles and later fields, with the fort on the summit in the background* (*NMRS B 17016*)

The cropmarks produced by the remains of ring-ditch houses of the type discovered on **Dunsinane Hill** and **Pole Hill**, along with those found on the north side of Strathmore on the Hill of Alyth and Middleton Muir (RCAHMS 1990, 52, no.129.2; 65, no.147.3), might be expected to differ from those of the hut-circles discussed above. Each is defined by a shallow ditch up to 3.5m broad. The **Dunsinane Hill** example has a causeway at the entrance, but on the Hill of Alyth the sunken floor extends into the hollow of the entrance; the cropmarks that formed above these two structures would be respectively penannular or annular. In the case of the Hill of Alyth example, it is worth noting that the ditch is shallowest on the uphill side, a common feature of ring-ditch houses in the Borders. The differentially erosive effect of ploughing such a structure on a hill-slope would tend, of course, to truncate and alter the basic shapes, as might other processes of decay and abandonment. The result would be to produce cropmarks ranging in shape from discs and rings to crescents.

As recently as fifteen years ago, the handful of surviving hut-circles and ring-ditch houses would have been the sole evidence for prehistoric houses in South-east Perth. Now, as a direct result of the aerial survey programme, there is a mass of new evidence, with a heavy preponderance of unenclosed rings, discs and crescents. These elements occur both singly and in clusters, and are found throughout the overall distribution of cropmarks. Clearly defined discs can be identified at no fewer than twenty-eight locations and crescents at twenty-six, and others may well be hidden in the irregularly-shaped maculae that occur at twenty-nine. The distinction between the different types should not be overstressed, however, and it is probably best to note that, to date, such markings have been recorded at as many as sixty sites, while the total continues to mount with every season of aerial survey. In addition, cropmark ring-ditches, many of which are also probably the remains of round-houses, have been identified at forty-five separate locations. Together, they point to the existence of large numbers of unenclosed settlements throughout South-east Perth, and, in this respect, there appears to be little difference between the lowlands and the hills to the north.

The factors which inhibit precise cropmark definition — local topography and geomorphology — also prevent accurate appraisal of the size and disposition of the unenclosed settlements that are being revealed by aerial photography. Nevertheless, the number of markings at each site is variable, ranging from single discs or crescents, to half a dozen or more; where the visible structures are more numerous, they are often very widely dispersed, and, in these cases, it is impossible to determine whether they should be regarded as a group, or as a series of entirely separate sites. Both linear groupings and clusters have been recorded, but it is still too early in the study of such sites to say whether, for example, linear groups are as common in the lowlands as they are in the hut-circle groups to the north.

The sizes of the discs and crescents are also very variable, as far as can be assessed. Relatively few are sharply defined and they tend to be rather diffuse around their edges. This problem is compounded by the fact that the shape of the marks may appear to alter at different stages of the crop development, and also from year to year. For instance, a mark some 12m across at **Wester Denhead** has been variously recorded as a disc or a crescent. Nevertheless, the majority of those for which a reasonable estimate may be made range from about 7m to 17m in diameter. These fall within the size range that has been recorded for prehistoric buildings, but in one or two instances the aerial photographs have revealed larger rounded marks whose nature is less easily determined.

For reasons that have already been outlined, it is difficult to be certain whether any of the single structures that have been recorded are really the only example of their type on that site, nor is it known if this apparent lack of local parallels is significant; hut-circle groups of any kind usually represent several phases of development, and may incorporate structures that were not habitations. For example, there appears to be only one solid disc at **Wester Denhead**, although some of the photographs also show other vague marks in the vicinity, and a large ring-ditch lies 30m to the east; the latter, which measures 20m in internal diameter, has no entrance, and, although no grave-pits are visible within the interior, it is perhaps best explained as a levelled barrow or some other kind of funerary site. Immediately adjacent to it, there is also a small mark about 3m square, which might even be a square barrow. Similar relationships can be found elsewhere: at **Kinloch** a well-defined disc 10m in diameter lies adjacent to a roughly square ditched enclosure measuring about 30m across, and there are other faint marks nearby, while a second disc lies about 90m to the south-east; another clearly defined disc has been recorded in the field immediately east of **Mains of Murie** farmhouse, but again other crescents and maculae, including a possible enclosed crescent, have been recorded in the field on the opposite side of the steading.

Most of the apparently single discs and crescents are probably merely outliers from more widely dispersed groups of cropmarks. The cropmarks at **Bonhard Park** are a good example of a scatter of discs, crescents and maculae extending across at least two fields. The markings also include at least one probable souterrain, but it is a noticeable aspect of this particular site that some of the maculae are apparently more rectangular than circular.

Several cropmark sites have provided evidence of clusters of markings which are quite difficult to distinguish from the remains of ploughed-out gravel-pits and the like. Some of these old pits form large interlocking markings, where rounded scoops or angular trenches have been driven into a bank of gravel; good examples of these have been photographed at **Hill of Errol** and **Paddockmuir Wood**. In other instances, however, the nature of the cropmarks is more ambiguous. The cluster of small rounded and angular pits revealed at **Balgarvie** is one such case, while similar markings at **Inchcoonans** are another. Even if some of these markings are quarries, however, this does not necessarily mean that all of the visible features are the result of quarrying. At **Ardgaith**, a row of marks along the crest of a low ridge includes three or four well-defined discs up to 13m in diameter, but towards the east the marks merge into one another and become much more angular. The discs at the west end of the ridge are almost certainly the remains of circular buildings, but the easternmost marks, which lie immediately adjacent to a road, may perhaps be gravel-pits. A similar juxtaposition occurs at **Middle Gourdie**, where a road runs past the north-east end of a line of at least four interlocking discs along a low ridge, with what is almost certainly the cropmark of a souterrain a further 10m to the south-west. It is worth bearing in mind, however, that geographical or topographical determinism may lie behind a pattern of communications, quarries and older settlements choosing the same ground.

Quarrying is less likely to be the explanation of diffuse cropmarks at certain other sites, notably the row of discs and crescents at **Easter Essendy**, or to the east of the **Grey Stone** at **Clashbenny**. Although the structures at the latter site are relatively poorly defined, and probably include oblong structures, too, the open side of one particular crescent is closed by an arc of pits, presumably the post-holes for the main structural timbers of the building. The problems of interpreting other sites stem from the complexity caused by several features merging together. A good example of this is at **Kilspindie**, where a crescent some 18m across, which is probably the remains of a ring-ditch house, lies at the west end of a mark some 60m in length and up to 30m in breadth. Further crescents can be detected within this mark on some of the photographs. A series of markings to the south include what are probably souterrains amongst a mass of maculae, some of which are quite angular. The cropmarks at **Middlebank**, which occur in two clusters, may also represent a series of overlapping discs and crescents. Both clusters are accompanied by narrow linear features, almost certainly small subterranean structures of the type discussed under the heading of souterrains. The western cluster includes an enclosed crescent, which not only intersects some of the discs, but also a ring-ditch some 15m in diameter. The eastern cluster is notable for a roughly circular setting of

A. **Balgarvie** (NO 147 262), cropmark maculae (NMRS A 64807)

B. **Clashbenny** (NO 2230 2132), unenclosed settlement (NMRS PT 2931)

six small pits, which are probably the post-pits for the structural timbers of a building.

Rather more spectacular are the cropmarks at **Pitroddie**, which are also referred to in the section on the souterrains. To the south of the Pitroddie Burn, and to the north-west of one of the souterrain complexes, there is a marked cluster of discs and crescents, while to the north of the burn there is a row of four or five. Immediately to the west of this row there is a further cluster of ring-ditches, some of which overlap. These ring-ditches range from 8m to 18m in diameter, at least four of them extending the arcs of crescentic features and presumably marking the line of the foundation trench for a timber wall. Several pits can be identified amongst this cluster of buildings, including four in a square setting.

The complexity of the cropmarks that reveal the various types of building at Pitroddie is rarely seen in extensive form amongst the settlements of South-east Perth. Yet even this level

58.

48A.

47D.

47A.

12.

46B.

47A.

47B-C.

66.

A. **Kilspindie** (NO 2210 2580), unenclosed settlement (NMRS A 29255)

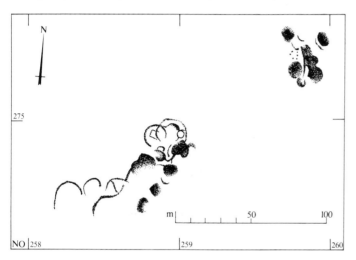

B. **Middlebank** (NO 258 274), settlement from the west, 1:2500 (NMRS DC 25072)

C. **Middlebank** (NO 258 274), settlement (NMRS PT 15272)

D. **Paddockmuir Wood** (NO 216 204), unenclosed settlement (NMRS PT 6144)

47D. is surpassed at **Paddockmuir Wood**, where a dense mass of features extends along the leading edge of a terrace above the Tay. At the westernmost limit they appear mainly as small pits, along with at least one crescent, while midway along the terrace a series of large subrectangular gravel-pits appears to have removed all earlier evidence. To the east of these, the character of the cropmarks changes, discrete features giving way to an almost indecipherable mass of narrow curved markings. The arcs appear to overlap each other and few complete rings can be discerned. As at Pitroddie, but much more intensively than there, the cropmarks almost certainly indicate the foundation trenches for a timber-built settlement whose buildings have a long history of construction and replacement. The extent of the complex is still far from clear, but the narrow band of ground on which the cropmarks have formed swings northwards to reveal further traces of narrow gullies and pits extending over a distance of 300m. Although only a relatively small portion of the Paddockmuir Wood site is therefore available for inspection, it is clear that, for density and extent of occupation, its parallels must be sought outside South-east Perth. Particularly apt comparisons may be made with other east coast complexes, notably: Mugdrum, only 3km distant on the opposite shore of the Tay; near Leuchars in north-east Fife; and at the mouth of the Lunan Water in Angus.

Isolated examples of the kinds of structural features recognised at **Pitroddie** and **Paddockmuir Wood** have been *48B.* recorded at **The Welton** and **Bankhead of Kinloch**, while *54A.* others may be represented amongst the ring-ditches, which form a substantial proportion of all the cropmarks that have been recorded. The uncertainties concerning the interpretation of many of these latter sites stem mainly from the unclear character of the relevant cropmarks. No fewer than thirteen of the ring-ditches are very indistinct markings, where either the whole area of the site lacks cropmark definition, or perhaps only one arc can be seen clearly. The aerial photographs currently available give the impression that the majority of the ring-ditches are isolated features in the landscape, although no great weight should be placed upon this observation. At several sites where there is one clearly defined ring-ditch, fainter traces of others can be detected in the vicinity. At **Islabank** for instance, arcs of two additional ring-ditches can be seen, while the clearly-defined example at **Lochlands** is apparently at the end of a row of three. Even with the few relatively well-defined ring-ditches, it is impossible to be certain whether the ditch is a continuous feature, the example 9m in diameter at **Myreside**, to the west of Blairgowrie, being the only one with a clear entrance causeway across the ditch.

It is worth emphasising again that the bulk of the cropmark material relating to settlement in South-east Perth comprises unenclosed circular buildings of one form or another, for this fact alone suggests that many of the structures that have been classified as ring-ditches belong in that category. Nevertheless, some will probably be the remains of funerary and ritual monuments, and this possibility is discussed in the appropriate *p. 17* sections of this volume.

Before describing the other types of settlement that have been recorded, mention should be made of one more aspect of the unenclosed settlements of South-east Perth. With the exception of the enclosed crescents described below, there is very little overlap between the local distribution of the unenclosed settlements and that of the enclosures, either rectilinear or curvilinear. For this reason, the discovery of a cluster of discs intersected by the ditch of an enclosure at **Middlebank** is of some significance. The enclosure measures *72B.* about 30m in diameter within a ditch 1.5m in breadth, and there is an annexe on the north-west side. Of the discs, three fall within the interior, where there is also an arc of what is either another ditch or a narrow subterranean structure, but a fourth, on the south, appears to be crossed by the enclosure ditch itself.

Enclosed crescents
49.

This type of settlement, which in traditional terminology would be classed as a homestead, comprises a single large crescent lying at the centre of a circular enclosure defined by the narrowest of cropmarks. The most clearly defined are at **The** *48B. 54A.* **Welton** and **Wester Drumatherty**, both of them in *50.* Strathmore. The group is not restricted to Strathmore, however, and the nine examples that can be identified with at least one confidence include at least one in the Carse of Gowrie at **Middlebank**, and possibly another at **Mains of Murie**. The *47B-C.* enclosing perimeters are very slight features on the aerial *48A.* photographs, and other examples doubtless await discovery, hidden till now by differential cropmark formation, as is shown by the most recent photographs of what were previously thought to be another cluster of unenclosed crescents at **The Welton**.

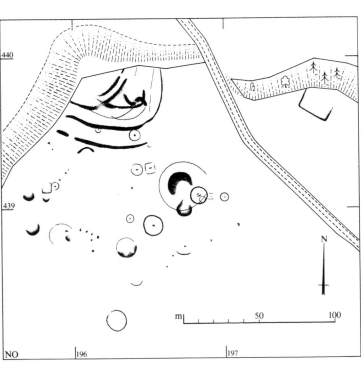

A. **Mains of Murie** (NO 2315 2206), enclosed crescent and cropmarks (NMRS PT 14412)

B. **The Welton** (NO 196 439), fort, settlement and square-barrow cemetery, 1:2500 (NMRS DC 25074)

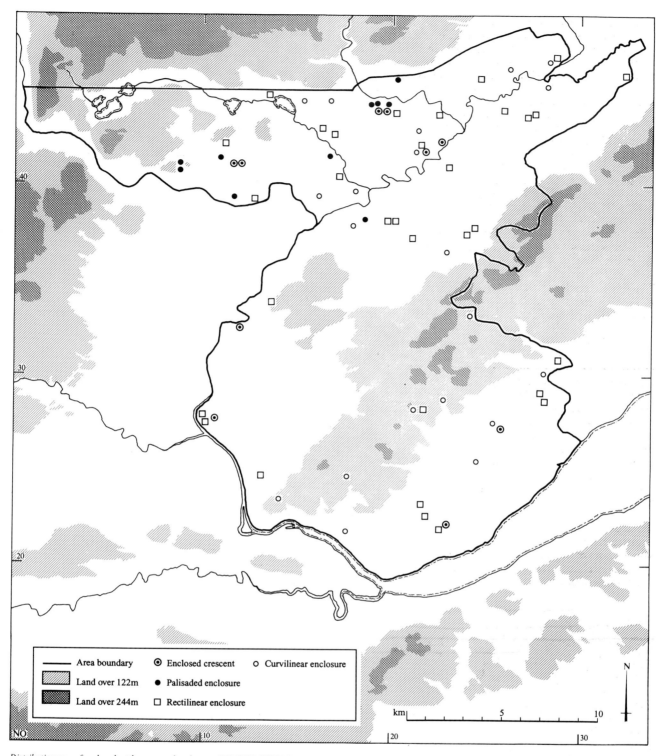

Distribution map of enclosed settlements and enclosures (NMRS DC 25073)

There is considerable variation in the size of both the enclosures and the crescents. The smallest of the group is at **Middlebank**, where the enclosure is about 20m in diameter and the crescent 12m, and the possible example at **Mains of Murie** is certainly no bigger. At 21m and 23m respectively, the enclosures at **Easter Bendochy** and **Sherifftown** are closely comparable, and the crescents that they enclose are about 14m in diameter. The enclosures of the other six examples are between 29m and 35m in diameter, the two at **The Welton** and **Wester Drumatherty** containing huge crescents, 17m and 18m in diameter respectively. The largest enclosure, at **Mudhall**, is exceptional in that it appears to contain an interrupted ring-ditch with an overall diameter of 23m (see below), but it is still possible to disentangle the arc of a crescent, some 18m across, from the rest of the markings in the middle of the interior.

The cropmarks of the enclosure perimeters are consistently narrow, in the case of **Sherifftown** appearing as little more than the outline of a faint halo around the crescent, from which it may be deduced that most of them are the remains of palisade trenches. The cropmarks of the perimeters at **The Welton, Wester Drumatherty** and **Easter Bendochy** are all of a similar scale, but others, such as at **Cambusmichael**, are a little wider and the possibility that they represent narrow ditches should not be discounted. This possibility would allow the curious double ring-ditch at **Woodhead**, which occurs adjacent to a cluster of interrupted ring-ditches, to be considered as a member of this group. In places, the rather indefinite cropmark of its outer ditch is at least 1.5m wide, enclosing an area about 25m in diameter; the narrower inner ring is about 16m in diameter.

49

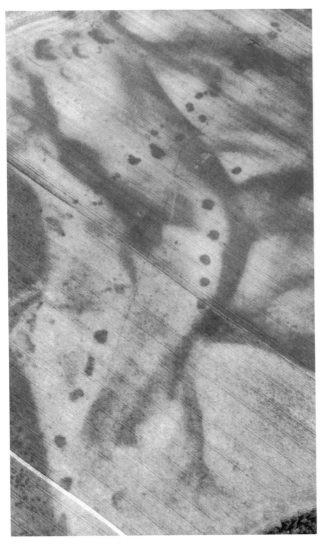

Wester Drumatherty (NO 1155 4119), settlement of enclosed and unenclosed crescents, together with the cropmarks of the Roman road and its flanking quarry-pits (NMRS PT 10687)

clearly visible in the crop; close examination of their relationship to the local topography revealed that the major portion of the crescent's north-eastern arc lies on the downslope side of the structure, a probable characteristic, as has already been shown, of a ploughed-out ring-ditch house. On the south, the perimeter intersects a penannular mark, which is probably the remains of another house, and, on the south-east, a ring-ditch containing two pits. The latter is probably a barrow, one of a cemetery which extends across this gravel terrace. Amongst the square and circular barrows of the cemetery, the cropmarks have revealed at least four other crescentic marks, which are presumably also the remains of circular buildings. One of these is of particular interest on account of the traces of a foundation trench for the timber wall extending around the open side of the crescent, thus delineating a building about 13m in diameter. A second arc of foundation trench some 16m in diameter can also be detected on some of the photographs, but in this instance there is no accompanying crescent. Apart from these features, there is a narrow curving mark, which was sampled by excavation in 1981 and shown to indicate the site of a souterrain-like structure, lying immediately outside the fort. The S-shaped mark of a broader souterrain, which appears to post-date one of the ditches of the fort, lies within the interior, where there is also evidence of at least two successive palisaded perimeters.

The second example of an enclosed crescent at **The Welton** lies about 300m to the west of the fort, on the edge of the same gravel escarpment. Previously, three crescents set in echelon had been recorded, but the most recent photographs show that the northernmost is enclosed by traces of a palisade trench some 25m in diameter. Of the other two crescents, one is intersected by the palisade trench and the southernmost lies outside the perimeter, indicating, as at **Wester Drumatherty**, some depth to the chronology of the site.

The example at **Middlebank**, in the Carse of Gowrie, forms part of the settlement complex that has already been described above, its enclosure apparently intersecting several other features of the settlement. Rather more simple are the cropmarks of the enclosed crescents at **Cambusmichael** and **Sherifftown**, where a second crescent occurs immediately outside each enclosure.

Palisaded sites

In addition to the enclosed crescents, eight other probable palisaded sites have been recorded as cropmarks in South-east Perth, and two other enclosures, **Upper Gothens** and **Old Mains of Rattray**, may also be assigned to this group. Two examples represent palisaded elements in the multiperiod defences of the forts at **Inchtuthil** and **The Welton**, at the latter exhibiting at least two separate periods of construction; five are circular, three of them falling in the size range of the enclosed crescents (0.03ha - 0.1ha); and the remaining example is a semi-circular enclosure backing on to the edge of a steep natural scarp to the north of **Spittalfield**. It is unclear whether the Spittalfield enclosure, which measures some 38m along the chord, is deliberately utilising the scarp as part of its perimeter, or has simply been eroded. What is perhaps surprising, is that, including the enclosed crescents, palisades make up over half of all the known curvilinear cropmark enclosures in South-east Perth. Furthermore, these relatively slight features have only been recorded on the most freely-draining soils, suggesting that palisaded enclosures are probably under-represented in the cropmark record.

Of the circular palisades, the smallest, at **The Welton**, measures only 22m in diameter (0.04ha), but there is also a second, larger enclosure here, only some 60m away to the south-east; the latter measures 42m in diameter (0.13ha), its perimeter enclosing one small crescent-shaped cropmark and intersecting two others. A similar pairing occurs on the summit of a prominent hill at **Stralochy**, but the larger of these two, which measures about 40m in diameter, is unusual in this part of Scotland, since it is defined by two concentric palisade

Wester Drumatherty represents the type-site for this group of settlements. Here, three crescents have been recorded in a row running roughly from north to south, with a fourth lying immediately to the west. The northernmost of the row is about 18m across and lies within a well-defined enclosure about 30m in diameter. This enclosure was tested by probing, the examination also showing that the feature forming the crescent was up to 1m deep (*DES 1982*, 33). On the south the enclosure adjoins the back of the second crescent, which also has traces of an enclosing halo. This crescent is about 15m across and its presumed enclosure, about 26m in diameter, also contains an L-shaped mark, which probably indicates the position of a souterrain-like structure about 5m in length and up to 2m in breadth. There can be no doubt that the two enclosures with their central crescents cannot have coexisted. It is also evident that the southern enclosure intersects the north side of the third crescent in the row. This crescent is comparable in size with the northernmost. At its south-eastern horn, however, there is a narrow mark forming three sides of a subrectangular shape some 6m in length, and there is also a rather angular macula a short distance to the south.

The first of the two examples that have been recorded at **The Welton** lies to the south-east of the ploughed-out fort (see below in the section on fortifications). It also forms part of an extensive complex of cropmarks, whose chronology cannot be fully understood without excavation. The enclosure measures 32m in diameter and the crescent some 17m. When the site was visited in June 1992, both the enclosure and the crescent were

trenches set 4m apart. The smaller enclosure lies some 65m to the south-south-west and is about 30m in diameter. The last enclosure of this group, at **Leyston**, also forms part of a larger settlement complex, and the course of its perimeter is difficult to disentangle from the other features of the site; it measures about 35m in diameter (0.1ha), and some of the photographs suggest the presence of an amorphous solid mark at its centre. On the north-east, the perimeter probably intersects an interrupted ring-ditch (see below), and there is possibly a second enclosure immediately to the east.

p. 59-62

The two enclosures at **Upper Gothens** and **Old Mains of Rattray**, are considerably larger than any of the sites described above, and in neither case can it be determined whether the perimeter is the remains of a large palisade trench or simply a narrow ditch. **Upper Gothens**, the largest of all the curvilinear enclosures in South-east Perth, measures about 62m in diameter (0.3ha); a scatter of flints has also been recorded from this area (*DES 1964*, 43). At **Old Mains of Rattray**, the interior of the enclosure, measuring about 54m by 42m (0.18ha), contains what are probably a souterrain and a circle of pits; this site is discussed further in the section on souterrains below.

58.

8A. 72A.

p. 68

76. ## Fortifications

Fortification is the one aspect of the settlement record of South-east Perth where the majority of the evidence is still drawn from upstanding structures. In the main, these are heavily defended forts, but, in the course of the survey, a previously unrecorded broch has been identified on the north flank of the Sidlaws, and also the remains of a stone-walled structure which appears to be some kind of ring-fort. Even here, however, aerial photography has made its contribution, providing evidence not only of four multivallate forts, but also of at least two single-ditched earthworks that appear to be of defensive character. The continuing programme of aerial reconnaissance will undoubtedly lead to the identification of other defensive earthworks, but those recovered to date form a very small proportion of the total number of cropmarks of all classes, and it is reasonable to suggest that they will always be relatively few and far between in this area, as elsewhere in eastern Scotland north of the Forth. It should be borne in mind, however, that palisaded phases have been identified in the defensive sequences of two of the forts, and some of the palisaded enclosures should also perhaps be regarded as fortifications.

The broch and the ring-fort are probably amongst the most exciting discoveries that were made in the course of the

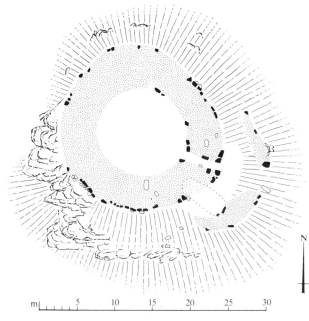

m |___|___5___|___10___|___15___|___20___|___25___|___30

Little Dunsinane Hill (*NO 2225 3253*), broch, 1:500 (*NMRS DC 25075*)

fieldwork in South-east Perth. Set on a small craggy knoll, high up on **Little Dunsinane Hill**, there is no doubting the exotic character of the broch. Circular on plan, with three courses of the outer wall-face surviving on the south-west, it measures 12m in diameter within a heavily-robbed wall 5m in thickness; the entrance, on the east-south-east, has been protected by an outer wall. The ring-fort, which stands on a low rise on the western rim of **Kilwhannie Den**, has also been heavily robbed, its wall now reduced to little more than a stony bank 4.5m in thickness, but enough survives to show that it measured about 21m in internal diameter. The structure is shown as 'Carquhanan old Castle, the remains of a round fortification' on an estate map of 1756 (SRO, RHP 1005), and it appears to have been identified as a medieval castle by local tradition (*NSA*, 10 [Perth], 221-2; Melville 1939, 149); the surviving remains suggest a considerably earlier date, pointing to parallels amongst the ring-forts of western Perthshire, or the structures that overlie the prehistoric fort on Turin Hill in Angus (Feachem 1977, 106).

51.

In addition to these two structures, a total of thirteen sites in South-east Perth can be identified as forts, to which may be added the two single-ditched earthworks. The emphasis of their distribution rests on the Sidlaws, with seven of the forts set in positions overlooking the major passes through the hills, and another two, both of them cropmarks, situated only a short distance into Strathmore to the north-east. Of the remaining four, three are well-known sites along the valley of the Tay, and the fourth is a complex fortification revealed by cropmarks close to Blairgowrie, at the mouth of Glen Ericht. Of the other two earthworks, one, known as **Gold Castle**, is situated some 2km north-west of Scone Palace, on a low-lying river terrace on the east bank of the Tay, while the other lies at the west end of the Carse of Gowrie, at **Tofthill**.

54B.

68A.

As a group, however, these fortifications share very few common characteristics, exhibiting a wide range of sizes, and considerable variation in the nature and strength of their defences. At one extreme there is the double-ditched cropmark fort at **The Welton**, or the small earthwork defended by two ramparts with external ditches at **Rait**, each about 0.05ha in extent; at the other, there is the enclosure of 2.16ha, defended by a single rampart on **Dunsinane Hill**. Leaving aside the large enclosure on Dunsinane Hill, the size of the forts shows a fairly even progression from **The Welton** and **Rait** up to **Law Hill, Arnbathie**, the latter enclosing an area of 0.96ha. At 0.4ha, the **Tofthill** earthwork falls within this span, but **Gold Castle** is significantly larger, enclosing about 1.5ha.

52B. 54.
53.

53. 56.

53.

The variation in the character of the defences partly reflects inherent differences between earthworks and stone walls or ramparts, but it is also a reflection of the sheer scale of some of the defensive systems in proportion to the size of the interior. The majority of the forts have multivallate earthwork defences, only three of them being entirely of stone. The smallest of these is **King's Seat**, Dunkeld, in which a variety of built terraces and annexes enclose a small citadel (0.06ha) crowning the summit of the knoll. The second is the fort of about 1ha on **Law Hill**, Arnbathie, which is demonstrably multiperiod and displays several unusual elements in its defensive system, including the remains of *chevaux de frise* at its northern end. The third fort, on **Dunsinane Hill**, probably the most spectacular of the forts surveyed, will be described in greater detail below.

53.

Three of the other forts, **Deuchny**, **Hill of Dores** and **Kemp's Hold**, Stenton, have a relatively small ditched component in their defences. The first two are both in modern forestry plantations and have been heavily disturbed. **Hill of Dores** (0.42ha) is defended by two earthen ramparts, while at **Deuchny** (0.25ha) only a fragment of a single rampart can be detected; this cuts across the east end of the ridge, where there is also an outer ditch. **Kemp's Hold** (0.12ha), set on a narrow rocky ridge overlooking the east bank of the River Tay at Stenton, has a virtually complete circuit of inner rampart, accompanied at the west end by two outer ramparts with

53.

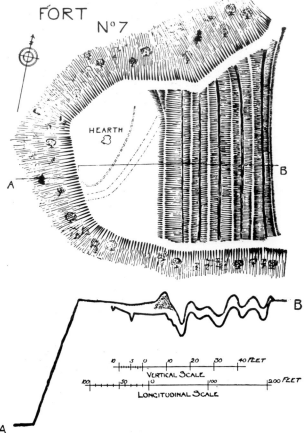

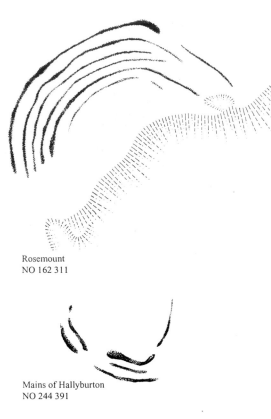

Rosemount
NO 162 311

Mains of Hallyburton
NO 244 391

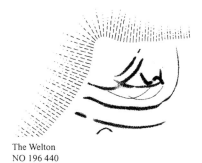

The Welton
NO 196 440

A. **Inchtuthil** (NO 1150 3928), plan and section from the report of the
excavations of 1901 (Abercromby, Ross and Anderson 1902)

internal quarry ditches, and at the east end by a shallow ditch
with a low counterscarp bank.

The rest of the forts appear to have been wholly protected by
earthwork defences, three of them still substantially intact and
four now only visible as cropmarkings. The three intact
53. earthworks are at **Rait**, **Inchtuthil** and **Evelick**, the first two
72C. occupying low-lying positions, and the last set high up on the
south-east side of the Sidlaws. As well as occupying similar
positions, **Rait** and **Inchtuthil** are also remarkably similar in
design, with a band of massive earthworks drawn straight
across the neck of a steep-sided promontory. At both, the
visitor will be struck by the massive scale of the defences in
comparison with the area that has been enclosed, even though
the interior of Inchtuthil (0.19ha) is four times that of **Rait**
91A. (0.05ha). At **Inchtuthil**, however, a close examination of the
defences leads to the suspicion that the innermost pair of
ramparts and their medial ditch represent a period of
construction distinct from that of the regularly spaced outer
banks and ditches. This suspicion is reinforced by the published
52A. section of a trench cut during the excavations of the Society of
Antiquaries of Scotland in 1901 (Abercromby, Ross and
Anderson 1902, 230-4). Although the vertical axis has been
grossly exaggerated, the surface and subsoil profiles across the
defences show a clear dislocation between the innermost pair of
ramparts and the outer earthworks. Furthermore, as drawn, part
of the innermost rampart appears to overlie its flanking ditch,
whose inner scarp has a curious stepped profile. This apparent
relationship between the rampart and the ditch should not be
overstressed; the work was carried out ninety years ago, and the
discipline of excavation, as may be clearly seen from the
photograph of a 'hearth' located in the interior, was still in its
infancy. At other early excavations, however, a step in the
profile of a ditch has been demonstrated to indicate a recutting
of the ditch, in this case perhaps indicating two periods of
refurbishment of the innermost defences. Apart from this

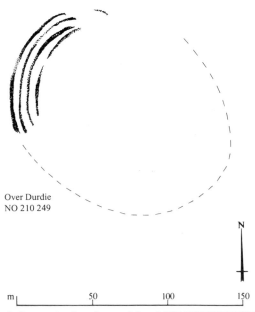

Over Durdie
NO 210 249

N

m   50   100   150

B. *Comparative plans of cropmark forts, 1:2500 (NMRS DC 25092)*

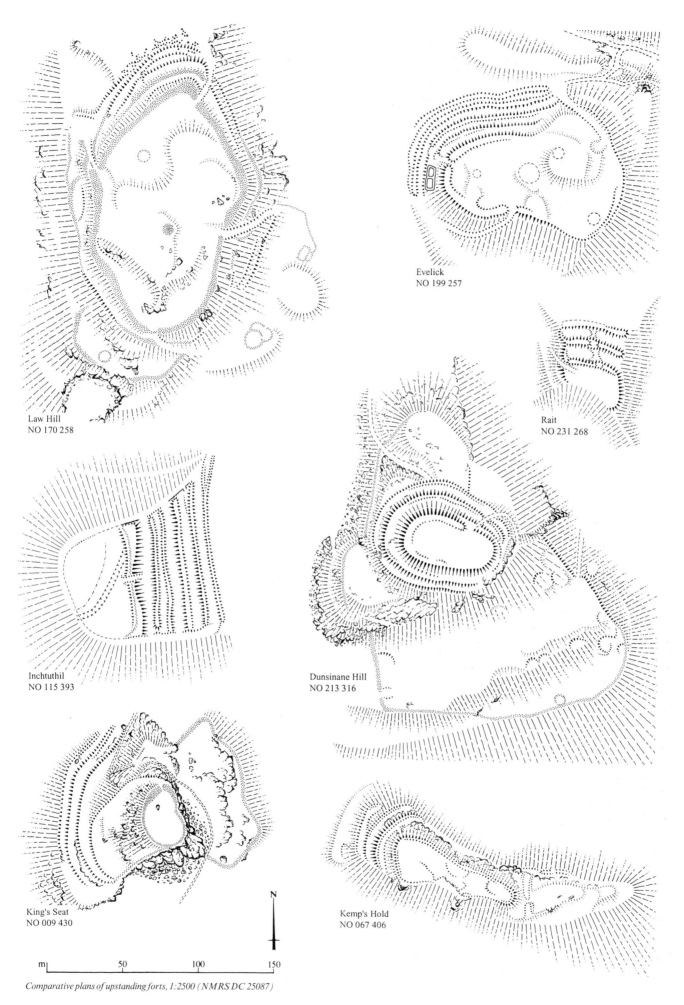

Law Hill
NO 170 258

Evelick
NO 199 257

Rait
NO 231 268

Inchtuthil
NO 115 393

Dunsinane Hill
NO 213 316

King's Seat
NO 009 430

Kemp's Hold
NO 067 406

N

m | 50 | 100 | 150

Comparative plans of upstanding forts, 1:2500 (NMRS DC 25087)

A. **The Welton** (*NO 196 439*), *fort and settlement complex*
(*NMRS B 22663*)

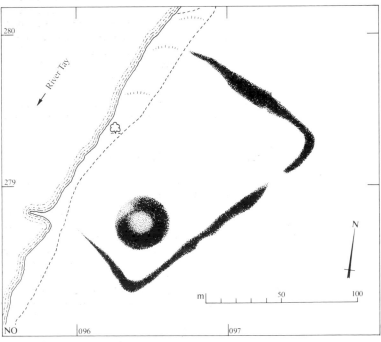

B. **Gold Castle** (*NO 0966 2788*), *earthwork, 1:2500*
(*NMRS DC 25093*)

slender evidence for several periods of construction in the visible defences, the excavations also recovered more compelling evidence of earlier occupation on the promontory, in the form of an arc of palisade and a ditch within the interior. These cut off the north-west corner of the promontory, but they lie eccentrically to one another and probably represent successive perimeters, the palisade presumably being the earlier. Nothing is now visible at ground level of either of these perimeters or of the 'hearth', although the major section cut through the massive inner rampart can still be seen. This rampart incorporates dressed blocks of Gourdie stone robbed from the Roman fortress lying to the east, and a single example was found in the cast of a wind-blown tree when the site was surveyed in 1989. The 'hearth' discovered in the interior was a substantial area of paving about 3m across, partly composed of squared blocks which were doubtless derived from a similar source. Although large quantities of charcoal were apparently associated with the paving, it is perhaps more likely to have been the floor of a building, part of whose wall survived to a height of 0.6m on the south-west.

53. 72C. **Evelick** (0.55ha), one of the larger forts in the area, has an impressive arc of defences cutting across the gentle north and west approaches. Again, a close inspection of the fort suggests that at least two periods of construction are represented, and the two outer banks and ditches appear to be an addition, blocking an earlier entrance through the inner defences on the west. The interior of this fort is probably the most remarkable of any of the forts in South-east Perth. A large ring-ditch house may be seen in the middle, and traces of several others can be detected elsewhere in the interior.

Meaningful comparisons between the earthworks that have been recorded as cropmarks and those that are still upstanding are very difficult to make. In their final form, however, the close-set ditched defences of **Evelick** can be paralleled in at 52B.
13B. least two of the cropmark sites, **Rosemount** and **Over Durdie**, the former (0.2ha) with an arc of at least five ditches backing on to the edge of a stream gully, and the latter (0.7ha) with a complete circuit of possibly four. The defences at both **Evelick** and **Rosemount** form a band about 35m deep, as against 20m at **Over Durdie**, but it should be remembered that the defences of the two cropmark forts may also reflect several periods of construction.

Of the other two multivallate forts, little is yet known of the 52B. defences of the fort at **Mains of Hallyburton**, but both of the 48B.
54A. two superimposed ditch-systems at **The Welton** are clearly of a different character. Although the complete layout of the defences at The Welton has yet to be recovered, enough has been recorded to show that this low rise on the edge of a river terrace is occupied by a complex sequence of structures. This not only includes the ditches of two successive forts, but also a mass of other settlement and funerary remains. This section, however, will only examine the defences of the forts and the structures that lie within them. The smaller of the forts comprises two ditches set some 3m apart, which cut off a small wedge-shaped promontory on the edge of the terrace; on the south-west, an area of the fort where the definition of the cropmarks is least clear, the defences intersect the inner ditch of what appears to be a triple-ditched work. The ditches of the latter are set about 10m apart, although the inner appears to diverge from the course of the other two and may represent a separate phase of enclosure. Arcs of two palisade trenches are visible between the inner and middle ditches, their intersecting courses showing that the palisaded and ditched defences were all built successively. By the very nature of cropmarks, however, it is almost impossible to be certain of the sequence of construction of the various perimeters. It may be a reasonable assumption that the palisades fall in the earlier part of this sequence, but it would be unwise to state this assumption too firmly. The relationship of the various perimeters to the other features that have been recorded is equally uncertain, although two conjoined souterrains are probably later in date than the triple-ditched fort, since the line of the wall of one of the

passages can be detected as a parchmark running through the cropmark of the innermost ditch.

The final cropmarks that should be mentioned here are those at **Tofthill** and **Gold Castle**, the first site only known from 54B. aerial photographs, but the second also recorded in the antiquarian literature. Gold Castle is first mentioned by Maitland, who describes a 'tumulus', standing within the earthwork, 'out of which a considerable quantity of gold coins have been dug' (1757, 199). Curiously, Roy (1793) does not depict the earthwork on his plan of the nearby Roman temporary camp at Grassy Walls. No trace of the tumulus, or the enclosing earthwork, are now visible on the ground, but cropmarks have revealed a ditch enclosing an area measuring 150m by 100m against the river bank, and there are also traces of a large disc-shaped mark at the southern end of the interior. A saddle quern has been discovered in the area of the earthwork (*DES 1964*, 38). **Tofthill** is rather smaller than Gold Castle, 68A. measuring 75m by 50m within a ditch about 5m in breadth, and it is notable for the cropmark souterrain that has been identified in the interior (see Souterrains).

There can be little dispute that the fort on **Dunsinane Hill** is 53. 56.
73B. the most spectacular of the fortifications in South-east Perth. Equally, it must always have been one of the more important sites of the area, commanding a wide sweep of country across the lower end of Strathmore. Its probable importance is also reflected in the remains themselves, which are unparalleled in the rest of the area, and the association of its name with Macbeth has led to the series of antiquarian excavations that now disfigure the interior. At the core, crowning the summit of the hill, there is a massively defended citadel, which almost certainly occupies the site of an earlier fort. The defences of the citadel comprise a substantial inner wall, possibly as much as 9m thick, accompanied by two outer ramparts, which together enclose an area of about 0.1ha, a relatively small area in view of the scale of the surrounding defences. The interior of the fort, particularly at the east end, has been extensively trenched by the early excavators, who also attempted to trace the outer wall-face, creating the narrow ledge visible at the foot of the wall today. The entrance is probably on the north-east, approached by a winding trackway that passes obliquely through the outer lines of defence. On the north side of the fort, the outer rampart blocks an earlier trackway, which, lower down the slope, passes through what is probably an original entrance in a heavily robbed rampart. The latter rampart, which takes in a series of terraces on the hill, must, therefore, predate the visible defences on the summit. Indeed, the present state of this rampart on the upper terraces of the hill leaves little doubt that it has been robbed to provide stone for the defences of the citadel. On the lower terrace, to south, it is in a considerably better state of repair, forming a stony bank 2.5m in thickness with several runs of outer facing-stones visible. In all, it encloses an area of 2.16ha, and there are traces of several crescentic scarps indicating the positions of timber houses on the terrace that forms the southern part of the interior. There is also a stone-walled hut-circle overlying the rampart on the south side of the fort.

The sequence of construction between the visible defences on the summit of the hill and the rampart taking in the surrounding terraces may be reasonably clear, but there is less certainty concerning the question of the presumed earlier fort on the summit. Indeed, there is little tangible evidence for such a fortification at all. The most persuasive evidence is the quantity of vitrified stone that is strewn about the inner defences and the three pieces that were identified in the course of the survey along the rampart enclosing the southern terrace. None of this material appears to be *in situ* and it can be argued that it has been robbed from an earlier timber-laced wall. To a certain extent, the case is sustained by the confused accounts of the antiquarian excavations on the hill, which do not appear to have located a vitrified core to the inner wall, but it would be unwise to imply a relationship between an earlier fortification on the summit and the rampart taking in the terraces on the

disturbed ground
cm cupmarked stone

m 10 20 30 40 50 60 70 80 90 100

strength of the three pieces of vitrified stone found on the south side of the fort. There can be little doubt that timber-lacing was a common construction technique in fort defences, and the dilapidated and grass-grown state of the rampart in question may yet hide evidence of a vitrified core.

In view of the historical associations of the place-name, it is not surprising that the fort has been the scene of two sets of antiquarian investigations. The first was carried out in about 1799 by James Playfair (Robertson 1799, 569-70, Appendix 12; Playfair 1819), and the second in 1854 by a Mr Nairne (Wise 1859), who then owned the hill. The results of these investigations are far from clear, and the published accounts are both confused and conflicting. Sketches by Skene (1834) and Stewart (1854), the latter published by Christison (1900, 88, fig.42), show that Playfair drove a trench from the entrance through the centre of the fort and dug a number of pits on the line of the wall. Nairne concentrated his efforts on trenching the east part of the interior, where he claimed to have found the base of a 'tower' and a two-chambered structure. The trenches and mounds of spoil that have resulted from these excavations give little clue to the nature of the structures that were uncovered, and the finds, which included a bronze spiral finger-ring (Brown 1873, 378-9) and a quern, have been lost. The excavations do show, however, that the deposits in the eastern part of the interior are quite deep, sufficient to bury the walls of the two chambers. The discovery of the skeletal remains of two adults and a child in a blocked off 'passage' between the two chambers may indicate that Nairne also broke into an earlier burial chamber set on the summit of the hill.

There can be little argument as to the disparate nature of this group of forts and earthworks, and, although it would usually be assumed that they are of prehistoric date, it is likely that some of these particular examples were occupied in the Early Historic period. The dressed Gourdie stone from the inner rampart at **Inchtuthil**, for instance, provides reasonably convincing evidence for at least one phase of the defences being later than the abandonment of the Roman fortress. Less certain is the identification of the fort on **Dunsinane Hill** with *Dunsion,* which is mentioned in the Pictish Regnal Lists (Alcock 1981, 173-4), or the attribution to this period of **King's Seat**, Dunkeld (Alcock 1987, 82). Conceivably, the earthwork at **Rait** may be of even later date, its proximity to the church suggesting the possibility of an earth-and-timber castle of medieval date. In this context, it should perhaps be noted that the earthwork at **Gold Castle** must have borne a superficial resemblance to a motte-and-bailey, although there is no documentary evidence to indicate the presence of such a castle in this area. However, by analogy with other defended sites where there is a coincidence with a souterrain, including the fort at **The Welton**, the **Tofthill** enclosure is quite likely to be prehistoric in date, as are most of the other forts. At least five of the forts betray evidence of multi-phase construction in their defences, and it should be anticipated that some of the individual sites remained in use, or were reoccupied on several occasions, over a very long period of time.

49. Enclosures

In addition to the fortifications and palisaded enclosures described above, about sixty simpler enclosures have been recorded in South-east Perth, the majority of them in the form of cropmarks. As a whole, they embrace a wide range of structures, and examples, such as the Neolithic long mortuary enclosure at **Inchtuthil** or the classic medieval moated site at **Hallyards**, will be found under all the main headings of this volume. Little is known about the rest; some are almost certainly the remains of settlements, others, such as at **Balgove** and **Woodside**, perhaps stock pens or old fields, and one, at **Peattie**, possibly even an old burial-ground, but the evidence of the cropmarks does not allow us to do much more than divide them into two basic groups — curvilinear and rectilinear — a classification that has no functional or chronological significance.

28A.
2. 108B.
58.

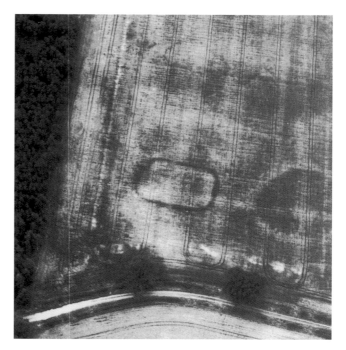

A. *Meikleour (NO 1618 3980), enclosure (NMRS PT 14730)*

B. *Nether Gothens (NO 1727 4054), enclosure (NMRS PT 14728)*

Of the curvilinear enclosures revealed by cropmarks, in only eleven cases is enough known for an accurate estimate of their size to be made. They range in shape from circular to oval and, with the exception of a small structure at **Links**, which measures only 16m by 8m (0.01ha), from 0.07ha to 0.14ha in internal area. The smallest of these is the circular enclosure, 30m in diameter, at **Middlebank**, which has already been described in the section on unenclosed circular buildings, and the largest is an oval example at **Plaistow**, measuring 50m by 36m. Of the rest little can be said. The entire circuit is seldom clearly defined, and it is rarely possible to identify the position of an entrance; nor have any traces of internal structures been recorded. The detail detectable at **Hallhole**, which measures 40m in internal diameter and has two opposed entrances, each defined by expanded ditch terminals, is the exception rather than the rule.

72B.

58.

58.

The sizes and shapes of the rectilinear enclosures are equally hard to assess, many of the cropmarks only revealing parts of their perimeters. At least eleven of them are relatively small, ranging in shape from rectangular to roughly square, and in size from about 17m by 12m (0.02ha) to 30m (0.09ha) across. Their

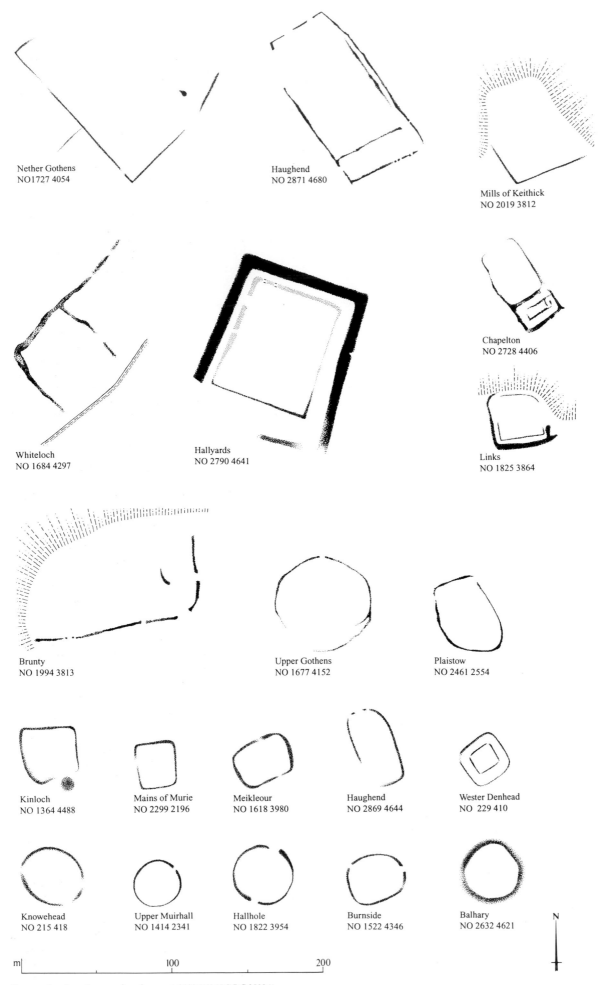

Nether Gothens
NO 1727 4054

Haughend
NO 2871 4680

Mills of Keithick
NO 2019 3812

Whiteloch
NO 1684 4297

Hallyards
NO 2790 4641

Chapelton
NO 2728 4406

Links
NO 1825 3864

Brunty
NO 1994 3813

Upper Gothens
NO 1677 4152

Plaistow
NO 2461 2554

Kinloch
NO 1364 4488

Mains of Murie
NO 2299 2196

Meikleour
NO 1618 3980

Haughend
NO 2869 4644

Wester Denhead
NO 229 410

Knowehead
NO 215 418

Upper Muirhall
NO 1414 2341

Hallhole
NO 1822 3954

Burnside
NO 1522 4346

Balhary
NO 2632 4621

N

m | 100 | 200

Comparative plans of cropmark enclosures, 1:2500 (NMRS DC 25094)

58

interiors tend to be featureless, but there are possible traces of a rectangular building at **Chapelton**, and complex sub-divisions at **Inchture**. The only other details worthy of mention are the gaps at the corners of the inner enclosure at **Wester Denhead**, a feature only parallelled in square barrows (see barrows and cairns), and what appear to be opposed entrances in the long sides of an enclosure at **Meikleour**. The latter, which measures about 36m by 24m (0.09ha) internally, appears to be defined by a rather more substantial ditch than the rest, and there is a possibility that it is another mortuary enclosure of Neolithic date.

The rest of the rectilinear enclosures offer few clues as to their purposes. Examples illustrated here include **Nether Gothens**, **Haughend**, **Mills of Keithick** and **Whiteloch**, which, by way of comparison, have been set against the moated sites at **Hallyards** and **Links**. The first three are all notable for their straight sides and sharp angles, contrasting with the less regular ditches at **Whiteloch**, where the shore of the loch apparently forms one side of the enclosure.

Not all the cropmark enclosures fall neatly into the curvilinear or rectilinear groups. The most notable of these, which is unparalleled in the rest of the survey area, has been recorded on the south side of a steep-sided gully at **Brunty**. The interior of the enclosure measures about 110m by 50m, defined by a single ditch on the east and south, and by steep natural scarps on the north and west. Several gaps in the ditch are visible, notably three close to the rounded south-east angle. While the gully lends considerable natural strength to this site, the ditch appears to be relatively narrow, and it is unlikely to be defensive in character.

Interrupted ring-ditches

The interrupted ring-ditches represent one of the most distinctive components of the cropmark settlement record in South-east Perth. The basic characteristics of these sites are a ring-ditch with one or more broad gaps in the perimeter and a curving mark either extending out through one of the gaps or intersecting the perimeter on one side. While some of the curving marks apparently associated with these ring-ditches are relatively slight, others are more substantial and almost certainly indicate the remains of souterrains. Indeed, the coincidence of cropmarks and antiquarian records at **Lintrose** has provided evidence of a souterrain with precisely this sort of spatial relationship to one of these ring-ditches. The Lintrose example is described in greater detail under the heading of souterrains.

A total of fourteen settlements of this type have been identified in South-east Perth, too few for variations in their local distribution to be held of much significance. Nevertheless, thirteen of the sites are scattered along Strathmore, the south-westernmost, at **Sherifftown**, falling within the Roman temporary camp at **Grassy Walls**, and the north-easternmost at **Jordanstone**, lying to the north-east of Meigle. Perhaps the most remarkable aspect of the distribution is that only one possible example has been recorded in the Carse of Gowrie, contrasting with the dense concentration of souterrains that have come to light in this part of the survey area. This apparent gap in the distribution is partly filled by the large C-shaped ring-ditch 18m in diameter at **Newton of Glencarse**, which also has two other rings adjacent to it. This site, and a similar structure some 15m in diameter at **Byres**, have some claim to inclusion in this group, since another example, at Dillavaird in Angus, has the characteristic curving mark extending out through its open side, although in this particular case the cropmarks have also revealed traces of a concentric palisaded enclosure.

Single examples of interrupted ring-ditches have been recorded at **Lintrose**, **Sherifftown**, **Leyston** and **Gallowflat**, and possibly at **Millhorn**, **Hatton** and **Hallhole**, but each is accompanied by traces of other features in the immediate vicinity. At **Sherifftown**, there is a cluster of maculae and linear features, including two lengths of causewayed ditch, and

some 80m to the north-east there is an enclosed crescent. At **Leyston**, the ring-ditch overlaps at least one palisaded enclosure (see above), with other diffuse markings close by, while at **Gallowflat** there are at least three curvilinear markings, which may include the remains of souterrains and the floors of circular buildings. Others of this type form groups, the largest being clusters of at least four at **Mudhall, Coin Hill** and **Grangemount**.

The internal diameters of the ring-ditches can be estimated in twenty-five individual cases. The smallest is the the **Sherifftown** example, with a diameter of only 13m, but the largest to be found, at **Grangemount, Jordanstone, Leyston, Mudhall** and **Coin Hill**, range from 20m to 24m. The breadth of the perimeter ditch is equally variable, at **Sherifftown** being perhaps no more than 1m, but at some of the larger examples in excess of 3m. The associated curvilinear features vary widely in size and shape, regardless of the size of the ring-ditch itself. At **Lintrose** and **Gallowflat** they are relatively broad, while in well-defined examples at **Coin Hill** and **Grangemount** the breadth does not exceed 1m.

One of the most impressive of the settlements of interrupted ring-ditches is the group at **Mudhall**. The cropmarks, comprise at least five discrete clusters of markings spread over a distance of 400m along a terrace between Mudhall and Red Brae, on the bank of the Isla. Each cluster comprises an interrupted ring-ditch with a curving appendage of the type discussed above. In four cases the curving marks are relatively slight features, but that associated with the north-easternmost ring is much broader. Detailed examination of the cropmarks shows that some of the ditched perimeters are themselves quite substantial features. The cropmarks here are also considerably more complex than on many of the other sites, an indication, perhaps, of a lengthy but episodic structural history. Clearer evidence of successive use is provided by the second ring from the south, which appears to coincide with at least one crescent marking, the latter probably contemporary with the concentric circular palisade (see enclosed crescents).

Since settlements of this type do not apparently survive on any of the neighbouring hills, and none has been excavated, their character must be deduced entirely from the evidence of aerial photographs. However, the sheer scale of some of the largest examples is in itself a clue. With the exception of two superimposed structures at Scotstarvit in Fife, whose character is in any case uncertain, the largest circular timber houses recorded in eastern Scotland are no more than 17m in diameter. It would therefore appear possible that the large interrupted ring-ditches are of a different character, the evidence strongly suggesting that activity was focussed within the interior. In a number of cases, there are traces of pits and diffuse discolouration of the crop within the interior, but it is rare for these features to form a coherent pattern. At **Coin Hill**, however, one of the ring-ditches is roughly concentric to a disc-shaped cropmark some 13m in diameter, and traces of a crescent may be visible in one of the others. At **Hallhole**, too, a clearly defined crescent can be detected within the interior of what is probably another interrupted ring-ditch. It is always possible that these discs and crescents are not contemporary with the rings at the centre of which they lie, but it is equally likely that they provide the evidence for the layout of the larger examples, with a free-standing circular timber building set within an enclosing ring-ditch.

It would be unwise to assume that all the interrupted ring-ditches conformed to this pattern. The smaller examples between 13m and 17m in diameter, like **Sherifftown, Woodhead** and **Cargill**, all of which are defined by relatively narrow ditches, fall within the known size range of circular timber buildings. These ring-ditches may well indicate the position of the bedding-trenches for successive phases of building. Excavation of a ring-ditch cropmark at North Straiton, in north-east Fife, which also displayed a curving mark leading out of the interior, showed that the relatively broad cropmark of the ditch had formed where the bedding-trenches for the walls

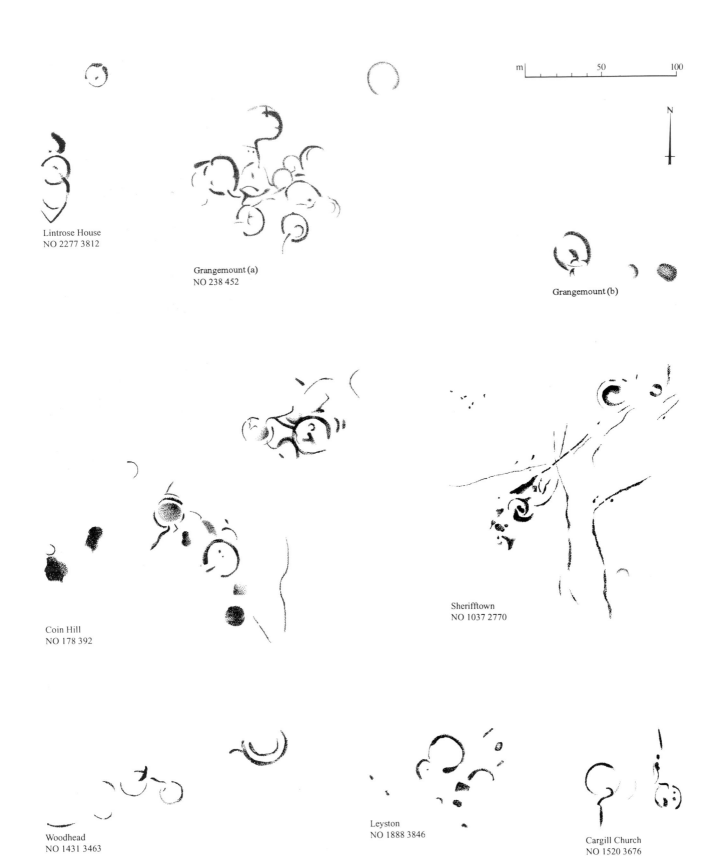

Lintrose House
NO 2277 3812

Grangemount (a)
NO 238 452

Grangemount (b)

m | 50   100

N

Coin Hill
NO 178 392

Sherifftown
NO 1037 2770

Woodhead
NO 1431 3463

Leyston
NO 1888 3846

Cargill Church
NO 1520 3676

Comparative plans of interrupted ring-ditches, 1:2500 (NMRS DC 25095)

A. **Sherifftown** (NO 1037 2770), viewed from the south-east, with the interrupted ring-ditch on the left side of the picture, and an enclosed crescent on the right, and traces of interrupted ditches between (NMRS PT 6815)

B. **Grangemount** (NO 238 452), complex of interrupted ring-ditches from the west (NMRS B 22704)

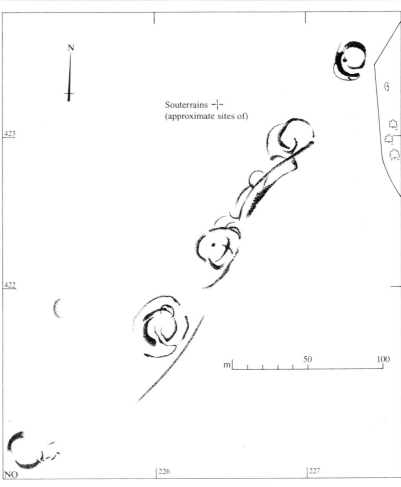

Souterrains -¦-
(approximate sites of)

C. **Mudhall** (NO 226 422), settlement, 1:2500 (NMRS DC 25096)

61

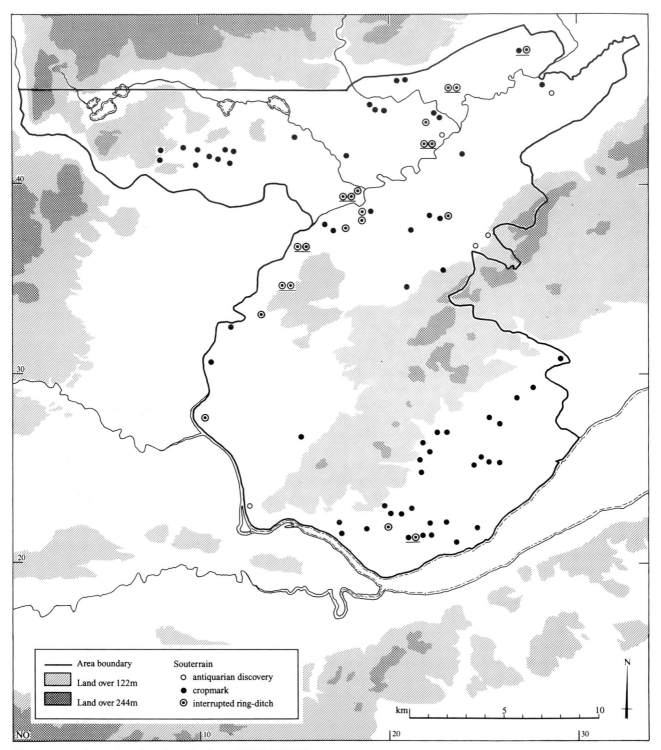

Distribution map of souterrains and interrupted ring-ditches (NMRS DC 25097)

60. 61B.

of successive timber buildings lay side by side.

The possibility that the interrupted ring-ditches may embrace two different types of structure raises the question of the function of the ditches of the larger examples. At **Grangemount**, for instance, the complementary arcs of ditch of the biggest ring-ditch rival some of the souterrain cropmarks for size, and the longest arc even appears to hook sharply into the interior at its north-west end. At least one of the arcs at **Leyston** narrows towards one end, while some of the arcs at **Jordanstone** are also closely comparable to the cropmarks of souterrains. This is perhaps how the larger examples might be interpreted, as an arrangement of subterranean structures around a central building. If this is the case, it is worth considering the possibility that the curving plan-form typical of so many souterrains owes its origin to this sort of arrangement,

although it requires to be explained why the regularly built and sinuously irregular types of 'embryo souterrain' appear to be broadly contemporary. Two further points should be observed: in several examples, notably at **Coin Hill**, the inner edge of the enclosing ditch is much more sharply defined than the outer, which may indicate that the former was much steeper; secondly, the suggested interpretation, creates a plan-form not dissimilar to that of the upstanding double-walled hut-circles of North-east Perth, with a circular house central to some form of enclosure. However, no features were recorded adjacent to any of these hut-circles that might provide a parallel for the curved appendages found in association with the interrupted ring-ditches.

60.

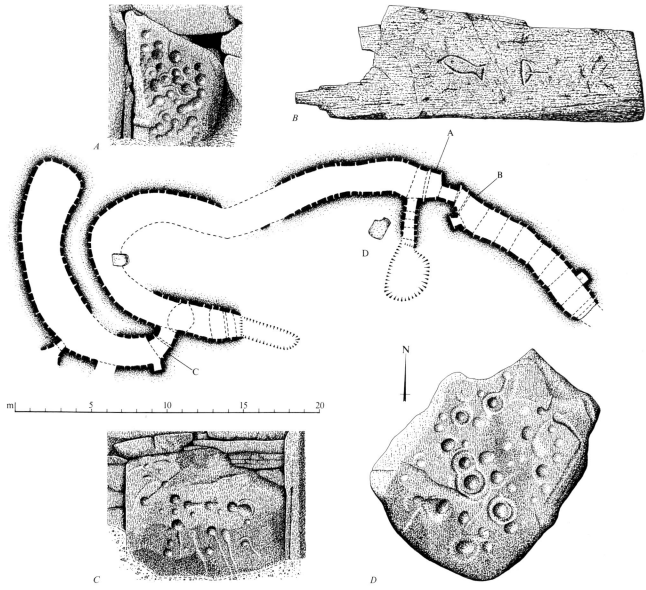

Pitcur (*NO 2529 3738*), *souterrain, 1:250* (*NMRS DC 25098*), *and carved stones A-D* (*NMRS DC 25270-3*)
A, C, and D, (*scale 1:25*)
B, (*scale 1:15*)

62. **Souterrains**

Souterrains were the only type of non-defensive settlement structure known in the lowlands of South-east Perth prior to the current campaigns of aerial reconnaissance. The context of their discovery has already been explored in the introduction to the patterns of survival and destruction within the survey area, but suffice it to say that from the late eighteenth century, quarrying, ploughing and road-building, had uncovered only a handful of examples. Pennant provides an account of the earliest of the discoveries, describing what must have been a curved passage about 2.7m broad with walls 1.5m high, which had been found some 0.6m below the surface of the ground near Coupar Grange (1776, 448-9). This site is often thought to be one of the those at **Mudhall** referred to by Playfair a little later in the eighteenth century, but it should not be forgotten that Pennant mentions a second example some 270m away and that several separate sites may be involved. Playfair describes one of the structures as having a curving passage with walls about 1.5m high, but he gives it a breadth of only 1.8m and goes on to mention paving on the floor (*Stat. Acct.*, 19 [1797], 359-60). The first edition of the OS 6 inch map (Perth, 1867, sheet 64) attributes the site of this discovery to the field to the north-east
61C. of Mudhall, and it is tempting to link the antiquarian accounts

to the cropmarks of the interrupted ring-ditches that lie in this area.

Fortunately, one of the souterrains discovered in the nineteenth century has survived virtually intact and can still be visited today. The **Pitcur** souterrain, which was extensively
63. trenched following its discovery in 1878 (MacRitchie 1900), provides a remarkable illustration of these curious underground passages. The boulder-faced walls of the passages still stand up to 2m high, and are corbelled inwards at the top to support massive stone roof slabs. Some of these slabs lie where they have fallen in the passages, but the whole of the eastern end of the souterrain retains its roof for a distance of 14m. The overall layout of the souterrain is not known, but the visible parts appear to comprise three interconnected passages, with a total length of at least 66m. Indeed, the broad western passage, with its two entrances and rounded terminal, might easily be identified as a souterrain in its own right. Surviving architectural details include doorways with rebated jambs leading from the central passage into the western and the roofed eastern passage, both of which also have aumbries built into their walls. No fewer than four stones decorated with cup-and-ring marks have been incorporated into the souterrain, together with another bearing some enigmatic graffiti of unknown date.

Lintrose (NO 2271 3800), souterrain and interrupted ring-ditch from the east (NMRS A 30624)

The potential of unroofed souterrains as targets for aerial survey has only been recognised quite recently. The greater part of the structure being set in a broad trench dug deep into the subsoil, it is not surprising that this gives rise to a response in a crop growing above. The shapes that might be anticipated range from the simple curved plan, tapering towards an entrance at one end, such as appears to have been recorded at **Mudhall**, to the more complex layout that was recovered from **Pitcur**, although it must be said that the complex plan of the latter was virtually unique prior to the aerial survey programme.

60. 64. Fortunately, the souterrain discovered at **Lintrose** in 1840 (*NSA*, 11, Forfar, 643-4) has also been identified by aerial photography, providing a sound basis for the interpretation of some of the cropmarks. The passage at Lintrose was about 15m long, narrowing from up to 2.4m in breadth at its inner end to 0.9m at the entrance, and it had a paved floor; the walls were 1.5m in height and the upper courses had been corbelled inwards. Although the account of the discovery at Lintrose only mentions one souterrain, the cropmarks have revealed two broad curving marks. The narrow end of the northerly one, however, hooks sharply round, and must surely be the entrance which 'winded half round' in the original description (*NSA*, 11, Forfar, 643-4). Immediately south of this souterrain, there is an interrupted ring-ditch with an internal diameter of 18m, its perimeter intersected on the south-east by the curving mark of the second souterrain. The curve of the second souterrain is then extended southwards by a much fainter mark to partially enclose the cropmarks of several other minor features. There are also traces of a smaller ring-ditch about 8m in diameter to the north. The north-eastern arc of this ring-ditch is considerably broader than elsewhere, creating a crescentic effect, and it may be reasonably identified as the remains of a circular house.

62. The distribution of cropmark souterrains is, of course, confined to the arable fields of Strathmore and the Carse of Gowrie, but it must be of some significance that the earlier discoveries were also made in the same areas. Despite the operations of the improvers on the Sidlaws, none have been recorded on the hills, and it was an aspect of the survey of North-east Perth that, apparently, the use of souterrains did not penetrate up Glenshee and Strathardle. Within the arable zone, the only areas where their absence is particularly noticeable is to the north-east of Perth itself, but this is not one of the areas noted for its free-draining soils, and the distribution of

cropmarks here is fairly sparse anyway. It should be remembered that a freely-draining site is a prerequisite for an underground structure such as a souterrain.

Many of the marks are very similar to the Lintrose example that has already been described, being no more than simple curving features, which taper towards one end, where they sometimes turn quite sharply. There is considerable variation in size, the smaller ones only measuring from 8m to 10m in length, while some of the larger ones exceed 30m. There can be difficulties in distinguishing some of the smaller examples from the crescents of circular buildings. In general terms, those that have been identified as souterrains have been adjudged to turn more sharply than could be accommodated by the wall of a circular building, and to exhibit relatively even cropmark definition along both sides and around one rounded end. This definition is no more than a general guide, and there is always the possibility that some small 'souterrains' are internal components of circular buildings. The variation in length is matched by the range of breadths that has been recorded, but the nature of the presumed construction-process makes any assessment of this dimension problematical. It is possible that in some cases it is the construction trench that produces the cropmark, not the souterrain, although the vast majority of the clearly defined examples appear to represent the passage itself. Indeed, in a few instances on exceptionally free-draining soils, it has proved possible to distinguish the lines of the passage walls within what may be the edges of the construction trench. Despite the problems of assessing the breadth of the underlying structure, there are a number of souterrain-like cropmarks that are very narrow, apparently representing small passages which do not conform to the pattern of broad curving structures that are so typical of the earlier discoveries.

Cropmark souterrains are found both in apparent isolation, and in close proximity to other structures, including other souterrains. The Lintrose and Mudhall examples have already been described, but juxtaposed features regularly include discs and crescents. There are also two examples which apparently occur within large ditched enclosures. The character of these relationships requires to be tested by excavation, as a matter of some urgency.

Many of the cropmarks are too indistinct to allow any detailed interpretation of the subterranean structures. Nevertheless, a wide range of specific architectural traits can be detected across the area as a whole. The squat curvilinear plans with sharply defined edges of **Spittalfield** or **Culthill**, for instance, are fairly typical of the smaller souterrains. At **Mains of Fordie**, there is a relatively broad example with a segmental appearance. It measures some 13m in overall length, narrowing to a sharply hooked entrance at the north-east end, but it is not clear whether the cropmark reflects a structure with two chambers, linked by a doorway, or simply results from the survival of some of the roofing slabs *in situ*.

In some cases, mainly from the Carse of Gowrie, remarkable levels of detail have been revealed by the cropmarks. At **Glencarse**, the wallhead on either side of a curving passage, some 26m in length by up to 2.25m in breadth, can be made out, and at both **Pitroddie** and **Rossie** a few lintels can also be detected *in situ*. A trial trench cut across the **Glencarse** souterrain in 1982 showed that the construction trench was about 5.3m wide at the top and that the space behind the walls had been packed with rubble (*DES 1982*, 33; Maxwell 1987, 37-40). In many ways, the simple plan and apparently isolated position of the Glencarse souterrain conforms with the traditional image of these passages, and it is the complex structures like **Pitcur** that appear to be the exceptions. The cropmark evidence increasingly challenges these perceptions. The **Glencarse** example is, in fact, not alone in the landscape; there is a second small souterrain within 60m of it, and yet another a further 100m beyond. More spectacular are the complexes at **Pitroddie**, **Rossie Priory** and **Rait**, while at **Peattie** and **West Buttergask**, both of them situated in Strathmore to the south-west of **Pitcur**, there are comparable,

65B.

66. 67A.
65A-C.

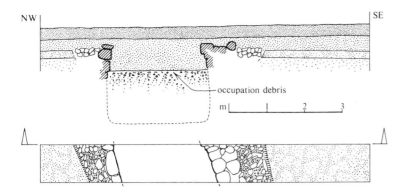

occupation debris

m | 1 2 3

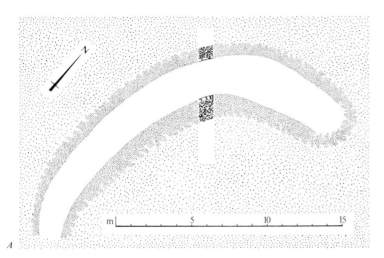

N

m | 5 10 15

A

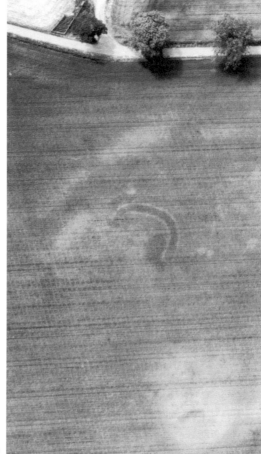

B

Glencarse (NO 2026 2243), souterrain

A. section and plans, 1:250 and 1:10 (NMRS DC 13686)
B. the cropmark of the souterrain, with traces of a second
   souterrain in the foreground (NMRS PT 10749)
C. the souterrain under trial excavation (NMRS A 36983)

but less clearly defined, clusters of markings. In short, the
cropmark evidence clearly shows that the distribution of
souterrains is much denser than was previously thought, both in
terms of a general pattern and the detailed composition of any
one settlement, and earlier interpretations are merely a
reflection of the causes of their discovery, not of the underlying
pattern of settlement.

66. 71.   The remarkable levels of definition at **Pitroddie** in particular
demonstrate the character of a souterrain complex to a degree
that was formerly only accessible through excavation. The
completeness of the information is especially evident in the
complex to the south-east of the road, where the wallheads of
the passages can be detected in the cropmarks. At the core of
the complex, a passage curls tightly away from a diffuse
macula. Within its arc there are traces of what is probably a
second passage or elongated chamber, which may well open off
it, while another two appear to spring from the outer wall of the
first on the south-west; parallel to the longer of these, but
extending for as much as 40m, there is a fifth passage, although
the markings suggest that this feature may have two separate
elements, possibly linked by a doorway, but with independent
entrances at opposite ends; this point can only be determined by
excavation. The souterrains are by no means the only markings
in the field and a series of shadowy arcs and crescents can also
be detected in the vicinity. It must be said, however, that there
is no clearly defined evidence of other settlement structures
around the mouths of the souterrains, possibly indicating that
the above ground structures associated with them were built of
stone or incorporated relatively light timber framing.

On the other side of the main road, some 180m distant to the
north-west, there is a second group of passages, which exhibit a

C

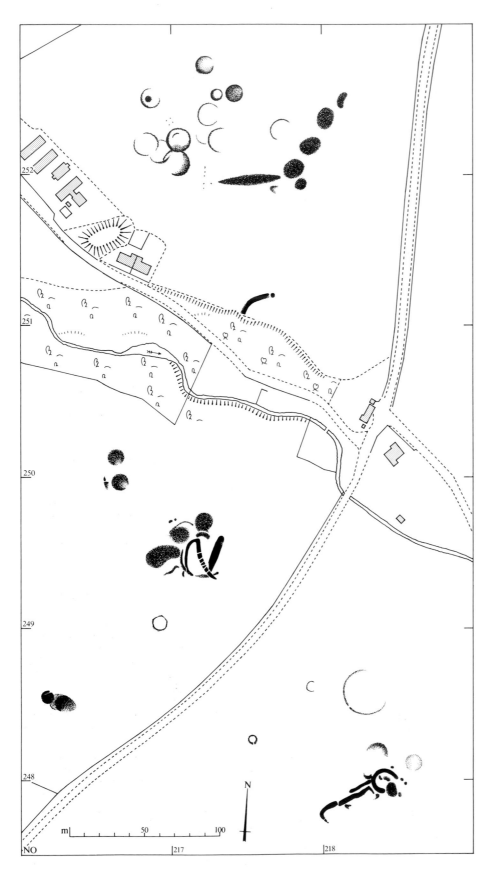

Pitroddie (*NO 21 24*),
souterrains and settlement, 1:2500
(*NMRS DC 25100*)

different degree of complexity from that just described. Pencil-thin lines of lighter cropmarking have again formed over the wallheads of two of the souterrains, but in this case the body of what appears to be the main passage is broken by a series of transverse marks, which are almost certainly caused by roofing slabs that still remain *in situ.* Unlike the first complex, this one appears to be the focus for several quite prominent circular and oval marks, which must be presumed to be the remains of

timber houses of one sort or another.

Another souterrain, this time apparently single, lies a further 150m to the north on the opposite side of the Pitroddie Burn, with a much more complex concentration of discs, crescents and ring-ditches on the slopes beyond. Amongst these there is yet another broad linear mark, whose character is such as to make precise identification impossible; it may conceivably be a length of hollowed trackway, as may a broad curving mark

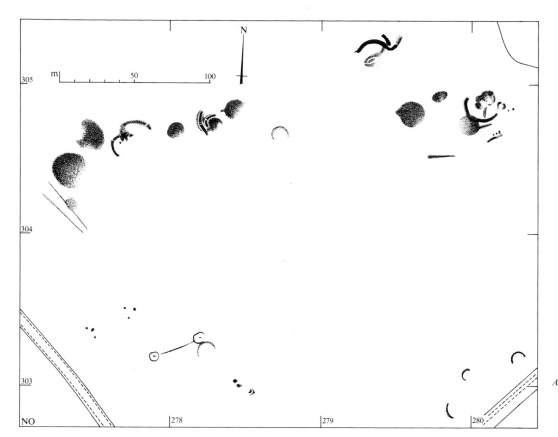

A. *Rossie Priory*
(NO 278 304),
souterrains and
settlement, 1:2500
(NMRS DC 25101)

B. *Gallowflat (NO 210 211), souterrains and probable interrupted ring-ditch,*
with serpentine marking in the foreground (NMRS B 05319)

some 30m in length and up to 5m in breadth on the slope above
112. the old parish church of **Cambusmichael**. The latter cropmark
has been mapped as a possible souterrain, but together these
two examples provide a timely reminder that our ability to
distinguish between souterrains and other curvilinear
cropmarks is often severely limited.

67A.   At **Rossie Priory**, however, we are again on firmer ground,
with further clusters including undoubted examples of
souterrains. The pattern detectable here is similar to that at
Glencarse and **Pitroddie**, with either single souterrains or
clusters occurring at intervals across a distance of 250m. The
easternmost appears as a single curving mark, with several
maculae lying within its arc and extending into a disc some
13m in diameter on the south-west; 60m to the north-west there
is a rather more complex mark involving at least two, and
possibly three, passages; a further 100m to the west there are

two more almost contiguous passages, in this case with traces
of not only the construction trench and the wallheads, but also
with several of the roofing slabs still in place; and another 30m
beyond them there are two conjoined curvilinear marks. Again
there is very little evidence of structures at the entrances of the
souterrains, although a series of discs, crescents and maculae
are woven in amongst them across the whole field. Other
cropmarks in the southern part of the field include what may be
the remains of several barrows, but the marks are too indistinct
to classify with certainty.

In addition to the souterrains that have been described so far,
there are several much narrower marks, which apparently
exhibit similar characteristics. Notable amongst these are a
serpentine marking some 25m in length at **Gallowflat**, in the   67B.
Carse of Gowrie, and a curving mark 14m in length which lies
immediately outside the ditches of the fort at **The Welton**. The   48B.
latter was subject of a trial excavation in 1981 (*DES 1981*, 88),   54A.
which showed that the underlying feature was U-shaped in
profile, measuring 1.1m wide at the top and 1.2m deep. It had
been deliberately filled with a mixture of earth and the burned
debris from a light wooden structure, but whether that structure
originally formed part of the lining cannot be determined
without full excavation. Evidence of timber linings was in fact
identified at Dalladies in Kincardineshire (Watkins 1981a),
during the excavation of several subterranean structures which
closely resemble some of the cropmark features recorded in
South-east Perth. Wooden revetments were also used to line the
outer walls in the sunken sectors of the ring-ditch houses at
Douglasmuir (Kendrick 1982), possibly indicating a common
architectural history. It is not known whether any of the larger,
developed souterrains were lined with timber, rather than stone,
but the possibility clearly exists.

Final comment in this section is reserved for the only two
souterrains to have been identified within large enclosures. The
first is at **Tofthill**, at the west end of the Carse of Gowrie, and   68A.
the second is immediately south of the public road overlooking
the laird's house at **Old Mains of Rattray**, in Strathmore.
Unfortunately, the cropmark of the **Tofthill** enclosure, which
has already been mentioned in the section on fortifications, is
not very well-defined, but it has evidently been a substantial

Tofthill
NO 176 213

Old Mains of Rattray
NO 203 456

N

A   m|_____50_____100|

A. **Tofthill and Old Mains of Rattray**, *comparative plans*
of the souterrains and enclosures, 1:2500
(NMRS DC 25102)
B. **Mains of Inchture** *(NO 2842 2871), enclosures, a*
possible building and two rectangular cropmarks
(NMRS PT 5999)   B

earthwork. In the southern portion of the interior, a broad
curving passage can be clearly identified, at least 25m in
length, with traces of the wallhead parching out along its sides.
Traces of what may be a second curving feature, either a house
or another souterrain, can be seen at the west end of the
interior, and perhaps at least one more souterrain outside the
entrance on the north-east. The **Old Mains of Rattray**
enclosure is of much slighter proportions, measuring 54m by at
least 42m within a narrow ditch which may even be the remains
of a palisade trench. The probable souterrain, which lies within
the western half of the interior, consists of a sharply defined
curving mark about 18m in length and 4m in breadth. Midway
along its length, the mark bifurcates, and a slightly more diffuse
feature extends northwards to the road. A circle of pits about
7m in diameter can be detected, eccentrically positioned within
the curve of the probable souterrain. A possible argument
against the identification of the curving mark as a souterrain is
that, according to the first edition of the OS six-inch map, it
roughly coincides with the position of some cists containing
burials, which were discovered in 1825. It is possible that some
of the markings are derived from gravel-digging, but on the
balance of probabilities the broad curving element of the
cropmarks should be identified as a souterrain, and it is likely
that the circle of pits marks the site of a timber building. There
are several other elongated pits within the interior of the
enclosure, one leading out of the southern end of the souterrain,
and it is always possible that the reference to the earlier
discovery, which was recorded forty years after the event, mis-
identified the remains of a smaller stone-lined pit, or even the
souterrain itself.

Cropmarks of rectangular buildings

Although the bulk of the solid cropmarks are circular or
crescentic, there are at least three that are clearly rectangular or
square. Furthermore, some of the diffuse marks that occur in
the unenclosed settlement sites are quite angular and might just
as easily represent the remains of sunken-floored rectangular or
subrectangular buildings as circular ones. In addition to the

handful of rectangular marks, there are another seven sites with
cropmarks revealing a ditch or bedding-trench defining what
may be a roughly rectangular building. The majority of these
cropmarks lie on the gravels in the Carse of Gowrie, and,
although it would be unwise to read any great significance into
this distribution, it is interesting that some of the best analogues
outside South-east Perth lie immediately to the east in Dundee
and Angus (RCAHMS 1992).

The most clearly defined of the solid rectangular markings
are at **Mains of Inchture** and **South Inchmichael**, in both
cases comprising two separate marks set at right-angles to each
other. At **Mains of Inchture**, the larger of the two marks
measures about 7m by 5m, and the smaller at least 4m by 3m.
About 50m to the east there is a rectangular outline measuring
at least 12m by 7m, and, beyond that, part of a large sub-
divided enclosure which should probably be associated with an
earlier layout of the village of Inchture. At **South Inchmichael**,
the two marks measure about 11m by 5m and 6m by 4m
respectively, and lie in a field which contains a scatter of
features ranging from pits to arcs of ditch and souterrains.
Another solid marking at **Rossie Priory** measures about 6m
square; it has a pit adjacent to it and the remains of a barrow
cemetery nearby.

There are also five other sites where possible rectangular
marks occur, but none of them is sufficiently well defined to be
confidently assigned to this category. These are at
Inchcoonans, **Mains of Murie**, **Hill of Errol**, **Bonhard Park**
and **Clashbenny**. The first of these lies in a cluster of maculae
which have both curved and angular edges and may even be the
remains of old gravel-pits. Similar possibilities exist with an
example immediately behind the steading at **Mains of Murie**,
while the photographs of a poorly-defined mark at **Hill of Errol**
are too oblique and distant for the shape of the mark to be
clearly seen. At **Bonhard Park**, however, there is a scatter of
solid markings, two of which appear to be fairly angular; others
of the marks are certainly circular and there is at least one
possible souterrain. A similar mixture has also been recorded at
Clashbenny, where subrectangular, square and straight-edged

68A.
72A.

68B.
118B.

69A.

46B.

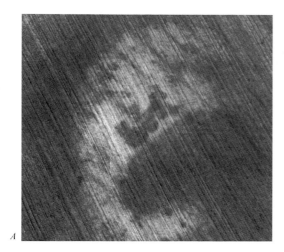

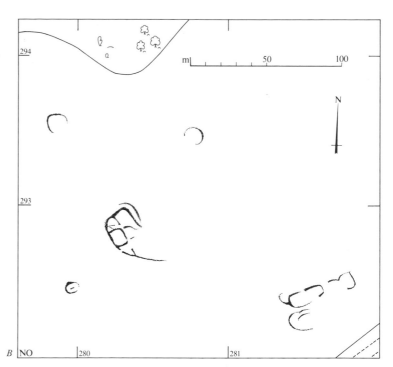

A. **Inchcoonans** (NO 2353 2353), rectangular maculae
(NMRS PT 10768)
B. **Inchture** (NO 281 292), lobate enclosure and enclosures,
1:2500 (NMRS DC 25103)
C. **Berryhill** (NO 1164 3198), possible buildings or mortuary
enclosures, with traces of a pit-alignment on the right side of
the picture (NMRS A 29252)

marks can be seen in close proximity to a circular example. At
the latter site, the long sides of the rectangular mark appear to
be bowed outwards, as at Mylnefield in Dundee District. Such a
feature has been noted in houses of the Early Historic period
elsewhere.

Of the possible buildings that are outlined by a ditch or
bedding-trench, five are simple shapes where at least three
sides can be identified. In at least three of these cases, **South
Inchmichael, Glencarse** and **Bankhead of Kinloch**, it is
possible that the cropmarks have simply revealed part of a
much larger enclosure, while a fourth, **Mains of Errol**, suffers
from the problem of oblique photography at long range. The
fifth is the example that has already been described at **Mains of
Inchture**. Despite these problems, all four must be considered
as possible examples of rectangular buildings. At 12m in
length, the **Glencarse** and **Mains of Inchture** structures are of
the same order of size, but the **South Inchmichael** example
would be considerably bigger with a length of about 25m.

Drawing a distinction between these trench- or ditch-defined
buildings and possible examples of long mortuary enclosures
described in the section on ceremonial and ritual monuments is
far from easy. Indeed, it must be admitted that the identification
of a ditched mortuary enclosure depends on evidence that can
only be recovered by excavation. The two structures at
Berryhill, which have been tentatively classified as mortuary
enclosures, are a case in point, and might just as easily be the
remains of buildings. The larger, measuring about 35m by 9m
within a mark up to 1.5m wide, has two entrances in one side
and two pits set on its axis. Only one end of the smaller
structure is clearly visible and this is about 7m in breadth. The
perimeters of both are quite broad features, and, if marking the
wall-lines, suggest the use of very large timbers. However, it is
worth noting that a large stone-walled building recorded on
Middleton Muir in North-east Perth (RCAHMS 1990, 116, no.
264.2) was apparently enclosed by a drainage ditch, and, like
the structure at Berryhill, also had two entrances in one side.

Finally, mention should be made of a complex cropmark at
Inchture, although its precise interpretation is hindered by the
lack of definition on the aerial photographs. The principal
feature that can be distinguished is what appears to be an
oblong building measuring about 23m in length by 8m in
breadth, but there are traces of what are either small enclosures
or fragments of other buildings clustered around it. Although
the cropmarks here are not very well defined, this building
should probably be identified as one of a small group of

C

structures that have been termed lobate enclosures; these are
distributed throughout eastern Scotland, and comprise an
oblong or sub-oval main element with a conjoined annexe
(Maxwell 1987). Another member of this group is to be found
amongst the cropmarks within the labour camp at **Inchtuthil**.
The main enclosure is oval, measuring about 26m by 13m
internally, the lobe of the subsidiary enclosure adjoining the
south-east portion of its perimeter. None of the lobate
enclosures have been excavated and their dates are not known;
it is perhaps worth noting, however, that, in plan at least, they
bear a superficial resemblance to some of the Pitcarmick-type
buildings of North-east Perth, which are also undated
(RCAHMS 1990, 12-13).

68B.
118B.

30B. 69C.

69B.

78.

69

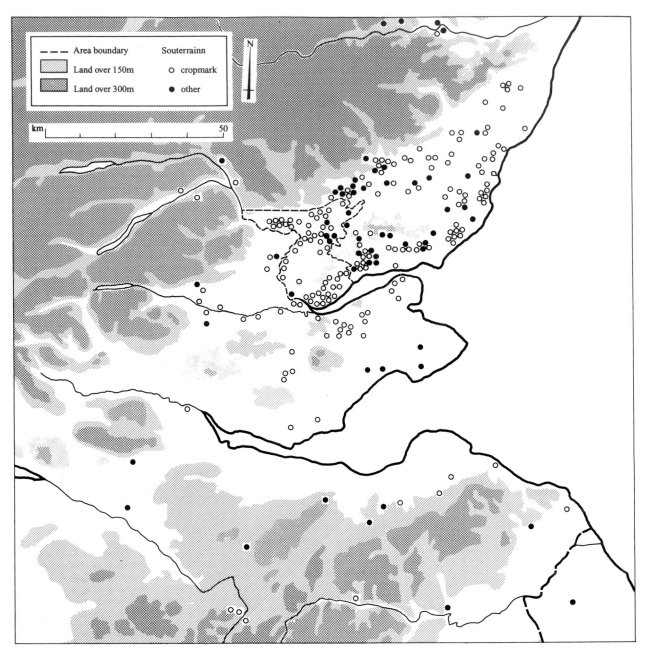

Distribution map of souterrains and souterrain-like cropmarks in eastern Scotland (NMRS DC 25105)

Chronology and context

The chronology of the various types of settlement remains that have been described is far from clear. With the exception of one of the hut-circles on **Law Hill, Arnbathie**, none of the structures that have been recorded in South-east Perth has been fully excavated, and the exploratory work carried out at **Wester Drumatherty**, **The Welton** and **Glencarse** has only been designed to clarify the nature of features underlying some of the cropmarks. None produced any dating evidence, and the only type of structure from which any dateable, and surviving, artefacts have been recovered are the souterrains at **Pitcur**. Despite this gloomy assessment of the dating evidence from within the survey area, there is a certain amount of comparative information available to suggest a broad chronological span for some of the settlement types. Furthermore, the patterns of occurrence and superimposition that can be identified tend to suggest that some of the settlement types represent distinct periods of settlement, rather than one long continuum that survived unbroken on a single site.

The most rewarding category to examine, with this in mind, are the souterrains, whose distribution has been much enhanced by the aerial survey programme. While this form of settlement

structure is still concentrated in Angus and Perthshire, the antiquarian discoveries can be seen to be a relatively minor component of the overall pattern, with cropmark examples now recorded in Fife, and even the Border counties. Despite this huge increase in knowledge, there is little more dating evidence available now than there was some fifteen years ago. Indeed, the two examples from **Pitcur** are amongst the few in the whole of eastern Scotland from which dateable finds survive. In both cases, these are fragments of Samian ware dating from the second century AD. Although it is possible that such finds might find their way into a souterrain at any time after its abandonment (Barclay 1981, 207), their use by the souterrain-builders is entirely consistent with discoveries elsewhere. Roman pottery and an amphora bung were recovered from the surface structures which were apparently associated with the excavated souterrains at both Carlungie and Ardestie in Angus (Wainwright 1963). The amphora bung at Ardestie was found within a building that went out of use at the same time that the souterrain was demolished, which has been taken to imply that the souterrain was in use during the Roman period. Radiocarbon dates from a souterrain at Newmill, which was excavated in advance of gravel-digging operations connected

63.

75.

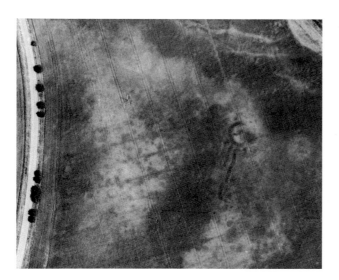

Pitroddie (NO 2181 2479), souterrain complex from the south-west (NMRS B 23267)

with the re-alignment of the A9 near Bankfoot, to the north of Perth, suggest that fully-developed stone-built souterrains of the type represented in Angus and Perth were in existence before the end of the first millennium BC (Watkins 1981b). How far back this development might be pushed is not known, although a single radiocarbon date from a small timber- and stone-lined subterranean passage at Dalladies in Kincardineshire falls in the third century BC (Watkins 1981a). The rest of the dates from this site are rather later, and, while it is possible such structures may prove to be early forms of the large stone-built souterrains, the two may equally be of broadly similar date.

If all the sites that remain to be found are as closely spaced as **Glencarse**, **Pitroddie** and **Rossie Priory**, then there can be little doubt that areas such as the Carse of Gowrie were densely settled by the end of the first millennium BC. Whether a souterrain was a standard component of every lowland settlement by that date is more difficult to assess, and it is conceivable that souterrains are simply the most durable element in a more complex pattern of settlement. The cropmarks have provided little convincing evidence of the surface buildings that must have accompanied them, and it is difficult to escape the conclusion that such structures would not be recognised in the cropmark record if they occurred in isolation. The structures excavated adjacent to the souterrains at Newmill, Ardestie and Carlungie, are perhaps themselves an indication that surface settlements of this period will only be revealed by cropmarks under exceptional circumstances. The post-holes of the superimposed timber buildings at Newmill, if indeed any of them were contemporary with the souterrain, can only be paralleled in the possible post-ring adjacent to the souterrain at **Old Mains of Rattray**, and relatively few examples of this type of structure have been recorded elsewhere in South-east Perth. The small stone-paved structures excavated at Carlungie are equally unlikely to provide well-defined cropmarks, particularly if later buildings had been superimposed upon them, as happened both there and at Ardestie.

Close examination of the distribution of souterrains in relationship to other types of cropmarks in South-east Perth does not reveal much evidence for some other kind of contemporary settlement structure. Certainly, the souterrains occupy the same general areas as other types of settlement, but, with the exception of the interrupted ring-ditches, there is no recurring pattern of juxtaposition. Thirty-four of the souterrains form elements in cropmark complexes, a term that means little more than a rash of features across a field, but at least twenty-four other examples are in apparent isolation, and a series of others are components of the fourteen sites with interrupted

ring-ditches. It is also noticeable that, while forming cropmark complexes in their own right, none of the interrupted ring-ditches have been recorded in the clusters of solid markings — discs, crescents, oblongs and squares — that characterise so many of the other cropmark complexes, although in two or three instances single discs or crescents have been identified within the rings.

On balance, the interrupted ring-ditches are the only sites where a clear chronological association between souterrain-like cropmarks and other settlement features can safely be inferred. It must be remembered, however, that none of the examples in South-east Perth has been excavated and none dated. Nevertheless, what may be a structure belonging to this group has been excavated at North Straiton, in North-east Fife (*DES 1987*, 15-16). There the ring-ditch element proved to be the remains of three successive timber houses, and the curved appendage a narrow ditch-like feature, which had varied between 5m and 15m in length at various stages of its five-phase history. No trace of any lining material was recovered from this feature, but it has been interpreted by the excavator as an early form of semi-subterranean souterrain. No dates are yet available for North Straiton, but the absence of any rotary querns has been taken to imply that the structures are considerably earlier in date than the conventional stone-built souterrains.

Prior to full publication of North Straiton, it would be premature to use the site as evidence that the interrupted ring-ditches were precursors of the souterrain settlements in use at the end of the first millennium BC. Furthermore, the structure at that site is clearly one of the smaller examples of this sort of site, which, as we have seen, may be of rather different character from the larger rings. The closest superficial parallel for the latter, is provided by the 'homestead' excavated at West Plean in Stirlingshire (Steer 1958), which is still virtually unique in that part of Scotland. Slightly larger than any of the interrupted ring-ditches in South-east Perth, it comprises a circular ditched enclosure with an external bank, but excavation revealed two gaps in the perimeter in the eastern arc and a multiperiod timber round-house at its centre. The excavations were limited to the enclosure itself, and further excavation may yet reveal evidence of associated subterranean structures, perhaps even in the ditch, whose excavated sections presented difficulties of interpretation. Dating evidence is limited to the upper stone of a rotary quern, but Roman artefacts were notably absent. Unfortunately, no cropmark example of an interrupted ring-ditch has been recorded in the intervening country between West Plean and South-east Perth, and the connection must be regarded as tenuous.

Although the origins of the souterrains and the interrupted ring-ditches are far from clear, there can be little doubt that the latter represent a break from whatever types of settlement preceded them. In virtually every case in South-east Perth, they form discrete clusters without any other discs or crescents occurring in the immediate vicinity. In several of the individual rings, there is evidence of a disc or crescent, possibly indicating reuse of the site, but more probably the remains of a central house. Only at **Mudhall** and **Leyston** is there clear evidence of a sequence of construction involving another type of structure, the former being associated with an enclosed crescent and the latter a palisaded enclosure, although in neither case can the sequence be determined from the cropmarks.

In at least one case, however, it can be shown that a souterrain has been cut through an earlier structure. This is at **The Welton**, where what appears to be a parchmark above the wallhead on one side of a passage can be detected running through the cropmark of a defensive ditch. Few examples of juxtapositions between souterrains and enclosed settlements have been identified anywhere in eastern Scotland, so this example, and also those at **Tofthill** and **Old Mains of Rattray**, are important additions to our knowledge. Interestingly, the inferred sequence at **The Welton**, is repeated at Hurly Hawkin, in Dundee District but overlooking the Carse of Gowrie, where

65. 66.
67A. 71.

75.

68A.
72A.

44. 49.
62.

61C.

48B.
54A.

68A.
72A.

a souterrain was constructed in the disused ditch of a fort (Taylor 1983), and a similar relationship was found at Castlelaw, Midlothian (Childe 1933).

In the absence of excavation, the dating of the enclosed crescents in South-east Perth is equally difficult. Nevertheless, the identification of what is almost certainly a ring-ditch house *48B.* in the interior of the example at **The Welton** suggests a *54A.* relatively early date in the first millennium BC, the uncalibrated radiocarbon dates for equivalent buildings at Douglasmuir, in Angus, falling between 450bc and 550bc (Kendrick 1982; Hill 1982, 40). What is not known, however, is how long this style of building remained in use in Angus and Perth. In South-east Perth, the enclosed crescents tend to form the nuclei for small clusters of structures, ranging from a single *112.* external crescent at **Cambusmichael** to a dense concentration *47B-C.* of markings at **Middlebank**, although in some cases it is quite clear that the perimeter of the enclosure cannot have coexisted with these additional buildings. This is an important point, implying some chronological depth on these sites, which, at *50.* **Wester Drumatherty**, has involved two successive palisades. In this respect, the cropmarks of South-east Perth may be compared with the upstanding earthworks of palisaded enclosures in the Border hills, which not only include examples with a single ring-ditch house in the interior, but also examples where ring-ditch houses are external to an enclosure or overlie its perimeter.

The occurrence of ring-ditch houses in the Border counties, however, is by no means limited to palisaded enclosures. Not only are they found in ditched earthworks, but also in unenclosed settlements, in some cases with ten or more separate buildings (see Hill 1982, 18-19). Although the only example of a ring-ditch house in a ditched earthwork in South- *53. 72C.* east Perth is the fort at **Evelick**, such a pattern is clearly detectable in Strathmore and the Carse of Gowrie, where discs with an enclosing palisade are a relatively rare component of the major groupings of unenclosed structures represented by the cropmarks of discs and crescents. Not all of these will be the remains of ring-ditch houses, of course, and excavations in north-east Fife are beginning to shed some light on the range of structures that lie below these markings, and on their date. At Easter Kinnear, for instance, a sunken-floored structure was uncovered, whose walls incorporated straight sections, but which appeared in cropmark form as a solid subcircular disc. The structure has produced rotary querns and is thought by the excavators to date from the middle of the first millennium AD *67A.* (*DES 1989*, 17-18; *1990*, 16-17). The presence at **Rossie Priory** of at least two examples of a solid disc, identical with the Easter Kinnear type, even to the presence of a small projection for an entrance on the uphill side, probably indicates a similar chronological context for some of the unenclosed settlements of South-east Perth. Not all of the discs need be sunken-floored structures of this type, and some of the crescents may be no more than the backs of circular house platforms. Thus, it can hardly be doubted that these unenclosed settlements cover a vast span of time from later prehistory into early history.

44. 62. Within this span, the differences in distribution between the souterrains and interrupted ring-ditches on the one hand, and the unenclosed discs and crescents on the other, point to periods of dislocation and reorganisation in the settlement record. Such a case is even more evident from the distribution of the *49.* curvilinear enclosures recorded in South-east Perth, both ditched and palisaded, which tend to form discrete sites within *73A.* the cropmark record, and have clearly played little part in the evolution of the individual unenclosed settlement sites recorded in the lowlands. It must be admitted that none of these enclosures has been dated and there is no evidence of any internal structures that might confirm their identification as settlements. Nevertheless, there can be little doubt that the majority of the simple palisaded enclosures, as distinct from the crescents enclosed by palisades, are the remains of settlements, by comparison with examples elsewhere, probably dating from

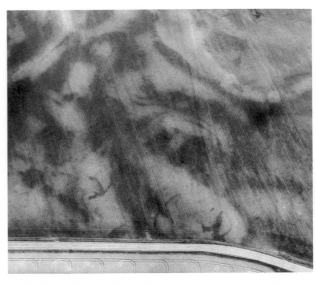

A. **Old Mains of Rattray** (*NO 2041 4570*), *enclosure containing probable souterrain and pit-circle from the north* (*NMRS B 22673*)

B. **Middlebank** (*NO 2543 2752*), *enclosure and round-houses* (*NMRS B 23998*)

C. **Evelick** (*NO 1997 2570*), *fort from the air* (*NMRS A 55972*)

relatively early in the first millennium BC. It is also noticeable that these palisaded enclosures fall into much the same size range as the bulk of the curvilinear ditched enclosures, perhaps suggesting that the distinction between the two groups is solely that of the classificatory system, and not necessarily one of function. Despite the uncertainty concerning their function, the discrete nature of their distribution can hardly be doubted, and it is for this reason that the coincidence of discs and souterrains with enclosures at **Middlebank**, **Old Mains of Rattray** and **Tofthill**, are so important for our understanding of the settlement sequence in this part of Scotland. These sites provide the opportunity for the excavator to explore the temporal relationship between enclosure and phases of open settlement.

Where the disparate group of forts, or for that matter the three crannogs, or man-made islands, fits into the pattern of settlement of South-east Perth is far from clear. In the context of the forts, however, the most significant observation that can be made is the massiveness of some of the defence-systems relative to the areas enclosed; **Rait**, **Inchtuthil**, **Rosemount** and the citadel at the core of **Dunsinane Hill**, all betray this characteristic. In the case of **Inchtuthil**, the area of the defences is about 2.6 times larger than the area of the interior, while the values for **Rait**, **Rosemount** and **Dunsinane Hill** are 2.7, 3 and 3.7 respectively. It would be unwise to push this sort of simple analysis too far, for it can be demonstrated that the

68A.
72A-B.

52B. 53.

73B.

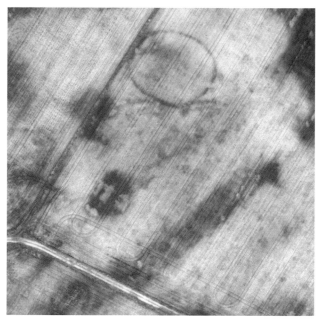

A. **Burnside** *(NO 1522 4346), enclosure (NMRS PT 5423)*

B. **Dunsinane Hill** *(NO 2137 3167), aerial view of the multivallate citadel of the fort from the north (NMRS A 55954)*

73

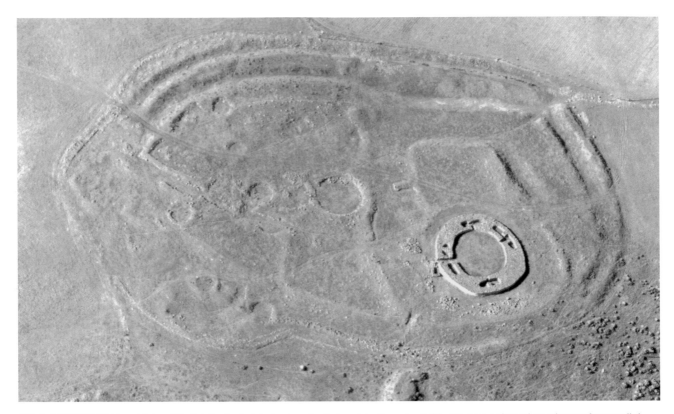

Edinshall (NT 7724 6031), aerial view of the fort showing the later broch or ring-fort overlying the west end of the interior, together with a settlement of stone-walled houses extending across the defences to the east (NMRS BW 2969)

defences of several of the forts are the result of more than one period of construction. However, with so few forts in the area, of whatever date, it can be confidently asserted that at no stage in prehistory or early history could they have accommodated the entire population, and it is reasonable, therefore, to identify these particular examples as the strongholds of an elite element in the local population. Other small forts in the area, for instance **Kemp's Hold**, the triple-ditched cropmark-site at **The Welton**, and possibly **King's Seat**, may well reflect the same phenomenon. In contrast, the bigger forts, like **Law Hill**, Arnbathie, could have housed a considerable population, but even here, the provision of *chevaux de frise,* a feature only recorded at five other sites in Scotland (Harbison 1971, 195-201), implies a high-status centre.

Such interpretations imply a level of organisation and control of the landscape for which there is no other evidence. Furthermore, the available chronological evidence, while on the one hand sparse, on the other suggests that this sort of organisation has considerable antiquity in the area. As we have seen, at least one phase of the defences of the fort at **Inchtuthil** can be dated to the Early Historic period, but it is equally clear that some of the forts are of earlier date. **Evelick**, for instance, with its internal ring-ditch houses, must surely belong in the middle centuries of the first millennium BC, and presumably occupied a peculiarly significant place in the social and political organisation of South-east Perth at that time. This sort of pattern, however, is by no means limited to South-east Perth. One of the most striking aspects of the archaeology of Strathmore, running north-eastwards through Angus to Kincardine, is the regular spacing of large, massively-defended forts, in several cases producing evidence of extensive vitrifaction, intermixed with no more than a handful of other fortified sites of various shapes and sizes. Radiocarbon dates from Green Cairn, Cairnton of Balbegno, in Kincardine (Wedderburn 1973), and Finavon, in Angus (MacKie 1969), show that some of these sites were in use very early in the first millennium BC, although in the case of Finavon, thermoluminescent dating suggests that the main rampart was only burnt in the middle of the first millennium AD (Sanderson, Placido and Tate 1988). There can be little doubt

that the large forts along Strathmore, which include **Law Hill**, Arnbathie, and **Dunsinane Hill** in South-east Perth, and Barry Hill in North-east Perth (RCAHMS 1990, 27-9, no. 102), were also major centres of power for long periods of time, almost certainly controlling the fortunes of many of the unenclosed settlements that have been revealed by aerial survey.

The single broch discovered in the course of the survey, one of only a handful known in eastern lowland Scotland, and the ring-fort, are perhaps another manifestation of this political organisation. Analogy with the other southern brochs, the nearest of which is situated at Hurly Hawkin, Dundee District, where a souterrain was constructed in the ditch of an earlier fort (Taylor 1983), would suggest that it dates from the early centuries AD. The dating of ring-forts is far less secure, although the examples at Turin Hill, in Angus (Feachem 1977, 106), overlie a large strongly-defended fort. While the ring-fort at **Kilwhannie Den** is considerably larger than the broch on **Little Dunsinane Hill**, it would be unwise to emphasise their differences. In comparison with examples from the broch heartlands of the north and west of Scotland, the latter structure, in common with most of the other outlying brochs in the lowlands, is by no means a typical example of this class of monument. The 'broch' at Edinshall, in Berwickshire, for instance, dwarfs the northern brochs, and should be regarded as some kind of ring-fort. Both the structures recorded in South-east Perth appear to represent the introduction of an exotic form of architecture into the area, possibly at much the same date. The social status of sites such as these cannot easily be determined. Tucked away in a position where its occupants could see without being seen, the broch on Little Dunsinane Hill might as easily be the remote fastness of a brigand as the hill-retreat of some warrior aristocrat.

The final aspect of the settlement sequence that must be considered concerns the abandonment of the souterrains and subsequent patterns of settlement. The few souterrains in eastern Scotland to have been excavated have produced remarkably consistent evidence relating to their abandonment. In each case, the roofs have been deliberately removed and the interior of the passage filled with earth and debris. At Newmill, which, according to the excavator, had been roofed in timber,

53.
56. 73B.

52B. 53.

52A.
91A.

53. 72C.

51.

74.

75.

Newmill (NO 0846 3238), composite view of the souterrain and the post-holes of the adjacent timber buildings after excavation (NMRS PT 5825)

the souterrain was probably dismantled and carefully infilled during the 2nd century AD. The very act of deliberate demolition, however, implies continuing settlement on or near the site, for there is otherwise little reason for the occupants to go to such effort. Indeed, it was suggested that one of the surface structures at Ardestie remained in use after the demolition, while both there and at Carlungie the remains of later buildings were recorded overlying the fill of the passages. Most of the cropmark souterrains, which by their very nature must be unroofed, probably exhibit the same process of demolition. It is tempting to see this pattern of demolition as a roughly synchronous event over a wide area, but there is still insufficient evidence to sustain such an interpretation. However, while some souterrains were demolished in antiquity, the sites of which they formed a part presumably still continuing in occupation, it is equally clear that others were abandoned with their stone roofs intact, suggesting that, even if a synchronous event, there was no uniform process of abandonment of these structures, or the settlements that they represent. Indeed, the recorded discoveries of so many roofed souterrains during the agricultural Improvements may provide a clue as to which of these settlement sites were simply abandoned, and which continued in occupation.

The character of the occupation that continued on some of the souterrain sites is a matter of surmise. The two best preserved examples of the structures which overlay the souterrain at Carlungie were oval, the larger measuring about 5.4m by 3.6m internally, with a stone wall and a carefully paved floor. No buildings of this sort have been recognised anywhere in South-east Perth, although they may well exist. Thus, there is no local evidence for occupation continuing unbroken at the sites of souterrains, or for the date at which the pattern of settlement that they represent was abandoned.

At some stage prior to the medieval period, rectangular buildings became a regular feature on settlements. When this change took place is not known, although the burnt remains of a rectangular building excavated at Easter Kinnear in Fife have been dated to the late sixth or early seventh century AD (Watkins and Freeman 1991, 32). The dating of the probable rectangular buildings that have been recorded amongst the cropmarks is fraught with difficulties, as was shown by the excavation of the timber hall at Balbridie in Kincardineshire, which was presumed to be of Early Historic date and proved to be Neolithic (Ralston 1982). It cannot even be assumed that they are the remains of domestic structures. The interpretation of the solid rectangular markings, which, although found elsewhere in eastern Scotland, belong to no known category currently recognised in Scottish archaeology, is equally difficult. The floors of some of the Pitcarmick-type buildings of North-east Perth were partly sunken (RCAHMS 1990, 12-13), but these would probably be more rounded than the recorded rectangular cropmarks, narrowing towards one end. Indeed, it is an interesting aspect of the cropmarks of South-east Perth that there is no obvious equivalent of the sunken element of the Pitcarmick-type buildings.

In conclusion, it can be justly claimed that the cropmarks provide the basic evidence for settlement in South-east Perth throughout later prehistory and early history. What is equally apparent is that the discrete nature of some of the settlement types points to the independent development of structural types in separate topographical niches, from which pattern there may be deduced episodes of desertion, dislocation and reorganisation. In this sense there is a direct parallel between the lowland archaeology of South-east Perth and the evidence that is being recovered by excavation in areas that are now marginal for agriculture. Such areas were only occupied in times of settlement expansion, their subsequent abandonment producing the pattern of dislocation implicit in the survival of deserted sites of all periods on the hills today. Thus, the similarities in the evidence from both North-east and South-east Perth go much further than shared structural traits, such as the use of sunken features and a general lack of enclosure. The patterns detected in the cropmarks show that settlements in the more favourable farming environment of South-east Perth display evidence of structural dislocation and may also have been prone to desertion, but whether the pressures responsible were governed by the same factors, at the same time, must be left to future research. What is clear, however, is that the patterns of survival and destruction in the lowlands may have removed all the recognisable evidence for some of the episodes of settlement that are represented by the hut-circles on the hills.

ROMAN MONUMENTS

Roman military operations first impinged on South-east Perth in about AD 79, at the end of a far-ranging campaign under the command of Gn. Julius Agricola (governor of Britain c.AD 77-89), which is said to have taken Roman arms from south of the Tweed to the very banks of the Tay (Tacitus, Agricola, 22). A further two years of consolidating conquest was spent to the south of the Forth, but then Agricola was compelled to deal with threats of a general rising in the north. By about AD 83 he had overwhelmed the North Britons in battle at Mons Graupius, a site still unlocated but probably lying some distance north-east of the survey-area (Tacitus, Agricola, 29-38; Maxwell

1990). The people living in South-east Perth at this time would probably have been considered by the Romans simply as inhabitants of *Caledonia,* but the territories of at least three tribes — the *Caledonii, Venicones* and *Vacomagi* — described by the Alexandrian geographer Ptolemy (Geographia, ii, 3, 12-14), may have encroached upon the survey-area. While the settlements of these peoples are undoubtedly represented amongst the cropmark evidence described in the previous section, no certain traces of Agricola's campaigns have yet been recognised in South-east Perth. Most of the works that can be assigned to the Flavian period appear to belong to the

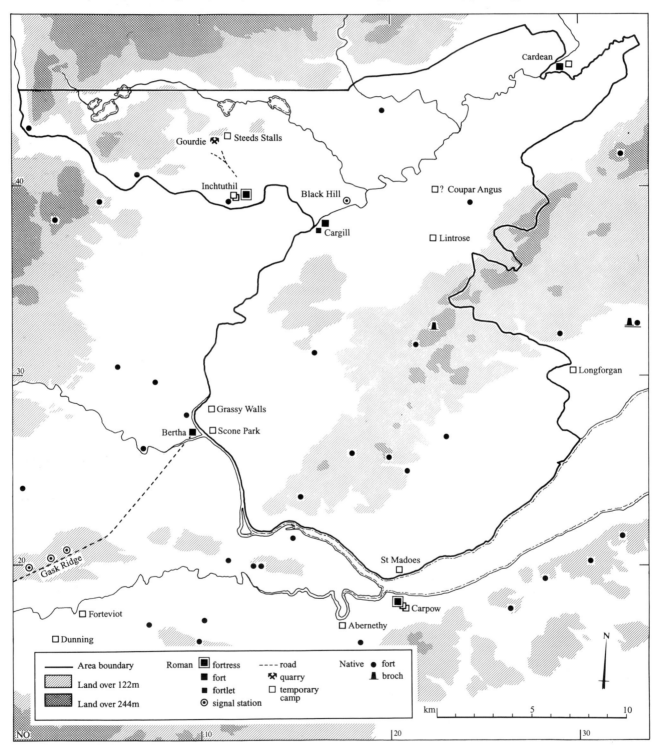

Distribution map of Roman monuments and native fortifications (NMRS DC 25104)

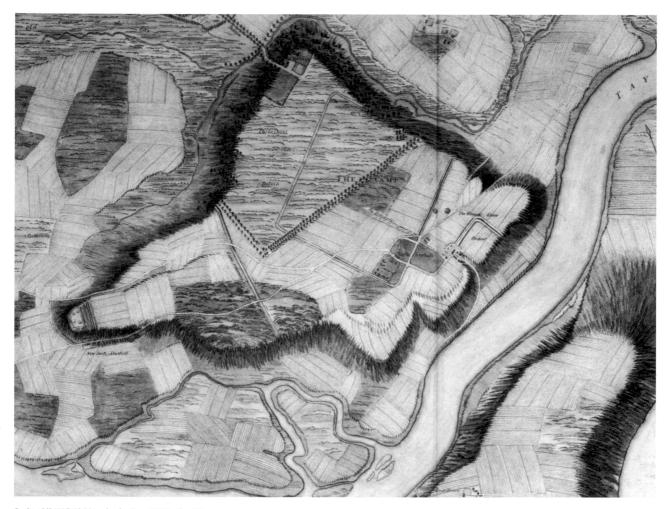

Inchtuthil (NO 1239), plan by Roy (1793, pl.xviii)

complicated process of occupation following the victory at
Mons Graupius. Into this relatively brief period, not extending
beyond AD 87, must be compressed, not only the construction
and demolition of the legionary fortress on the **Inchtuthil**
plateau, but also the institution and overhaul of a
complementary outer screen of auxiliary forts, fortlets and
minor installations. Of the latter, the two posts at **Cargill** and
the watch-tower at **Black Hill**, Meikleour, fall within South-
east Perth.

The evacuation of the frontier posts in Strathmore presaged a
complete withdrawal from Scotland by the early years of the
second century. With the accession of the emperor Antoninus
Pius (AD 138-61), however, orders were given for a re-advance
into Scotland. Victory had been achieved by AD 142/3, and the
new frontier, the Antonine Wall, was established across the
isthmus between the Forth and the Clyde. No structures of the
Antonine period have been identified in South-east Perth,
which then lay immediately outside the buffer-zone that
bestrode the northern approaches to the new frontier. The
Antonine occupation of Scotland was to be no more permanent
than that of the Flavian period, and within about twenty-five
years the Roman army had retired to the line of the wall
constructed across northern England during the early years of
the reign of the emperor Hadrian (AD 117-38).

Early in the third century Roman armies again advanced into
Scotland, this time under the personal command of the emperor
Septimius Severus (AD 194-211). The course of his campaigns
against the restless northern tribes can be traced across South-
east Perth by the distribution of third-century Roman marching-
camps. These have been divided into two categories, 25.5ha
and 52.6ha in area respectively (St Joseph 1973, 230-33), and
examples of both classes have been identified within the
survey-area.

In the context of the historical sequence outlined above, for
which a more wide ranging discussion may be found elsewhere
(Hanson and Maxwell 1983; Hanson 1987), it has been deemed
appropriate to discuss the Roman military structures of South-
east Perth under three main headings: the Flavian fortress and
adjacent earthworks at **Inchtuthil**; the outlying installations of
the Flavian frontier; and the marching-camps, all but one of
which are thought to belong to the Severan period.

Inchtuthil

It would be difficult to exaggerate the importance of Inchtuthil,
whether as the linch-pin of the Flavian outer limes in North
Britain, or as a source of archaeological information revealed
by excavation and aerial survey (Pitts and St Joseph 1985). As
regards the latter, it represents a unique body of evidence for
the gradual development of a major military base on the
imperial frontiers. From the primary site-assessment, planning
and earth-moving — with due provision of temporary quarters
for the legionary work-force and its supervising officers — to
the building of the defences and erection of almost the entire
complement of internal structures, no phase of activity goes
unattested by structural remains. This extends even to the
winning of the materials needed for construction. The quarry
that provided the building stone has been identified, together
with the road that led to it and the temporary outpost which
may have accommodated the quarriers. More remarkable still,
the very processes of abandonment — the dismantling of the
stone revetment of the curtain-wall, the blocking of the
drainage-system with discarded material, the burying of surplus
nails and metalwork — were all recorded during the
excavations.

The fortress itself lies at the core of a series of temporary
compounds and construction camps on an isolated plateau of

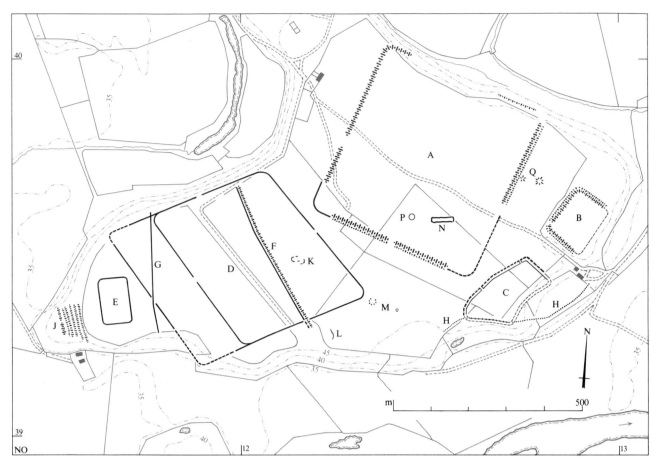

A
Q
P O
N
B
F
C. J K
G
D
C
H
E
J
H
H
M
L

Inchtuthil (NO 12 39), general plan of the plateau, 1:10,000
(NMRS DC 25106)

A. fortress, B. Redoubt, C. officers' compound, D. labour camp,
E. temporary camp, F. Western Vallum, G. masking work,
H. early defensive line, J. native fort, K. lobate enclosure,
L. linear cropmark, M. pit-circles, N. Neolithic mortuary enclosure,
P. ring-ditch, Q. post-Roman barrows

fluvio-glacial sands and gravels. The plateau rises about 15m above the flood-plain of the Tay, and its area has been reduced since Roman times by lateral erosion from one or other of the successive river channels. The effect of this erosion is most dramatically illustrated on the north-east, where a stretch of about 250m of the fortress defences has been destroyed. Portions of the two compounds that lie to the south-east of the fortress and the large labour camp to the south-west have also been removed, and, more importantly, all traces of approach roads leading across the immediately adjacent plain. Consequently, it is impossible to determine which of the many river-channels was active in Roman times.

The association of the site with Roman military operations in the late first century AD was part of popular tradition as early as the beginning of the sixteenth century (Boece 1526, iv, 14), but its true character was not recognised until about the middle of the eighteenth century. By this time, increasingly intensive cultivation of the plateau had brought to light objects of brick, iron and lead, as well as the first structural traces (Maitland 1757, 199; Pennant 1776, 67-70, pl.vii). The first measured plan of the site, executed in 1755 by Roy (1793, pl.xviii), records one stage of the process of destruction, when most of the north-west half of the fortress lay within the enclosed parklands of Delvine House, and much of the rest of the plateau was occupied by rig-and-furrow cultivation associated with the small fermtoun of 'Inchstuthill'.

In the first excavations, which were conducted under the auspices of the Society of Antiquaries of Scotland and directed by the Hon. John Abercromby, work was concentrated on the defences of the fortress and the temporary compound known as 'The Redoubt', which lies near the eastern corner of the plateau. The area to the south-east of the south angle of the fortress was also sampled, revealing another ditched compound, containing wooden barrack-buildings and a handsome stone bath-house; the linear earthwork that cuts across the plateau to the west of the fortress, which is known as the 'Western Vallum', was examined too. As a result of these excavations, the Roman origin of the visible works on the plateau was put

beyond doubt, and it was possible to suggest that they belonged to a single, relatively brief, occupation, late in the first century AD.

Aerial reconnaissance in the 1940s, particularly during the dry summer of 1949, revealed a wealth of structural detail and confirmed the possibility, first recognised by Richmond (1943, 47), that at Inchtuthil the entire plan of a single-period legionary fortress of Flavian date might be recovered. In the well-planned series of excavations conducted by Richmond and St Joseph between 1952 and 1965, that goal was very largely attained; in addition, by means of a continuing programme of aerial survey, integrated with ground inspection, the significance of the related works to the south-west of the fortress was also determined.

By the very nature of excavation, however, it is rarely possible to establish the temporal relationships of all the features recorded, particularly at a site as extensive as Inchtuthil. The sequence of construction between the various temporary works that were erected in the course of the construction of the fortress, and of the outlying defensive earthworks that its tactical situation required, cannot be established with certainty, and it is far from clear which, if any, may have functioned in the process of demolition and withdrawal. While most of the layout of the earthworks on the plateau can be recovered from aerial photographs, there are several that are only known from the excavation trenches. These include a relatively early defensive work beneath the temporary compound discovered by Abercromby, and also a ditch beneath The Redoubt (Pitts and St Joseph 1985, 204, 207-11). The early defensive line comprised a timber 'breastwork', possibly a revetment to a low bank, with an external ditch no

77.

81.

82.

81.

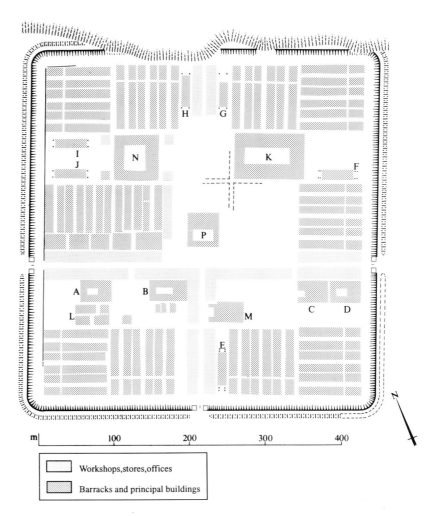

Inchtuthil *(NO 124 397), fortress, 1:5000*
(NMRS DC 25107)

A-D. Tribunes' houses
E.   granaries
K.   hospital
L.   senior doctor's quarters
M.   possible workshop and stores building
N.   main workshop
P.   headquarters building

Workshops, stores, offices

Barracks and principal buildings

more than 1.4m wide. The ditch was traced for a distance of 430m (not the 615m as published in Pitts and St Joseph 1985, 207) along the edge of the south-east escarpment of the plateau and terminates on the east in a butt-end overlooking the approach to the south-east gate of the fortress. The fact that this defence was rapidly superseded by the compound, suggests that it was never conceived as any more than a temporary work. Nevertheless, it must have been a key tactical defence, securing the southern flank of the labour force in the initial stages of the occupation of the plateau.

The fortress, the permanent base of at least 5,500 legionary troops and their support staff, encloses an area of about 21ha on the north-east portion of the plateau; it faces south-west, however, a possible indication that, then as now, the main river-channel of the Tay ran on this side, crossed by a wooden bridge, long since swept away. The original defences consisted of a turf rampart 5.2m in maximum thickness, and 4.9m in front of it lay a single, V-profiled ditch 6.1m wide and nearly 2m deep; the upcast from the ditch was piled up to form an external bank *c.*7m thick, which heightened the counterscarp by about 0.9m and was itself crowned by a series of wooden obstacles. In a secondary phase of construction, following hard upon the first, the outer face of the turf rampart was cut back for the insertion of a stone wall about 1.5m thick, which would have stood to the level of the sentry-walk, a height probably in the order of 4m.

There were four gates, of which three survive, but only one (the *porta principalis sinistra,* on the south-east) has been fully excavated. It is probable, however, that all were of the same massive plan, being built entirely of timber, with a double portal set back from the line of the fortress wall and flanked by towers with guard-chambers on the ground floor. The interior of the fortress was divided into the standard pattern of rectangular blocks by a grid of gravelled streets. The main streets, leading to the gates, were flanked by colonnaded rows

of partly open-fronted buildings, which, as elsewhere in the fortress, appear to have served mainly as store-rooms, workshops, or even offices. Like all the other internal buildings, they were timber-framed and clad with either wattle-and-daub panelling or clapboard; the presence of these relatively simple structures reflects the wide range of duties and ancillary services required for the effective functioning of such a large garrison. The combatant elements of that garrison, the legionary troops themselves, were housed in the long barracks that occupy most of the built-up area of the interior, grouped in ten blocks — one for each of the legion's cohorts; these are disposed around the perimeter immediately within the *via sagularis,* which separates the internal buildings of the fortress from the defences. Nine of the blocks comprise three pairs of opposed, narrow barrack-buildings, which together accommodated the six centuries of a standard cohort; each barrack is divided into fourteen double rooms for individual messing-units of eight men apiece *(contubernia)*, with a larger suite of rooms for the centurion's quarters at the end nearest the defences. Along the front of the *contubernia* ran a veranda in which were located wicker-lined pits for the disposal of food-refuse. The tenth block of barracks is made up of eleven and a half rows of colonnaded *contubernia,* with five large peristyle-houses at their south ends, which reflects the fact that these were the barracks of the first cohort, comprising five double-centuries under the command of five centurions; the largest of the centurions' houses, on the south-east, was provided with a hypocaust, indicating that these were the quarters of the *primus pilus,* the senior centurion of the legion. The occupants of the one and a half barracks at the south-east end of the block may have been craftsmen *(fabri)*, or, just possibly the unit of 120 cavalry *(equites)* which was part of every legionary establishment.

Accommodation for the senior officers of the legion was provided by a series of peristyle-houses even larger than those of the first cohort. Four in number, they lie in the front portion of the fortress *(praetentura)*, immediately south-west of the *via principalis*. The largest probably belonged to the *praefectus castrorum*, second in command to the legionary legate, while the other three housed tribunes. It would thus appear that only half of the full legionary complement of six tribunes had been posted to Inchtuthil before its evacuation.

To maintain the effectiveness of the legion, its troops required more than simply accommodation and protection. A plentiful supply of fresh water would have been a necessity and was clearly planned. Conduits and terracotta water-pipes have been discovered in various places in the interior, but the only water supply-link so far discovered appears to have been of a temporary nature. The corn which formed the legionaries' main food-supply was stored in granaries *(horrea)*, eight of which were probably planned at Inchtuthil, but only six were actually erected. Massively built and provided with tiled roofs, the remains of the granaries are easily recognisable by the close-set pattern of twenty-nine parallel foundation trenches in which their complicated timber sub-structures were based. Each had a covered loading-area at both ends, but the structure of the loading-areas suggested by excavation (Pitts and St Joseph 1985, 116-22), is not wholly borne out by the evidence of air photography. At the south-west end of one granary, and at each end of another, the cropmarks of two isolated pairs of post-pits can be detected on some prints. The loading-areas might thus be reconstructed as incorporating two bays, rather than one, the inner being occupied by a platform, level with the granary-floor, and the outer providing covered space for the grain-delivery wagons; this represents an interesting variation of the double-bay design suggested by Manning (1975, 114).

Much of the preparation of the food provided may have been carried out on hearths inside the barracks, but each century appears to have been assigned a cooking-oven set against the rear of the rampart, roughly opposite the end of its barrack. The ovens were circular on plan, with walls and corbelled dome built mostly of thin sandstone slabs covered with earth and turf; a hob projected from the mouth of the oven across the free space of the *intervallum* outside the *via sagularis*. Fifteen ovens, most arranged in clamps, were located during excavation (Pitts and St Joseph 1985, 195-200), and cropmarkings of several others have been identified at various points along the perimeter of the *intervallum*. All of the excavated examples showed evidence of use, but none appeared to have been rebuilt, reflecting the relatively brief period of occupation.

The paramount importance of the physical well-being of the garrison is even more convincingly demonstrated by the fact that the largest building is the hospital or *valetudinarium*, situated in the south-east half of the rear portion of the fortress *(retentura)*. Its plan is the same as that of all known legionary hospitals, comprising a central open quadrangle surrounded by two ranges of rooms divided by an internal circulating corridor. The ranges contained, in all, about thirty-two pairs of individual rooms or wards, each pair being separated by a passage or anteroom connecting directly with the main corridor. Remarkably, in view of the concern shown by its builders for ensuring the peaceful convalescence of patients, the hospital does not seem to have been equipped with a built latrine; indeed the absence of such facilities throughout the fortress is equally noteworthy, although, without a copious supply of running water to flush them, they would have been of limited use.

There is, moreover, no provision of accommodation inside the hospital for the medical officer in charge, and it has been suggested (Pitts and St Joseph 1985, 145) that his probable equestrian rank justified the allocation of a separate suite of buildings in the north-west half of the *praetentura*. However, the remoteness of these from the hospital, unlike the examples cited at the fortresses of Bonn and Vindonissa, makes this identification less credible. The absence of accommodation for senior medical staff within the hospital is, perhaps, simply

another indication of the incompleteness of the fortress facilities on evacuation.

In the south-east portion of the *praetentura*, giving on to the *via praetoria*, there is a large basilican building. It was entered from the north-west, through a gravelled court and porch which led directly to a colonnaded hall; the outer court and the aisles of the hall were flanked by ranges of rooms, one of which was traversed by a pipe-duct feeding a timber-lined water-tank. Although originally identified by Richmond (1960, 213) as a *basilica exercitatoria*, or drill hall, the building seems more likely to have been used as a workshop *(fabrica)* — hence the water-supply — with part of the area given over to storage.

The legion's main *fabrica* is situated in the *retentura* opposite the hospital; it had a colonnade extending along its south-east front, on either side of the main entrance. The centre of the building was occupied by an open courtyard, which was also surrounded by a colonnade. On the south-east side of the courtyard there lay a suite of five rooms, and aisled halls were ranged along the other three sides. A smithing-hearth, a slag-pit and the possible emplacements for a heavy-duty work-bench indicated the character of the metal-working operations carried out here, and the well-marked ruts in the road outside bore testimony to the density of wheeled traffic plying to and from it. During the final dismantling of the fortress, the rectangular pits within the *fabrica*, originally used for disposing the waste-products of manufacture, were filled with demolition-refuse and unwanted metal objects. One pit, situated near the south angle of the building was found on excavation to contain approximately 10 tonnes of iron nails, as well as nine iron cart-tyres; the whole deposit was sealed by 1.8m of gravel to prevent its discovery and use by local tribesmen after the Roman withdrawal.

Occupying a central position in the fortress, at the middle of the *via principalis*, opposite its junction with the *via praetoria*, is the headquarters building *(principia)*. Paradoxically, although of standard plan, this operational nerve-centre is the smallest example of its type known in any legionary fortress and occupied less than a quarter of the space allocated to it within the fortress street-grid; it may consequently be assumed that it was designed from the outset as a temporary structure, ultimately to be rebuilt in stone at full scale. Despite its temporary nature, the *principia* had to be capable of accommodating the administrative and official functions of the legion's senior officers. It thus contained all the elements to be found in permanent examples: an open, colonnaded courtyard occupying the front half of the building, and a *basilica*, or cross-hall, separating the courtyard from the symmetrically-arranged rear suite of rooms, with the chapel of the standards *(aedes)* and the unit's treasury-strongroom at its centre.

The empty spaces immediately to the north-east and south-east of the *principia*, levelled but never built upon, demonstrate even more graphically the unfinished nature of the legionary construction-programme: the former was probably intended to be the site of the main bath-building *(balneum)*, the latter to be the palatial residence *(praetorium)* of the legion's commanding officer. The absence of the *praetorium* does not, however, necessarily mean that the legate himself was absent, accommodation for him having been tentatively identified within the temporary compound discovered by Abercromby on the south-east margin of the plateau.

81.

The full significance of this compound was not realised until more extensive examination by Richmond and St Joseph in 1963-4 (Pitts and St Joseph 1985, 207-22). An irregular polygon covering 1.5ha on plan, it was defended by a turf rampart with an external ditch; there were two single-portal gateways, both facing north-west towards the site of the fortress. The structures within the interior comprise: a handsome (but incomplete) suite of baths; a pair of timber barracks, one overlying an even earlier example; an elaborate timber-framed house, incorporating offices as well as a dining-room and stone-built hypocausts; a shed or stores building lying parallel to the house; and a pair of 'offices' resembling the

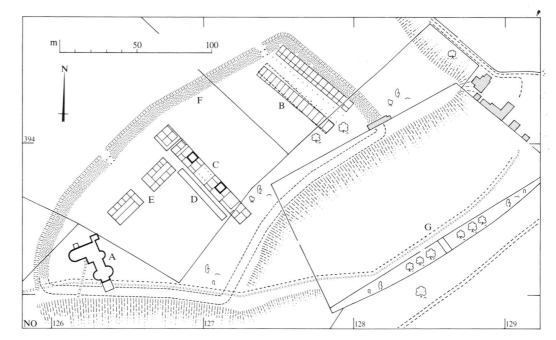

Inchtuthil
(NO 1271 3937),
the officers' compound,
1:2500
(NMRSDC 25108)

A. *bath-house*
B. *barracks*
C. *house and offices*
D. *stores building*
E. *centurions' quarters*
F. *turf rampart*
G. *early defensive line*

centurion's quarters of the fortress barracks. There were at least two periods of use, in the first of which there was only one barrack and no bath-house; during the second period, the defences were at least partially levelled, a pair of barracks replaced the singleton, and the bath-house (a simple *Reihentyp,* but well-built and provided with an extra hot-room or *laconicum*) was constructed in the south-west angle of the compound, encroaching upon the slighted defences.

The structures identified in this compound imply that its intended occupants were of some importance. Initially, perhaps, it was to house the second-in-command of the legion, but the doubling of the guard in the second phase of use and the provision of a private bath-house suggest that it may have been refurbished for the legate himself. As such, its use must have spanned the major part of the Roman occupation of the plateau, although the discovery of the earlier defensive line beneath the south-west side shows that it was by no means the first of the structures to be erected. If the intended occupants have been correctly identified, it is reasonable to assume that the buildings of this compound remained in use until the abandonment of the plateau.

78.	The other temporary compound, The Redoubt, is a strongly defended enclosure of about 1.4ha, whose rampart still stands up to 1.5m in height and is accompanied by an external ditch. Erosion of the escarpment has destroyed all traces of the defences on the south-east, but excavation by Richmond and St Joseph in 1965 (Pitts and St Joseph 1985, 202-6) showed that there had probably never been more than a rampart on this side. There was one single-portal entrance, situated in the north-west side, unusually near the west angle, but about the closest point in the defences to the south-east gate of the fortress. The Roman date of The Redoubt is proved beyond doubt by associated pottery, but its function is far from clear. The absence of structures within the interior suggests that its occupation was only a transient phase in the sequence of events on the plateau. A direct connection with the fortress may be indicated by the unusual location of the entrance, but whether it belongs to an early stage in the construction-programme, or to the demolition phase, cannot be determined.

78. 82.	The main labour force working on the construction of the
86.	fortress was undoubtedly housed in the large temporary camp that has been revealed by cropmarks occupying most of the western part of the plateau. Initially, it enclosed an area of 19.9ha and faced north-east towards the site of the fortress; subsequently it was reduced in size to 14ha and a new south-west side was drawn across the rear portion, or *postica,* of the original camp.

The length of the construction-programme upon which the

occupants were engaged has made it inevitable that they left more obvious traces of their stay than would be expected in a more transitory marching-camp. The wealth of evidence recorded by air photography within the interior makes it a unique source of evidence for reconstructing the internal layout of a temporary camp-site. Study of the air photographs, combined with the evidence of the excavations, has enabled Frere to offer a plausible interpretation of the complex internal cropmarks, correcting earlier attempts based on the air photographs alone (Pitts and St Joseph 1985, 223-44; Maxwell 1981). Two types of marking are particularly significant: those indicating the positions of ovens and cooking-places just behind the presumed rampart; and those of smaller size disposed in lines running parallel to one or other of the main axes of the camp, which were proved by excavation to be rubbish-disposal pits associated with the tent-lines of the encamped garrison. Of the latter it is possible to identify two pairs of double-lines traversing the *postica* of each period, which appear to define the course of roadways, and one or two double-lines delimiting shorter streets in the right *praetentura.* From these identifications, which prove beyond question that the *via quintana* was lacking in both periods, it is possible to specify the areas occupied by individual cohorts and to assess the strength of the force under canvas. In its first phase, the camp appears to have held the equivalent of some 30 cohorts (*c.*15,000 men); the reduction of the area by about a third in the second phase might thus represent the departure of ten cohorts (a complete legion), perhaps to take up occupation in the permanent fortress.

78. 86.	This camp is not the only temporary camp that has been revealed by aerial photography on the plateau. Between the south-west side of the labour camp and the earthworks of the native fort that occupies the western tip of the plateau, there is a small camp of about 0.9ha. Although not securely dated, its Flavian date must be presumed from its context, and it has been suggested (Pitts and St Joseph 1985, 225, 243) that it may be the bivouac of an independent auxiliary force, perhaps a cavalry *ala,* which arrived at Inchtuthil after the large labour-camp had been laid out.

77. 78.	At some stage the labour camp was evacuated, its perimeter was deliberately slighted, and the linear earthwork known as the 'Western Vallum' was constructed across its interior from side to side of the plateau. First planned by Roy in 1755, this earthwork has now been reduced to a low bank with a barely detectable hollow marking the line of the ditch on its south-west side. A second earthwork of similar character lies a further 300m to the south-west, but is only known from aerial photographs. It has been suggested that this particular

Inchtuthil (NO 12 39), aerial view of the plateau from the south-east, showing the legionary fortress on the right, with the area of the labour camps centre top; the Neolithic mortuary enclosure is visible within the fortress (NMRS PT 5404)

earthwork was contemporary with the reduced phase of the labour camp (Pitts and St Joseph 1985, 245), but its proximity to the western angle of the camp makes this interpretation less easy to accept. It is more likely that it supplemented the scheme of tactical defences represented by the Western Vallum. It would be unusual for earthworks of this sort to be part of the permanent defences of the fortress, and it is more likely that they were simply to provide additional protection to the fortress while it was still some way from completion.

The activities involved in the construction of the fortress were not limited to the plateau, and materials must have been drawn in from far and wide (see Pitts and St Joseph 1985, 45-7). The winning and transportation of stone was in itself no mean achievement, but there is also the extraction of substantial quantities of timber to be considered. A source of lime for

mortar would have been essential to the project, while the laying of drains in the fortress speak of the intentions of tapping a suitable source of running water. This aspect of the construction project not only required immense powers of organisation, but also a detailed knowledge of the resources available in the hinterland of Inchtuthil. It should not be forgotten that the force of 15,000 men also required feeding, a burden that could not have been sustained indefinitely on the long lines of communication stretching southwards. By implication, the surrounding landscape must have been a hive of activity, with work details dispatched on tasks that ranged from quarrying to simply servicing the logistical requirements of the troops.

Clearly, some kind of road network would have been necessary for the transportation of heavy loads of stone and timber. To a certain extent this requirement may have been met by a road coming up from the south of the Tay, although no trace of this has yet been discovered. The stone for the fortress, however, was probably quarried on the **Hill of Gourdie** to the north-west, and aerial photography has revealed a short sector of Roman road heading in this direction across the gravel plateau to the west of **Wester Drumatherty** (Pitts and St Joseph 1985, 47, 256). The link between this sector and the north-west gate of the fortress has now been lost, but, having crossed the plain to the north-west of Inchtuthil, traces of the road can be detected on Redgole Bank, the southern scarp of the gravel plateau to the north. Here a much-eroded causeway and cutting (NO 1151 4097), now obscured by tipping and dense vegetation, are visible. The road-alignment across the cultivated fields beyond Redgole Bank at first points directly at what is probably the Roman sandstone-quarry on **Hill of Gourdie**, but about 200m to the north-west the road bifurcates, the east branch bending a little to the north and the west branch inclining towards the west. To the south of the fork the road is intermittently visible as a low bank 5m in average width, although both here and elsewhere the parched corn above road-metalling and the cropmarks of roadside quarry-pits indicate its track more clearly. The east branch continues northwards and descends to a crossing of the Millhole Burn by way of a broad cutting. The cropmarks of the quarry-pits indicate the course of the west branch for a further 500m before it too reaches the north scarp of the gravel plateau.

Excavation in 1983 demonstrated that the road had been metalled with rammed gravel, beneath which there was a bottoming of large river-cobbles and an *agger* of compacted earth and turf 6m wide. The robust construction of the road gives every reason to believe that it catered for quarry traffic proceeding to and from the **Hill of Gourdie**; a small quadrate block of Gourdie sandstone, unlike any material observed in the subsoil of the plateau, was in fact found during the 1983 excavation close to the west side of the road. The bifurcation may indicate that unladen vehicles were provided with a steeper, more direct access (the eastern branch) to the quarry.

The quarry for which the east branch of the road was making is situated on the lower cultivated slopes of the steep south-east face of **Hill of Gourdie** (Pitts and St Joseph 1985, 61, 255-6). It comprises a large amphitheatre-like hollow, which measures about 190m by a maximum of 65m and about 9m in greatest depth and is most unlikely to be of natural origin; it has been

estimated that in excess of 30,000 cubic metres of rock has been quarried from the site.

About 730m to the north-east of the quarry, on the gently sloping east shoulder of Hill of Gourdie, there is a small Roman temporary camp, which was probably associated with the quarrying operations. Known as **Steeds Stalls** on account of the curious earthworks within its interior, the site has long been associated with the operations of the Roman army under Agricola (*Stat. Acct.*, 19 [1797], 367-71; Crawford 1949, 75-6). The cropmarks that alone betray its outline were first recorded in 1941, and more recent photography has shown that the camp measures about 145m square. The interior has been divided into two roughly equal parts by a ditch that springs from the north-east side immediately south of what may be an original entrance; the dividing-ditch itself is broken by a causeway at its mid-point to give passage between the two halves. The northern portion of the south-eastern half is occupied by the seven elongated hollows whose resemblance to the stalls of a stable gave the site its name. Cropmarks, however, not only indicate that there were originally at least twelve such features, but also more clearly demonstrate their character. All appear to have been roughly keyhole-shaped, with a round head about 4.5m in diameter and up to 6m deep approached by a level passage 4m in average width. The purpose of the 'stalls' has never been convincingly explained, but the sheer quantity of stone required for the fortress, as testified by the quarry to the south-west, makes it unlikely that they were individual quarries providing material for the construction programme. The layout of the camp suggests a more specialised function, and it is perhaps worth remembering that the closest parallels for the stalls are provided by relatively recent clamp kilns for lime-burning, which are commonly found in the limestone areas of Fife and the Borders. The construction of the fortress undoubtedly required the operation of kilns for the production of lime or the firing of bricks and tiles, operations that would have required a major installation well away from the timber buildings of the fortress and the tents of the encamped work force. Indeed, the choice of site for such an installation would probably have been determined by the location of the raw materials or the fuel. Despite the attractions of such an interpretation, it must be admitted that there is no physical evidence to support this kind of use and it is by no means certain that the camp and the 'stalls' are even contemporary.

The excavations on the road leading up to **Hill of Gourdie**

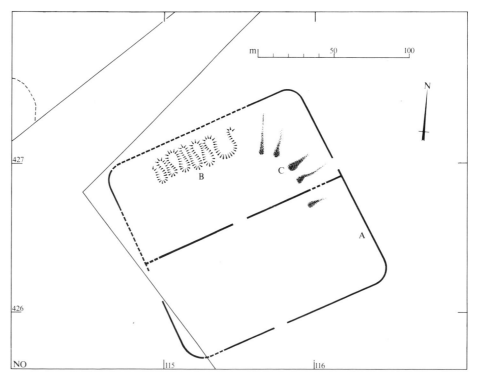

Steeds Stalls (*NO 115 427*),
temporary camp, 1:2500
(*NMRS DC 25109*)

A. *perimeter ditch*
B. *upstanding 'stalls'*
C. *cropmark 'stalls'*

in 1983-4 may also have shed some light on a temporary water supply established early on in the construction of the fortress. The evidence for this supply is provided by a narrow linear cropmark which adjoins the east side of the road and follows the western branch for a distance of some 800m towards the north-west. When sectioned, the feature proved to be a channel with a U-shaped profile about 1m wide and not more than 0.85m deep, and may have been intended to hold wooden water-pipes (Pitts and St Joseph 1985, 191). The linear cropmark is apparently broken by the metalling of the eastern branch of the road, possibly indicating a sequence of construction between the two branches and the channel. How the water was supplied across the flood plain of the Tay to the army encamped on the Inchtuthil plateau is not known.

The Flavian frontier
Despite the detailed knowledge that has been achieved at Inchtuthil, it is difficult to assign the fortress a securely fixed place in the general sequence of events relating to the Flavian occupation. It is not known whether Inchtuthil was planned (or even begun) by Agricola before his departure in AD 83/4. Construction may have been initiated by his successor, perhaps after a further period of campaigning. But by that time, work would already have started on the series of outlying permanent garrison-posts, and the addition of a legionary base might well have occasioned a change affecting these posts too.

85A-B.   The identification of both a Roman fort and a fortlet some 250m apart at **Cargill**, certainly suggests that a change of strategy took place, since it is unlikely that the two were contemporary. Indeed, the results of trial excavation of the two posts, both of which were first identified from the air by Eric Bradley in 1941, suggests that the development of the frontier 85B.   may have been yet more complex. The fortlet, whose double ditches enclose an area of about 0.5ha, appears to have been deliberately abandoned after a brief period of occupation (*DES* 84. 85A.   *1965*, 30). At the fort, on the other hand, excavation in 1980 and 1981 revealed a complicated sequence of construction or repair (Maxwell and Wilson 1987, 16; Maxwell 1989, 108). Two structural phases were identified in the small parts of timber buildings that were exposed in the interior, and at least three phases were recognised in a limited examination of the relationship between the rampart of the fort and an annexe, which extends down to the banks of the Isla on the north-west. The absence of the ditch-system on this side of the fort indicates that the annexe had been planned from the first. Few dateable artefacts were recovered from the excavations at either site, but the layout of the defences leaves no doubt that both are Flavian in date. An assemblage of Samian ware later discovered by chance near the south-west gate of the fort points to the abandonment of this particular post not long after AD 85.

Although the relationship between the two posts cannot be demonstrated archaeologically, it is likely that the fort was constructed first, but, even within the brief period of its occupation, the size of the garrison or the role of the post altered significantly. The Cargill fort presumably guarded a crossing point on the Isla, and it has been suggested that it supported an as yet undiscovered fortlet set at the mouth of the Ericht gorge near Rattray (Pitts and St Joseph 1985, 273-6). This suggestion stems from the discovery of a fortlet at the mouth of Glen Clova in Angus (Maxwell and Wilson 1987, 15-16), which raises the possibility that there may have been two series of Flavian garrisons in Strathmore. In this scheme larger units of at least regimental strength would have occupied mid-valley positions, as at Cardean and Stracathro in Angus, while smaller vexillations guarded the mouths of the side valleys that breach the southern face of the Grampian massif. The fort at Cargill would be one of the mid-valley posts.

When Inchtuthil was nearing completion, the build-up of legionary strength may have made the presence of a full auxiliary regiment at Cargill unnecessary. The position would then have been more appropriately guarded by a smaller garrison, perhaps the unit that had occupied the presumed

Cargill (NO 1661 3790), the cropmarks of the fort showing the annexe ditches extending down to the river and what are probably arcs of later trackways cutting across their line (NMRS PT 8668)

Ericht outlier in the earlier organisation of the frontier. The new base to the south-west of the fort may be closely compared, in plan and size, with other Flavian fortlets, especially those at Inverquharity at the mouth of Glen Clova and Gatehouse of Fleet in Galloway (St Joseph 1973).

The precise temporal and strategic position of the watch-tower at **Black Hill**, Meikleour in the development of the   85C. Flavian frontier is not known. The hypothesis that it guarded a gap in the Cleaven Dyke (Richmond 1940, 37), which was then thought to be Roman in date (see ceremonial monuments), is no longer safely tenable. Set on a glacial knoll some 18m high, the remains of this small subrectangular earthwork command an imposing prospect, and are readily visible from Inchtuthil, the forts at Cargill and Cardean, and even the presumed fortlet on the Ericht. Excavation in 1939 (Richmond 1940, 37-40) revealed the post-holes of a timber tower enclosed by a turf rampart with an external ditch and a counterscarp bank. Of the external ditch little more than a terrace can now be seen around the shoulder of the knoll, but originally it was of V-profile, 5.2m wide and interrupted by a narrow entrance causeway on the north-north-west. None of the Roman artefacts recovered in 1939, or during an earlier excavation in 1903 (Abercromby 1904), could be closely dated (unless the fragment of 'wavy glass' mentioned by Abercromby belonged to a pillar-moulded bowl of the type common in Flavian times). Watch-towers, whether as isolated posts or ranged in series, were a common element in Flavian frontier-systems in North Britain, and also on the Rhine and the Danube from even earlier times.

By AD 87 at the latest, the Flavian frontier posts in Strathmore appear to have been peacefully abandoned. The defences and internal structures of the fortress were systematically demolished and any material likely to be of use or value to the enemy was buried in rubbish pits and disused drains. The work of destruction was apparently as unhurried as it was thorough, indicating that the reason for withdrawal had little, if anything, to do with enemy pressure in north Britain. Indeed, strikingly uniform numismatic evidence (Pitts and St Joseph 1985, 283-5) provides strong grounds for believing that this was part of a wide-ranging and drastic reduction of the frontier forces in Scotland. Few, if any, garrisons were then left north of the Southern Uplands, and all those surviving in the south were housed in totally reconstructed forts. By the early years of the second century these, too, had been withdrawn.

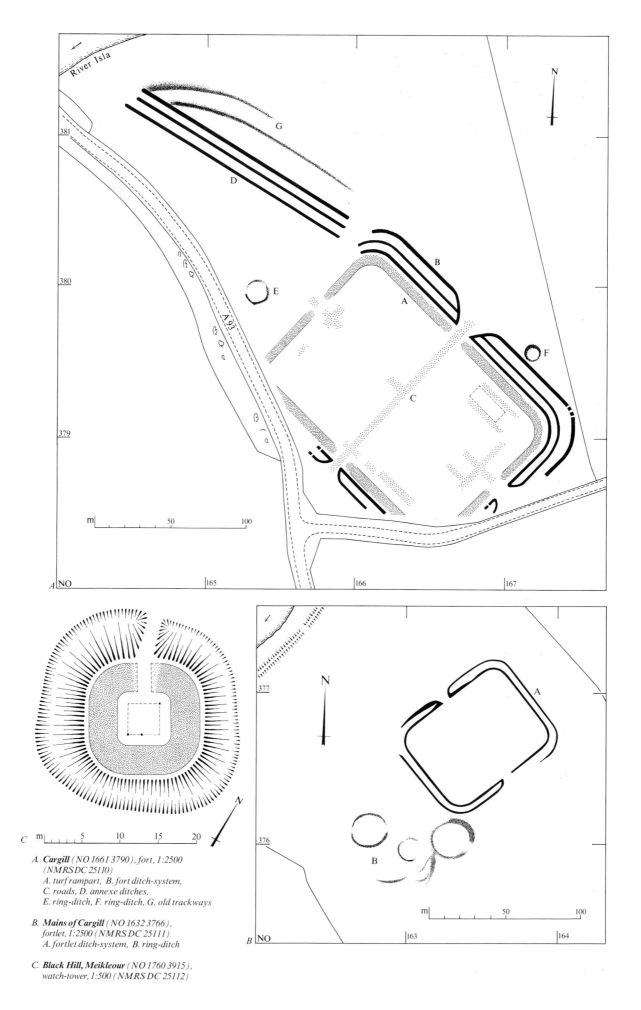

River Isla

381

380

379

A93

G

D

B

E

A

F

C

N

m   50   100

A NO |165 |166 |167

N

C m 5   10   15   20

377

376

N

A

B

m   50   100

B NO |163 |164

A. **Cargill** *(NO 1661 3790), fort, 1:2500*
  (NMRS DC 25110)
  A. turf rampart, B. fort ditch-system,
  C. roads, D. annexe ditches,
  E. ring-ditch, F. ring-ditch, G. old trackways

B. **Mains of Cargill** *(NO 1632 3766),*
  fortlet, 1:2500 (NMRS DC 25111)
  A. fortlet ditch-system, B. ring-ditch

C. **Black Hill, Meikleour** *(NO 1760 3915),*
  watch-tower, 1:500 (NMRS DC 25112)

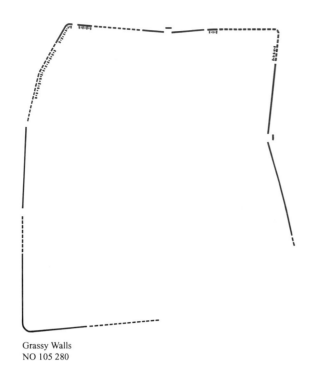

Grassy Walls
NO 105 280

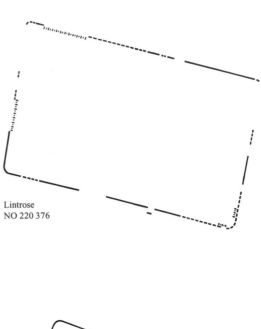

Lintrose
NO 220 376

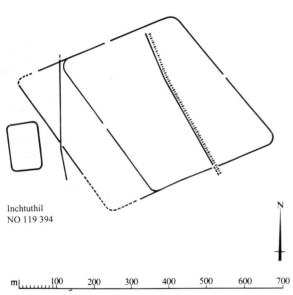

Inchtuthil
NO 119 394

N

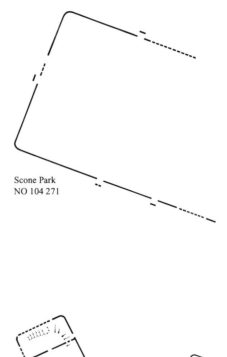

Scone Park
NO 104 271

m |_____| 100   200   300   400   500   600   700

Comparative plans of the temporary camps, 1:10,000 (NMRS DC 25113)

Steed Stalls
NO 115 427

St. Madoes
NO 209 196

76. 86. **Temporary camps**

Apart from the various temporary works associated with the construction of the fortress at Inchtuthil, there are at least four other temporary camps within South-east Perth. Two of them, *3A.* **Lintrose** and **Grassy Walls**, were discovered in the eighteenth century and have already figured in the account of the antiquarian tradition in the area, while the other two, **Scone Park** and **St Madoes**, were revealed by aerial photography in the 1950's and 1960's. In addition to these, however, there is also the possibility that a temporary camp existed at **Coupar Angus**, where Maitland recorded the remains of a large earthwork enclosure in the middle of the eighteenth century (1757, 199-200). The earthworks that he noted may well reflect the presence of a major Cistercian foundation there, but it has long been appreciated that Coupar Angus lies on a natural line of advance for an army moving up Strathmore, and, although discounted by Crawford (1949, 82-5), the perimeter he traced out in the modern field- and property-boundaries can be compared in proportions and size with marching camps of

probable Flavian date elsewhere in Strathmore.

The largest of the proven camps is **Grassy Walls**, which encloses about 52ha and is one of a series of large camps thought to have been built to accommodate the entire field army of the emperor Septimius Severus in the campaigns of AD 208-11. A second series of smaller camps, which also probably date from these campaigns, includes **Lintrose** (c.26ha) and **Scone Park** (at least 23.7ha), but the fourth camp at, **St Madoes** (3ha), is significantly smaller, and its date is unknown.

Although nothing can be seen on the ground of the two camps discovered by aerial photography, fragments of the ramparts of both **Grassy Walls** and **Lintrose** can still be seen today. **Grassy Walls** in particular, provides a good impression of the scale of the temporary defences that might be erected by a Roman army in the field. The best preserved sectors are near the north-west angle and to either side of the north-east angle, where the rampart forms a grassy bank 6m in thickness and standing up to 0.6m above the bottom of an external ditch 3m

86. 87.

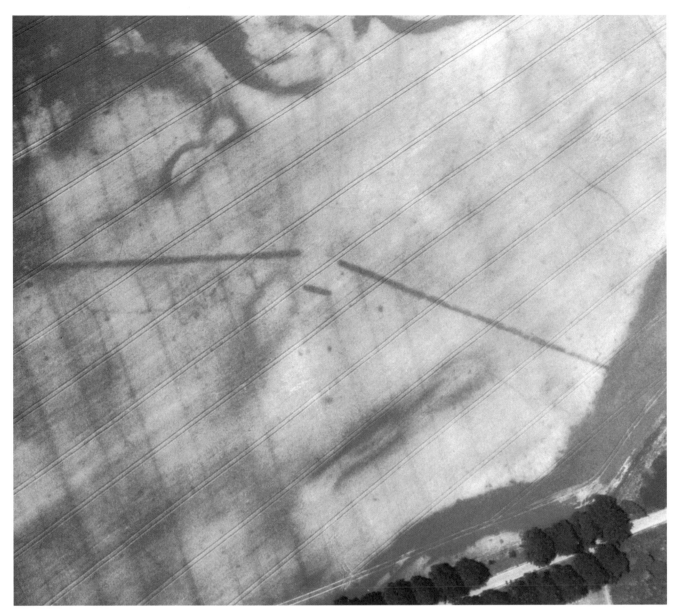

Grassy Walls (NO 105 280), cropmarks of the east side of the camp showing a gateway guarded by a traverse (NMRS B 22630)

broad. The camp itself presents a markedly irregular quadrilateral on plan, the result of difficulties experienced by the Roman military surveyors, who had chosen to lay out their camp on an awkwardly-contoured piece of high ground. The positions of two of the camp's six gates have been identified; at both there is a marked re-entrant angle and an external traverse has been recorded.

It was Roy's knowledge that the Romans had crossed the Tay at Bertha that led him in 1771 to discover the remains at Grassy Walls. Aerial survey in the twentieth century, which resulted in the discovery of the smaller camp on the haughland of the Tay, no more than 400m to the south, was guided by similar considerations. A predominantly clay subsoil has restricted the amount of information that can be gleaned from cropmarks in these parts, the more so because most of the camp lies within the grounds of Perth Hunt Race Course. Trial excavation, however, has helped to confirm the whole of the camp's north-west side and parts of the long north-east and south-west sides. Three gates, each probably guarded by a traverse, have so far been identified, and these allow the overall proportions of the camp to be estimated.

The second of the smaller series of camps, **Lintrose**, lies about a day's march towards the north-east of the Tay crossing. When it was planned by Roy, in 1755, about three-quarters of the perimeter could still be seen on the ground, but only a few

short stretches of the enclosing rampart and ditch now survive. The most notable of these are the short sectors of the sides immediately adjacent to the south-east angle, where the rampart appears as a bank 6m thick, and about 100m of the north side near the north-west angle. Cropmarks recorded on aerial photographs, however, confirm and add to the plan drawn by Roy, a gate with a traverse now being known in the east half of the south side, while the slight change in alignment of the defences 160m to the east probably indicates the position of another. Another entrance with a traverse was depicted by Roy midway along the west side.

The temporary camp that has been identified at **St Madoes** (St Joseph 1969, 110-11) is too small to have housed part of the field-army associated with the Severan operations. Nevertheless, its situation on the north bank of the Tay opposite the legionary vexillation-fortress of Carpow, has been seen by some as indicating construction in the early third century AD, perhaps to guard the northern landfall of a Tay crossing. In the absence of excavation, its use as a coastal station in the Flavian period cannot be ruled out. All that has been recorded of the camp is the north-west angle and approximately 60m of the north side and 90m of the west side, the latter including a gate guarded by a traverse. However, the position of the gate so close to an angle suggests that the camp was not of great extent, probably not exceeding 3ha.

86.

86.

86.

3A.

86.

EARLY HISTORIC

88. In the Early Historic period South-east Perth formed part of the Pictish province of Atholl, which was divided into the districts of Atholl and Gowrie (Henderson 1975, 8-9). The precise boundaries of these areas have not been established, but both lay to the east of the River Tay, with Atholl to the north of the River Isla, and Gowrie to the south, its eastern boundary perhaps following the border between the former counties of Perth and Angus. To the west of the Tay lay the province of Fortriu, which, at some stage, may also have incorporated the district of Gowrie (Anderson 1980, 139-41). The power centre of Atholl was **Dunkeld**, but the identification of a corresponding centre for Gowrie is more difficult, possibilities including **Scone** or, perhaps, the fort on **Dunsinane Hill**.

56. 73B.

There are, however, considerable difficulties of assessment in this period of proto-history, where the chronological framework is derived from Pictish king-lists and annals, few of which are contemporary. Nevertheless, it is possible to draw together several of these threads to identify certain key sites in the landscape of South-east Perth. Archaeological evidence allows several undocumented centres to be identified, while place-names hint at the pattern of rural settlement across the area. The most striking of the archaeological monuments are

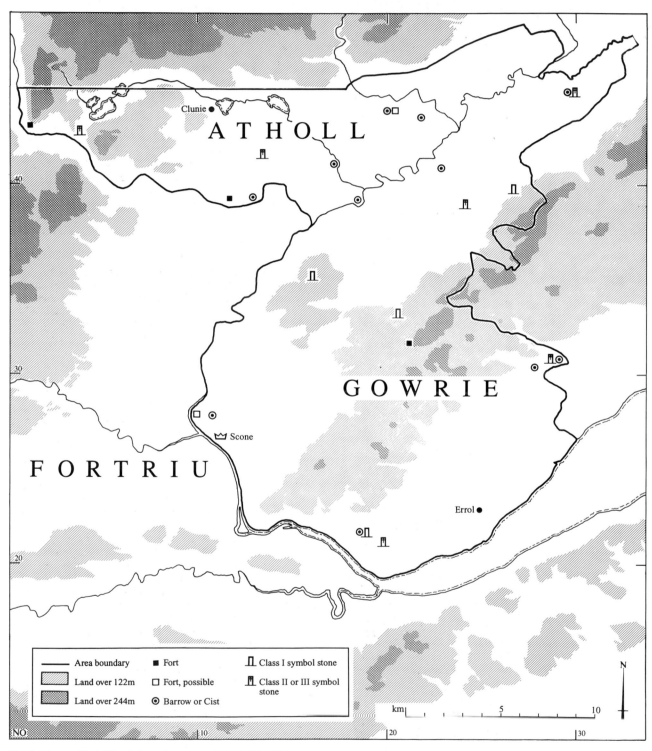

—— Area boundary	■ Fort
▨ Land over 122m	□ Fort, possible
▨ Land over 244m	◉ Barrow or Cist

Ⴖ Class I symbol stone

Ⴖ Class II or III symbol stone

Distribution map of Early Historic sites and monuments (NMRS DC 25114)

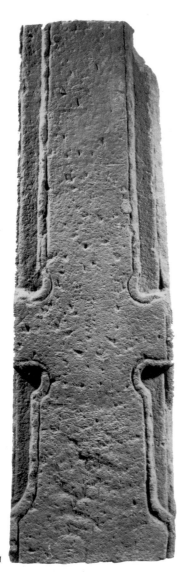

Dunkeld Cathedral
(NO 0237 4259)

A. cross-slab
(NMRS B 1351)

B. Apostles Stone,
cross-slab
(NMRS B 1402)

A

B

undoubtedly the Pictish carved stones, which, more than any other category of evidence, reflect the wealth and importance of South-east Perth between the sixth and ninth centuries. Some of the stones remain as monuments in the countryside, while others are gathered into museums, most notably at **Meigle**. The *98-102.* significance of the collection there goes far beyond the carvings themselves, reflecting the status of what was possibly an important monastic centre (see Cruden 1957; Henderson 1982), and certainly a burial-place of powerful Christian patrons. This material is discussed here in three sections: the first concerns the documented centres at **Dunkeld** and **Scone**; the second, the evidence for other centres and rural settlement; and the third, the carvings on the Pictish stones.

Dunkeld and Scone

The importance of **Dunkeld**, and the probable key to its emergence as the centre of Atholl, stems from its geographical location at the foot of the Highland Edge, dominating the lines of communication northwards and westwards by way of the valley of the Tay. The derivation of its place-name (Gaelic *Dun Chailleann* 'fortress of the Caledones', Jackson 1954, 14-16) has led to the assumption that Dunkeld was a prehistoric tribal centre. Whether such a centre should be identified with the fort on **King's Seat** is uncertain, but it is possible that this *53.* was the seat of royal power in Atholl during the Early Historic period. Documentary evidence, however, sheds little light on the nature of the kingdom, and such information as is available needs to be treated with care. The first known king of Atholl was Talorgan, son of Drostan, whose death by drowning at the hands of the Pictish overlord Oengus, son of Fergus, is recorded in the Annals of Ulster for 739.

In a late note in the Gaelicised version of the Pictish king-list, it is recorded that Constantine, son of Fergus, who died in 820, founded Dunkeld (Anderson 1980, 194). This is inexplicable in the context of the royal centre, but may refer to the establishment, or revival under royal patronage, of a monastery. With Kenneth MacAlpin's accession to the joint kingship of the Picts (843-58), there was undoubtedly a shift in the political status of peripheral kingdoms such as Atholl; while the significance of Dunkeld as a royal stronghold may well have waned with these changes, its rising fortunes as an ecclesiastical centre can be inferred from surviving records. According to the *Scottish Chronicle*, Kenneth 'brought relics of Saint Columba to a church that he built' in about 848-9, and, although the name of the church is not given, it is thought to have been at Dunkeld. It appears that Kenneth intended that Dunkeld should be the primary centre of the church in eastern Scotland, a significance probably reflected in the record in the Annals of Ulster of the death in 865 of Tuathal, son of Artgus, principal bishop *(primepscop)* of Fortriu and abbot of Dunkeld. In affairs of state, Dunkeld was thus placed on a par with the royal centre at Forteviot in Fortriu, Kenneth's adoptive capital. Structural evidence for this early ecclesiastical centre, however, *89 A-B.* is lacking, although two decorated stones and a large cross-slab *96 B-C.* (probably ninth or tenth century), which may have come from *97 D.* its precincts, are preserved within the medieval abbey.

As the chief centre of the church in Scotland, Dunkeld undoubtedly prospered materially. This may have been the attraction for a Danish expedition, which plundered the town and monastery in 903. The Annals of Ulster and other sources also show much Danish activity in eastern Scotland in the 860s-870s. This onslaught on Pictish territory by the grandson of Ivar was eventually halted by the 'men of Fortriu' in Strathearn, this possibly the triumph ascribed by the Scots to the power of Columba's crozier borne before them in battle (Anderson 1922, i, 408). Evidence for the Danish presence close to Dunkeld is, however, only provided by a plain-ringed, polyhedral-headed pin (Fanning 1983, 338, no.29), but its find-spot is not known. Whatever the consequences of the Danish raid, monastic life at Dunkeld seems to have continued. Thereafter, in common with other houses in Scotland, the community was secularized, and probably maintained by a dynasty of lay royal abbots (Cowan & Easson 1976, 47). One of these was Crinan, an abbot of Dunkeld and father of King Duncan I, slain by Macbeth in 1040. By 943, however, Kilrimont (St Andrews) had wrested the ecclesiastical primacy from Dunkeld, whose secular status was also in decline. In 966 Dubdond, the ruler of Atholl, is simply *'satrapos'* or governor. According to the Annals of Ulster, Dunkeld was burnt again in 1027, but seventy years later Donald Ban (1093-7) is said to have been buried there (although his remains were later transferred to Iona), and the presence of a church community in the twelfth century seems to be confirmed by a reference (1214 x 1229) to *macleins et scolloci* (students and scholars)(Cowan & Easson 1976, 47).

The origins of **Scone** are altogether uncertain, the documentary evidence casting little light on the subject. Much that has been said in the past is pure speculation, and the level of inference that can reasonably be achieved on the basis of the existing sources is limited. Like Dunkeld, however, topography and communications are probably the key factors which underlie its emergence as a regional centre. If the original focus of Scone occupied much the same position as the Augustinian abbey, this would have afforded the site a degree of elevation when viewed from the river, but there is no rock-girt fortress comparable to those found at some other notable centres of royal lordship in the Early Historic period. In this respect, Scone is perhaps no different from Forteviot, simply illustrating how little is known of the character of lowland royal centres in this period.

The first reference that can be used to imply the existence of a centre in the vicinity of Scone is in the Annals of Ulster for 728. In that year, Alpin was ignominiously put to flight as the result of a battle between the Pictish factions at *Castellum Credi,* 'the fortress of Crede'. Attempts have been made to identify the Moot Hill at Scone as *Castellum Credi* (Anderson 1922, 224, n.1), but whatever its original purpose, and irrespective of whether it is natural or artificial, this mound has nothing to commend it as a defensive work. In fact, the only known defensive site close to Scone is the ploughed-down earthwork at **Gold Castle**, some 2km to the north-west. However, the date of this earthwork, and, furthermore, of the 'gold coins' from which the site derives its name, is not known.

In the king-lists, Kenneth MacAlpin is credited as 'the first king from among the Gaels' to assume the kingdom of Scone. It is not clear whether this implies the presence of a discrete district dependent on Scone or relates to Gowrie as a whole, but in the seventh year of his reign Scone was unambiguously established as a recognized place of assembly and inauguration. The elevated stance offered by the Moot Hill may well have provided the focus for such gatherings, possibly continuing a tradition from earlier in the Pictish period (Anderson 1980, 199), although there are apparently no Pictish carvings from Scone to attest its importance.

In 858, Kenneth died at the royal palace *(palacium)* at Forteviot, which was probably the principal seat of royal power in the realm, but other royal centres almost certainly existed elsewhere. Some versions of the Dalriadic king-lists, for instance, record the death of Donald, Kenneth's brother, at *Rait Inveramon,* probably at the Roman fort at Bertha, on the right bank of the Tay, but it is not known what stood there, or on the opposite side of the river at Scone, at this time. In 906, however, a meeting took place at Scone between Constantine II and Bishop Cellach (of Kilrimont), at which the rights of the church were affirmed in conformity with the customs of the Scots (Anderson 1982, 127ff). The meeting took place *'in colle credulitatis prope regali ciuitati Scoan'* (Anderson 1980, 251). *Collis credulitatis,* 'Hill of Faith', is probably to be identified as the Moot Hill. At this date Scone is clearly a royal centre.

Other centres and rural settlement
Other than Scone and Dunkeld, few sites are referred to in the early texts and little is known of the accompanying pattern of secular lordship. The reference to the Danish expedition against

126.

54B.

A

B

***Meigle** (NO 2872 4459)*

A. Pictish cross-slab (NMRS B 1479)
B. architectural fragment (NMRS B 1530)

Dunkeld in the *Old Scottish Chronicle* in 903 mentions **Clunie**, implying that this was a place of some note, perhaps a centre of some political and administrative importance, a role which conceivably continued to the twelfth century when it emerged as the site of a royal castle (Alcock 1981, 161). But what stood here in the late ninth or early tenth century is not known, and none of the visible earthworks around the Castle Hill can be attributed to this period. It is even possible that the caput of Clunie at this time was on the crannog, or artificial island,

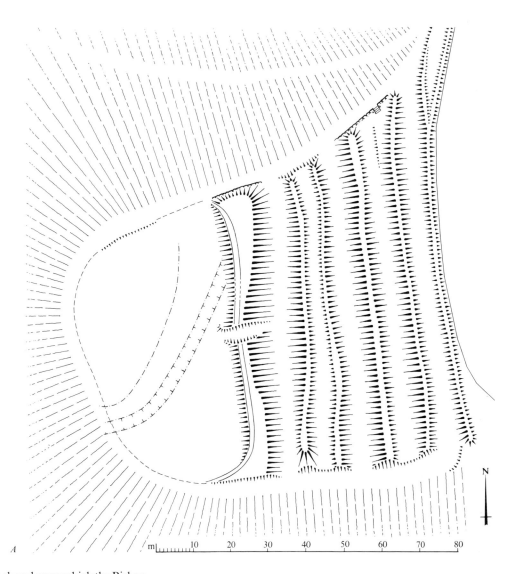

A. **Inchtuthil** *(NO 1150 3928),*
fort, 1:1000
(NMRS DC 25090)   *A*

| m | 10 | 20 | 30 | 40 | 50 | 60 | 70 | 80 |

recorded in the neighbouring loch and upon which the Bishop
of Dunkeld's tower-house was subsequently built. The use of
crannogs as high status centres, whether secular or
ecclesiastical, may have been widespread, as in Ireland. Danish
raiding could conceivably provide a context for the loss, or
deposition, of two penannular brooches, perhaps the
possessions of a Pictish aristocrat, which are said to have been
91B-C. found near **Clunie Castle** (Youngs 1990, 114-15, nos. 109-10).
The fragment of a third, cast in silver and decorated with gold
filigree, was discovered in 1990 on the north-east side of the
Castle Hill.

By far the greatest weight of archaeological evidence for a
90A-B. key centre of this period, survives at **Meigle**. By any standards,
94B-D. its collection of sculptured monuments is exceptional and must
98-102. surely indicate a centre of considerable power and influence
dating from at least the eighth century. Orientated long-cist
burials have been found within the burial-ground of the present
90B. church, but the presence of at least two architectural fragments
within the collection of stones points to a more elaborate
structure standing here, a stone building, possibly, but not
necessarily, a church. The surviving monuments, together with
a documentary reference to the work of Thana, son of
Dudabrach, probably a scribe at Meigle in about 840, though he
need not have been permanently resident there, would be in
accord with a monastery founded in the eighth century
(Anderson 1922, i, 267; Davies 1982, 272, n.47). It is likely
that Meigle had acquired powerful royal patrons to become an
important dynastic centre, perhaps with an accompanying
church and burial-ground, although the presence of a monastery
established on either a 'British' (dynastic), or an 'Irish'

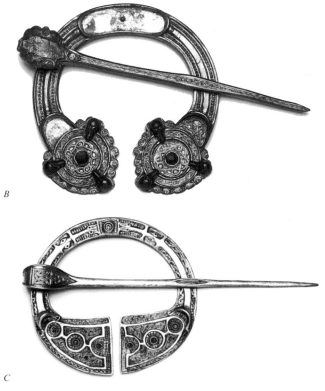

B,C. **Clunie** *(NO 110 440), penannular brooches (NMS WA 5091-2)*

B

C

91

(monastic) model, would provide a sufficient context for the burials.

In addition to Meigle and Clunie, several of the forts may have provided the focus for Early Historic centres. The prehistoric fortress on **Dunsinane Hill**, for instance, was conceivably occupied in the late tenth century, when the scene of a slaying seems to be identified as *apud Dunsion*, but no elements of its defences can be attributed to this period with any degree of confidence. At **Inchtuthil**, however, whilst corroborative documentary evidence is lacking, there can be little doubt that elements of the defences of the native fort are post-Roman date. Excavation in 1901 showed that the fort had been remodelled on several occasions, the initial phases probably dating from pre-Roman times, but the innermost rampart incorporates slabs of dressed Gourdie stone looted from the Roman fortress. The barrows to the east, one of which overlies Roman earthworks, point to the presence of a funerary complex in the vicinity (see Fortifications, and Barrows and Cairns), the two elements — a small fortification and a cemetery — perhaps providing a glimpse of the archaeological components that might be anticipated of a minor caput of this period.

While forts are relatively few and far between in the area, what may be Early Historic barrow cemeteries are an increasingly common aspect of the cropmark record. Typically, these cemeteries comprise scatters of both round and square barrows, but evidence is now coming to light to suggest the presence of more elaborate square burial-enclosures. The identification of these structures is discussed more fully in the section dealing with barrows and cairns, but good examples of barrow cemeteries have been recorded at **Rossie**, for instance, and, close to Scone, at **Sherifftown** and **Blairhall**. Some of these may yet prove to be pre-Roman but the majority are probably later (Close-Brooks 1984, 91-2; Maxwell 1987, 34-5), perhaps indicating the locations of other minor centres in the area. Indeed, the juxtaposition of a barrow cemetery with the multiperiod fort at **The Welton** provides a remarkable parallel with **Inchtuthil**.

The most enduring monuments of this period, however, are the carved stones, some of them possibly indicating the locations of other cemeteries. Burials have been found in association with, or close to, three out of the five examples of Class I stones, the **Inchyra** slab, for instance, covering what was probably an extended inhumation (Stevenson 1946). With the exception of the cross-slab built into the tower-house at **Lethendy**, all the Class II stones and later cross-slabs in this area have been found in medieval parish churches or their burial-grounds, a pattern which, as in other areas, is not repeated in the occurrences of Class I stones. The overall distribution of both classes of stones, however, appears to be closely related to the pattern of medieval parishes. Although only a small sample, it is possible that, in South-east Perth, these monuments are facets of a broadly contemporary landscape, the one perhaps denoting foci of secular activity, the other ecclesiastical centres. This is to go much further than an orthodox distinction of these monuments as the successive products of non-ecclesiastical and Christian milieus; but, if the two classes of Pictish stones in South-east Perth do represent such a chronological development, some overlap in their distribution might be anticipated, and this does not seem to be the case. The association between the cross-slabs and medieval churches, however, should say something about the status of these sites in the Pictish period, and may well indicate places which, by the eighth century, were at least recognized centres of Christian burial, and may even have had churches of their own. Whilst this sort of interpretation can be no more than supposition, the presence of other pre-parochial district churches might be denoted by the surviving *kil-, annat* and *eccles* place-names (Barrow 1983): Kilspindie; Annat Burn, Scone (MacDonald 1973, 139); and Clashbenny (*Ecclesdouenauin,* 1202 x 14; Barrow 1983, 10). A twelfth-

A   *B*

A,B. *Inchyra* (*NO 1904 2120*),
Pictish symbol stone
(*NMRS B 3058, B 3060*)

C. **Cargill** (*NO 1477 3623*),
Pictish symbol stone
(*NMRS B 1458*)

C

century reference to the *abthania* of Rossie, in conjunction with the impressive cross-slab, would also seem to hold the promise of an early church site, perhaps that of a Celtic community, though this is by no means certain.

The evidence for accompanying rural settlement, however, is sparse and difficult to interpret. Attention can be drawn to what appears to be cropmark evidence for rectangular sunken-floored structures (see Settlement section) but none has been excavated and their date is unknown. The same problems are encountered with the remains of other types of buildings that have been revealed by cropmarks, including those that have been described as lobate enclosures at both **Inchtuthil** and **Mains of Inchture**. Nevertheless, the extent of rural settlement can be assessed from the distribution of place-names which incorporate either the prefix *pit-* (denoting a share, a piece of land) or the element *bal-* (Gaelic *baile,* farmstead or township). In many cases the second part of the *pit-* name is Gaelic, which would imply a bilingual context and a ninth- or tenth-century threshold for naming of such places, perhaps indicating a late,

56. 73B.

91A.

p. 19

pp. 17-20

67A.
18A.
17C.
26A.

48B.
54A.

92A-B.
93. 95A.

94A.
97E.

pp. 68-9

78. 69B.

but peaceful, Gaelicisation of these areas (see Nicolaisen 1979, 123-4, 149-60).

Although the place-names have been mapped throughout the area of the survey (Whittington and Soulsby 1968; Whittington 1977; see also Cottam and Small 1974, and Alcock 1987, 82), much more work will be required before this form of evidence can be used to generate a settlement model applicable to Strathmore. At face value, there is an impression that the *pit*-names favour better quality soils, while the *bal*- prefix is more common in the less agriculturally rich areas of Tayside, but the comparison of past place-names with modern land-capability maps may be misleading, and any inferred pattern of land-use and historical succession should be treated with extreme caution (cf. Alcock *et. al.* 1987, 264). Pitmiddle, for instance, in the hills overlooking the Carse of Gowrie, occupies a marginal position in respect to the escarpment (Perry 1988), as it probably did in earlier times. Its situation, however, may be compared with those of Kilspindie and Rait, centres which survived into the medieval period, when they became kirktouns, and it is these latter which characterize the settlement pattern on the Braes of Gowrie.

Pictish and Early Christian stone carving

The Picts are renowned for their legacy of carved stone monuments. The carvings make use both of a series of closely defined symbols, some of which may have originated before the adoption of Christianity, and of decorative patterns and Biblical imagery betokening a wider range of artistic influence. The interpretation of such symbols has given rise to much speculation (Thomas 1964; Jackson 1984). The symbols may have been intended to convey information about tribal affiliation, rank, lineage, or occupation; the stones themselves have been seen as memorial stones, territorial markers and commemorative statements of marriages or political alliances. Symbols may be found together, possibly implying that they form messages or statements (e.g. Thomas 1964, 82-8); they may also be found associated with a cross and other Christian motifs, and this juxtaposition implies that their meaning was compatible with Christianity.

The chronology of Pictish and Early Christian monuments may be interpreted in several ways, some scholars preferring a long stylistic development and others a much shorter creative period; Stevenson provides a table of relative chronologies (1961, 54-5) and the matter is further discussed by Henderson (1982, 1990). In broad terms, however, many of the simpler stones, those bearing symbols alone — Allen and Anderson's Class I (1903) — were certainly being carved in the seventh and eighth centuries, although a few may be of earlier date.

95D. Fine examples of Class I stones include those from **Fairygreen,**
92A-B. **Collace** and **Inchyra**, the last of which also bears four ogam
93. 95A. inscriptions. Ogam is a system of writing, invented in Ireland, in which individual letters are represented by groups of incised lines cut across a long medial line (or the edge of a stone), either at right angles or at a slant. Most of the inscriptions in the Pictish areas appear to belong to the seventh and eighth centuries and to incorporate elements of personal names, but, although they may be transliterated, most remain unintelligible (Jackson 1955, 138-42).

The first half of the eighth century saw the appearance of Class II stones; these are symbol-bearing cross-slabs carved in relief, which combine abstract ornament similar to that found on metalwork and illuminated manuscripts of the seventh to ninth centuries with symbols, animals, horsemen or hunting scenes, the latter often on the back of the slab. Most notable are
C. 103J-K. the cross-slabs from **St Madoes** and **Rossie**. The latter, preserved in the old parish church of Rossie, now the mausoleum of the Kinnaird family, is decorated in relief and is not only unusual in bearing a cross on both faces, but also in the variety and detail of its monsters. The four recumbent slabs
100A-B. at **Meigle** have sockets at the head end, which were presumably
D-E. designed to hold an upright cross, although, with one possible

Inchyra (NO 1904 2120),
ogham inscriptions (NMRS B 3054-5)

exception, no upright stones in the collection have an appropriate tenon.

The cross-slabs at Meigle are remarkable not only for the *90A.* complexity of their interlace, fret and spiral ornament, but *94D.* particularly for the range of their animal art. Dr Isabel *98-102.* Henderson has commented that 'the theme of violence, between animals and between animals and men, dominates the collection. Such imagery has a counterpart in the biting and distorted animals and men that ornament the Book of Kells but the capacity of the Pictish sculptor to express naturalistic muscular action gives their motifs remarkable power' (Henderson 1982). The single surviving example of Biblical imagery, Daniel with the lions, is part of this iconography in a negative way, representing the violence tamed by divine intervention. The centaur, gryphon and other fabulous animals may be based on an illustrated manuscript of animal lore. These animals, and the depictions of ecclesiastics, are part of the artistic repertoire of other Pictish centres, but the Meigle sculptors, unlike those of Easter Ross, do not share motifs with the sculptors on Iona. The iconography of David the Psalmist at **Lethendy**, on the other hand, though considerably later (tenth century), is widely represented in Pictland. A number of major monuments at **Meigle** do not display Pictish symbols, a fact which may support the view that by the early ninth century integration between the Picts and the Scots was under way (Anderson 1980, 194), or that carving continued through the ninth century. The hogback monument, with the pecularities of its ornament applied to an asymmetrical stone (Lang 1975, 214-15, 229), is evidence for the production of sculpture at Meigle in the tenth century.

94A.
97E.

94C.
100C.

A

B

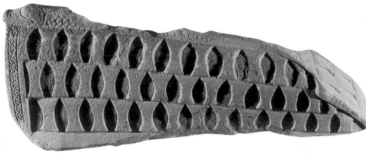

C

D

E

A. **Lethendy** (NO 1405 4170), cross-slab (NMRS PT 2384)
B. **Meigle** (NO 2872 4459), top of the recumbent monument (NMRS B 1549)
C. **Meigle** (NO 2872 4459), side-view of the hogback monument (NMRS B 1540)
D. **Meigle** (NO 2872 4459), cross-slab (NMRS B 1469)
E. **Rossie** (NO 2915 3080), cross-slab (NMRS B 3039)

Comparative drawings of the Pictish and Early Christian stone carvings

This section contains drawings of all the extant Pictish and Early Christian stone monuments in eastern Perth, all of them reproduced at the same scale (1:15). Where appropriate, the system of numbers adopted by Anderson and Allen (1903) has been incorporated into the captions.

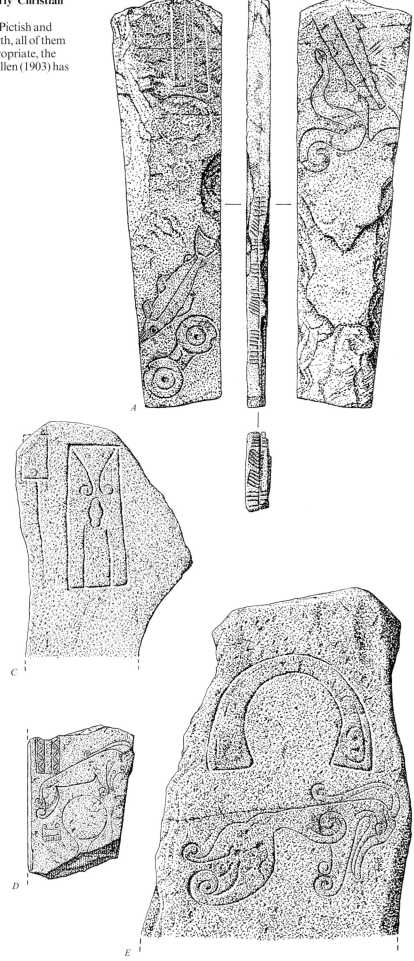

A. **Inchyra** (now in PMAG), Pictish symbol stone bearing ogam inscriptions, found covering an inhumation in 1945 (NMRS DC 25222)

B. **Keillor** (NO 2733 3976), Pictish symbol stone standing on a burial-cairn adjacent to the public road (NMRS DC 25221)

C. **Cargill** (now in the garden at Balholmie House, NO 1477 3623), Pictish symbol stone which formerly stood in a plantation wall to the north-west of West Whitefield Farm (NMRS DC 25223)

D. **Fairygreen, Collace** (now in ABDUA), fragment of a Pictish symbol stone ploughed-up in 1948 (NMRS DC 25224)

E. **Bruceton** (NO 2898 5039), standing stone bearing Pictish symbols (RCAHMS 1990, 87, no 19; NMRS DC 13926)

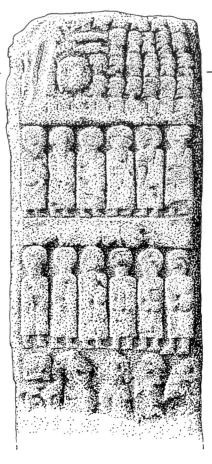

B

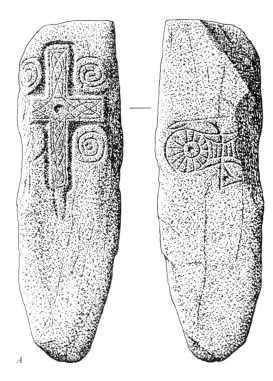

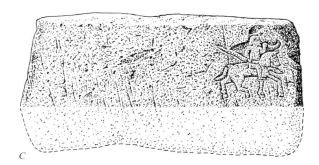

A

C

This page

A. **Alyth** *(now in the porch of Alyth High Kirk, NO 2432 4875), found in 1887 when the ground in front of the manse was levelled (RCAHMS 1990, 87, no. 189; NMRS DC 13925)*

B. **Dunkeld** *No. 2 (now in the Chapter House Museum), the Apostles' Stone, fragment of a cross-slab which was formerly used as a gate-post at the entrance to the churchyard (NMRS DC 25226)*

C. **Dunkeld** *No. 1 (now at the cathedral in the ground floor of the tower), decorated stone from the grounds of Dunkeld House (NMRS DC 25225)*

Opposing page

D. **Dunkeld** *No. 4 (now in the Chapter House Museum), cross-slab which shows evedence of re-use as a gate-post (NMRS DC 25227)*

E. **Tower of Lethendy** *(NO 1405 4170), fragment of a probable cross-slab in re-use as a lintel above a staircase in the tower-house (NMRS DC 25229)*

F. **Kettins** *(now in the burial-ground of Kettins parish church, NO 2378 3906), cross-slab formerly used as a footbridge over the Kettins Burn (NMRS DC 25228)*

G. **New Scone** *(now in PMAG), cross-slab which was found in 1978 in the garden at 19 Angus Road, but is thought to have come from the burial-ground adjacent to St Johns Kirk, Perth (NMRS DC 25230)*

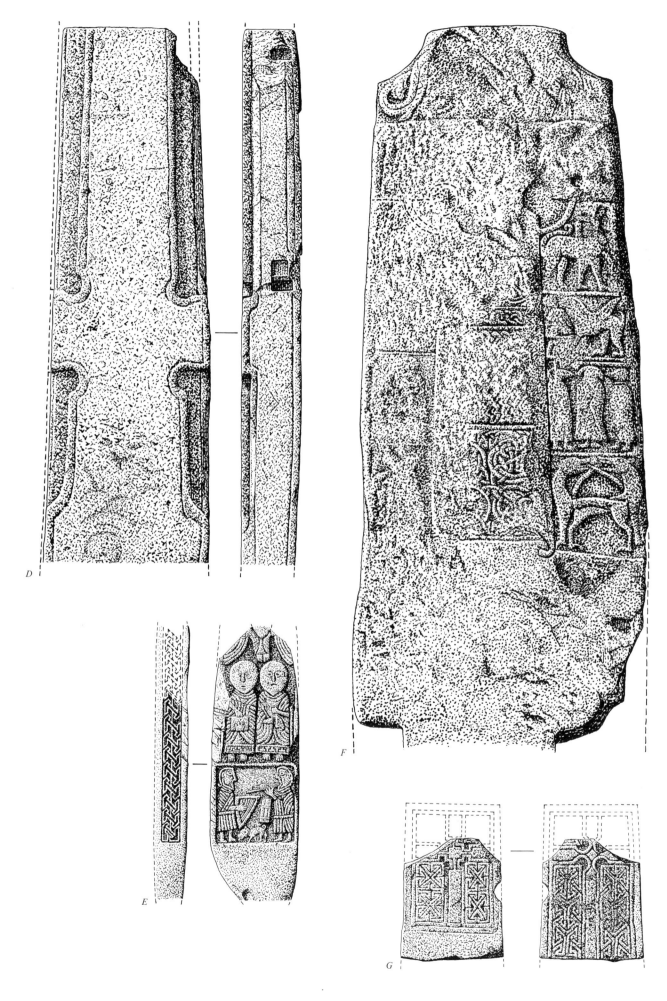

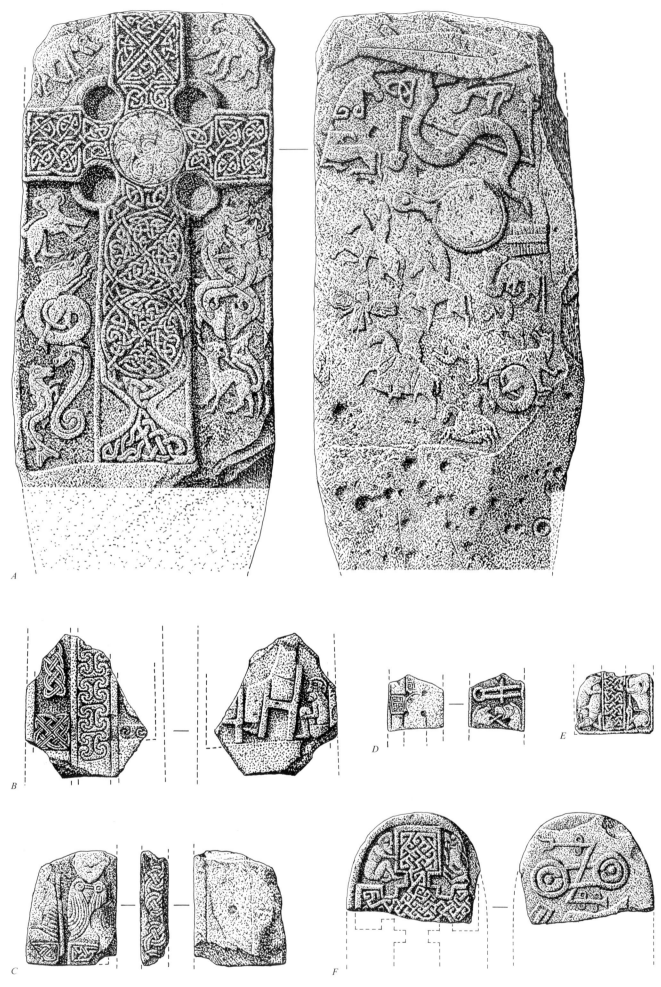

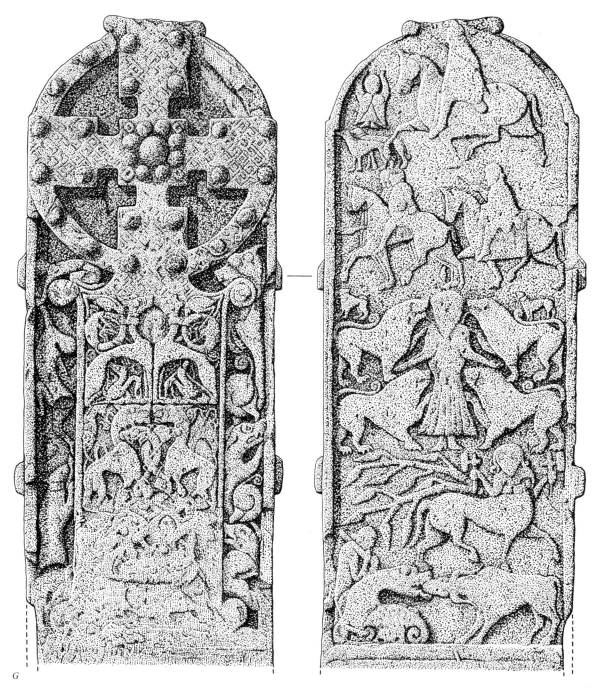

G

Meigle *(NO 2872 4459)*
The stones displayed in the Meigle Museum, all of which were found in or near the parish church, form one of the most important collections of Pictish sculpture in eastern Scotland. Some formerly stood in a group on a mound on the north side of the church, a location that caused some antiquarian speculation, but it is by no means certain that these were in their original positions. Others were built into the walls of the church and burial-ground, and many of these had been broken into manageable building-blocks. The church, however, was burnt down in 1869 and, although some previously recorded stones appear to have been lost, several other slabs were recovered in the course of the salvage and re-building operations. Yet more stones were found in the fabric of a malt-kiln at Templehall, a property some 70m north of the church, when it was demolished in 1858.

Opposing page
A. *No. 1, cross-slab which formerly stood on the right-hand side of the gateway into the burial-ground (NMRS DC 25231)*
B. *No. 27, fragment of a cross-slab recovered from the church in 1869 (NMRS DC 25254)*
C. *No. 29, fragment of a probable cross-slab (NMRS DC 25256)*
D. *No. 8, fragment of a cross-slab found outside the museum building in 1889 (NMRS DC 25239)*
E. *No. 15, bottom part of a cross-slab formerly built into the wall of the old church (NMRS DC 25246)*
F. *No. 7, upper part of a cross-slab recovered from the church (NMRS DC 25238)*
This page
G. *No. 2, cross-slab which formerly stood on the left-hand side of the gateway into the burial-ground (NMRS DC 25233)*
H. *No. 23, cross-slab found at Templehall in 1858 (NMRS DC 25251)*

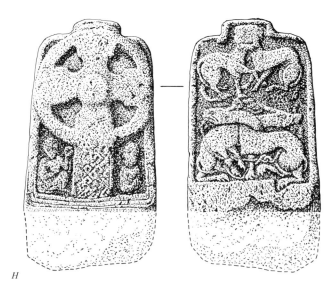

H

99

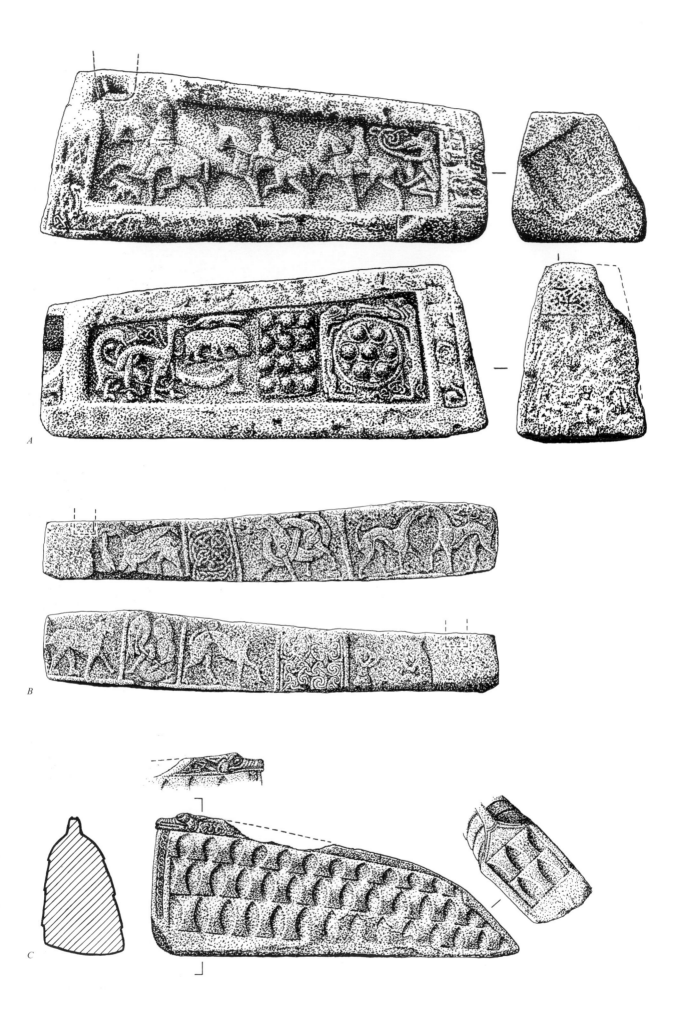

A

B

C

Meigle (NO 2872 4459)

Opposing page

A. No. 11, recumbent monument formerly built
   into the old church (NMRS DC 25241-2)
B. No. 9, recumbent monument which formerly
   rested on a modern pedestal in the
   churchyard (NMRS DC 25240)
C. No. 25, hogback monument
   (NMRS DC 25252)

This page

D. No. 26, recumbent monument recovered
   from the church in 1869 (NMRS DC 25253)
E. No. 12, recumbent monument which
   formerly lay in the garden of the manse
   (NMRS DC 25243-4)
F. No. 33, carved fragment found in the burial-
   ground in 1988 (NMRS DC 25260)
G. No. 28, lower part of a cross-slab
   (NMRS DC 25255)
H. No. 32, fragment of a cross-slab
   (NMRS DC 25259)
I. No. 14, fragment of a cross-slab; another
   fragment of this slab, now lost, was
   formerly built into the old church
   (NMRS DC 25254)

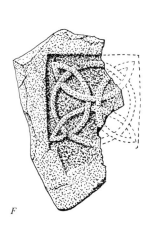

D

E

F

G

H

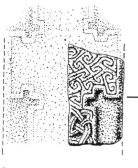

I

101

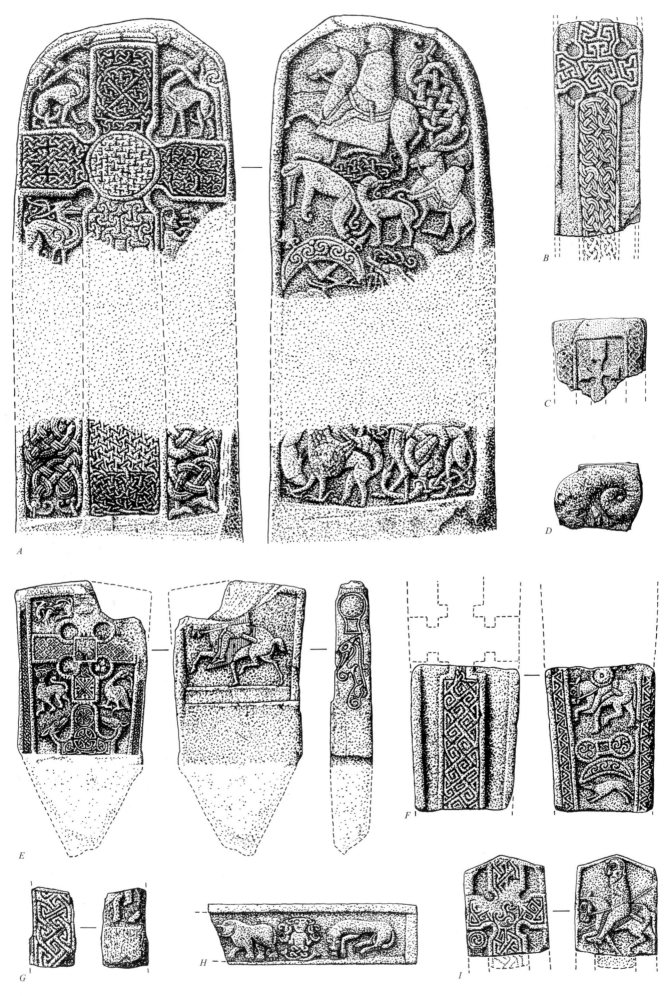

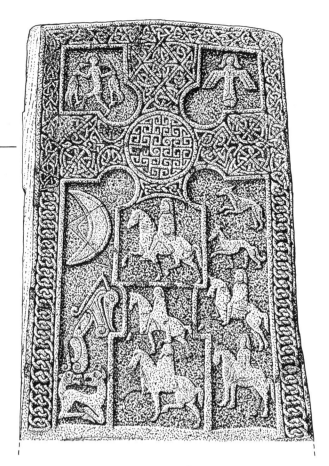

J

K

SETTLEMENT AND LANDSCAPE FROM THE TWELFTH TO THE EIGHTEENTH CENTURY

This period opens and closes with events which were formative in the development of both the landscape and the social structure of South-east Perth. The foundation of the priory of Scone between 1114 and 1116, and Coupar Angus Abbey in 1164, transformed large parts of the area from royal demesne into monastic estate, and much of the rest was converted into secular lordships, often in the hands of newly-arrived Anglo-Norman families. The situation thereafter was not static, perhaps the greatest single development being the return of church lands to secular ownership, culminating in the feuing movement, which, particularly in the sixteenth century, transformed many tenants into small landed proprietors. Eventually, however, in the second half of the eighteenth century, the nature of farming, the farming landscape, and rural society were to be transformed, as the Improving movement

reached its climax, and the pattern of the modern landscape was ushered in.

Various strands of evidence for these developments can be distinguished in the landscape of South-east Perth. Some of it is purely archaeological, but much of it is historical. This section reviews the evidence, looking in turn at the early estate centres, the monastic lands and the rural settlement. However, the tower-houses and churches, which are also components of this landscape, have been dealt with in separate sections. *pp. 124-46*

Early castles *107.*

The centres of a number of twelfth-century estates may be identified by the presence of earth-and-timber castles, often taking the form of a motte-and-bailey, or, rather less commonly, a ringwork. The motte-and-bailey, as it normally survives, comprises an earthen mound (the motte), which was the strongpoint of the castle, with, at its base, a courtyard (the bailey) enclosed within a bank and external ditch. The ringwork appears as an enclosure defended by a substantial bank and external ditch. Such earthworks frequently survive only in an eroded state, belying their roles as the substructures of potentially sophisticated timber castles. These castles were introduced into South-east Perth by incoming Anglo-Norman families, such as the Montfiquets at Cargill, the Hays at Errol, and Ruffus at Kinnaird. There are mottes, apparently unaccompanied by baileys, at **Murie, Lawton, Meikleour,** and *104A-B.* **Barton Hill, Kinnaird**; a ringwork at **Cargill**; and a motte *105B.* with two baileys at **Rattray**, now irrecoverably mutilated by

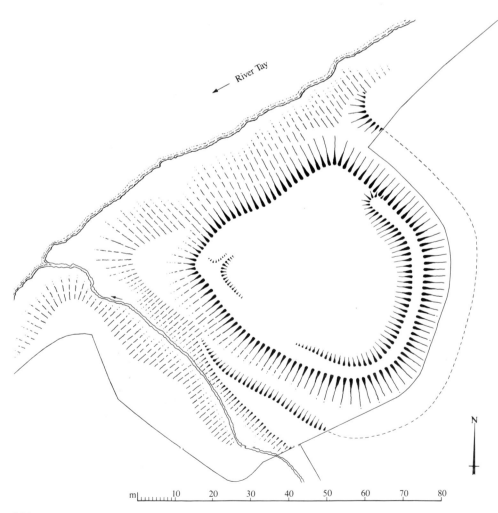

A. **Murie** *(NO 2315 2238), motte, 1:1000 (NMRS DC 25115)*

m |ₗₗₗₗₗₗₗₗₗ| 10   20   30

B. **Cargill** *(NO 1579 3743), ringwork, 1:1000 (NMRS DC 25119)*

River Tay

m |ₗₗₗₗₗₗₗₗₗ| 10   20   30   40   50   60   70   80

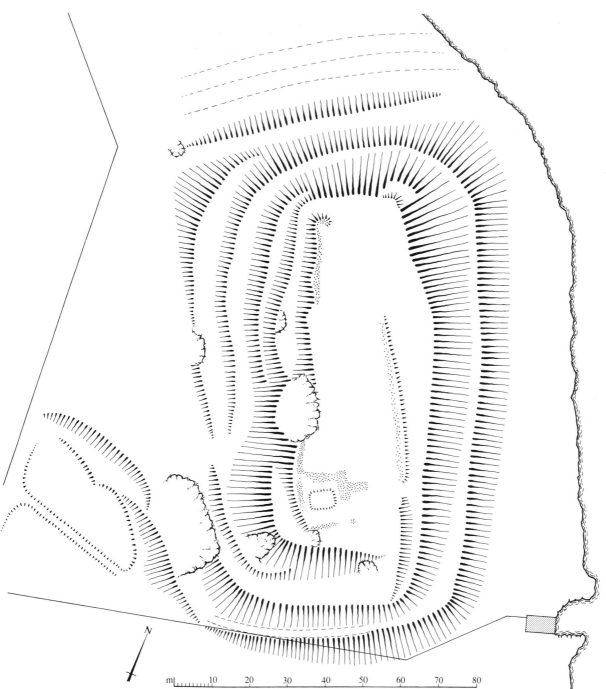

A. **Clunie Castle** (*NO 1107 4403*), *1:1000* (*NMRS DC 25121*)

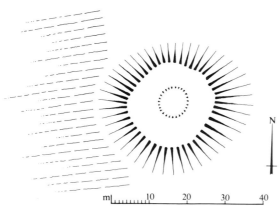

B. **Meikleour** (*NO 1536 3869*), *motte, 1:1000* (*NMRS DC 25117*)

quarrying. The first phase of the royal castle of **Clunie** may also have been of timber, utilising the advantages of the entirely natural Castle Hill, although this can only be demonstrated by excavation.

The only one of these to have been excavated is at Kinnaird, where the motte, fashioned from a natural knoll (**Barton Hill**), was examined in 1971, in advance of the construction of a house upon its summit. The excavation revealed four large post-holes and seven smaller ones, interpreted by the excavators as the settings for a rectangular timber tower within a post-and-log fence (Stewart and Tabraham 1974). A narrow drystone wall on the southern edge of the motte was thought to be the revetment to a bank of turves, designed to support a palisade, whilst at the base of the motte, on the west, there was a flat-bottomed ditch. The castle may be that of Ralph Ruffus, who was granted the barony of Kinnaird between 1172 and 1174 (*Reg. Reg. Scot.*, ii, no.135).

The motte at **Murie**, held by the Hays of Errol from about 1180 (*Reg. Reg. Scot.*, ii, no.204), is a simple inverted 'pudding

105A.
106.

113A.

104A.

Loch of Clunie (NO 110 440), a view across the loch from the east, with Clunie Castle in the centre of the picture, the parish church beyond it, and the tower-house on the island in the foreground (NMRS A 65066)

105B. basin' 8m high, with a summit area measuring 13m by 11m, whilst that at **Meikleour**, held by the earls of Strathearn at the beginning of the thirteenth century (*Reg. Reg. Scot.*, ii, nos.399 and 472), stands to a height of 5m and has a roughly circular summit 22m in diameter. At Lawton a circular flat-topped mound known as **Macbeth's Law** has been identified as a prehistoric burial mound, but could equally well be interpreted as a motte, and indeed might have served as both. As a motte it would make a suitable centre for the small estate of Buttergask, where, between 1211 and 1214, Hugh of Calder gave to Scone Abbey forty acres of cultivated land, common pasture and other easements, and one toft and croft in the toun (*Reg. Reg. Scot.*, ii, no.508). The origin of the name 'Macbeth's Law' is unclear, but a Macbeth was Sheriff of Scone at the end of the twelfth century, possibly the same Macbeth, judex of Gowrie, who was cited alongside Hugh of Calder in a charter granted by William I (1165-1214) to Coupar Angus Abbey (*Reg. Reg. Scot.*, ii, no.420). The name Macbeth also occurs in connection with the earthwork at **Cairnbeddie**, sometimes referred to as Macbeth's Castle. It formerly comprised a roughly rectangular enclosure some 70m by 60m within a broad ditch, and with a circular, flat-topped mound in its southern corner (OS 6-inch map, Perthshire, 1st ed., 1867, sheet 86; Christison 1900, 46). Nothing can now be seen but the ploughed-down remains of the mound, part of which was removed in the early nineteenth century, when 'horse shoes... handles of swords and dirks' were found (*NSA*, 10, Perth, 873-4). The earthwork must have borne a superficial resemblance to a motte-and-bailey, but its position in a natural hollow is not suited to defence, which places considerable doubt upon such an identification.

The only earth-and-timber castle in South-east Perth to which specific reference is made in contemporary documents is 104B. the ringwork at **Cargill**. Cargill was granted to Richard de

Montfiquet by William I between 1189 and 1195, and the castle is mentioned in a charter between 1195 and 1199 (*Reg. Reg. Scot.*, ii, nos.334 and 377). It is set on the left bank of the River Tay, at the top of a steep scarp, which provides the only defence on the north-west. The enclosing bank is up to 10m thick and 2m high, but the visible remains of the external ditch have largely been removed by ploughing. The reasons why a ringwork was constructed, rather than a motte-and-bailey, are never likely to be known. It may have been a measure of economy, mottes being expensive to raise, or simply the preference of the Montfiquets, who perhaps felt sufficiently secure without the strongpoint of a motte to fall back upon. The site seems to have remained in use into the fourteenth century, when the barony of Cargill passed to the Drummond family, who established their seat at **Stobhall**.

What was probably the earliest stone castle in South-east Perth stood upon the flat and elongated summit of Castle Hill, on the west shore of Clunie Loch. Although there may have been a fortified site at **Clunie** as early as 849 (Alcock 1981, 105A. 10 161), the present castle was established about 1141 as a hunting seat to accompany the royal forest of Clunie, in the hills to the north (Lawrie 1905, no.136). Unfortunately, the castle has been largely demolished, and in the early sixteenth century it was a source of building materials for the Bishop of Dunkeld's tower-house on the island in the loch (*Dunkeld Rentale*, 187). Its plan was largely determined by the topography of the hill, and what little survives might be interpreted as the remains of a tower, from which traces of a curtain wall extend northwards. The approach to the castle was by means of a terraced trackway on the south, but it is not clear to what period other terraces on the flanks of the hill belong. An interesting parallel for Clunie is the royal castle of Alyth, which comes on record between 1196 and 1199 (*Reg. Reg. Scot.*, ii, no.410) and which accompanied

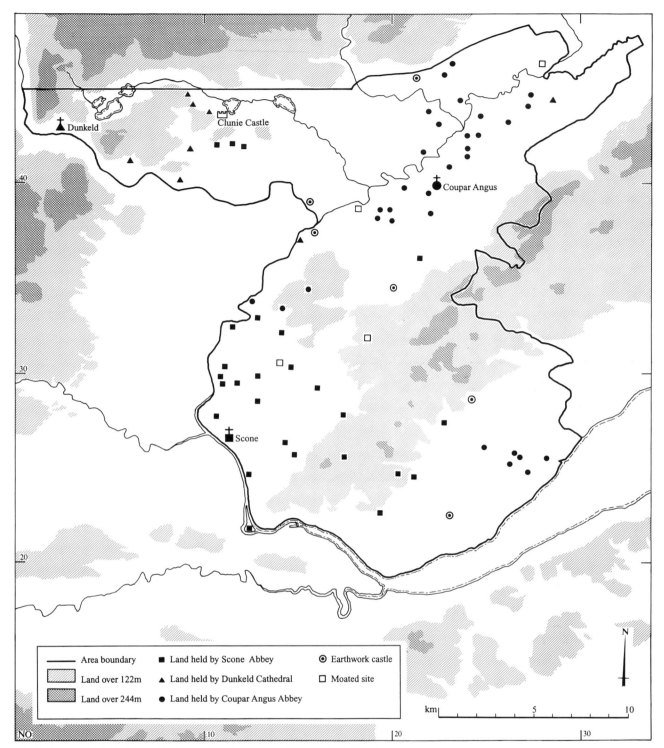

Distribution map of ecclesiastical land-holdings, early castles and moated sites (NMRS DC 25123)

the forest established by William I at Alyth. Alyth castle, and the castle of Inverquiech, are probably one and the same, and at Inverquiech the visible remains suggest a simple curtain wall enclosing an area determined by the topography of the site (RCAHMS 1990, p.91, no.207). The irregular form of both Clunie and Inverquiech contrasts with the precisely square ground-plan of the royal castle of Kinclaven, which stands on the west bank of the Tay opposite Cargill. Kinclaven was built between 1210 and 1236, following the destruction in a disastrous flood of what was probably an earth-and-timber castle at Perth (Dunbar and Duncan 1971, 11-13).

107.   When the distribution of the early castles is compared with that of the lands of the abbeys, the pattern of landholding in the twelfth and thirteenth centuries begins to emerge. Gaps in that pattern point to the presence of other possible estates, whose

administrative centres have yet to be identified. Unlocated, for example, is the caput of the barony of Kettins, held by Hugh de Ever in the late thirteenth century (*Coupar Angus Charters,* no.63), as is the residence of Simon de Meigle, who, before 1183, granted the parish church of Meigle to the priory of St Andrews (*Reg. Reg. Scot.*, ii, no.201). It should not be assumed that these were all earth-and-timber castles, however, and some might have been no more than halls, perhaps set within a relatively slight earthwork or palisade. Such sites are not only more susceptible to the effects of continual ploughing than most mottes, but are also more difficult to detect amongst the cropmark evidence. It is salutary to reflect that an unenclosed hall such as that belonging to Coupar Angus at **Campsie** (see *111B.* pp. 110-11) is unlikely to leave anything decipherable as a cropmark after the site has been levelled.

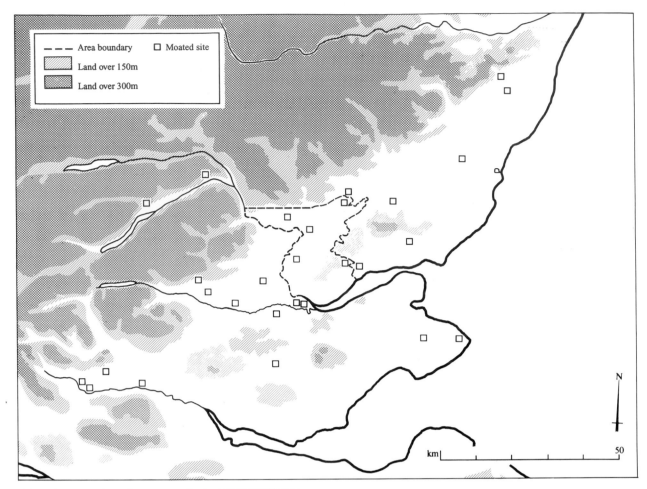

A. *Distribution map of moated sites in eastern Scotland (NMRS DC 25124)*

107. Moated sites

Fortunately, a number of estate centres were enclosed by broad ditches or moats, and it is possible to identify some of these as either upstanding earthworks or cropmarks. These identifications, however, are not without problems, since there is a possibility that rectangular ditched enclosures may have an earlier, even prehistoric origin. This is particularly true in eastern Scotland south of the Forth, but, fortunately, to the north, enclosed settlements of any shape are relatively uncommon, and some sites can reasonably be dated to the medieval period on the basis of form alone. The social range ascribed to moated sites in England has yet to be established in Scotland, though they were probably limited to the seigneurial levels of society, either lay or ecclesiastical. A superficial examination of record-sources suggests that they fall within areas generally accepted as those in which Anglo-Norman penetration occurred, and where earth-and-timber castles are also to be found. They appear in the south-west, the central valley, the eastern Borders, and on the eastern coastal plain north of the Forth.

Within the survey area, moats have been securely identified at **Hallyards** and **Links**, whilst others at **Moncur**, **Gourdie** and **Friarton** may be tentatively suggested. **Hallyards** is undoubtedly the most impressive, if only on the basis of the cropmarks which it has produced, the visible remains being severely wasted by ploughing; it measures about 85m by 80m over a stone wall, and has a ditch 8m broad. It is unfortunate that so little is known about its history, beyond the fact that Hallyards is on record in 1506 (*Dunkeld Rentale,* 76), and the site was still occupied as late as 1727, when the house was described as being protected from the floodwaters of the Isla 'by ditches encompassing it'(Macfarlane 1906, 110).

The moat at **Links**, which is set on the edge of a terrace

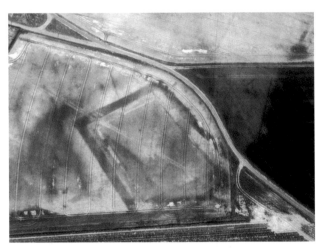

B. *Hallyards (NO 2790 4642), cropmarks of the moated site from the south-west (NMRS B 22708)*

overlooking the River Isla, is known only from cropmarks. It measures some 30m across within a ditch up to 5m broad, and there is evidence of an internal palisade. Whilst no documentary evidence can be attached to this site with any certainty, it is tempting to suggest that it may have been held by William, son of Alexander (see below), who at the end of the twelfth century was granted lands in the barony of Cargill by Richard de Montfiquet, lands which included an oxgang and toft beside Leyston (*Reg. Reg. Scot.,* ii, no.377). The farm of Links was formerly known as Easter Hatton, which is on record by the sixteenth century (*Reg. Mag. Sig.,* iii, no.1560), and it is possible that the buildings which stood within the moat were the origin of the 'hall' element in the Ha'toun place-name (see below).

108A.

2. 108B.
109A.

109A-B.

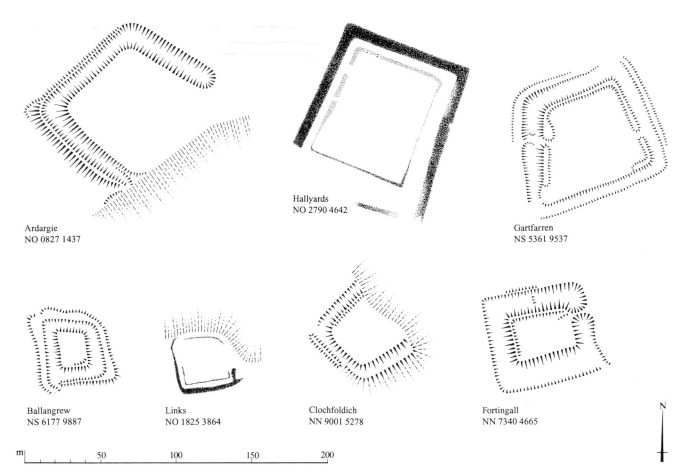

Ardargie
NO 0827 1437

Hallyards
NO 2790 4642

Gartfarren
NS 5361 9537

Ballangrew
NS 6177 9887

Links
NO 1825 3864

Clochfoldich
NN 9001 5278

Fortingall
NN 7340 4665

N

m | 50   100   150   200

A. Comparative plans of moated sites in South-east Perth and eastern Scotland (NMRS DC 25125)

B. Links (NO 1825 3864), cropmarks of the moated site from the south (NMRS B 16597)

109A.   When **Hallyards** and **Links** are compared with a group of upstanding Scottish moats, the contrast in size between the two enclosures is immediately apparent. Whether or not this results from a difference of status or function cannot be determined, but, if the moat at Links was that of William, son of Alexander, it would appear that he was a very minor landholder, with a holding constituting only one twentieth part of a knight's fee.

     The identification of the other possible moats in South-east Perth poses considerable problems. At **Friarton**, where the lands were held by Scone Abbey, cropmarks reveal two sides of a rectangular ditched enclosure, but the view is too distant to allow the enclosure to be conclusively identified as a moat. Problems also arise at **Moncur Castle** and **Gourdie**, where it is not clear whether cropmarks have revealed moats or parts of formal gardens. Finally, it is worth mentioning that in 1546 there was a 'moat called Newhall of Kinrossie' (*Reg. Mag. Sig.*, iv, no.12), although there are no visible remains of the site, and its precise nature is unclear.

144C.

Granges and the church lands

107.

Despite the creation of the various secular lordships, the abbeys of Scone and Coupar Angus, and Dunkeld Cathedral, were the greatest landowners in South-east Perth from the twelfth century to the Reformation. The founding of an abbey was an enormous undertaking, which went far beyond the provision of a site upon which the monks could build. Not only did the immediate building requirements have to be met, but a supporting economy had to be set up. Food, clothing, fuel and the needs of future building and maintenance programmes all had to be guaranteed if the foundation was to succeed. These were normally met by gifts of land and properties in return for prayers for the souls of their lay donors, or, in cases of great generosity, perhaps for burial within the abbey precincts. During the twelfth century, the zeal and commitment of the reformed orders struck a chord in the religious feelings of vast numbers of people across Europe, and donations flowed in, allowing many abbeys to build up extensive estates. The initial austerity of the Cistercians, made them the order most attractive to benefactors, and they led the great monastic farming movement. Seeking seclusion and self-sufficiency, wherever possible they attempted to consolidate their holdings into farms, known as granges, managed by lay brethren (Platt 1969).

     The Cistercians of **Coupar Angus** were fortunate in having royal patronage, which provided them with consolidated holdings at the outset, and a grange system must have come into operation relatively quickly. The Melrose Chronicle records that, on the 17th October 1215, a badly fixed candle caused a fire which burned one of the best Coupar Angus granges, 'full of grain', a laybrother perishing in the conflagration (*Chron. Melrose*, 61). In South-east Perth, granges were established at Coupar Grange, Aberbothrie, Keithick, Balbrogie, and Carse Grange, the remaining Coupar Angus granges being at Tullyfergus and Drimmie in North-east Perth, and Kincreich and Airlie in neighbouring Angus.

Although the Cistercians sought solitude for their houses and were notable as reclaimers of the wastes, they can seldom have settled in a totally empty landscape, and many of the gifts were undoubtedly of lands which were already being farmed by peasant communities. Such may well have been the case with most of the initial Coupar Angus endowment. Malcolm IV (1153-65) gave Coupar, Balbrogie, Tullyfergus, and pasture in the royal forest of Drimmie, together with rights to timber, charcoal and pannage in the royal forests of Drimmie and Clunie (*Reg. Reg. Scot.*, i, no.226). William I, as well as giving a site for the abbey, gave Persie, Aberbothrie, Keithick, Campsie and the marsh of Blairgowrie (*Reg. Reg. Scot.*, ii, nos.10, 397 and 420). The marsh of Blairgowrie was probably intended as a source of peat for fuel, and the only specified waste is associated with Campsie.

Carse Grange, however, represented a major reclamation project. Its core comprised the lands of Edderpols, granted by William de la Hay and confirmed by William I between 1187 and 1195. The character of the location of the grange, between the Bog Mill Pow and the Grange Pow, is well conveyed by the name Edderpols, meaning 'between the pows', a pow being a slow-moving, ditch-like stream, flowing through carse-land (*Reg. Reg. Scot.*, ii, no.322). In fact, all the land lies below the 15m contour, and was marginal to the main Hay holdings on the higher ground to the south-west, where the medieval parish church of Errol stood. This low-lying, marshy, position is further emphasised by the 'inches' to the west and north-west, namely Inchcoonans, Megginch, Inchmichael, Inchmartin and Inchture, and in about 1225 it was necessary to build a causeway from Inchture to the grange (*Coupar Angus Charters*, no.37). Some of the haughlands on granges like Aberbothrie and Balbrogie are also likely to have required drainage.

The development of monastic granges in England has been studied by Platt (1969), and there is, as yet, no reason to assume that their development in Scotland took a radically different course. Not a great deal is known about the earliest Cistercian granges, though they were probably quite humble affairs, designed to meet the basic requirements of accommodation for lay brothers, labourers, farm equipment and livestock, and storage for agricultural produce. However, the passage of time, different economic circumstances and the relaxation of aspects of the monastic rule brought about changes. Chapels, for example, were originally discouraged on Cistercian granges, so as not to detract from the focal position of the mother house, and to avoid conflict with the interests of the local parish churches. Full attendance was sought at the principal celebrations of the monastic calendar, and it was initially stipulated that granges must be no more than one day's journey from the abbey. However, in the late thirteenth century and the first half of the fourteenth century, there was a drastic decline in both the numbers and quality of the lay brethren, in some cases necessitating the employment of choir monks on the granges, and it became common for the granges to serve as rest and resort centres for choir monks. It is possible that the chapels, which increasingly appeared on Cistercian granges, were to meet the needs of these monks. In time, facilities in general seem to have improved, but there was no attempt to create monasteries in miniature, or to mirror the monastic plan.

Changing circumstances also led to more dramatic changes in grange structure. The medieval economy, flourishing in the twelfth century, began to falter; climatic deterioration had a serious impact upon farming, political instability developed, and, in the middle of the fourteenth century, there was appalling pestilence. It was no longer practicable for the abbeys to manage their estates in the same way, and it became increasingly the practice for grange lands to be leased to secular tenants. Certainly the leasing of Cistercian granges was normal practice by the fifteenth century.

It is unfortunate that there is so little information relating to the management of the Coupar Angus lands before the fifteenth and sixteenth centuries. However, the *Coupar Angus Rental*, which survives from 1443, contains a large collection of leases of what were formerly granges, by then subdivided into several smaller holdings, and provides some information about what structures were to be found on the granges. The fullest account is contained in a lease of Cowbyre, a part of the grange of Keithick, in 1463 (*Coupar Angus Rental*, i, no.113), although given the proximity of Coupar Angus to Cowbyre, the buildings listed are probably those at the abbey itself. Nevertheless, some abbey lands were kept in hand, frequently for pasturing cattle, and it is likely that at least some grange buildings were maintained. Mentioned in the Cowbyre lease are the principal barn of the grange, the great stable, the seed house, the kitchen, the brewhouse and the bakehouse. Elsewhere, references are much less full, but they include: chapels at Balbrogie, Keithick and Carse; and mills at Aberbothrie, Coupar, Keithick (where there was also a waulk mill), and Carse. Mills or millsteads are still to be found at Coupar Grange, Keithick and Carse Grange, though we do not know if they occupy the sites of their medieval precursors. Mill sites could change, and a lease of the mill of Aberbothrie in 1449 refers both to the new mill and the place where the mill was formerly built (*Coupar Angus Rental*, i, no.52). In 1473 the miller of Keithick was permitted to move the mill to a place of greater convenience, if he thought this to be necessary (*Coupar Angus Rental*, i, no.220). The same lease, which charges him with building a mill house of stone and mortar to accommodate goods brought to the mill by the tenants, illustrates not only the character of the structures, but also the potential for archaeological recovery. Dovecots may also have been common to all or most of the granges, but only one, on Carse Grange, is mentioned in the Coupar Angus documents. In 1473, David Gardner, who held the orchards of the grange, was charged with the maintenance of the Carse dovecot, and with digging ponds deep enough for eels and fish (*Coupar Angus Rental*, i, no.232). Unfortunately, the two surviving dovecots at Carsegrange are of eighteenth-century lectern type.

The only upstanding remains on a Coupar Angus property are at **Campsie**, but at **Coupar Grange** cropmarks have revealed part of a large rectilinear ditched enclosure. The cropmarks are multiperiod and complex, showing not only the enclosure itself but adjacent rig-and-furrow cultivation, numerous linear features, large numbers of pits, and at least one prehistoric circular house. One of the most striking aspects of the cropmarks, however, are the large, apparently sunken features, in the east corner of the enclosure, whose sharp angularity may indicate the remains of substantial rectangular buildings.

In contrast to the large enclosure at Coupar Grange, all that can be seen at **Campsie** is a group of five buildings, reduced to their stone wall-footings, and ranged around a yard. William I granted his chase of Campsie, together with the waste belonging to it, to the abbey between 1173 and 1178, to be held in free forest (*Reg. Reg. Scot.*, ii, no.154), and whilst Campsie is never referred to as a grange, it provided the abbey with the meat products of the chase, fish from the River Tay, timber from the woods, and pasture for the abbey's cattle. It provides a model for other types of grange arrangements, and, more intriguingly, perhaps for the residences of the minor aristocracy who did not live in earth-and-timber castles or moated enclosures.

By the fifteenth century, Campsie had been leased to secular tenants, although the buildings and a small amount of land

111A.

111B.

A. **Coupar Grange** *(NO 2253 4313), a view of the cropmarks from the south (NMRS B 22697)*

around them were retained to serve as a resort, or rest house, for the abbot and monks. In 1474 Robert Pullour, who had leased half of the abbey's fishings, was allowed to live in the abbot's mansion until proper provision could be made for him (*Coupar Angus Rental*, i, no.299). In 1551 the abbot's residence comprised a hall, chapel, chamber, kitchen, bakehouse and brewhouse, and Alexander M'Brek, the tenant of what was then known as Nether Campsie, was responsible for its maintenance. The house was to be kept ready for occupation, furnished with four feather beds and four other beds for servants, as well as bed clothes, towels, pots, pans, plates, dishes and other necessaries (*Coupar Angus Rental*, ii, no.66). Certainly, Campsie must have been a very pleasant resort, lying as it does at the top of cliffs overlooking a spectacular stretch of the River Tay known as Campsie Linns.

The local holdings of the abbey of **Scone** were consolidated in the south-west corner of South-east Perth, marching with Coupar Angus at Campsie on the north, and then sweeping round in a broad arc to Fingask on the east. It is unclear if granges as such were ever established on Scone lands, but cropmarks at **Cambusmichael**, lands given to the abbey by David I (1124-53), should probably be considered in this context. The cropmarks reveal two parallel ditches, which spring from the river cliff on the north, and the deeply incised gully of the Cambusmichael Burn on the east, enclosing about 1.5ha around the ruinous medieval church and its burial-

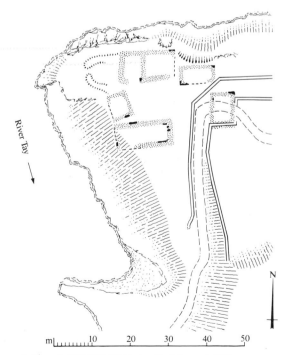

B. **Campsie** *(NO 1243 3394), the abbot's house, 1:1000 (NMRS DC 25126)*

church

N

Cambusmichael
(NO 115 324),
cropmarks of the probable
grange and prehistoric
settlements, 1:2500
(NMRS DC 25128)

ground; about 180m to the south-south-east of the church there is what may be a rectangular ditched enclosure. There is nothing intrinsically medieval in the appearance of these cropmarks, but it seems entirely possible that they represent the remains of the Augustinian estate centre. However, the abbey was clearly being granted a functioning estate, complete with tenants, and the possibility that the cropmarks relate to this earlier period cannot be discounted. Of course, not all the centres of monastic holdings need have been on this scale, and the possible moated site at **Friarton** might reasonably be identified as the focus of the abbey's lands there. Reference should also be made to the holding at Clein, given to the abbey by Alexander I (1107-24), and mentioned in a charter of 1567, which reserves to the abbey the mansion, with chapel, orchards, three acres called the Gardener's Land of Clein, and pasture for two cows (*Reg. Mag. Sig.*, iv, no.1778). By 1668 the house was ruinous (*Retours,* Perth, no.780), and its site may now be occupied by the eighteenth-century house of Glendoick (NO 2075 2361).

The **Dunkeld Cathedral** lands north of the Forth were consolidated into the barony of Dunkeld, and those to the south into the barony of Aberlady. The bulk of the northern lands lay to the west of the Tay, and, within South-east Perth, were confined largely to the area east of the abbey, between Dunkeld and Clunie. There is little surviving documentary evidence to suggest how the estate was organised in the earlier middle ages,

but by 1500 the barony of Dunkeld was being administered by sergeants at Dunkeld and at Tibbermore (*Dunkeld Rentale*), the latter lying outside the survey area, to the west of Perth, but probably identifiable as the moated site partly underlying the farm of Peel. Clunie also served as a collecting centre, and the only example of an ecclesiastical estate building, albeit residential, to survive in South-east Perth in anything like its original form is the on **Clunie Loch**. A granary lay immediately to the east of the tower, but it is unclear whether the stables and barn mentioned in the *Dunkeld Rentale* (162-89) stood on the island, or at a separate mains farm. The tower may well have been the successor to the castle at Laighwood, in North-east Perth, said to have been built by Bishop William Sinclair (1309/10-1337), and 'fortified on all sides by ditches filled with water'(RCAHMS 1990, p.91, no.209).

The pattern of rural settlement

The granges did not exist in isolation. They were large farms, with workers and their families to be housed, and on the estates of a number of religious houses in Yorkshire an association of grange and settlement earthworks has been noted (Platt 1969, 88). In the absence of upstanding sites this cannot be seen in South-east Perth, where most of the evidence for settlement has to be drawn from documentary sources, or by inference from the presence of other medieval structures.

The churches are the most obvious settlement indicators, and

106.
140C-G

the kirktons, the touns which developed around them, were possibly amongst the earliest settlements to be established. Many of these have survived, either as fully-developed villages like Kettins or Inchture, or simply as small clusters of houses like Collace and Lethendy, but some churches, like

130A-B. **Cambusmichael** and **Bendochy**, now stand in isolation, and no visible traces of any surrounding settlement survive.

The earth-and-timber castles may have acted similarly as the focus for settlements of the twelfth and thirteenth centuries.

113A. Associated with the motte of **Kinnaird** and its adjacent church were 'the toft and houses in the toun', confirmed to Geoffrey, son of Richard steward of Kinghorn, by William I between 1205 and 1211 (*Reg. Reg. Scot.*, ii, no.470), whilst one of the earliest references to settlement in South-east Perth is in association with the earth-and-timber castle of **Cargill**. Between 1195 and 1199 the king confirmed a grant by Richard de Monfiquet to William, son of Alexander (see above), of a toft and croft between the castle and the church, an oxgang and one toft beside Leyston, and a half ploughgate in Whitefield (*Reg. Reg. Scot.*, ii, no.377). The centre for William's small

109B. estate has been tentatively identified with the small moated site overlooking the Isla to the east of **Links**. In the fourteenth century the estate passed from John to Philip Meldrum (*Reg. Mag. Sig.*, i, app.2, no.1104), and at the end of the fifteenth century, when it comprised Leyston, Leystonshiels and Easter Whitefield, the estate was exchanged for the barony of Kinloch by Walter Cargil of Leyston (*Reg. Mag. Sig.*, ii, no.2508).

113B. In the late twelfth century, therefore, it is reasonable to suggest that within the barony of Cargill there was a toun at Cargill itself, presumably around the church, a farmstead somewhere between the church and the castle, and touns at Leyston and Whitefield. Unfortunately, further settlement is not recorded until the fifteenth century, when Leystonshiels and Easter Whitefield are mentioned. However, by the 1530s the barony was made up of some thirteen touns, namely the Kirkton, Balholmie, Easter and Wester Hatton, Leyston, Gallowhill, Whitefield, Wolfhill, Woodhead, Redstone, Brakywell and Stobhall, and Whitelees (*Reg. Mag. Sig.*, iii, no.1560). Many, if not all of these touns, probably existed before the sixteenth century. Elsewhere in the parish of Cargill, there were places such as Buttergask, where, in about 1212, Hugh of Calder granted to Scone Abbey forty acres of cultivated land, with rights to the common pasture and a toft and croft in the toun near the marches with Peattie (*Reg. Reg. Scot.*, ii, no.508).

Immediately south of Cargill was the Coupar Angus holding of **Campsie**, which is better recorded, and the *Coupar Angus Rental* provides some interesting insights into the medieval landscape along this stretch of the Tay. Although the abbot's

111B. house, chapel and associated buildings at Campsie remained in the hands of the abbey, as mentioned above, the lands had been leased to secular tenants by the middle of the fifteenth century. They were set on a series of five-year tacks, usually to three or four tenants, and there were fishermen to maintain the abbey's supply of fish, a granitar (official in charge of a granary) and a forester. In 1471 it was stipulated that the forester, Andrew Hughson, was to live with the cotters at the head of the wood (i, no.293). The area had been well-wooded in the twelfth century, but by the fifteenth century the state of the woods had become a major concern to the abbey. In 1460 Thomas Robertson and David Anderson were fined for sale and destruction of the wood (i, no.72), and Campsie leases contained stipulations about woodland management beyond those which became standard in the fifteenth century. In 1471, the wood was to be divided into four equal parts, each the responsibility of a tenant. Cattle were to be excluded altogether, and no one was to 'burn any of the wood except it be from the ditch nearer the ploughed land, if any should be pulled up' (i, no.293). Walls around the wood are referred to in 1479 (i, no.319), and in 1483 the tenants were being instructed to 'build walls around a half of the forest within two years', (i, no.361). The woods appear to have been reasonably open; in 1474, Robert Pullour, who had

A. **Kinnaird** *(NO 243 286), aerial view of the toun from the north, with the parish church and burial-ground in the centre of the picture, and the motte (under excavation) above left (NMRS PT 6925)*

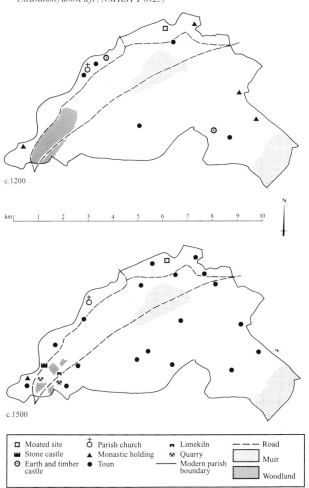

□ Moated site	✛ Parish church	⌐ Limekiln
⛫ Stone castle	▲ Monastic holding	⚒ Quarry
⊙ Earth and timber castle	● Toun	

--- Road
— Modern parish boundary

Muir

Woodland

B. Map of The Barony of Cargill in about 1200 and 1500 (NMRS DC 25129)

been granted one half of the fishings of Campsie, did not have sufficient grazings for his cattle, and was given licence to pasture them in the west part of the wood (i, no. 299). Similarly, in 1479, the tenants were given leave to cultivate within the walls of the wood (i, no.319). Evidently there was enclosed and unenclosed woodland, for in 1558 John Crago and his wife were given rights of common pasture only in the open woods of Campsie, and not in the woods enclosed or being enclosed (ii, no.220). When the lands of Campsie were divided, probably in 1477, the toun of Over Campsie or Wolfhill was created on the higher ground above the woods.

A. *Plan of the fermtouns and unenclosed rigs around Inchtuthil by Roy in 1755 (1793, pl.xviii)*

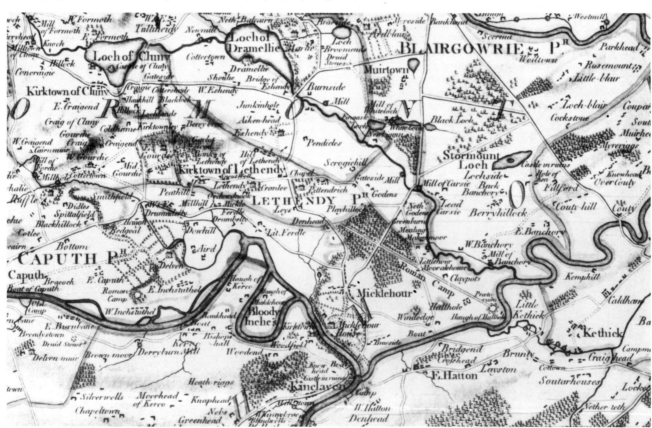

B. *Stobies map (1783) of a large area around Inchtuthil showing several 'kirktons', 'hattons' and cottertouns (National Library of Scotland)*

The rental books also provide some good illustrations of toun splitting, the process whereby the lands of a toun were divided and additional settlements created; this usually resulted in two or more settlements with a common surname, but distinguished by prefixes such as Easter, Wester, Nether and Over. On the grange of Balbrogie for instance, five separate holdings were created, although the grange of Aberbothrie appears only to have been split into two. It cannot always be assumed that these divisions resulted in the creation of new settlements, although in 1463 a lease of Cowbyre on the Grange of Keithick describes such a procedure (i, no.113). The lease specified that in the first year each tenant should settle one cotter on the north side of the grange, in a place determined by the abbot, and that in the third year three of the tenants, with their habitations, should transfer there. The division of Cowbyre suggests the creation of a nucleated settlement, but this was not always the case, and elsewhere in the rental there are references which point to the creation of dispersed settlements. In 1464, for example, the grange of Keithick was set for two years to seven husbandmen, who, if they wished to remain beyond that term, were to divide the grange into 'just portions', and each one thereafter 'with domicile and cottar' was to 'maintain himself separately at his own part' (i, no.136).

It is likely, therefore, that there was a mixed settlement pattern in South-east Perth, comprising the kirktons, and a number of larger fermtouns and cottertouns, together with a wide scatter of smaller fermtouns and individual farmsteads. A number of the touns attained the status of burgh (see Pryde 1965), the first to do so being Dunkeld (before 1511) and the former Coupar Angus grange of Keithick (1492). Later came Coupar Angus itself (1607), Meigle (1608), Errol (1648), Meikleour (1665) and Kinnoull (1706). Whilst burghal status conferred limited privileges to hold markets and fairs, and to allow craftsmen, bakers, brewers, fleshers and so on to ply their trades, these settlements remained essentially rural in character.

This is the pattern that existed when reliable map information becomes available in the middle and late eighteenth century. The maps of Stobie (1783) and Ainslie (1794) postdate the onset of the agricultural improvements, yet both depict elements of the earlier landscape, most notably the survival of the traditional fermtoun. Also depicted are a number of cottertouns, communities of cotters who held only small amounts of land and worked on the farms of the tenants, or perhaps had some craft such as shoemaker or wright.

The pre-Improvement landscape is described by James Playfair, who was minister of both Bendochy and Meigle at the end of the eighteenth century. He recounts that the farmhouses of the area were grouped together in clusters, and that 'each field was divided into as many parts or ridges as there were farmers in the village; by which the good and bad land was equally divided among all; and in winter, or when in grass, all the ground was common pasturage... There were formerly balks

125.
144D.

114B.

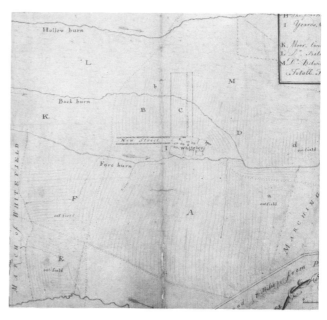

A. **Whiteley** *(NO 189 362), plan of the fermtoun in 1763 (SRO RHP 3410)*

between the ridges; there was no grass private property but what grew on the balks... Formerly they ploughed with eight oxen, or with four oxen and two horses before them... What corn they had was not much inferior to what grows at present. They ploughed always deep, cleaned the ground in the spring, and dunged it for barley. The whole of the dung was laid on the infield. The outfield, which was the greater proportion, never got any dung. It yielded a crop now and then, after lying several years in grass, or rather in a state of nature; the crop was private property, but the grass was common pasturage. Formerly they used tumbler sledges for carts; the wheel and axle being all of one piece' (*Stat. Acct.*, 19 [1797], 346-7).

A visual image of this landscape is provided by Roy's Map (1747-55), although it is a stylised and schematic representation, and a more detailed impression can only be obtained from estate plans of the period. The fermtoun of Whiteley, which was cleared to make way for a planned village to house retired soldiers, provides a good example of such a plan. Whiteley belonged to the Drummond family, whose estates were forfeited to the Crown after the 1745 Jacobite rising. The rents and profits from such estates were to be used to remove some of the causes of discontent in the Highlands, to develop industry and manufacturing on the forfeited estates themselves, and to promote Protestantism and loyalty to the Crown. Prior to the necessary improvements being carried out, the estates were surveyed, in order to assess their condition and the resources that were available. The plan of the toun of

114A.

115A.

B. **Scone**, *John Slezer's view of the house and toun at the end of the seventeenth century (NMRS B 41585)*

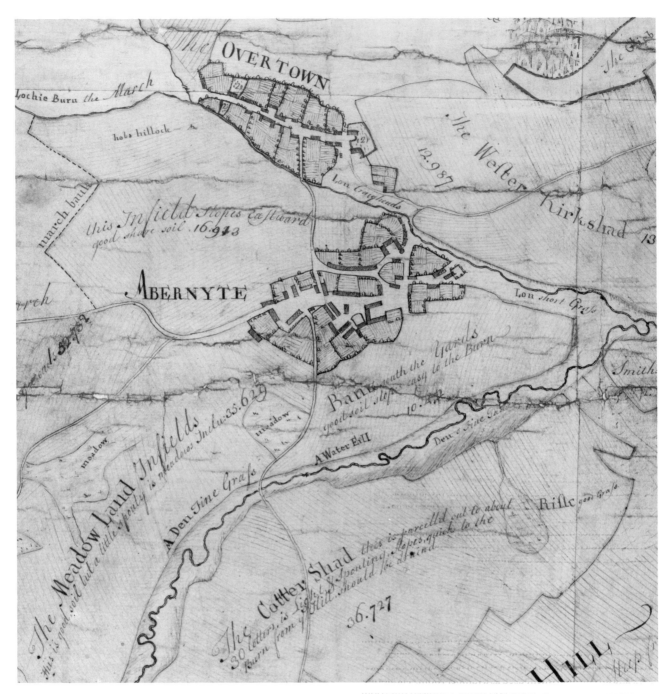

Abernyte (NO 257 311), plan of the toun, and Overtown, in 1756 (SRO RHP 1005)

Whiteley and its lands, drawn in 1763 before the clearance, confirms the picture painted by Playfair, of furlongs of rig-and-furrow cultivation in an unenclosed landscape, in this instance, with broad grass baulks between every second ridge. Of a total of 460 acres, only 180 acres constituted infield, of which 120 acres lay in 'The Great Field' on the south side of the fermtoun. Only 75 acres constituted outfield, the remainder being dry moorland covered with short heath. The fermtoun itself comprised some twelve buildings and six enclosures, their somewhat random disposition contrasting markedly with the regimented appearance of the proposed street (Lesslie 1763).

In the case of the larger touns of Abernyte and Overtown, the plan drawn in 1756 reveals striking differences between the two. Overtown comprises a relatively ordered street, on either side of which stand single houses with gardens to the rear. At Abernyte, there are single buildings, either houses or agricultural buildings, two pairs of buildings set parallel to each other, two U-plan steadings, and at least one long terrace reminiscent of that depicted on Slezer's late seventeenth-

century view of Scone. As at Whiteley, the landscape is still unenclosed and divided between infield, outfield and pasture; of a total of some 994 acres, 201 acres were classed as infield, and 309 as outfield. The field immediately south of the Abernyte Burn is named 'The Cotter Shad' on the plan, and its thirty-six acres were parcelled out amongst thirty cotters (Winter 1756).

It is unfortunate that so few of the tenants' houses and farm buildings depicted on such estate maps survive in South-east Perth, and those that do have been so heavily altered that their origins are not easily discernible. What are probably the wasted remains of such buildings are to be found on the Sidlaws, but in the absence of excavation, evidence for rural housing must be drawn largely from documentary sources, combining descriptions by travellers and agricultural writers with information contained in estate papers. It is only in the eighteenth century that descriptions specific to this or neighbouring areas start to appear, and these have to be viewed with caution, as they are often highly critical, written from the

116.

115B.

120.

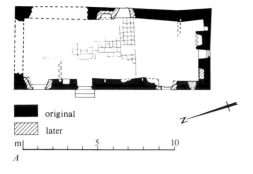

original

later

m |_____| 5 |_____| 10

A

Cargill (NO 1505 3693),

A. cruck-framed cottage,
   1:250 (NMRS DC 25131)
B. view of the north-west end of
   the cruck-framed cottage, showing
   the cut-back cruck, an aumbry and
   the doorway (NMRS B 14624)

B

117A-B.

standpoint of people interested in the Improving movement. An account of the state of farmhouses, and their evolution, is provided by the Board of Agriculture Survey of the county of Forfarshire. It describes the houses of the 1750s as cruck-framed, the crucks resting upon the ground, presumably upon post-pads. The walls were about 1.5m high, constructed of alternating layers of turf and stone, and the roofs were also of turf, sometimes with a covering of thatch. The internal arrangements were those of the byre-dwelling, with people occupying one end of the building and animals the other, both entering by the same central doorway. The fire, around which the family slept, was centrally placed on the floor and the smoke escaped through a vent in the roof. The first improvement was the addition of a screen between door and fireplace, subsequently provided with a wooden window which was eventually glazed. A small external window of up to four panes was also a later addition. Wooden box-beds, when eventually provided, served as a screen between the fireplace area and an end apartment used as a lumber room. The addition of a fireplace with stone-and-clay chimney allowed this room to become a private chamber for the farmer and his family, the other room, now designated the kitchen, being used by the servants (Headrick 1813, 127-8).

The Agricultural Survey of Perthshire is less forthcoming, but what little is said confirms the Forfarshire description (Robertson 1799, 51). Only on the Carse of Gowrie is a distinction noted, with the use of clay as a walling material rather than stone and turf. Indeed clay-walled houses, if properly rendered, were thought to be exceptionally warm and durable, and examples of such buildings are still to be found in the area. In the 1790s the minister of Errol, noting the survival of some old clay-walled houses 'in a tolerable state of repair', was of the opinion that the techniques of constructing such buildings were being lost; instead of building up the wall in layers between wooden shuttering, it was apparently becoming the practice to mould the clay into bricks (*Stat. Acct.*, 4 [1792], 490).

Such then was the nature of vernacular housing in the eighteenth century. The difficulty is whether or not this can be projected backwards into earlier periods. Travellers in the seventeenth century were generally of the opinion that the

quality of housing was low. In 1661, for example, John Ray described the 'ordinary country houses' as 'pitiful cots, built of stone and covered with turfs, having in them but one room, many of them no chimneys, the windows very small holes, and not glazed' (Hume Brown 1891, 231). One of the earliest accounts is from the reign of James I (1406-37), and, whilst rather vague and generalised, it follows the line taken by later writers; 'The roofs of the houses in the country are made of turf, and the doors of the humbler dwellings are made of the hide of oxen' (Hume Brown 1891, 26-7). It is an interesting reflection of these descriptions that at Keithick, in 1464, the tenants and cotters of Coupar Angus Abbey were not permitted to 'upturn the meadows or pasture lands for their divots, except only for repairing of houses' (*Coupar Angus Rental,* i, no. 136).

Descriptions such as these have led to the conclusion that, before the agricultural Improvements, the overwhelming majority of the population of rural Scotland lived in poor housing. This conclusion has been reinforced by two further assumptions: firstly, that before the Improvements leases were generally short, tenancy insecure, and, therefore, there was no incentive for tenants to build durable houses; and secondly, that, outside the ranks of the aristocracy, Scottish rural society was uniformly impoverished. However, sufficient evidence is available for the blanket application of these views to be challenged; in South-east Perth, at least, tenurial insecurity was not the problem that it has been taken to be, and there was also a wide range of wealth and resources within rural society.

The Coupar Angus leases have been analysed by Sanderson (1982, 46-8), who found that in the period from 1464 to 1516 five-year leases were the norm. Of the 418 issued in that period, eighty-seven were for life and only twenty-three were for less than five years. But even relatively short leases did not necessarily imply insecurity of tenure, and though the Grange of Aberbothrie was set on six-year tacks, three of the seven tenants named in 1448 were still there twenty years later (*Coupar Angus Rental*, i, nos. 51 and 122). In the period between 1539 and the Reformation life-leases were usual, and around 1560 most of the lands of Coupar Angus and Scone were feued. The tenants of Scone seem to have fared better in this process than those of Coupar Angus. On the Scone estate 77% of land was feued to previous occupants as opposed to

117

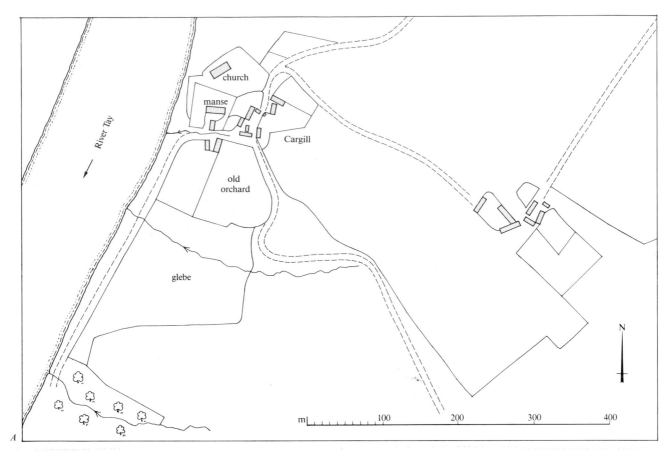

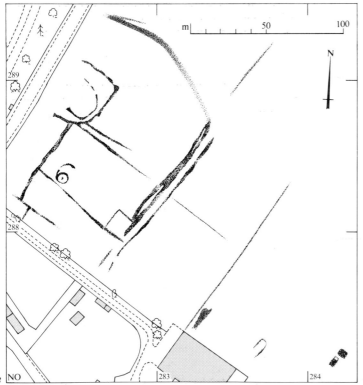

A. **Cargill** *(NO 150 369)*,
plan of the kirkton about 1750,
1:5000 (NMRS DC 25133)

B. **Mains of Inchture** *(NO 284 287)*,
enclosures, buildings and ring-ditch,
1:2500 (NMRS DC 25130)

57% on the Coupar Angus estate (Sanderson 1982, 81).

Furthermore, Scottish rural society was of varied composition, embracing a range that extended from small proprietors through tenants, sub-tenants and cotters down to landless labourers, and the testaments examined by Sanderson reveal that this was accompanied by considerable differences in wealth. Some tenants were moderately wealthy and lived with a reasonable degree of comfort. Patrick Robertson of Finmouth, for example, who died in 1560 and was perhaps of middling wealth, possessed '4 standing beds, 5 feather beds, 8 bolsters, 24 cods (pillows), 6 pairs of blankets, 2 pairs of linen curtains (probably for beds), 2 counters or trestle-type tables, 12 table cloths, 24 serviettes, 6 washing cloths, a Flanders cist, a kist for meal, an iron chimney, a basin, a dozen pewter plates, a dozen pewter trenchers, 3 quart stoops, 3 tin pint stoops, 3 silver spoons, an iron pot of three gallons capacity, 6 chandellars, 6 great trees of ash sawn for cuppillis, 3 chairs, 2 forms, and 2 spits, with 12 sacks, 3 canvases containing 12 ells each, 2 sowing sheets, 6 harrows and 6 sleds' (Sanderson 1982, 173). By way of comparison, it is worth noting that the range of furnishings is not dissimilar from those in use in the abbot's house at Campsie. Testaments took account only of moveable wealth, and the inclusion of the cruck-couples (pairs of timbers curved inwards from the outer walls to support the roof), if they were in use in an existing house, suggests that it could have been dismantled relatively easily. Of course the couples may simply have been in store, or purchased for the construction of another building.

Work on the agricultural buildings of Strathmore (Walker 1983, 152-9) has, indeed, pointed to manifestations of social distinction in rural buildings, which might well mirror the gradations of wealth revealed by Sanderson. Appraising tickets (assessments of the condition of buildings at the change of leaseholder) indicate the presence of halls on several of the farms of two Angus estates. One at Mill of Glamis (NO 386 467), for instance, which was appraised in 1726, was estimated by Walker to be some 9.7m in length, possessing a clay partition, a board partition, a clay chimney, two doors, three windows, one of which had glass, and an east chamber 7.3m long. The same ticket records a number of much smaller houses, but also one 9.7m long with three windows, and another 12.9m long with a two-leafed entrance door, a back door, three chamber doors, three glass windows, three little windows, a big clay chimney and a clay partition wall.

The hall at Mill of Glamis was described as the 'Old Hall', and Walker points out that in only one instance on the Glamis Estate do appraising tickets refer to a building as 'new built'. Such evidence implies a pre-eighteenth-century tradition. Furthermore, the place-name Hatton, or 'Hall Toun', is frequently of antiquity, some eleven appearing in the Register of the Great Seal between 1424 and 1513. Although the nature of the implied structures is unclear (see above), excavation of the fifteenth-century Ha'ton House, which stood upon the summit of the motte at Lumphanan in Aberdeenshire, revealed the remains of a building measuring 18m by 7m (*DES 1975*, 6; *1976*, 5-6).

Attempts to answer the questions raised here are beyond the scope of this volume, but this is clearly an area which requires a great deal of further research. Objective evidence from contemporary estate-papers must be set alongside both the descriptions of travellers and the accounts of the agricultural writers. The former may sometimes have sought to impress their readers with the outlandishness of the places to which they had journeyed, while the latter were sometimes keen to discredit things which they considered to be associated with bad farming practices.

The pre-Improvement landscape, within which these buildings stood, was itself subject to fairly constant and gradual change, but the later decades of the eighteenth century saw an unparalleled reorganisation of farming. The multiple-tenancy fermtouns and their cottertouns were swept away to be replaced by consolidated single-tenant farms, and the swathes of unenclosed rig-and-furrow disappeared beneath the orderly pattern of hedged or stone-walled fields so familiar today.

The process was recorded by the ministers of the various parishes of South-east Perth in the *Statistical Account* of the 1790s. The minister of Kinnaird parish noted that 'the population of the parish has been gradually decreasing for many years past; owing in a great measure to the monopolising of farms; 10 or 12 small farms, which supported as many families, having been at different times added to larger ones, in the cultivation of which the farmers employ not cottagers, but young unmarried men'. The number of farms in the parish had been reduced by half within the previous fifty or sixty years (*Stat. Acct.*, 11 [1794], 235-6). In St Martins, several villages occupied by pendiclers, who farmed their small land-holdings in runrig, had been demolished, and fewer tenants subsequently occupied larger farms (*Stat. Acct.*, 18 [1796], 501-2). As the leases expired in Cargill, it was the policy of the landowners to convert several smaller farms into one larger one, and the

population decreased because of the abolition of cotters and pendiclers. Here, too, the labour was mostly carried out by servants living in the farmer's house, as they were less expensive than cotters, who were thought to pay more attention to their homes and families than was consistent with their master's interests. The practice in Bendochy was to import workers from the Highlands, rather than keeping cotters (*Stat. Acct.*, 19 [1797], 357-8).

In Abernyte, the population of the parish declined by about a hundred over the course of the eighteenth century, and, apart from scattered houses, the parish contained only three hamlets, with a total of forty-one houses. Two villages, which formerly had sixty houses each, had shrunk to thirty each by 1790, whilst one village of eight or nine houses had declined to just one. The reason given for this decline is the expulsion of cotters, not, as seems normally to have been the case, because of the amalgamation of farms, but because lands which had formerly been held by four farmers were divided into five larger farms and eight or ten smaller ones; the tenants of the latter had other trades, and ran the farms with the help of large families. Those who took on workers preferred, like the tenants in Cargill and Kinnaird, to employ single people rather than cotters (*Stat. Acct.*, 9 [1793], 142-3).

Clearly, this reorganisation resulted in the desertion of large numbers of settlements across South-east Perth, but, except on the Sidlaws, subsequent agricultural activity has largely removed all surface traces of them, and there are considerable difficulties in identifying their sites. Modern farms frequently preserve medieval place-names, but whether or not they stand upon the sites of pre-Improvement precursors can only be demonstrated by excavation.

The cropmark evidence for rectangular buildings is discussed in the settlement section (pp. 68-9). It includes both sunken-floored structures, and what may be buildings outlined by a bedding-trench or a drain, but on no occasion can they be shown to be of medieval date. Indeed, from what is known of pre-Improvement buildings, they are unlikely to produce cropmarks, and it is more probable that the presence of a medieval settlement will be indicated by its accompanying enclosures, perhaps like those photographed to the east of **Inchture** church. Ploughed-out rig-and-furrow, ubiquitous on aerial photographs, might also offer some clues, gaps in rig systems possibly indicating settlement sites. To progress any further along this line, however, will require a more intensive programme of aerial photography to record and map the cropmarks of rig-and-furrow.

One means of identifying the approximate locations of settlement sites is provided by early maps, such as those of Timothy Pont (about 1600), and later Roy and Stobie. On the surviving estate plans of the eighteenth century, however, the sites of some abandoned fermtouns may be located with a higher degree of precision. The plans of Whiteley and Abernyte (see above), can be used to identify the locations of both houses and steadings in what are now open fields. Whiteley, is of particular importance, because it was abandoned relatively early in the eighteenth century, and has documentary evidence taking it back into the sixteenth century. The archaeological potential of sites such as these has been demonstrated by excavations in both Angus and the Borders (Pollock 1987; Dixon 1988).

There is also considerable potential in the extant kirktons. Cargill, which has already been discussed, was an estate centre by the late twelfth century, with both earth-and-timber castle and church. The kirkton is mentioned specifically in 1538 (*Reg. Mag. Sig.*, iii, no.1560), and it appears on an estate plan of about 1760 (SRO, RHP 3422). The detail of this plan is still evident on the ground today, and several of the eighteenth-century buildings can be identified, most notably the ruins of a cruck-framed cottage. Elsewhere, the remains of earlier buildings may be hidden in the fabric of cottages and houses still occupied today, and Walker (1981) has been able to demonstrate, for example, that a stone-walled terraced cottage

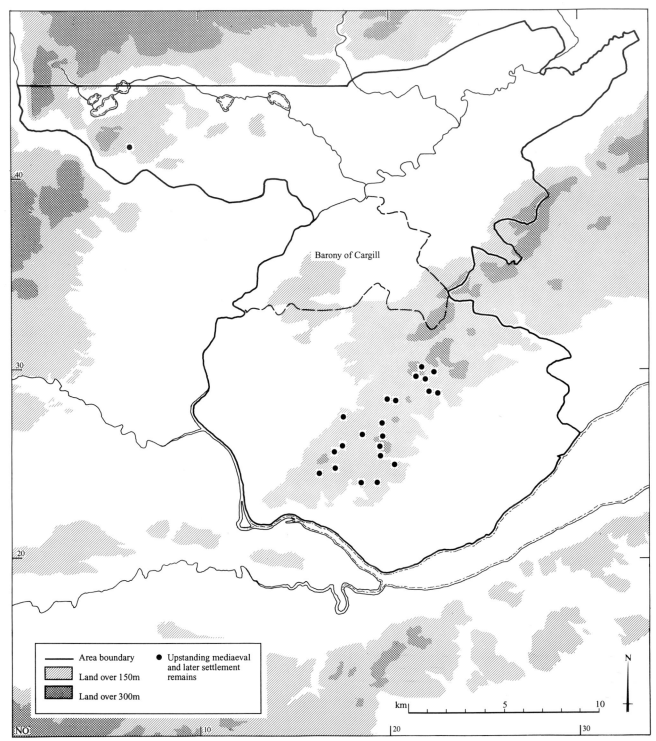

Distribution map of the upstanding pre-Improvement settlement remains (NMRS DC 25135)

in the kirkton at Rait originated as a turf-walled building.

120.   Of the twenty-two upstanding sites recorded in the Sidlaws, only one may be classed as a fermtoun, and six as farmsteads. Most of the remainder, isolated buildings and small huts, were probably herds' bothies or shielings. The fermtoun is situated immediately beyond the improved fields, to the north-north-

121C. east of the farm of **Arnbathie**, on lands held in the middle ages

122A. by the abbey of Scone. It comprises at least six buildings and

123. their associated enclosures. The buildings, the largest of which measures 17.8m in overall length, now survive only as grass-grown wall-footings, and what appear to be middens are to be found alongside two of them. A further two buildings lie on opposite sides of an enclosure some 110m to the north, whilst to the north and north-north-east there are three large fields of rig-and-furrow cultivation. Ridging is also visible to the north

of the fort on Law Hill.

    Of the farmsteads, the plans of only two examples are presented here, **Over Fingask** and **Franklyden**. At **Over** *121B.* **Fingask**, close to the foot of a prominent natural knoll, there are the remains of five buildings and at least two enclosures. On the summit of the knoll there is a possible earthwork of unknown date, but there is no reason to assume that the two sites are associated. At **Franklyden**, adjacent to a number of *121A.* small enclosures, there are two buildings and a kiln. Around both of these sites, and elsewhere in the Sidlaws, there are extensive traces of rig-and-furrow cultivation and field banks, amongst which some chronological depth is detectable. At **Over Fingask**, where there is a well-preserved system of large *122B.* rectangular fields defined by earthen banks, several of the banks overlie rig, and within one of the fields there are traces of

120

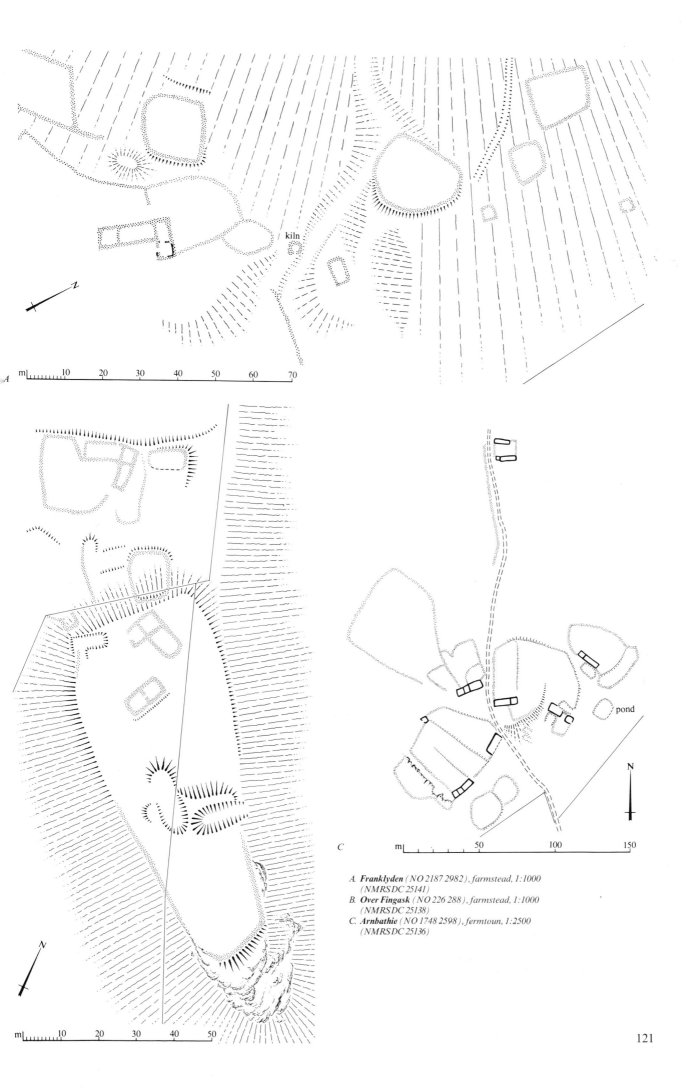

kiln

A m |⌞⌟⌞⌟⌞⌟⌞⌟⌞⌟⌞ 10   20   30   40   50   60   70

N

N

pond

N

C m | ⌞⌟⌞⌟⌞ 50   100   150

A. **Franklyden** *(NO 2187 2982), farmstead, 1:1000*
   (NMRS DC 25141)
B. **Over Fingask** *(NO 226 288), farmstead, 1:1000*
   (NMRS DC 25138)
C. **Arnbathie** *(NO 1748 2598), fermtoun, 1:2500*
   (NMRS DC 25136)

m |⌞⌟⌞⌟⌞⌟⌞⌟⌞⌟⌞ 10   20   30   40   50

121

A. **Arnbathie** (*NO 1748 2598*), *aerial view of the fermtoun and surrounding cultivation remains from the north-north-east (NMRS B 17015)*

B. **Over Fingask** (*NO 221 289*), *aerial view showing field-system and ploughed-down enclosure, with a farmstead and possible earthwork in the background (NMRS A 55965)*

Arnbathie (NO 1748 2598), deserted fermtoun and settlement (NMRS B 17010)

an earlier enclosure 40m in diameter.

The dates of the various settlement remains on the Sidlaws are unknown. Three sherds of medieval pottery were recovered from mole-casts in the course of the survey, one from near each of the sites described above, but none was associated with any structural remains. Probably of greater significance is the limited amount of documentary evidence that is available for sites like **Arnbathie**, which was known as 'Arybothy' in the middle of the fifteenth century *(Scone Liber)*. This place-name incorporates the Gaelic prefix 'airigh', implying its origin as a shieling site. Here, perhaps, is the clue to the main use of the Sidlaws in this period, and a context for some of the huts and bothies, but it should not be forgotten that the extensive areas of ridging point to at least one occasion when permanent settlement expanded out of the lowlands on to the hills.

ECCLESIASTICAL MONUMENTS

The transfer of so much of South-east Perth into the hands of the church in the twelfth century had a profound influence upon the medieval landscape. As with so many of the other medieval buildings, however, there has been a heavy toll on the churches and chapels of the district, firmly placing the emphasis of the present survey on the archaeological potential of their sites. Nevertheless, something of the wealth and prosperity of the district during this period can be gleaned from the handful of churches that survive, amongst them the imposing remains of **Dunkeld Cathedral**, and also from the architectural fragments and other carved stones that have been removed from church sites for re-use elsewhere.

The evidence is set out under four headings, examining in turn the major ecclesiastical foundations, the parish churches, the chapels, and, in a final section, furnishings and decoration.

Major religious foundations

The political importance of South-east Perth in the twelfth century, combined with the relative prosperity of the district, is almost certainly reflected in the establishment of its three leading ecclesiastical foundations, **Dunkeld Cathedral**, the Augustinian abbey of **Scone**, and the Cistercian abbey of **Coupar Angus**. Dunkeld was already by this date a long-established ecclesiastical centre, Scone a key political and royal centre, and both were appropriate locations for major ecclesiastical foundations. Coupar Angus Abbey, the only certain foundation of Malcolm IV (1153-65), was endowed with one of the four royal manors of Gowrie.

Each of the three has evident archaeological potential, but only at **Dunkeld**, whose ecclesiastical associations extend back to the mid-ninth century, if not earlier, are there substantial

124.

Dunkeld Cathedral *(NO 0237 4259), looking west along the nave (Historic Scotland A 2349-7)*

architectural remains. The see was revived in the reign of Alexander I (1107-24), but, on structural evidence, work on the existing cathedral was not begun until the thirteenth century and nothing is known of any earlier buildings on the site. The choir was completed in the fourteenth century and work extended to the nave in the early fifteenth century. Between 1450 and 1475 the west tower, the south porch and the chapter-house were all added.

The archaeological potential at Dunkeld extends beyond the immediate confines of the cathedral itself. The boundary wall which extends from the Tay on the south-east side of the cathedral incorporates a number of blocked door- and window-openings, and the foundations of eighteenth-century buildings have occasionally come to light when trenches have been dug on the south side of the cathedral. Indeed, traces of these buildings are sometimes still apparent as parched outlines in the turf. Moreover, excavation over a wider area around the cathedral might reveal the key components of a cathedral burgh, the bishop's palace, the canons' houses, and to the east, within the present town, the site of the medieval hospital of St George. Tithe barns and other agricultural structures should be added to the list, together with the service buildings that would be necessary for such a centre, and the houses of the lay population.

The town of Dunkeld was all but destroyed by fire after an attack by the Covenanting forces in 1689, and, consequently, our knowledge of the topography of the medieval burgh is principally derived from documentary sources. The bishop's palace is on record in the early fifteenth century and is described by Myln as a 'rambling structure in the highland fashion' (*Dunkeld Rentale,* 117, 315, 336). According to the author of the *New Statistical Account* (10 [Perth], 972-3) it stood to the south-west of the cathedral. It was replaced with a tower-house by Bishop Robert de Cardeny (1398-1436), who is also credited with having built a 'hall with larder and granary underneath', possibly a reference to the same building. Bishop George Brown (1483-1514) added a west wing and oratory. The tower is probably that depicted by Slezer (about 1678) to the west of the cathedral (1693, plate 24). The medieval hospital, dedicated to St George, is said to have stood at the corner of Cathedral Street and High Street and was refounded by Bishop Brown in 1506 (*Dunkeld Rentale,* 80, 82, 242, 312; Cowan & Easson 1976, 175). Accounts in the rental suggest that the building was of clay-bonded rubble masonry with a slated roof, its character perhaps little different from many contemporary domestic vernacular buildings. Although burnt down in 1689, it seems to have been rebuilt and was demolished about 1750; in 1798 it was described from memory as a group of 'low ruinous cottages' (*Stat. Acct.,* 28 [1791], 428n; *NSA,* 10 [Perth], 993). Of town-houses pre-dating the Covenanters' attack, only Deans House has survived. It is a seventeenth-century T-plan building, altered in the eighteenth century, but with an original arched fireplace in the basement.

The Augustinian priory at **Scone** was founded about 1114 by Alexander I. Its dedication to the Trinity has been taken to suggest that there may have been an earlier Culdee community on the site, but this is unverified. In 1164, the priory was elevated to the status of an abbey, and amongst its possessions was the 'Stone of Destiny', which was removed from Scone by Edward I in 1291. Both the abbey and the bishop's palace are said to have been burnt by the Reformers in 1559. What remained must have provided a ready source of quarryable building material, and the site itself was ultimately landscaped when the eighteenth-century policies of **Scone Palace** were laid out.

Whilst no structural remains of the medieval abbey can now be seen *in situ*, substantial portions of the major buildings probably survive beneath the ground. The pattern of chance

125.

126.

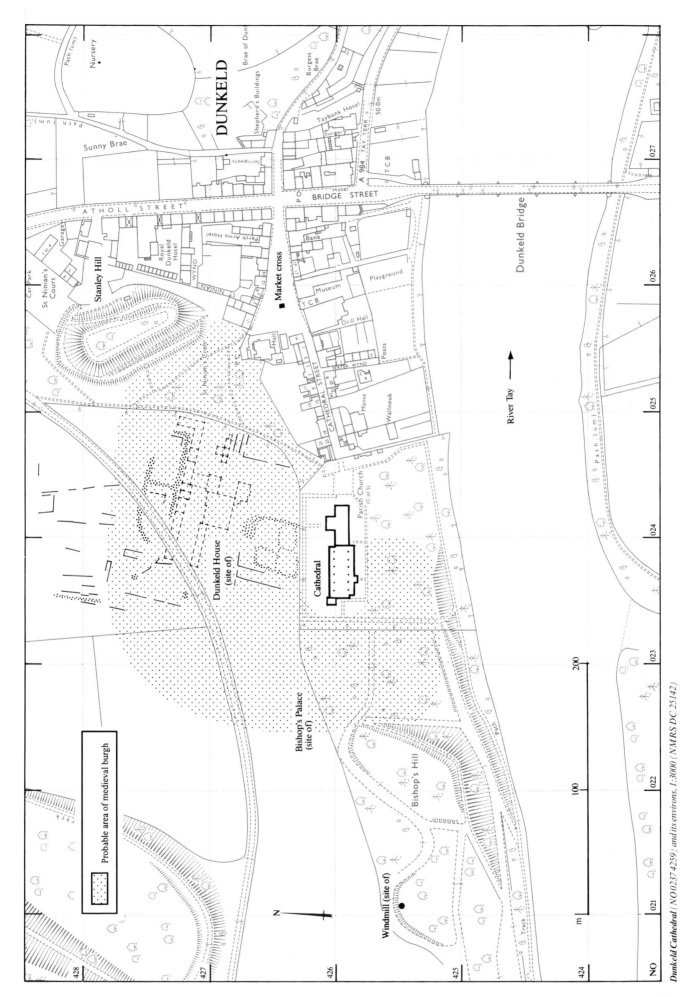

Dunkeld Cathedral (NO0237 4259, and its environs, 1:3000 (NMRS DC 25142)

125

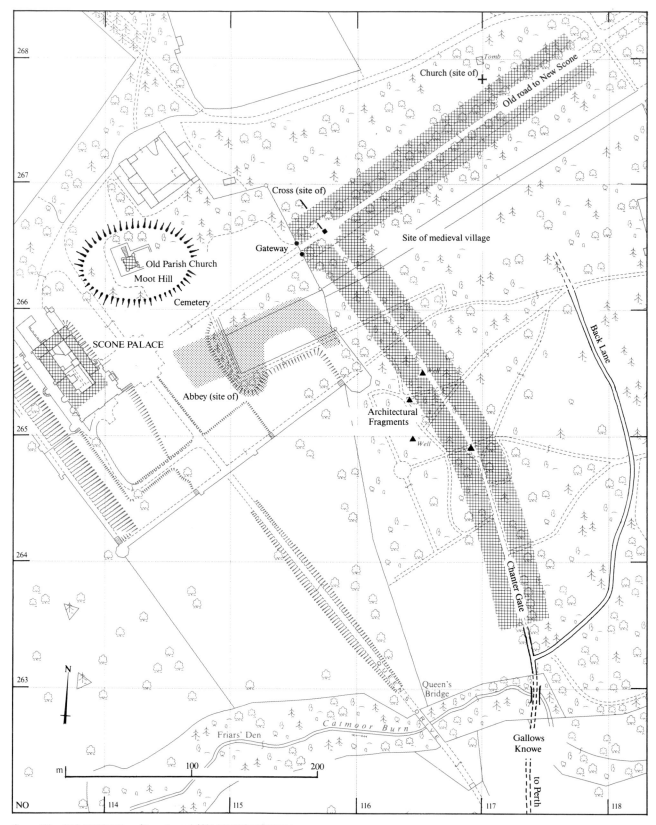

Scone Abbey (NO 1146 2654), and its environs, 1:3000 (NMRS DC 25143)

discovery recorded in the *Statistical Account,* indicates that the precincts of the abbey enclosed 4.8ha. The walls abutting the remodelled seventeenth-century gateway on the main drive were believed by Skene (1870, 70) to have been built on the foundations of those defining the abbey precinct, but there is no visible evidence to demonstrate this.

For various reasons it is believed that the original priory church stood to the south of the Moot Hill and west of the present burial-ground, and, unless the cemetery was in two places, that the monastic cemetery lay between the church and the Moot Hill (Skene 1870, 70-1). This appears to be confirmed by the author of the *Statistical Account* (18 [1796], 83, 85-6), who notes 'the vestiges of the old abbey church about 100 yards due east from the south-east corner of the house'. Furthermore, the *New Statistical Account* (10 [Perth], 1062-3) notes the discovery of a cemetery 'between the present palace and the churchyard' in about 1841-3. The cemetery comprised 'a great many stone coffins, some rough, and others in some

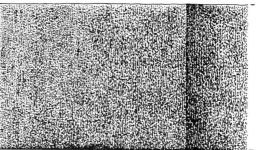

A. **Scone Abbey** (*NO 1146 2654*), *Romanesque capital, 1:15 (NMRS DC 25265)*

B. **Coupar Angus** (*NO 2233 3980*), *an engraving from the south*

C. **Coupar Angus** (*NO 2233 3980*), *abbey gateway and parish church (NMRS B 14637)*

D. **Charlestown** (*NO 2450 2761*), *fragment of tracery (NMRS B 14766)*

degree hewn, in which the skeletons were very entire', but there were also 'many skeletons without any coffin' close by. Some of the coffins appear to have had coped grave-covers. One stone sarcophagus survives, together with a large slab, which covered a stone-lined grave and bears an inscription commemorating 'Alexander Mar, Abbot'. Since 1970, other skeletal remains have been found in this area.

The topography at Scone, together with the distribution of seventeenth- and eighteenth-century gravestones, seems to support the assumption that the present burial-ground (NO 1153 2658) is the site of the abbey church. If this is the case, it is likely that the claustral ranges lay on the south side of the burial-ground, and that it was a portion of these that workmen found there in 1841, while altering the layout of a garden terrace. They uncovered 'one apartment, which seemed to be a sort of cell... was surrounded by stone seats, about 15 inches broad, and might be from 10 feet to 12 feet in dimension'; close by 'two stone coffins in good preservation' were discovered (*NSA*, 10 [Perth], 1062-3). A parish church, however, is not on record until 1624, and it is possible that part of the abbey church was retained for public worship.

Large numbers of architectural fragments are gathered together at various points within the policies, and these document building episodes from the twelfth to the sixteenth *127A.* century. They include a very fine Romanesque cubic capital,

probably from a door or window of the original priory church, a double-cap of the twelfth or thirteenth century, probably from the abbey's cloister arcade, and fragments of tracery, mullions, vaulting bosses, and arch- and rib-mouldings of thirteenth- to fourteenth-century date. Fragments of mouldings and masonry are also incorporated in the gateway and precinct walls on the north drive (NO 1115 2664), while other dressed and carved stone fragments have been identified still farther afield. Most notable of these is a substantial fragment of curvilinear tracery, part of a circlet in a major window, which was discovered about 1970 near the farmhouse at **Charlestown**, on the Carse *127D.* of Gowrie. It is probably of fifteenth-century date, and was presumably removed from the abbey, along with other building materials, some time after its destruction at the hands of the Reformers.

Although monks from Melrose were established at **Coupar Angus** before September 1162, and a full convent arrived in 1164, it was not until 1173 x 78 that William I (1165-1214) granted a half ploughgate for the site of the abbey. Whether this grant reflects *de facto* recognition of an existing situation, or that the site selected by the original community lay elsewhere, are questions not easily resolved. There would appear to have been a pre-existing parish church, since the Bishop of St Andrews surrendered his rights in it to the abbey, but its site is unknown, and may even have lain at **Bendochy**, rather than **Coupar Angus** itself. The royal manor of Coupar Angus, given to the abbey in its foundation charter, may have embraced the joint parochial area of Coupar Angus and Bendochy, and formal recognition of the two parishes perhaps only followed later.

All that remains visible of the abbey is a ruinous gateway at *127C.* the south-west corner of the modern burial-ground. The site of *128A.* the abbey church is probably occupied by the present nineteenth-century parish church, itself replacing a church built in 1681, whilst the claustral buildings stood to the south, within what is now the burial-ground. Part of the monastic cemetery was uncovered in the late eighteenth century, when 'digging at the west end of the church' revealed at least twelve stone

A. *Coupar Angus (NO 2233 3980), aerial view of the site of the abbey and its precincts from the west (NMRS PT 14934)*

coffins (*Stat. Acct.,* 17 [1796], 10-11). Later, in 1887, two more stone coffins and a possible long cist were found in the burial-ground (Hutcheson 1888, 146-8). The abbey precinct appears to have lain within a much larger enclosure, and the grass-covered remains of what was probably a substantial perimeter wall can be traced across the field to the north-east of the burial-ground for a distance of 280m. The *Statistical Account* refers to the enclosure as 'nearly a regular square of 24 acres' (17 [1796], 10-11). Maitland described it some forty years earlier as 'an equilateral quadrangle of four hundred yards, fortified with two strong ramparts and large ditches, still to be seen on the eastern and southern sides, and on part of the northern; but the western by agriculture, is demolished' (1757, 199-200). As Crawford pointed out (1949, 82-5), much of the perimeter is probably indicated by modern field- and property-boundaries, which confirm the description of its shape and show that it measured about 370m from north-east to south-west by at least that distance transversely. The possibility that the outer work had a Roman origin, discounted by Crawford, should not perhaps be altogether dismissed.

128A.

p. 86

As at Scone, surviving architectural fragments and carved stones within the present church and burial-ground can be used to document building episodes between the thirteenth and the sixteenth century. Likewise, a number of carved stones and architectural fragments from **Coupar Angus** have travelled further afield, either in the form of building materials for re-use, or simply to satisfy an antiquary's whim. Several architectural fragments of late thirteenth- and fourteenth-century date, and a seventeenth-century pediment, have been incorporated in the **Old Bridge of Dean**; a capital, a column-base and a window jamb can be found in the burial-ground of **Kettins** parish church; and there are also a number of fragments in the south wall of the steading at **Easter Bendochy**. It is just possible that the last may have been removed from **Bendochy** parish church, rather than from the abbey. They include: a zoomorphic head carved in high relief,

128B-C.

B. *Easter Bendochy (NO 2215 4198), architectural fragment (NMRS B 14651)*

C. *Easter Bendochy (NO 2215 4198), architectural fragment (NMRS B 14649)*

possibly Romanesque, but the surface is too shattered for certainty; an early thirteenth-century keel-moulding; a weathered torso also carved in high relief; and a seventeenth-century framed panel, presumably detached from an armorial bearing the royal arms. A small fragment from a decorative panel of fifteenth- or sixteenth-century date was also recovered from the rockery beside the farm cottage. The significance of the royal arms at **Coupar Angus** at this date is not clear. After the Reformation there is a tradition in churches of erecting the arms in place of the rood cross, and this is possibly what happened at Coupar Angus or in the church at **Bendochy**. A feature of the detached panel is that the Saltire is placed uppermost. This has been seen as symptomatic of the resentment felt by the people of Scotland, in having their flag

A,B. **Arthurstone**
(NO 2612 4310),
capitals
(NMRS B 14925-6)

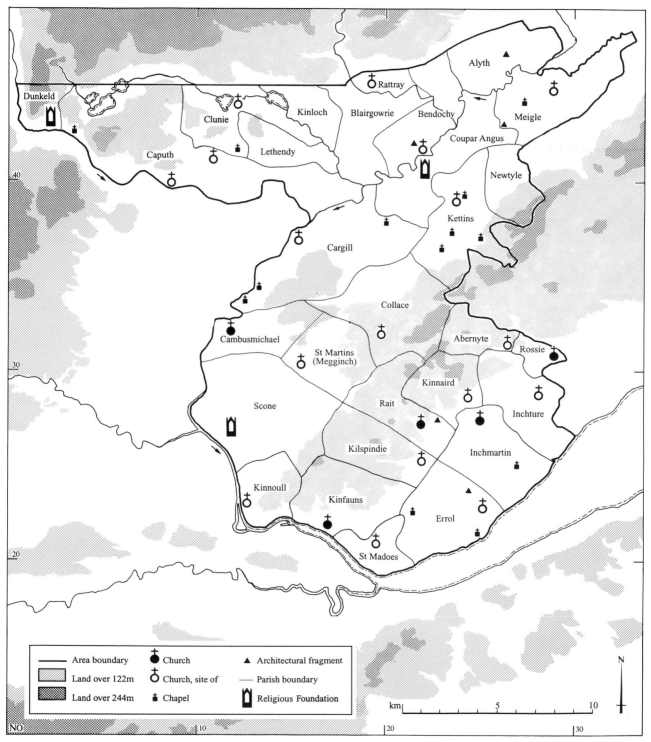

——	Area boundary	●	Church	▲ Architectural fragment
▨	Land over 122m	○	Church, site of	—— Parish boundary
▨	Land over 244m	⚑	Chapel	⌂ Religious Foundation

C. Distribution map of medieval parishes and ecclesiastical sites (NMRS DC 25146)

placed beneath the cross of St George after the Union of the Crowns. Consequently, the flags were often reversed in Scotland (Grant 1952, 140).

129A-B.
136B.
A notable collection of material derived from the abbey, including a fine funereal slab which will be discussed later, has been preserved in re-use in the walled garden and outbuildings at **Arthurstone**. A seventeenth-century lectern dovecot was removed and re-erected there in 1883, and it is likely that the rest of the material arrived at about this time too. The preserved fragments, including voussoirs, rib-sections, part of a mullion, capitals and other moulded stones of transitional and late thirteenth- or fourteenth-century date, are clearly of vital importance to an understanding of the abbey's architectural history. In addition, there are a number of late-medieval fragments, including a scalloped capital in re-use in the dovecot, a sundial-head, and a dormer pediment bearing the name COLINE CAMPBELL, together with the Campbell arms.

129C.
Parish churches
Although the evidence is slight, parochial formation in South-east Perth seems to have been a gradual process. Some of the churches which ultimately attained parochial status may well have enjoyed an independent existence before 1100, but most of the medieval churches were proprietorial, built and endowed by a lord for the use of his family and retainers. The physical juxtaposition of a church and an earth-and-timber castle provides the most visible clue to this kind of patronage in the twelfth century, and there are particularly good examples of *106.* this relationship at **Clunie**, **Cargill**, **Errol** and **Kinnaird**. *113A.* Proprietary churches were often subsequently granted to a cathedral or abbey, the appropriated revenues either being redirected for the elaboration of the mother church, or else used for the support of its dignitaries and clergy. Unfortunately, the surviving fragments of these churches are in many cases not closely datable on the basis of their architectural detail, and, since we rarely know the foundation date, first records are of little help in understanding parish formation. In the twelfth century, five parish churches are on record in South-east Perth, a further seven in the thirteenth century, one in the fourteenth century, and five in the fifteenth century, including three that were formerly chapels of Scone. In the case of **Clunie** and *132D-E.* **Collace**, however, surviving architectural fragments indicate that these churches were in existence well before their presence is confirmed by documentary evidence.

Little, however, is known of the ecclesiastical buildings of South-east Perth prior to the reign of David I (1124-53). Some level of continuity from earlier times might be inferred, with the maintenance, albeit in decay, of the probable monastic centres at places like **Meigle**, and possibly **Rossie**, their churches adapted to the requirements of a community of Culdees or other secular priests. A reference in 1153 x 59 to the *abthania* (abbey lands) of Rossie, taken together with the presence of the Pictish cross-slab found in the burial-ground *94E.* about 1890, may indicate that this was the site of an earlier *103J.* ecclesiastical foundation. **Meigle** is on record about 1178 x 87, and it is perhaps surprising that no Romanesque architectural detail was apparently found when the collection of Pictish *98-102.* sculptured stones was recovered from the ruins of the old parish church burnt down in 1869. That such fragments are absent, suggests the possibility that the church standing within the burial-ground in the twelfth century was rather earlier, and *90B.* perhaps the source of the possible eighth- or ninth-century *102H.* architectural fragments in the collection. Although at present this is no more than speculation, it serves to remind us that nothing is known of the early churches of Southern Pictland and that some may have been fairly grand and elaborate buildings. A church is reputed to have been built by Kenneth MacAlpin at **Dunkeld** in 848, but nothing is known of the materials used in its construction, or the derivation of its prototype (whether western Scottish/Irish or Northumbrian). The handsomely carved stone arch found at Forteviot (MacGibbon & Ross 1897, 623-4), possibly part of the fabric of

another early stone church in Perthshire, may serve as an instructive parallel (*cf.* Alcock 1982, 218-29). Therefore, whilst documentary evidence may provide a rudimentary chronology of the use of a church in the medieval period, the presence of a Pictish or later cross-slab, may ultimately prove a better guide to the date of its foundation.

Of the eighteen pre-Reformation parish churches that are *129C.* known to have existed in South-east Perth, only four have survived as standing buildings, and all of these are roofless shells. To a certain extent, however, the demolition of so many of the churches is offset by the survival of a fourteenth- or fifteenth-century chapel at **Stobhall**, and the presence of *131E.* medieval fabric incorporated into several of the churches that have been remodelled since the Reformation. The Stobhall chapel, which retains much of its medieval character and period detail, provides an important yardstick for the architectural features of the other churches in the area. This is particularly important in the consideration of those churches which have undergone radical alteration since the Reformation and yet retain something of their medieval core. Accordingly, the description of Stobhall is included here alongside the other churches rather than under the heading of chapels.

Of the surviving medieval churches, three, **Rait**, **Cambusmichael**, and **Kinfauns**, originated in the twelfth century as chapels of **Scone** and only attained parochial status in the fifteenth century. Each consists of a plain rectangular block, with no structural distinction drawn between nave and chancel. The least informative of the three is at **Rait**, its ivy-clad ruin measuring 20.1m by 6.1m overall. The east gable is still entire, but the rest of the walls have been reduced to a height of 2.5m. However, a higher standard of craftsmanship and structural refinement can be detected elsewhere, as at **Cambusmichael**, where the shell of the church which *112.* accompanied the monastic estate centre stands within its burial- *130A-B.* ground on a bluff overlooking the Tay. Marginally smaller than the church at Rait (15.5m by 6.4m overall), its walls incorporate numerous ashlar blocks, possibly in re-use from an earlier building on the same site, and it has evidently been remodelled more than once. The gables stand to their full height and have chamfered offsets, which coincide with projecting eaves courses, now largely vanished, on the side walls. The doorway is placed towards the west end of the south

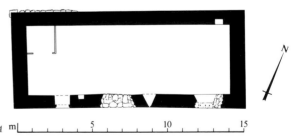

Cambusmichael (NO 1156 3258),
A. church, 1:250 (NMRS DC 25147)
B. view from the south (NMRS B 14753)

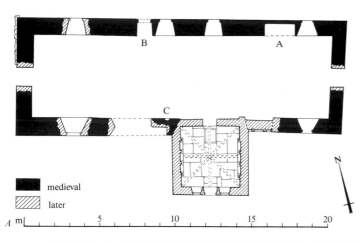

Kinfauns (NO 1666 2226),
A. church, 1:250 (NMRS DC 25151)
B. view from the south-east (NMRS C 14501)
C. Easter Sepulchre (NMRS B 14705)
D. south doorway and ogival-headed recess (NMRS B 14710)

wall. It has a semicircular head, wrought with a broad chamfer, and the lintelled doorway-embrasure incorporates a medieval grave-cover. Central to the south wall, there is a small round-headed window, with the remains of two larger window openings to either side. The church was ruinous by 1711 (*Stat. Acct.*, 13 [1794], 505)

The church at **Kinfauns**, which attained parochial status in 1419, is perhaps quite close in date to **Cambusmichael** and shares a number of its architectural features. It too has been remodelled on several occasions, but the fabric still incorporates medieval work. It measures 21.6m by 7.9m overall, and its walls, which are up to 1.2m in thickness, preserve the remains of chamfered offsets at each gable, a semicircular-headed Easter Sepulchre and a round-headed doorway in the north wall, and an ogival-headed recess midway along the south wall, immediately above the present ground-level. There are also several medieval coped grave-covers. One, bearing a floriate-headed cross and shears, stands against the west end of the south wall, and a second is in re-use in the lintelled embrasure of the north doorway; what may be a third has been cut to serve as the lintel of a square-headed window at the east end of the south wall. A roofed burial-aisle bearing the date 1598 adjoins the church on the south. It has a ribbed and groin-vaulted ceiling and cartouche panels on the east and west

131A-B

131C-D

135 I.

E. Stobhall (NO 1320 3435), chapel from the east (NMRS B 39089)

walls, one of which records that the aisle was built for John Charteris and Janet Chisholm.

The chapel at **Stobhall** is also a simple rectangular building, standing on a promontory amongst a group of medieval and later buildings. It is of fourteenth- or fifteenth-century date and was probably built for the Drummonds, who had owned Stobhall since before 1384. Although altered several times, and then restored in 1840, the chapel still retains much of its medieval character and period detail. Measuring 13.4m by 6.8m overall, it has chamfered eaves-courses and low-level offsets to the gable walls. At the south-east angle there is a zoomorphic skewput. A deeply splayed trefoil-headed window in the north wall is probably original and the fenestration on the south side, which was remodelled in the nineteenth century, may reflect an earlier scheme. In 1578, the chapel was converted for secular use and, uniquely, became the ground-floor hall attached to a tower-house. An arch-pointed doorway, reset at the entrance of a basement created beneath the west end of the chapel, is probably the original doorway. Now restored to its original function, the chapel retains a fine, but heavily repainted, ceiling of 1642, as well as its original aumbry door, stoup, and altar slab.

While the upstanding evidence suggests that many of the churches in South-east Perth were unicameral, two churches on the Carse, **Westown** and **Rossie**, appear to have been bicameral from the first, and the presence of a chancel arch at nearby Dron, City of Dundee District, almost the sole surviving

131E.
142C.

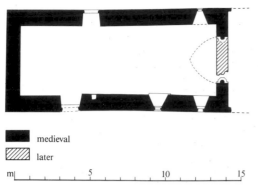

A. *Westown* (NO 2493 2746), church, 1:250 (NMRS DC 25153)

medieval

later

m 5 10 15

B. *Westown* (NO 2493 2746), church and burial-ground from the south (NMRS B 14699)

fragment of this church (MacGibbon & Ross 1897, 497-9), suggests that a bicameral layout may have been more common. The interiors of the simple rectangular buildings would also have been liturgically divided, and the length of the church at **Kinfauns** would certainly allow for the provision of a timber rood-screen. The ruins of the late-medieval church of **Inchmartin** parish stand on a ridge at **Westown** in the Carse of Gowrie. Although originally comprising a nave and chancel, the latter has been largely removed. The masonry is of snecked squared rubble, built to a course, and incorporates some re-used ashlar; put-log holes pierce the walls at regular intervals. The west gable has a chamfered offset at the height of the main wall-head, a slit window above, and a bellcot. In the north wall, there are a round-headed doorway with roll-mouldings, and a lancet window with cusped head and moulded surround. The south wall has a doorway with a chamfered arris and two square-headed windows; the windows all have glazing-grooves. The pointed chancel arch, now blocked, has simple respond capitals and a chamfered main rib. A stoup seems to have been removed from beside the south door, and joist sockets roughly central to this wall may indicate the position of the pulpit at the time of Reformed worship.

Comparison of **Rossie** old parish church with the church at **Westown**, and the detail of the chapel at **Stobhall**, suggests that the building retains a substantial medieval core. It is situated on the crest of a scarp overlooking the site of the village of **Rossie**, which was cleared in the late eighteenth century as part of the improvements to the Rossie Priory estate. The present building, which comprises a nave and chancel with an overall length of 20.5m, was apparently rebuilt on an earlier plan in about 1870 for use as a memorial chapel of the Kinnaird family. The fabric of the north and east walls, however, is

largely medieval. There is a gable-offset at the height of the main wall-head, and the north doorway, although restored, is probably original. A church at Rossie is on record by 1160 x 62.

Sadly, the majority of medieval churches in South-east Perth have either undergone more radical alteration since the seventeenth century, or have been demolished and replaced, in some cases more than once. However, surface traces within the burial-ground indicate the positions of a number of them. At **Caputh**, for example, the church site is indicated by a depression measuring 22m from east to west by 7.8m transversely, at the east end of which there is a nineteenth-century burial-vault said to incorporate the remains of the chancel. Similarly, at **Cargill,** the outline of the church can be detected, although a burial-enclosure has been built upon its east end. Whilst the medieval church at **Bendochy** has been reduced to little more than a terrace on the south side of the present church, extending from within the burial-ground into the manse garden, there are a number of dressed and moulded stones here; some of these may be medieval and are probably derived from the old parish church, whose seventeenth-century bellcot has been re-erected on the manse lawn.

Yet despite the removal of so many of the medieval churches, their accompanying burial-grounds all survive, and it is important that the archaeological potential of these sites is recognised. Indeed, two of the most important architectural fragments in south-east Perth, albeit restored or reconstructed, are to be found on sites where visible traces of the medieval church have otherwise been removed. At **Clunie** an arched doorway of late twelfth- or early thirteenth-century date has been re-used in a small detached building to the south-west of the nineteenth-century church, whilst at **Collace**, a fine

C. **Bendochy** (NO 2184 4145), bellcot from the old church (NMRS A 63076)

D. **Clunie** (NO 1095 4405), fragments of Transitional detail incorporated in an outbuilding to the south of the church (NMRS A 63064)

E. **Collace** (NO 1970 3198), processional doorway from the old church (NMRS B 14631)

processional doorway of late twelfth- or early thirteenth-century date has been incorporated into the middle of the south wall of the nineteenth-century Nairne of Dunsinane aisle. The high quality of the **Clunie** capitals is particularly noteworthy, and may even indicate the use of masons from Dunkeld.

129C. **Chapels**
Apart from **Stobhall** and the chapels which later attained parochial status, the only historically attested chapel site in South-east Perth that can be identified with any confidence is at
111B. **Campsie**, where a cluster of five ruined buildings overlooking the River Tay at Campsie Linns is all that remains of a residence of the abbots of Coupar Angus (see granges and the church lands above pp. 109-12). Several other chapels are known to have served the Coupar Angus granges, but none of these can now be located. A chapel dedicated to St Mary at **Carsegrange** is attested in the late fifteenth century, but the only possible clue to its location is a tradition of a burial-ground in the orchard to the east of the smithy (Melville 1935, 104). Similarly, the tradition that the mausoleum of the Kinlochs of Kinloch at **Chapelton** is erected on the site of a pre-Reformation chapel may indicate the location of a chapel of St Mary, on record in 1472, on the grange of **Balbrogie** (Name Book, Perth, No.54, p.9; *Coupar Angus Rental*, i, no.207). In this particular case it is possible that the chapel was not beneath
58. the mausoleum but in the field to the south, where cropmarks have revealed a rectilinear enclosure containing traces of what may be a building. However, there is nothing inherently ecclesiastical in either the building or the enclosure, and, until tested by excavation, such an interpretation must be regarded as no more than speculation.

Many early identifications are based upon the flimsiest of evidence. For example, a shallow subrectangular depression on a low rise in boggy ground to the north-west of Clunie parish church is said to be the remains of a chapel, a suggestion given credence by the recorded presence of a chapel of St Catherine at Clunie, endowed by Bishop George Brown. However, this chapel was probably situated in the tower-house on **Clunie Loch**, and the remains on the rise might equally prove to be those of an island dwelling or even a summer-house. Similar problems attend the site of St Ninian's chapel in **Dunkeld**, today commemorated by a plaque in a public square (NO 0263 4272), but which appears to have been part of the south aisle of the cathedral (Eeles 1915, 34, 38).

These cases should counsel caution in the consideration of the remaining supposed chapel sites of South-east Perth, even in the two instances where traces of a building survive. In the north-west corner of an overgrown stone-walled enclosure on the south side of Brae Street, **Dunkeld,** there are the wasted remains of a rectangular building, largely obscured by field-clearance, but measuring at least 9.6m by 5.3m overall. It is known locally as 'the Red Chapel', dedicated to St Jerome, and was ruinous by 1843 (*NSA*, 10 [Perth], 985). The remains of the second alleged chapel (see Allen 1881, 86-7), lie in a knot of trees some 180m to the south-west of **Over Kincairney** steading. Enclosed by a low stony bank, the building measures 11.8m by 5.3m over grass-grown stone wall-footings, and there is a probable entrance at the west end of the south wall. The building was trenched about 1938, but no finds were recovered.

The last of the chapel sites that must be accounted for are in the parish of **Kettins**. An early eighteenth-century description of the parish (Macfarlane 1906, 280-1) states that there were six chapels dependent upon the church of Kettins and lists their locations, but none now survives. It is difficult to know what to make of this tradition, which seems like a distant memory of a pre-twelfth-century minster, with its extensive *parochia* and large number of dependent chapels (*cf.* Stobo, Peeblesshire, Cowan & Easson 1976, 53). While this is theoretically possible, the size of the parochial area of Kettins bears no comparison with those of known examples, and the comparison strains credulity. The description, however, also stated that 'most have had inclosures about them for burying places, as appears from

the vestiges of them remaining and the bones of men that sometimes are cast up'. It may be significant that at the only one of these locations that can now be identified, the large burial-cairn at **Peattie** (Name Book, Perth, No.52, p.48), cropmarks have revealed traces of an adjacent enclosure.

Furnishings and decoration
Although period detail is to be seen within a number of the upstanding medieval churches of South-east Perth, only the chapel at **Stobhall** preserves *in situ* any evidence of its internal fittings and decoration. Myln's *Vitae,* however, give some idea of the furnishings of the high altar and side chapels in **Dunkeld Cathedral**. For example, Bishop Brown presented to the cathedral a tabernacle (probably a carved wooden canopy) for

A. **Errol** (*Perth Museum*), *effigy* (*NMRS B 39093*)
B. **Coupar Angus** (*NO 2233 3980*), *effigy* (*NMRS B 14997*)

the altar, which was imported from Flanders, a four-sided lectern of brass with figures of the four Evangelists each supporting one of the desks, a brazen figure of Moses holding a desk in his arms, and, behind it, a brass candlestick with three branches. The same bishop had 'the upper parts of the choir stalls painted and completely renewed the rood-loft, with the altars of St. Michael and St. Martin and the choir-screens: there were carved paintings of the Apostles and paintings of saints on front and back, and on the back were painted the figures of kings and nobles who were benefactors and of bishops, so that the choir might call them specifically to mind in prayer' (Myln's *Vitae,* 314). The prebendary of Menmuir, Walter Leslie, adorned the altar of St. John Baptist with silk coverings and curtains, and a 'pendant candlestick of brass', while the prebendary of Forgandenny, Walter Brown, provided the altar of St Martin with coverings and a silver gilt chalice. At the newly founded parish church of **Caputh**, Bishop Brown built

A

B

C

This page

A. **Dunkeld Cathedral** (NO 0237 4259), table-chest and effigy
believed to be of Alexander Stewart, Wolf of Badenoch
(NMRS B 39068)

B. **Coupar Angus** (NO 2233 3980), panel of weepers
(NMRS B 14998)

C. **Meigle** (NO 2873 4460), detail of the decoration on the font
(NMRS B 5907)

Opposing page

D. **Dunkeld Cathedral** (NO 0237 4259), early sixteenth-century
graveslab commemorating Alexander Douglas,
Rector of 'Munidi' (Moneydie) (NMRS B 1389)

E. **Bendochy** (NO 2184 4145), graveslab of Nicholas Campbell,
originally from Coupar Angus (NMRS A 63073)

F. **Bendochy** (NO 2184 4145), graveslab of John Cumming
(NMRS A 63074)

G. **Tower of Lethendy** (NO 1405 4170), graveslab
(NMRS PT 2383)

H. **Inchture** (NO 2812 2878), graveslab (NMRS B 14972)

I. **Kinfauns** (NO 1666 2226), graveslab (NMRS B 14970)

D

E

F

G

H

I

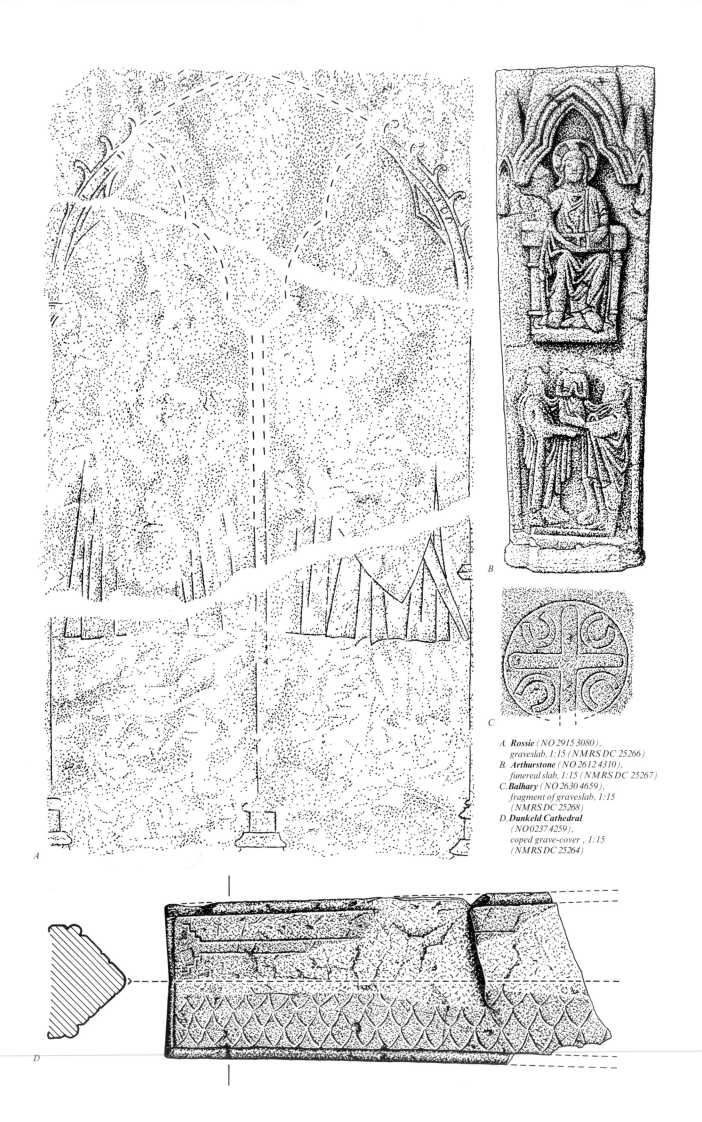

A. **Rossie** (*NO 2915 3080*),
   graveslab, 1:15 (NMRS DC 25266)
B. **Arthurstone** (*NO 2612 4310*),
   funereal slab, 1:15 (NMRS DC 25267)
C. **Balhary** (*NO 2630 4659*),
   *fragment of graveslab, 1:15
   (NMRS DC 25268)*
D. **Dunkeld Cathedral**
   (*NO 0237 4259*),
   *coped grave-cover , 1:15
   (NMRS DC 25264)*

A

B

C

D

A. *Stormont Mausoleum, Scone (NO 1145 2665), funerary monument to David, 1st Viscount of Scone (died 1631) (NMRS B 85834)*

and adorned the choir at his own expense; there was glass in the windows and a painted reredos.

To see such survivals today, it is necessary to turn to churches like Fowlis Easter in City of Dundee District, where part of an original timber rood-screen survives, along with an elaborate sacrament house and some painted decoration. Nevertheless, there are occasional survivals within South-east Perth which serve to show the quality of the detail that has been lost. At **Dunkeld** itself, for example, it is possible to detect the positions of some of the screens which enclosed the altars. There is a fourteenth-century effigy of Bishop William Sinclair, the tomb of Bishop Cardeny (died 1436) with its fine architectural canopy, and the tomb-chest and highly polished

134A. effigy believed to be that of the Earl of Buchan, 'the Wolf of Badenoch' (died 1406). Comparable in date is an effigy of a

133A. knight from **Errol**, now in Perth Museum, and another from

33B. 134B. **Coupar Angus**, where there is also the side panel of a tomb-chest with weepers, comprising two knights, a man-at-arms, two figures in civilian dress, and a sixth figure bearing an axe (Caldwell 1988, 57), by any standards exceptional representations of figure and costume. The incised graveslab of Abbot John Shanwell (died 1506) is also to be found in the church at Coupar Angus, but the most remarkable piece from this site is to be found amongst the collection in the annexe to

136B. the walled garden at **Arthurstone**. Here, a tapered slab, now set in a mural recess, bears in high relief the figure of Christ in Majesty below a richly moulded and pinnacled trefoil-headed canopy. Below are two robed figures, standing, and holding aloft a soul in prayer. The slab is probably funereal, evidently for a person of distinction, and may be of late thirteenth- or fourteenth-century date.

In **Bendochy** church, there is a beautifully ornamented sacrament house bearing the initials VT, probably William Turnbull, Abbot of Coupar Angus (1507-1523/4), whilst in the floor of the chancel in **Rossie** old parish church, now the *136A.* Kinnaird family mausoleum, there is a slab of Tournai marble bearing a framed depiction of a knight and a lady and dating from about 1260. The slab is possibly the product of a workshop in southern England, and aptly conveys the resources available to the wealthier patrons. A number of fonts also survive in the area, the most elaborate being that in the church at **Meigle**, which is octagonal, each face carved in false relief *134C.* with a symbol of the Passion. However, the octagonal font at **Stobhall**, ornamented with a plain band of interlace and what may be a defaced sheela-na-gig (an erotic female figure), was brought from Perth by the present Earl of Perth.

Finally, medieval graveslabs are to be found in many of the district's burial-grounds, whether set up within the ruins of the old parish church or incorporated into the fabric of the church, or buildings close by. These include the two slabs noted at **Cambusmichael** and **Kinfauns**, and others at **Inchture**, *134 I.* **Collace** and **Errol**. The **Inchture** slab is coped, bearing a disc-*135H.* headed cross on the upper face, with a sword on one side and an incomplete inscription beginning *hic iacit* in Lombardic capitals, whilst in the cathedral at **Dunkeld** there is what is *136D.* probably a thirteenth-century coped grave-cover, tegulated on one face, and displaying the remains of the lower part of a long-shafted Calvary cross on the other. Graveslabs removed from **Coupar Angus Abbey** and now set in the south wall of **Bendochy** church, include those of Nicholas Campbell of *135E.* Keithick (died 1587), Leonard Leslie, Commendator of Coupar (1565-1605), and John Cumming of Couttie (died 1606), whose *135F.* monumental graveslab bears the effigy of a knight in armour, an archaic but fitting testimony to a long-established sculptural tradition.

A particularly handsome slab, bearing a floriate-headed cross, is in use as a lintel in the dovecot at **Kinnaird**, some 200m to the north-north-west of the parish church. Also serving as a lintel, above the staircase in **Lethendy** tower-house, there *135G.* is a graveslab, probably of early sixteenth-century date, which bears the incised outline of a figure in civil dress (of which only part is visible) and the letters '..NBUL..'; this is conceivably the tombstone of Dean William Turnbull, who is on record in 1503. Finally, what is probably a fragment detached from a medieval graveslab of unknown provenance is set in a framed panel over the north door to the walled garden at **Balhary**. It *136C.* bears the incised outline of a Greek cross within a circle, with a penannular ring or horseshoe between each arm.

Exceptionally fine examples of post-Reformation tombs are to be found at **Kinnoull** and **Scone**. In the north aisle in **Kinnoull** churchyard is the tomb of the 1st Earl of Kinnoull, Lord Chancellor Hay (died 1634), which incorporates a standing effigy of the earl and combines spirited carving with Jacobean detail, whilst in the mausoleum at **Scone** is that of *137A.* David, 1st Viscount Stormont, which was probably imported from London. Elsewhere in South-east Perth, many of the burial-grounds preserve collections of seventeenth- and eighteenth-century headstones (see Willsher 1987).

B. *Cargill (NO 1501 3699), panel from a post-Reformation table-tomb (NMRS B 14719)*

137

FORTIFIED AND DOMESTIC ARCHITECTURE

The tower-house, which typified castellated architecture in Scotland from the later fourteenth to the seventeenth centuries, was undoubtedly built with security in mind, but its other functions were equally important. It was a lord's dwelling, adaptable in size and ostentation to individual status and wealth, and, in its capacity as an estate centre, was an important symbolic and working component of the medieval landscape. Indeed, it is essential to consider them alongside the churches, chapels, mottes, moats, granges, fermtouns and farmsteads.

The evolution of tower-house architecture reflects changing social and political conditions throughout Scotland, and improving domestic standards. The first part of this section traces the general themes of tower-house development through the handful of surviving examples in South-east Perth, from the massive and severe solidity of **Balthayock**, to buildings like **Megginch**, which are better described as fortified houses rather than towers, and ultimately into laird's houses such as **Old Mains of Rattray**. The second part summarises the evidence that shows where other towers and houses once stood.

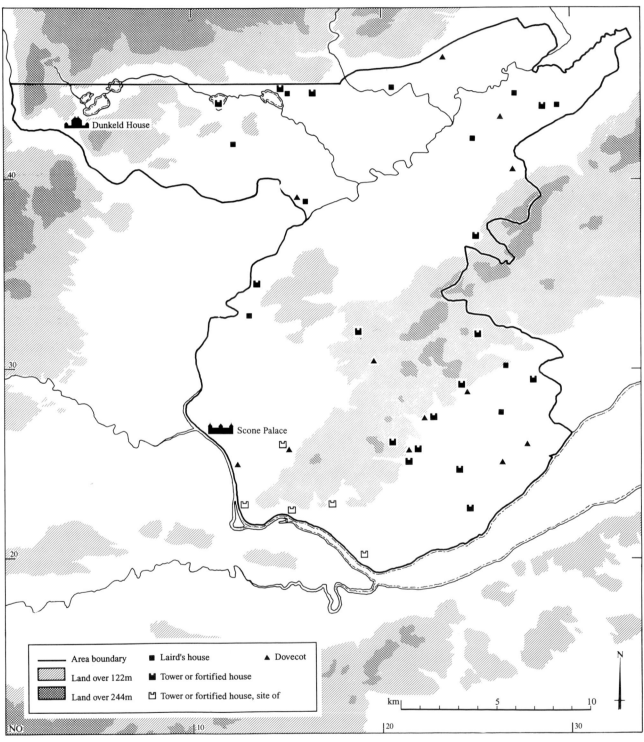

Distribution map of fortified and domestic architecture dating from before 1700 (NMRS DC 25156)

A

C

D

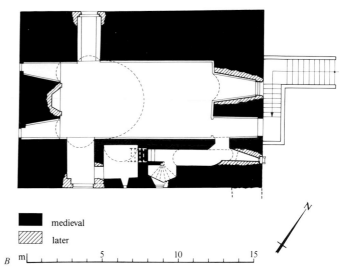

B

■ medieval

▨ later

m |⎿_____5_____10_____15⎤

Balthayock (NO 1741 2295),
A. a view from the north-east (NMRS B 14614)
B. first-floor plan, 1:250 (NMRS DC 25158)
C. a pencil sketch from the north-east, with white ink shading, dating from 1850
  (Perth and Kinross District Library)
D. a view from the north, engraved in about 1840 (NMRS B 7700)

dwelling to the west; in each illustration the tower appears as it was before restoration. The buildings ancillary to the tower were demolished about 1870, when the policies were laid out around the present house (now derelict). While Balthayock survives as a free-standing structure, the tower at **Belmont Castle**, which is probably of fifteenth century date, is now immured in a sprawling mansion. It, too, has at least three storeys, and although much altered, both the ground- and first-floor vaults remain, together with a number of mural chambers and a turnpike stair between first and second floors. External detail is hidden by harling, but a circular loop, possibly not an original feature, lighting a first-floor chamber is visible in the north wall.

Various changes were taking place in the architecture of towers in the late fifteenth and early sixteenth century. The earlier solidly-walled structures, albeit with their walls punctuated with mural chambers, gave way to less austere buildings with narrower, and often loftier elevations. Communication between floors was rationalized, sometimes by the provision of an integral stair-wing; loop-holes were applied more sparingly and windows used in increasing numbers; continuous parapet walks and machicolations were used more sparingly, and corbelled rounds, or bartizans, appeared at the wall-head, often in company with a cap-house, a simple box-machicolation sufficing for the entrance. These changing architectural fashions can be detected in three of the tower-houses of South-east Perth, **Kinnaird**, **Pitcur** and **Loch of Clunie**.

Of these, only **Kinnaird Castle** is still occupied, standing on a prominent rock outcrop which overlooks the Carse from the Braes of Gowrie. Its main block stands four storeys and a garret high, and to the east there is a gabled block containing a ground-floor kitchen. An entrance at first-floor level may have given access to the wall-walk of a barmkin which enclosed the west side of the tower. A mid-nineteenth century sketch (NMRS, PT/13931), made prior to the restoration, shows the tower with a corbel-course and machicolation at the main wall-head, but does not show the garret. The ruined tower-house at **Pitcur** is of L-plan type, but was later remodelled with the addition of a semicircular stair-turret in the re-entrant angle. The main block is vaulted at both the ground- and first-floor level, and surviving details include a series of keyhole loops (later blocked) in the basement, as well as the moulded jambs and tusking for a canopied fireplace on the first floor; the fireplace is flanked by two high-level windows, a feature

140A.

140B.

138. **The surviving towers and houses**

The earliest stage in the development of tower-house architecture is represented in South-east Perth by only two examples, namely **Belmont Castle** and **Balthayock**, the latter

139A-B. being a particularly fine example of an early tower. Dating from the late fourteenth or early fifteenth century, it is rectangular on plan with walls over 3m thick, and three storeys in height, and the open parapet was carried on continuous corbelling. The vaulted ground and first floors were linked by a straight mural stair in the south-east wall, while a turnpike stair gave access to the top floor and wall-walk. The entrance, which is now approached by a nineteenth-century forestair, is at first-floor level, and tusking at the eastern angle of the block

139C. indicates the former presence of a barmkin. A drawing of about 1850 depicts an L-plan range of late seventeenth- or early eighteenth-century date to the north-east of the tower, and an

139D. engraving of about the same date shows a single-storeyed

A. **Kinnaird Castle** *(NO 2412 2889), from the south-west*
   (NMRS B 39103)
B. **Pitcur Castle** *(NO 2515 3699), from the north-east*
   (NMRS B 14946)

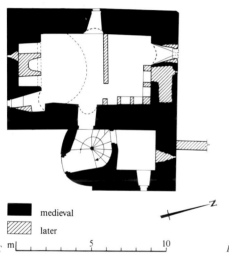

medieval

later

Loch of Clunie *(NO 1132 4402),*
C. ground-floor plan, 1:250 (NMRS DC 25161)
D. from the south-east in the early twentieth century (NMRS Lindsay Collection PT 3946)
E. rom the south (NMRS B 39044)
F. ground-floor vault and kitchen fireplace (NMRS B 39042)
G. aerial view from the south (NMRS A 65054)

A. **Ardblair** (*NO 1636 4453*),
   from the south-east
   (*NMRS A 62968*)
B. **Ardblair** (*NO 1636 4453*),
   entrance and panel
   (*NMRS A 62969*)
C. **Lethendy** (*NO 1405 4170*),
   from the south
   (*NMRS A 62949*)

reminiscent of **Balthayock**. The kitchen was in the ground-floor of the wing.

140C-G.   The third member of this group stands on a small island in the **Loch of Clunie**, and it is almost the sole surviving example of ecclesiastical estate architecture in South-east Perth. Built for the bishops of Dunkeld, a remarkable record of its construction is preserved in the Granitar's and Avenar's accounts of the *Dunkeld Rentale*. In the time of Bishop Thomas Lawder (1452-76), the island and the old castle on the western shore of Clunie Loch appear to have been a refuge of robbers (Myln's *Vitae*), but they seem to have been evicted, and by 1506 the ground-floor vault of the tower was in place. Although much of the material for the earliest phase of construction was derived from the old castle, the accounts for the period 1502-12 show that materials were being drawn from much farther afield, including stone and lime from across the Tay, and timber from the Wood of Stobhall. A granary seems to have been built immediately to the east of the tower, an arrangement reminiscent of the Bishop's palace at Dunkeld, and the accounts include references to the construction of an outshot on the western side of the tower in 1512 and a new pier in 1512-13. By 1507, provision had been made for a chapel, which was dedicated to St Catherine and is said to have stood on the north side of the tower, an area where human bones were found in the late eighteenth century. However, a more likely location for this chapel is provided by a chamber with independent access adjoining the first-floor hall, an arrangement paralleled in the

mid- to late-fifteenth-century tower at Affleck, in Angus.

The ruins of the tower show that it was an L-plan, with a   140C.
main block of three storeys and a wing of five. The entrance, protected by a high-level machicolation, is in the re-entrant angle and opens on to a newel stair. The vaulted ground floor of the main block was originally lit by a series of slit-windows and was furnished with a large kitchen fireplace. A straight   140F.
mural stair in its north wall, now blocked, seems to have provided independent access to both the first-floor hall and the chamber identified above as the chapel in the wing. In the mid to late sixteenth century the building was remodelled; additional fireplaces were introduced, and pedimented half-dormers were added to the west front. Subsequent alterations in the eighteenth and nineteenth centuries included extensive renovations to the upper side-walls of the main block, the blocking of the mural stair, provision of large first-floor windows, subdivision of the vaulted basement, and remodelling of the fireplaces; a single-storeyed kitchen range was added on the north side of the tower. A survey of the submerged portion of the island, undertaken by Dr Nicholas Dixon in 1990, indicates that it is probably artificial, and has been enhanced and extended on more than one occasion. The edge of the island is enclosed by the remains of a low rubble wall and on the south there is a small well-constructed quay (Dixon and Andrian 1991).

Amongst the tower-houses built after the Reformation, there are several which display a common development on plan, although the tower at **Stobhall** is unique in South-east Perth. **Lethendy**, which is incorporated into the rear of a nineteenth-   141C.
century house, and **Ardblair**, are both conventional L-plans, while **Evelick** and **Fingask** are both stepped L-plans, with a stair-turret extruded between the main block and the wing. **Ardblair** tower, which is probably of late sixteenth- or early   !41A.
seventeenth-century date, occupies the north-west angle of a courtyard, with seventeenth-century and later ranges on three sides, and a screen wall on the north, the latter incorporating an arched gateway surmounted by a pediment dated 1688. Although remodelled, the tower retains some original detail, including a fine pedimented Renaissance doorway and armorial   141B.
niche in the re-entrant angle.

The lands of **Evelick** had been the property of the Lindsays   142A.
since at least 1497, but the ruined tower-house that stands beside the farm is of late sixteenth-century date. The entrance and stair are in a semicircular tower in the south-east re-entrant angle, and, in common with **Balthayock** and **Ardblair**, a need for additional accommodation later in the seventeenth century was met by a two-storey ancillary range, whose position is indicated by tusking and openings in the tower's east gable.

A. **Evelick Castle** *(NO 2039 2595), from the south-east (NMRS B 14653)*

B. **Fingask Castle** *(NO 2280 2745), from the south (NMRS B 14773)*

C. **Stobhall** *(NO 1320 3435), tower-house and chapel from the north-west (NMRS B 39090)*

promontory overlooking the Tay in 1578. The site had been the family seat until about 1487, and the presence of an earlier building, a medieval chapel, appears to have exercised a profound influence on the design of the tower. In place of the standard plan, with basement, first-floor hall and apartments above, the entire chapel was converted into a ground-floor hall, and a basement was dug out beneath its west end; a three-storey accommodation tower was added on the north-west. In the late sixteenth or early seventeenth century a single-storey laundry range, with a brewhouse and a bakehouse in the basement

131E.

D. **Moncur Castle** *(NO 2835 2952), from the west (NMRS B 39085)*

E. **Megginch Castle** *(NO 2418 2460), from the west (NMRS B 14960)*

beneath, was added to the north of the tower, and in the late seventeenth century a two-storey dower-house was built across the neck of the promontory. Formal policies are depicted at Stobhall by Archer about 1685.

143A.

The need to increase the accommodation offered by a tower-house, brought further architectural developments in the late sixteenth and early seventeenth century, leading to the emergence of buildings which are best described as fortified houses. **Megginch Castle**, which is still occupied, and **Moncur**, now no more than a ruined shell, are notable examples. **Megginch Castle**, dating from the late sixteenth century, is a Z-plan building, which has been enlarged and remodelled several times. The main block has a kitchen and two vaulted cellars on the ground floor, with a hall and chamber on the floor above. A wing containing a scale-and-platt stair is stepped out from the south-west angle of the block and the entrance is set in the south-east re-entrant angle. On the north side of the block there is a semicircular tower, which incorporates a newel service-stair and is corbelled square at the wall-head to accommodate a caphouse.

142D.
144C.
142E.

The break with the tower-house tradition, which is heralded by the two-storey ancillary ranges at **Ardblair**, **Evelick** and **Balthayock**, and the dower-house at **Stobhall**, is finally made manifest with houses like **Old Mains of Rattray**. This two-

143B.

142B. **Fingask**, which is still occupied, dates from 1594, but was converted to a T-plan in 1674, and further enlarged and remodelled in the eighteenth and nineteenth centuries. For all this, it retains much of its original character and period detail, and is a fine example of its type.

142C. The tower at **Stobhall** was built for the Drummonds on a

A. **Stobhall** (*NO 1320 3435*), *the dower-house from the west* (*NMRS B 39092*)

B. **Old Mains of Rattray** (*NO 2065 4525*), *from the south-east* (*NMRS A 78130*)

C. **Old Mains of Rattray** (*NO 2065 4525*), *south-east skewput* (*NMRS B 14937*)

storey house is of late seventeenth-century date, but was remodelled and extended in 1720 and about 1800, and was roofless at the time of the survey. It is rectangular on plan, with a symmetrical five-bay frontage, and the weathered lintel over the entrance bears the name and arms of David Chrichton, together with the date 1694. Other details include cavetto-moulded skews carved with human heads, and an original ground-floor fireplace. The roll-moulded surrounds of the attic windows may be contemporary with the house, but it is as likely that they have been re-used from an earlier building. A keyhole gunloop has been incorporated into the kitchen outshot of 1720, and a second can be seen in an outbuilding some 30m to the west.

143C.

Another house of this date survives at **Marlee**, but other examples in South-east Perth are few. Indeed, they seem to have survived less successfully than the towers and have largely been removed, or hidden within later buildings.

'Lost' towers and houses

Despite the heavy toll of demolition, there are often sufficient clues available to allow the former presence of a tower or house

to be detected, although not always its precise location. Re-used carved stones and architectural fragments can often be found in later buildings nearby, while others were simply discarded, awaiting discovery in some rockery or heap of field-clearance. Surviving dovecots provide another clue and, in some instances, evidence of the policies has been recovered by aerial photography; in one particular case the ground plan of a vanished house has been recorded as a cropmark.

On the ground, it is the discovery of architectural fragments that provides the major source of evidence. At **Kilspindie**, for instance, where a tower-house is believed to have stood on or close to the nineteenth-century farmhouse, a late seventeenth-century lectern dovecot stands in the field to the north-west of the steading. A dormer pediment, bearing an armorial and the initials WL/MB, has also been incorporated into the steading, and a moulded slab has been re-used as a lintel over the tail-race of the mill. Other fragments, including parts of two armorials, are incorporated into an outbuilding adjoining the manse, whilst stones in the fabric of the church, although not necessarily from the tower itself, point to at least one building of late sixteenth- or seventeenth-century date in the vicinity. The dovecot itself incorporates a fragment of medieval tracery

145B.

D. **Gourdie House** (*NO 1210 4195*), *architectural fragment* (*NMRS B 14657*)

E. **Pitroddie** (*NO 2148 2521*), *inscribed lintel* (*NMRS B 14736*)

above the rat-ledge in the south wall. Fieldwork elsewhere in the area has revealed fragments belonging to towers or houses that once stood at **Pitkindie**, **Pitroddie**, **Mains of Rattray**, **Inchmartin**, **Keillor**, **Kinloch**, **Newbigging**, **Viewbank**, **Gourdie**, **Fullarton** and **Baledgarno**.

143E.

143D.

The last is a particularly interesting example of this type of survey work. An early castle in the vicinity is attributed by Boece to King Edgar (1094-1107), and, on the same authority, said to have been repaired in the reign of Alexander I (1107-1124). In the nineteenth century, 'foundations and pavements' were discovered on the site of the steading, whilst Melville (1939, 85) notes that 'many years ago an Errol mason… when building a huge wash tank or cesspool in an adjoining field about 20 yards (18.29m) to the south of the dovecot at the farm buildings, came upon extensive foundations which undoubtedly bore the character of an extensive keep'. Whilst the possibility of an early castle cannot be completely dismissed, the carved stones incorporated in the court of offices and steading at Castlehill, which include a bull-nosed moulding, two stones with rounded upstands, two chamfered rybats and a lintel, a datestone of 1658 and a framed panel bearing the depiction of a cow, are more likely to derive from an unidentified laird's dwelling, possibly a tower-house, of sixteenth- or seventeenth-century date.

In some cases, on the other hand, fieldwork recovers

A. **Scone Palace** *(NO 1135 2655), from the north, engraved by A Rutherford in 1775 (NMRS B 10588)*

B. **Scone Palace** *(NO 1135 2655), remodelled sixteenth-century gateway from the east-north-east (NMRS PT 3908)*

C. **Moncur Castle** *(NO 2835 2952), the surrounding cropmarks from the north-east (NMRS PT 14385)*

144A-B.

fragments from houses whose existence is already well-known from documentary sources. The present palace at **Scone**, which was built between 1803 and 1812, is the latest in a series of houses on this site. Work is known to have started on a house here in 1581, when Scone was erected a temporal lordship for William, Lord Ruthven, but this building was superseded in the seventeenth century by a house built for David Murray, Lord Scone. A survey by Andrew Cock (1798) shows it divided into two courts, and it is usually assumed that the northern court incorporated most of the work of about 1581. Little of the fabric from either period of construction can be identified in the walls of the present palace, but a seventeenth-century dormer pediment is incorporated in the Stormont mausoleum, what may be another lies at the foot of the mercat cross, and other architectural fragments probably from the house can be found in stone-heaps at various points in the grounds.

142D.
144C.

Our knowledge of these lost or dramatically altered buildings in South-east Perth has been considerably enhanced by aerial photography. At **Moncur**, for instance, which was abandoned after a fire in the early eighteenth century, cropmarks have revealed traces of a ditched enclosure surrounding the castle, and also what are presumably fragments of the policies. In contrast, the house at **Fullarton** does not

D. *John Slezer's 'Prospect of the Town of Dunkeld' (Theatrum Scotiae 1693) (NMRS B 41586)*

survive, but aerial photography has recorded the cropmarks of a network of ditches which almost certainly belong to the policies. Trial excavation has recovered sherds of seventeenth-century pottery from some of them (Strong 1987). A house with policies is depicted here by Roy (1747-55, sheet 18/3), but these had been removed prior to 1867. However, a number of dressed and moulded stones are incorporated into **South West Fullarton** steading. These include chamfered window rybats, and a pediment bearing a shield and the initials of Dame Margaret Erskine, widow of Sir William Fullarton of Ardo, who is mentioned in a bond of 1620. Three other pediments removed from the steading are incorporated in the walls of a house in **Meigle**: one bears the inscription YIS.HOVS.IS.BVLDS B[ ] ELESOBETH. BETOVN L.FVLLERTOVN and the initials EB WF, which should probably be identified as Elisabeth, daughter of Robert Bethune of Balfour, who married David Lindsay in 1609, and died in 1666 (Paul 1908, 405; Jervise 1882, 405); the second bears the quartered arms of Balfour and Beaton; and the third pediment the arms of Fullarton of that ilk and the initials WF, probably signifying William Fullerton, who married, on or before 1648, Margaret, eldest daughter of Elizabeth and David Lindsay (Paul 1911, 108-9).

A similar coincidence of cropmarks, architectural fragments and a missing house occurs at **Gourdie**, but here the aerial photographs suggest the presence of what may be a more substantial rectangular ditched enclosure, and possibly the foundations of a building too. A house and policies are again depicted by Roy (1747-55, sheet 17/3), and a dormer pediment and a lintel, bearing 1661 GN MK, and 1674 DK (David Kinloch) respectively, have been built into the wing of the eighteenth-century house at Gourdie.

Perhaps the most remarkable instance of cropmark evidence concerns **Dunkeld House**, the former seat of the Dukes of Atholl. The first house was destroyed by Commonwealth troops in 1653, but was remodelled, or possibly rebuilt, about 1679. The latter is the house depicted by Slezer (1693, plate 24) and by Stobie (1783), and shown, with its offices, outbuildings and policies, on a plan made after 1821 (Atholl Muniments, D3.34). Cropmarks have not only confirmed the location of the house to the north of the cathedral, but have also revealed the foundations of 'Dunkeld New Palace', which was begun in the 1820s, some 400m to the west, but demolished incomplete, on the death of the fourth Duke of Atholl.

While dovecots, architectural fragments and cropmarks may be used in this way to identify the site of a house or its policies, it should not be forgotten that dovecots are often fine and elegant structures in their own right. The fashion for such structures originates in medieval times, when landowners set up deer parks, rabbit warrens and dovecots, to ensure a fresh supply of meat over the winter months. By the sixteenth century, if not earlier, dovecots were being constructed in stone, beehive types being popular in Fife and the lectern type in Angus, Kinross and Perthshire (Walker and Ritchie 1987, 22).

With one exception, all the surviving dovecots of South-east Perth are of lectern type, invariably of random-rubble build and sometimes harled. Rat-ledges extend along the fronts and are stepped up at the sides. Flight-holes are occasionally paired, but more often these are arranged in a continuous string-course, either directly above the rat-ledge or breaking forward from the roofline. Most have a single compartment, with stone nesting-boxes lining all the available wall-space, but there are examples with two, each with a low-level doorway in the front or side. The rear walls rise above the pitch of the roofline and are generally capped with a simple coping, but that at **Polcalk** is crenellated, while **Newbigging** (1733) and **Waterybutts** are stepped and finialled. The Waterybutts dovecot is also notable for its original iron-framed doors and iron yetts.

The one exception to these lectern-type dovecots is that which stood on the motte at **Meikleour**, but it is not possible to say whether this was a sixteenth-century beehive type, or a later

143D.

144D.

145C.
146A-B.

A. **Kinnaird** (*NO 2412 2889*), *dovecot from the west-south-west* (*NMRS B 39106*)

B. **Kilspindie** (*NO 2190 2577*), *interior of the dovecot* (*NMRS B 14662*)

C. **Polcalk** (*NO 2326 4638*), *dovecot from the west* (*NMRS B 63049*)

A

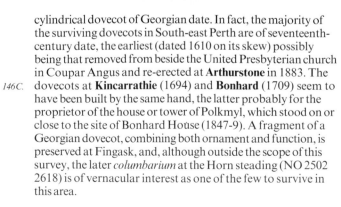

B

C

A. *Waterybutts* (*NO 2766 2592*), *dovecot from the south* (*NMRS B 14941*)
B. *Newbigging* (*NO 2645 2518*), *dovecot from the south-west*
(*NMRS B 14686*)
C. *Bonhard* (*NO 1484 2573*), *dovecot from the south-west* (*NMRS B 14955*)

146C. cylindrical dovecot of Georgian date. In fact, the majority of the surviving dovecots in South-east Perth are of seventeenth-century date, the earliest (dated 1610 on its skew) possibly being that removed from beside the United Presbyterian church in Coupar Angus and re-erected at **Arthurstone** in 1883. The dovecots at **Kincarrathie** (1694) and **Bonhard** (1709) seem to have been built by the same hand, the latter probably for the proprietor of the house or tower of Polkmyl, which stood on or close to the site of Bonhard House (1847-9). A fragment of a Georgian dovecot, combining both ornament and function, is preserved at Fingask, and, although outside the scope of this survey, the later *columbarium* at the Horn steading (NO 2502 2618) is of vernacular interest as one of the few to survive in this area.

146

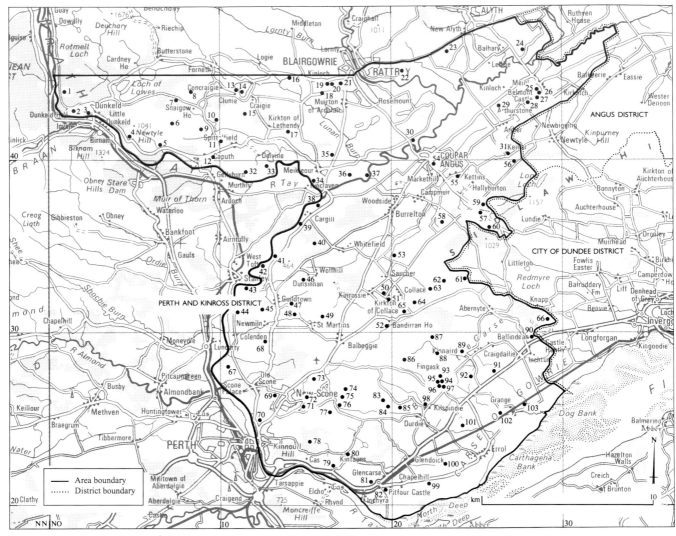

Principal upstanding monuments in South-east Perth

1   King's Seat, Dunkeld, fort
2   Dunkeld House, standing stone
3   Dunkeld Cathedral and Early Christian stones
4   Newtyle, stone pair
5   Kemp's Hold, Stenton, fort
6   East Cult, stone alignment and cup-markings
7   Ninewells, cairn
8   Over Kincairney, cup-markings and chapel
9   Mains of Fordie, cairn
10   Cairn Muir, Caputh, cairn
11   Glendelvine House, barrow and cairn
12   Caputh, cairn
13   Clunie, church, burial-ground and castle
14   Loch of Clunie, tower-house
15   Steed Stalls, Roman temporary camp
16   Kinloch, cairn
17   Tower of Lethendy, tower-house and
      cross-slab
18   Leys of Marlee, stone circle
19   Ardblair Castle, tower-house
20   Ardblair, enclosure
21   Fir Hillock, cairn
22   Old Mains of Rattray, house
23   Polcalk, dovecot
24   Hallyards, moated site
25   Meigle Museum, Pictish and Early Christian
      stones
26   Belliduff, Belmont Castle, cairn
27   Belmont Castle, standing stone
28   Macbeth's Stone, Belmont, standing stone and
      cup-markings
29   Arthurstone, dovecot
30   Knowehead, cairn
31   Keillor, tower-house and dovecot
32   Inchtuthil, fort
33   Inchtuthil, Roman legionary fortress,
      compounds, temporary camps, linear
      earthworks and barrows

34   Meikleour, motte
35   Cleaven Dyke, cursus
36   Black Hill, Meikleour, Roman watch-tower
37   Hallhole, square barrow
38   Cargill, Castle Hill, ringwork
39   Balholmie, cup-and-ring markings and Pictish
      symbol stone
40   Newbigging, cup-and-ring markings
41   Stobhall, tower-house and chapel
42   Campsie, chapel and abbot's house
43   Cambusmichael, church and burial-ground
44   Colen, stone circle and cup-markings
45   Druids' Seat Wood, stone circle
46   Loanhead, stone pair
47   Blackfaulds, stone circle
48   Tammieteeth, cairn
49   Brownies Knowe, stone circle and
      cup-markings
50   Kirkton of Collace, cairn
51   Collace, old parish church and burial-ground
52   Bandirran, dovecot
53   Macbeth's Law, Lawton, barrow
54   Coupar Angus, abbey
55   Kettins, cross-slab
56   Keillor, cairn and Pictish symbol stone
57   Pitcur Castle, tower-house
58   Peattie, cairn
59   Pitcur, souterrain and cup-and-ring markings
60   Hill of Dores, fort
61   Kilwhannie Den, Glenbran, ring-fort
62   King's Seat, cairn
63   Little Dunsinane, broch
64   Dunsinane Hill, fort
65   Bandirran, stone circle and stone pair
66   Rossie Priory, church and cross-slab
67   Grassy Walls, Roman temporary camp
68   Ardgilzean, cairn
69   Sandy Road, New Scone, stone circle

70   Kincarrathie, dovecot
71   Bonhard, tower-house and dovecot
72   Murrayshall, standing stone
73   Shianbank, stone circles
74   Shien Hill, cairn
75   Law Hill, Arnbathie, hut-circles
76   Law Hill, Arnbathie, fort and fermtoun
77   Murrayshall Hill, cairn
78   Deuchny Hill, fort
79   Kinfauns, church and burial-ground
80   Balthayock Castle, tower-house
81   Witch Knowe, Inchyra, cairn
82   Pitfour, stone pair and cup-markings
83   Pole Hill, cairn
84   Evelick, fort
85   Evelick Castle, tower-house
86   Whitemyre, hut-circles
87   Culfargie, ring-cairn and cairn
88   Over Fingask, farmstead and field-system
89   Kinnaird Castle, tower-house and dovecot
90   Moncur Castle, fortified house
91   Inchmartin House, standing stone
92   Westown, church and burial-ground
93   Fingask Castle, tower-house
94   Fingask Castle, standing stone
95   Rait, church and burial-ground
96   Rait, cup-markings
97   Rait, fort
98   Kilspindie, dovecot
99   The Grey Stone, standing stone
100   Law Knowe, motte
101   Megginch Castle, fortified house
102   Newbigging, dovecot
103   Waterybutts, dovecot

GAZETTEER

This gazetteer contains a list of the recorded sites and monuments in South-east Perth, complete to April 1992. Several sites discovered since that date have also been included, but it has not been possible to incorporate the results of aerial survey for 1992, which was a particularly rewarding year.

The organisation of the gazetteer reflects the main headings under which the sites are dealt with in the text and thus relate directly to the distribution maps. Sites which appear in more than one section, such as a stone circle which incorporates a cupmarked stone, will have more than one entry. The entries in each section are by alphabetical order of name, and comprise the appropriate National Grid References, followed by the National Monuments Record of Scotland record numbers, which provide unique references to site-descriptions, photographs and plans held in the archive. However, the classifications that have been used to order the material within this volume are not necessarily those that will be found in the

NMRS, which has a more general classificatory system, designed for a much wider application in Scotland than the detailed study of the archaeology of one district. This particularly affects the cropmark material in the settlement section, most of which is held in the archive under the classifications of unenclosed settlement, ring-ditches and enclosures. Where computer-aided transcriptions are available for cropmark sites, the National Grid References for individual structures are quoted to eight figures, but these plots should be treated with caution since their metrical accuracy cannot be guaranteed. Short Harvard-style references have also been included in the entries, and these are expanded in the full bibliography at the end of this volume.

The principal upstanding monuments in the area are plotted on the map of South-east Perth opposite. The majority are in private ownership, and the visitor must seek permission for access locally.

FUNERARY MONUMENTS

Barrows and cairns

Culfargie, ring-cairn
NO 2239 2977   NO 22 NW 45

Abernyte Parish, cairns
NO c.26 31   NO 23 SE 36
Stat. Acct., 9 (1793), 153.

Ardgilzean, cairn
NO 1264 2951   NO 12 NW 3

Beech Hill, Coupar Angus, cairn
NO 2201 4040   NO 24 SW 8
Food Vessels (3), Grooved Ware, bronze pin, bone pommel, bone toggle and 'urn';
Stat. Acct., 17 (1796), 11;
Coutts 1970, 8; *DES 1989*, 63-4;
Stevenson 1989.

Belliduff, Belmont Castle, cairn
NO 2890 4421   NO 24 SE 15
Pennant 1776, 179;
Stat. Acct., 1 (1791), 505-6;
Jervise 1859, 246;
Coutts 1970, 8.

Blairhall, barrow cemetery
NO 116 281   NO 12 NW 32, 43

Cairn Muir, Caputh, cairn
NO 0983 4233   NO 04 SE 3
Stat. Acct., 9 (1793), 504;
NSA, 10 (Perth), 675;
Name Book, Perth, No.13, p.30;
Coutts 1970, 9.

Caputh, cairn
NO 0953 4033   NO 04 SE 16

Culfargie, cairn
NO 2233 2973   NO 22 NW 47

Dalreichmoor, cairns
NO c.19 27   NO 12 NE 28
Melville 1939, 124.

Duff's Knowe, cairn
NO 2775 4330   NO 24 SE 24
Pennant 1776, 177.

East Cult, cairn
NO 0724 4198   NO 04 SE 4
Name Book, Perth, No.13, p.116.

Evelick, cairns
NO 2037 2602   NO 22 NW 8
NSA, 10 (Perth), 1164;
Name Book, Perth, No.38, p.25.

Fir Hillock, cairn
NO 1712 4451   NO 14 SE 32
Name Book, Perth, No.11, p.91.

Glencarse, barrow
NO 1974 2200   NO 12 SE 29

Glendelvine House, barrow
NO 0995 4129   NO 04 SE 13
Simpson 1868, 15; Abercromby,
Ross and Anderson 1902, 202-3.

Glendelvine House, cairn
NO 0987 4115   NO 04 SE 39

Greenbank Cottage, Blairgowrie, cairn
NO 1741 4484   NO 14 SE 3
Name Book, Perth, No.11, p.92;
NSA, 10 (Perth), 914.

Haer Cairn, Rattray, cairn
NO 1926 4551   NO 14 NE 4
'Dagger';
Name Book, Perth, No.70, p.37.

Hallhole, barrow
NO 1862 3899   NO 13 NE 53

Hillpark, Barnhill, cairn
NO 1288 2207   NO 12 SW 33

Inchtuthil, barrows
NO 1274 3968 &   NO 13 NW 7
1279 3968
Stat. Acct., 9 (1793), 505-6;
Abercromby, Ross and Anderson
1902, 197-202.

Innerbuist, cairn
NO 1107 2932   NO 12 NW 5
Name Book, Perth, No.75, p.96.

Keillor, cairn
NO 2733 3976   NO 23 NE 3
Skene 1832 (NMRS, SAS 464);
Stuart 1856, 34-5;
Warden 1880, 27.

King's Seat, Collace, cairn
NO 2306 3300   NO 23 SW 11
Pennant 1776, 179;
Stat. Acct., 9 (1793), 154;
Name Book, Perth, No.15, p.51.

Kinloch, cairn
NO 1407 4485   NO 14 SW 2

Kirkton of Collace, cairn
NO 1952 3215   NO 13 SE 10

Knowehead, cairn
NO 2121 4110   NO 24 SW 18
NSA, 10 (Perth), 1189.

Law Hill, Arnbathie, cairn
NO 1703 2586   NO 12 NE 43
Watson 1930b, 271.

Leys of Marlee, barrow
NO 1561 4397   NO 14 SE 46

Macbeth's Law, Lawton, barrow
NO 2015 3446   NO 23 SW 6
Stat. Acct., 13 (1794), 537;
Name Book, Perth, No.15, p.32;
Crawford 1949, 152.

Mains of Fordie, cairn
NO 0893 4182   NO 04 SE 5
Stat. Acct., 9 (1793), 504;
NSA, 9 (Perth), 675-6;
Name Book, Perth, No.13, p.12.

Mains of Pittendriech, cairn
NO 1557 4186   NO 14 SE 19
Name Book, Perth, No.41, p.52.

Murrayshall Hill, cairn
NO 1647 2535   NO 12 NE 13

Murrayshall Hill, small cairns
NO 1590 2498   NO 12 SE 59

Ninewells, cairn
NO 0757 4360   NO 04 SE 1
Name Book, Perth, No.13, p.25.

Peattie, cairn
NO 2294 3641   NO 23 NW 8
Name Book, Forfar, No.52, p.48.

Pitcur, cairn
NO c.25 36   NO 23 NE 5
Stat. Acct., 17 (1797), 17;
NSA, 11 (Forfar), 643.

Pitcur, cairn
NO c.23 36   NO 23 NW 62
'Urn';
Stat. Acct., 17 (1797), 17;
NSA, 11 (Forfar), 643.

Pitroddie, cairns
NO 218 249   NO 22 SW 8
Cowan 1904, 23.

Pole Hill, cairn
NO 1955 2606   NO 12 NE 6
Coutts 1970, 15.

Rannaleroch, cairn
NO 2532 4620   NO 24 NE 25
Name Book, Perth, No.5, p.101.

Rossie, barrow
NO 2946 3066   NO 23 SE 20

Shien Hill, cairn
NO 1735 2667   NO 12 NE 5
Name Book, Perth, No.37, p.8;
Coutts 1970, 15.

Stobcross, barrow
NO c.245 419   NO 24 SW 10
Sword and socketed spearhead;
NMS DG 1 (spearhead);
Name Book, Perth, No.18, p.9;
Stat. Acct., 17 (1796), 11;
Archaeologia Scotica,
5 (1890), part 3, p.19.

Tammieteeth, cairn
NO 1440 3109   NO 13 SW 21
Scott 1911, 35.

West Buttergask, cairn
NO 2075 3428   NO 23 SW 7
Name Book, Perth, No.15, p.45.

Whirley, cairn
NO c.079 413   NO 04 SE 26
Stat. Acct., 9 (1793), 504.

Witch Knowe, Cronan, cairn
NO c.24 43   NO 24 SW 48
Stat. Acct., 17 (1796), 11.

Witch Knowe, Inchyra, cairn
NO 1894 2118   NO 12 SE 14
'Urns';
Name Book, Perth, No.45, p.5;
Coutts 1970, 13.

Hallhole, square barrow (probable)
NO 1862 3908   NO 13 NE 10
McOmie 1784;
Chalmers 1887, 175;
Abercromby 1904, 87-96.

Monkmyre Burn, square barrow (possible)
NO 2169 4352   NO 24 SW 39

Rossie, square-barrow cemetery
NO 2947 3081   NO 23 SE 21

Rossie, square-barrow cemetery
NO 277 302 to   NO 23 SE 31
282 303

Sherifftown, square-barrow cemetery
NO 109 279   NO 12 NW 10

The Welton, square-barrow cemetery
NO 196 438   NO 14 SE 39

Wester Denhead, square barrow (probable)
NO 2292 4102   NO 24 SW 46

Burials and cists

Abernyte House, cists
NO 2617 3125   NO 23 SE 13
Name Book, Perth, No.4, p.3.

Beech Hill, cist
NO 2208 4042   NO 24 SW 9
Name Book, Perth, No.18, p.20.

Belmont Castle, cist
NO c.28 43   NO 24 SE 21
Food Vessel; NMS EE 129;
Proc Soc Antiq Scot,
73 (1938-9), 331.

Blackfaulds, cist
NO 1448 3224   NO 13 SW 13
'Urn';
Name Book, Perth, No.74, p.7.

Bridge Farm, cist
NO 1710 3889   NO 13 NE 2
**Beaker/Food Vessel and flint
blade**; PMAG 215, 215a;
Ritchie 1935.

Bully Quarry, burial
NO 2607 3606   NO 23 NE 14
Stat. Acct., 17 (1796), 18.

Burnfoot, cist
NO 1635 2205   NO 12 SE 8
Food Vessel; PMAG 213;
Coates 1919.

Cairnbeddie, cists and burials
NO c.149 310,   NO 13 SW 3
1493 3109,
1452 3109,
1448 3084 &
c.144 310
'Urns';
Name Book, Perth, No.74, p.18;
Callander 1919a, 16.

Castle Hill, Rattray, cist
NO 2097 4541   NO 24 NW 52
Food Vessel; DUNMG 1980.271;
Thoms 1980.

Cleaves Farm, burial
NO 163 433   NO 14 SE 30
DES 1981, 48-9.

Colen, cist
NO 1084 3031   NO 13 SW 23
Name Book, Perth, No.75, p.96.

Colenden, cist
NO 1094 2995   NO 12 NW 4
Name Book, Perth, No.75, p.96.

Coupar Angus, cists
NO c.222 404   NO 24 SW 11
The Scottish Antiquary,
13 (1899), 183.

Easter Essendy, cist
NO 1557 4272   NO 14 SE 23
Food Vessel and jet neclace;
DUNMG 1974.561-2; Thoms 1980.

Easter Essendy, cist
NO 1552 4287   NO 14 SE 44
Food Vessel; DUNMG 1980.270.1;
Thoms 1980.

Easter Rattray, cists
NO 2036 4568   NO 24 NW 20
Name Book, Perth, No.69, p.39.

Fingask, burial (probable)
NO c.22 27   NO 22 NW 20
Beaker; present whereabouts
not known;
Proc Soc Antiq Scot,
86 (1951-2), 208-9, fig.2;
Clarke 1970, vol.2, 289, no.74.

Flawcraig, cist
NO c.236 276   NO 22 NW 22
Food Vessel; NMS EE 105;
Coates 1919, 149-50.

Flowerdale, cists
NO 1989 3300   NO 13 SE 11
Name Book, Perth, No.17, p.9.

Greymount, cist
NO 2322 4696   NO 24 NW 15
Coutts 1966, 158, 163-4;
DES 1962, 37.

Hangie's Well, burial
NO 1587 3557   NO 13 NE 13
Name Book, Perth, No.15, p.17.

Inchture, burials
NO c.28 29   NO 22 NE 22
Melville 1939, 86.

Inchtuthil, burials
NO 1261 3989   NO 13 NW 5.5
Cinerary Urn; NMS EA 251;
Longworth 1984, 312;
Pitts and St Joseph 1985, 313.

Keillor Hill, burials
NO c.28 38   NO 23 NE 6
Warden 1884, 17.

Leyston, cist
NO 1795 3812   NO 13 NE 11
'Urn';
Name Book, Perth, No.15, p.10.

Little Keithick, burials
NO 1948 3938   NO 13 NE 1
**Cinerary Urns (4) and Accessory
Vessel**; PMAG 218-9, 221.

Little Keithick, cists
NO 18 38   NO 13 NE 12
Name Book, Perth, No.15, p.3.

Lochlands, cist
NO 2128 4549   NO 24 NW 3
Aitken 1964.

Moor of Blairgowrie, burial
NO c.182 437   NO 14 SE 50
**Cinerary Urn and Accessory
Vessel**; NMS EC 5-6;
Fraser 1878;
Cowie 1978, 131, 140, fig.3.

Muirhall Farm, cist
NO 142 249   NO 12 SW 85
Flint knife; PMAG 1977. 2622;
DES 1970, 36.

Ninetree Brae, cists
NO 2560 2508   NO 22 NE 1
Name Book, Perth, No.26, p.35.

Old Pickstonhill, cist
NO 1321 2542   NO 12 NW 24
Name Book, Perth, No.75, p.95.

Pitroddie, cists
NO c.215 249   NO 22 SW 8
Cowan 1904, vol.1, 23.

Rossie, burials
NO 2934 3077   NO 23 SE 8
Stat. Acct., 19 (1797), 560.

St Martin's Mill, cist
NO *c.* 148 306   NO 13 SW 58
Scott 1911, 35-6.

Sandy Road, New Scone, burial
NO 1327 2646   NO 12 NW 28
Cinerary Urn; PMAG 1993.75.1-3;
second **Cinerary Urn**, on
loan to PMAG, attributed to this
site but not mentioned in the
excavation report;
Stewart 1966.

Sherifftown, burial
NO 1049 2801   NO 12 NW 15
Food Vessels (3);
PMAG 214, 216-17; Callander 1918.

Sherifftown, cist
NO 1050 2798   NO 12 NW 29
Callander 1918.

Upper Muirhall, cist
NO 1454 2405   NO 12 SW 114
Beaker; PMAG 1984-641;
Reid, Shepherd and Lunt 1987.

Williamston, cist
NO 1416 3074   NO 13 SW 16
Bronze armlet; PMAG 1473,
Callander 1919a; Coles 1971a, 89.

Williamston, burial
NO 1414 3072   NO 13 SW 22
Name Book, Perth, No.74, pp.17-18.

RITUAL AND CEREMONIAL MONUMENTS

Cursus monuments

Blairhall, cursus
NO 1160 2800   NO 12 NW 43

Cleaven Dyke, cursus
NO 1754 3976 to   NO 13 NE 89,
1540 4094   14 SE 80
Pennant 1776, 68;
Abercromby, Ross and
Anderson 1902, 234;
Richmond 1940, 41;
Adamson and Gallagher 1986;
Maxwell 1989, 106.

Milton of Rattray, cursus
NO 197 448   NO 14 SE 82

Mortuary enclosures

Berryhill, mortuary enclosure (possible)
NO 1164 3198   NO 13 SW 48

Carsie Mains, mortuary enclosure (possible)
NO 177 417   NO 14 SE 84

Inchtuthil, mortuary enclosure
NO 1254 3956   NO 13 NW 5.6
Pitts and St Joseph 1985, 248-51;
Barclay and Maxwell 1992.

Littleour, mortuary enclosure (possible)
NO 1734 4024   NO 14 SE 59

Upper Gothens, mortuary enclosure (possible)
NO 169 413   NO 14 SE 85

Pit-settings

Ardmuir, pit-setting
NO 1947 4311   NO 14 SE 66

Ardmuir, pit-setting
NO 193 431   NO 14 SE 86

Pitroddie, pit-setting
NO 2170 2523   NO 22 NE 44

Whiteloch, pit-setting
NO 167 428   NO 14 SE 87

Pit-circles

Carsie Mains, pit-circle
NO 177 417   NO 14 SE 88

Inchtuthil, pit-circle
NO 1235 3936   NO 13 NW 35

Inchtuthil, pit-circle
NO 1241 3934   NO 13 NW 39

Middlebank, pit-circle
NO 2597 2754   NO 22 NE 14

Old Mains of Rattray, pit-circle
NO 2041 4570   NO 24 NW 44

The Welton, pit-circle
NO 1886 4406   NO 14 SE 76

Pit-alignments

Ardblair, pit-alignment
NO 160 439   NO 14 SE 58

Ardmuir, pit-alignment
NO 196 428   NO 14 SE 65

Balendoch, pit-alignment
NO 2853 4743 to   NO 24 NE 42
2855 4745

Berryhill, pit-alignment
NO 1159 3190 to   NO 13 SW 64
1172 3196

Berryhillock, pit-alignment
NO 181 414   NO 14 SE 62

Dunkeld Park, pit-alignment
NO 016 430 to   NO 04 SW 27
016 429

Glencarse, pit-alignment
NO 196 219   NO 12 SE 29

Hallhole, pit-alignment
NO 1852 3903 to   NO 13 NE 70
1869 3939

Millbank, pit-alignment
NO 179 402   NO 14 SE 64

Sherifftown, pit-alignment
NO 104 277   NO 12 NW 42

Spittalfield, pit-alignment
NO 1076 4139 to   NO 14 SW 72
1077 4148

Tay Farm, pit-alignments
NO 150 404   NO 14 SE 4

Henges

Mains of Gourdie, henge (possible)
NO 1201 4189   NO 14 SW 18

Whiteloch, henge (possible)
NO 1676 4284   NO 14 SE 37

Stone circles and settings

Bandirran, stone circle
NO 2091 3099   NO 23 SW 3
Skene 1832 (NMRS, SAS 464);
Stewart 1966, 20-1;
Burl 1976, 195;
Barnatt 1989, 313.

Blackfaulds, stone circle
NO 1413 3167   NO 13 SW 15
Scott 1911, 38; Burl 1976, 362;
Thom, Thom and Burl 1980, 360-1;
Barnatt 1989, 313.

Brownies Knowe, stone circle
NO 1606 3093   NO 13 SE 15
Baxter 1892, 223-4.

Colen, stone circle
NO 1106 3116   NO 13 SW 19
Name Book, Perth, No.74, p.12;
Baxter 1892, 222-3;
Coutts 1970, 18;
Burl 1976, 195, 362;
Thom, Thom and Burl 1980, 345-5;
Barnatt 1989, 315.

Druids' Seat Wood, stone circle
NO 1248 3132   NO 13 SW 20
Name Book, Perth, No.74, p.13;
Baxter, 1892, 223;
Burl 1976, 362;
Thom, Thom and Burl 1980, 354-5.

East Cult, stone circle
NO 072 421   NO 04 SE 27
Stat. Acct., 9 (1793), 504.

East Whitefield, stone circle
NO 1729 3514   NO 13 NE 37
Name Book, Perth, No.15, p.30.

Gallowhill, stone circles
NO *c.* 16 35   NO 13 NE 30
Pennant 1776, 451-2.

Leys of Marlee, stone circle
NO 1599 4388   NO 14 SE 15
Coles 1909, 115-20;
Coutts 1970, 19;
Burl 1976, 362;
Thom, Thom and Burl 1980, 330-1;
Gibson 1988; Barnatt 1989, 309.

Sandy Road, New Scone, stone circle
NO 1327 2646   NO 12 NW 28
Coles 1909, 126-30;
Stewart 1966;
Coutts 1970, 20-1;
Burl 1976, 363;
Thom, Thom and Burl 1980, 360-1;
Barnatt 1989, 326-7.

Shianbank, stone circles
NO 1556 2729   NO 12 NE 7
Name Book, Perth, No.72, p.75;
Stewart 1966, 16;
Burl 1976, 363;
Thom, Thom and Burl 1980, 358-9;
Barnatt 1989, 327.

Stockmuir, stone circle
NO 2422 3285   NO 23 SW 13
Stat. Acct., 9 (1793), 154;
NSA, 10 (Perth), 221;
Name Book, Perth, No.4, p.13;
Melville 1939, 149-50.

Williamston, stone circle
NO 1383 3106   NO 13 SW 14
Name Book, Perth, No.74, p.17.

Commonbank, four-poster setting
NO 1749 2484   NO 12 SE 23
DES 1964, 44; *1973*, 44.

Stone alignments

Commonbank, stone alignment
NO 1749 2484   NO 12 SE 23
DES 1964, 44; *1973*, 44.

East Cult, stone alignment
NO 0725 4216   NO 04 SE 2
Stat Acct., 9 (1793), 504;
Allen 1881, 82-4;
Coles 1908, 148-52;
Stewart 1967, 142-3.

Gallowhill Wood, stone alignment
NO 1681 3604   NO 13 NE 20

St Martins, stone alignment
NO 1592 3122   NO 13 SE 9
Burl 1976, 363;
Barnatt 1989, 326.

Stone pairs

Bandirran, stone pair
NO 2107 3096   NO 23 SW 2
Stewart 1967, 142-3;
Coutts 1970, 18.

Loanhead, stone pair
NO 1477 3286   NO 13 SW 12
Scott 1911, 38-9;
Stewart 1967, 142-3.

Moonshade, Newbigging, stone pair
NO 1614 3576   NO 13 NE 21
Stat. Acct., 13, 537;
Name Book, Perth, No.15, p.18;
Simpson 1868, 59-60.

Newtyle, stone pair
NO 0449 4106   NO 04 SW 7
Coles 1908, 147-8;
Stewart 1967, 144-5.

Pitfour, stone pair
NO 1970 2098   NO 12 SE 20
Allen 1882, 95-8;
DES 1967, 44-5;
Stewart 1967, 144-5;
Coutts 1970, 19-20.

Standing stones

Arthurstone, standing stone
NO *c.*261 429   NO 24 SE 27
Headrick 1813, 178;
Mackay 1876, 46;
Warden 1884, 8.

Belmont Castle, standing stone
NO 2858 4366   NO 24 SE 18
Jervise 1859, 246;
Wise 1859, 94.

Dunkeld Park, standing stone
NO 0144 4299   NO 04 SW 6
Coles 1908, 145-6.

Fingask Castle, standing stone
NO 2293 2716   NO 22 NW 9

Glendelvine House, standing stone
NO 0997 4130   NO 04 SE 13
Simpson 1865, 15; Abercromby,
Ross and Anderson 1902, 202.

The Grey Stone, standing stone
NO 2217 2131   NO 22 SW 6
NSA, 10 (Perth), 384-5;
Name Book, Perth, No.26, p.85.

Hangie's Stone, standing stone
NO 1575 3557   NO 13 NE 14
Name Book, Perth, No.15, p.17;
Coles 1909, 123-4.

Inchmartine House, standing stone
NO 2614 2759   NO 22 NE 6
NSA, 10 (Perth), 384-5;
Name Book, Perth, No.26, p.8.

Macbeth's Stone, Belmont, standing stone
NO 2799 4346   NO 24 SE 16
Pennant 1776, 177;
Stat. Acct., 1 (1791), 505-6;
NSA, 10 (Perth), 234;
Name Book, Perth, No.54, p.18;
Coutts 1970, 18.

Moncur Castle, standing stone
NO *c.*28 29   NO 22 NE 5
NSA, 10 (Perth), 832.

Murrayshall, standing stone
NO 1520 2627   NO 12 NE 8

Cup- and ring-markings

Balholmie, cup-markings
NO 1480 3636   NO 13 NW 2
Baxter 1892, 224.

Balmalcolm, cup-markings
NO 2154 3227   NO 23 SW 27

Brownies Knowe, cup-markings
NO 160 309   NO 13 SE 28
Baxter 1892, 223-4.

Cairnbeddie, cup-markings
NO *c.*15 31   NO 13 SW 53
Scott 1911, 37.

Colen, cup-markings
NO 1106 3116   NO 13 SW 19
Baxter 1892, 222-3;
Burl 1976, 195, 362.

Commonbank, cup-markings
NO 1749 2484   NO 12 SE 23
DES 1973, 44.

Commonbank, cup-markings
NO *c.*177 247   NO 12 SE 42
DES 1973, 44.

Commonbank, cup-markings
NO 1735 2481   NO 12 SE 55

Dunsinane Hill, cup-markings
NO 2133 3166   NO 23 SW 1

East Cult, cup-markings
NO 0725 4216   NO 04 SE 2
Stat Acct., 9 (1793), 504;
Allen 1881, 82-4;
Coles 1908, 148-52.

Easter Essendy, cup-markings
NO 1557 4272   NO 14 SE 44
Thoms 1980.

Gallowhill, cup-and-ring markings
NO *c.*167 359   NO 13 NE 16
NMS IA 26;
Baxter 1897.

Gallowhill Wood, cup-markings
NO 1681 3604   NO 13 NE 20

Goddens, cup-markings
NO 1985 2591   NO 12 NE 42

Inchture, cup-markings
NO *c.*281 287   NO 22 NE 3
Simpson 1868, 61.

Macbeth's Stone, Belmont, cup-markings
NO 2799 4346   NO 24 SE 16
Coutts 1970, 18.

Meigle Museum, cup-and-ring markings
NO 2872 4459   NO 24 SE 25.1
Cruden 1964.

Newbigging, cup-and-ring marking
NO 1558 3521   NO 13 NE 17
Simpson 1868, 60;
Coles 1909, 124-6;
Barclay *et al.* 1983.

Newbigging, cup-markings
NO 1597 3528   NO 13 NE 15
Simpson 1868, 60.

Newbigging, cup-and-ring markings
NO 1615 3576   NO 13 NE 21
Simpson 1868, 59-60;
Stat. Acct., 13 (1794), 537.

Newbigging, cup-and-ring markings
NO *c.*15 35   NO 13 NE 18
Simpson 1868, 60.

Newbigging, cup-markings
NO *c.*15 35   NO 13 NE 19
Simpson 1868, 60.

Ninewells, cup-markings
NO 0757 4360   NO 04 SE 1

Over Kincairney, cup-marking
NO 0833 4398   NO 04 SE 17
Allen 1881, 86-7.

Pitcur Souterrain, cup-and-ring markings
NO 2529 3738   NO 23 NE 1.2-5
Young 1938, 143-9;
Wainwright 1963, 202-4;
Coutts 1970, 45-6.

Pitfour, cup-markings
NO 1970 2098   NO 12 SE 20
DES 1967, 44-5;
Allen 1882, 95-8;
Coutts 1970, 19-20.

Rait, cup-markings
NO 2275 2677   NO 22 NW 52

Sherifftown, cup-markings
NO 1049 2801   NO 12 NW 15
Callander 1918.

South Friarton, cup-and-ring markings
NO *c*. 146 299   NO 12 NW 47
Scott 1911, 37-8.

Stockmuir, cup-markings
NO 2422 3285   NO 23 SW 13
Melville 1939, 149-50.

West Whitefield, cup-and-ring markings
NO *c*. 16 34   NO 13 SE 2
Hutcheson 1884.

Williamston, cup-and-ring markings
NO 1416 3074   NO 13 SW 52
NMS IA 20;
Callander 1919a, 22-3;
Hutcheson 1889, 142-3.

SETTLEMENT

Flints

Carsie, scatter of microliths, arrowheads, scrapers, etc
NO *c*. 17 42   NO 14 SE 14
NMS AA 220-26; AB 1820-51;
AD 1552-56; AD 1798;
Proc Soc Antiq Scot,
65 (1930-1), 259.

Nethermuir of Pittendreich, scatter of knives, scrapers, and debitage
NO 158 411   NO 14 SE 25
PMAG 1982.319.1-13;
1983.670.1-9; 1984.326.1-12;
DES 1977, 43; *1982,* 37;
1983, 37; *1984,* 40.

The Gothens, scatter of microliths, arrowheads, scrapers, etc
NO 168 414   NO 14 SE 20
PMAG 1981.35; NMS AA 295-6;
AB 2990-3001; AD 2383-7; *DES 1964,* 43;
Proc Soc Antiq Scot,
107 (1975-6), 333.

Tulloch Ard, scatter of microliths, arrowheads, scrapers, etc
NO *c*. 21 31   NO 23 SW 16
PMAG 7/1967.

Guildtown, microlith
NO 132 316   NO 13 SW 73
PMAG 1978.1695.

South West Fullarton, microlith and chip
NO 294 438   NO 24 SE 61
Present location not known;
Strong 1987.

Beech Hill, Coupar Angus, hollow-based arrowhead
NO 2002 4040   NO 24 SW 8
DES 1989, 63-4.

Binn Hill, hollow-based arrowhead
NO 158 225   NO 12 SE 27
PMAG 3/1967; *DES 1967,* 41.

Bridgend, barbed-and-tanged arrowhead
NO 125 243   NO 12 SW 91
PMAG 23/1960;
Trans Proc Perths Soc Natur Sci,
11 (1963-5), 51.

Coupar Angus, barbed-and-tanged arrowhead
NO 219 403   NO 24 SW 56
With finder; *DES 1985,* 53.

Dunkeld, barbed-and-tanged arrowhead
NO *c*. 02 42   NO 04 SW
NMS AD 580;
Cat Nat Mus Antiq Scot, (1892), 14.

Kinnoull Hill, leaf-shaped arrowhead
NO 135 230   NO 12 SW 37
PMAG 11/1956;
Trans Proc Perths Soc Natur Sci,
11 (1963-5), 51.

Loch of Lowes, leaf-shaped arrowhead
NO *c*. 15 04   NO 04 SE 15
PMAG 3/1965.

Murray Royal Hospital, leaf-shaped arrowhead
NO 129 240   NO 12 SW 66
Trans Proc Perths Soc Natur Sci,
6 (1914-18), 153.

Pole Hill, flat-based triangular arrowhead
NO 195 260   NO 12 NE 11
PMAG 1811.

Seaside Farm, barbed-and-tanged arrowhead
NO 280 242   NO 22 SE 19
PMAG 23/1966; *DES 1967,* 41.

Stormontfield, leaf-shaped arrowhead
NO 109 298   NO 12 NW 39
PMAG 1985.22; *DES 1985,* 54.

Blairgowrie, knife
NO *c*. 17 45   NO 14 NE 30
NMS AA 254;
Glasgow Art Gallery and Museum
1951, 27, no.154.

Blairgowrie, knife
NO *c*. 17 45   NO 14 NE 31
NMS AB 480;
Proc Soc Antiq Scot, 24 (1889-90), 382.

Carsie, knife
NO *c*. 17 42   NO 14 SE 13
PMAG 26 & 2440
Trans Proc Perths Soc Natur Sci,
8 (1923-29), 145.

Deuchny Wood, spearhead
NO 156 240   NO 12 SE 2
Lost;
Proc Soc Antiq Scot,
57 (1922-23), 306.

Hillpark, Barnhill, knife
NO 1288 2207   NO 12 SW 33
PMAG 18 & 2389.

Muirhall, knife
NO 142 249   NO 12 SW 85
PMAG 1977.2622; *DES 1970,* 36.

Murray Royal Hospital, knives
NO 129 240   NO 12 SW 66
Trans Proc Perths Soc Natur Sci,
6 (1914-18), 153.

Arnbathie, scraper
NO 1696 2580   NO 12 NE 3
NMS EQ 565;
Proc Soc Antiq Scot,
82 (1947-8), 317.

Barnhill souterrain, scraper
NO 1248 2271   NO 12 SW 67
NMS HD 279;
Hutcheson 1904, 541-7.

Blairgowrie, scraper
NO *c*. 17 45   NO 14 NE 90
PMAG 17 & 2976.

Blairgowrie, scraper
NO *c*. 17 45   NO 14 NE 91
PMAG 22 & 3110.

Carsie, scraper
NO *c*. 17 42   NO 14 SE 12
PMAG 19 & 1418;
Trans Proc Perths Soc Natur Sci,
7 (1918-23), 127.

Colen, scraper
NO 108 304   NO 13 SW 34
PMAG 4 & 2392.

Corsiehill, scraper
NO 138 235   NO 12 SW 35
PMAG 3a & 2405.

Coupar Angus Abbey, scraper
NO *c*. 224 397   NO 23 NW 66
NMS AB 2761.

Kinloch Hotel, scraper
NO 149 448   NO 14 SW 23
PMAG 21 & 1488.

Kinnoull Hill, scraper
NO *c*. 13 22   NO 12 SW 68
PMAG 3 & 1414;
Trans Proc Perths Soc Natur Sci,
7 (1918-23), 127.

Kinnoull Hill, scraper
NO 135 230   NO 12 SW 36
PMAG 3/1950.
Trans Proc Perths Soc Natur Sci,
11 (1963-5), 50.

Marlee, scrapers (2)
NO *c*. 14 44   NO 14 SW 1
PMAG 25 & 2437-8;
Trans Proc Perths Soc Natur Sci,
8 (1923-9), 145.

Murray Royal Hospital, scraper
NO 129 240   NO 12 SW 76
PMAG 2021;
Trans Proc Perths Soc Natur Sci,
7 (1918-23), 146.

Parkfield, scraper
NO 146 250   NO 12 NW 50
PMAG 8 & 1512;
Trans Proc Perths Soc Natur Sci,
7 (1918-23), 134.

St Madoes Kirkyard, scraper
NO 196 212   NO 12 SE 66
PMAG 1990.148; *DES 1990,* 42.

Bridge Farm, Meikleour, blade
NO 1710 3889   NO 13 NE 2
Found in cist; PMAG 215a;
Ritchie 1934.

Abernyte Parish, flake
Unlocated   NO 23 SE 3
PMAG 2 & 1417;
Trans Proc Perths Soc Natur Sci,
7 (1918-23), 127.

Blairgowrie, core
NO *c*. 18 45   NO 14 NE 27
PMAG 24 & 2439;
Trans Proc Perths Soc Natur Sci,
8 (1923-29), 145.

Deuchny Hill, flakes (2)
NO 1522 2367   NO 12 SE 3
One of chalcedony; now lost;
Watson 1923, 307.

Law Hill, Arnbathie, flint-knapping pebbles, gouge, and quartz flakes
NO 171 259   NO 12 NE 60
PMAG 1992.502.1-4.

Pitcur, flake
NO 2478 3657   NO 23 NW 9
NMS HD 3; MacRitchie 1900, 211.

Wester Drumatherty, chert core
NO 115 411   NO 14 SW 30
With finder; *DES 1984,* 38-9.

Stone tools

Aberbothrie, axe
NO 237 463   NO 24 NW 71
PMAG 1992.9; *DES 1992,* 77.

Balbeggie, axe
NO *c.*16 29   NO 12 NE 22
PMAG 1986.80; *DES 1986,* 40.

Blairgowrie, axe
NO *c.*14 45   NO 14 NE 8
PMAG 71;
Trans Proc Perths Soc Natur Sci,
9 (1929-38), 120, pl.30, no.8.

Blairgowrie, axe
NO *c.*14 45   NO 14 NE 33
NMS AF 587;
Proc Soc Antiq Scot,
32 (1897-8), 382.

Blairgowrie, axe
NO *c.*17 45   NO 14 NE 93
NMS AF 447.

Cargill, axe
NO 150 369   NO 13 NE 36
PMAG 78.

Carsie, axe
NO *c.*17 42   NO 14 SE 7
PMAG 69 & 2741.

Carsie, axe
NO *c.*17 42   NO 14 SE 8
PMAG 76 & 1447;
Trans Proc Perths Soc Natur Sci,
7 (1918-23), 129, pl.17, no.11.

Carsie, axe
NO *c.*17 42   NO 14 SE 14
NMS AF 702;
Proc Soc Antiq Scot,
65 (1930-31), 259.

Collace Burn, axe
NO 204 323   NO 23 SW 18
PMAG 1992.835;
Trans Proc Perths Soc Natur Sci,
8 (1923-29), 264.

Corsiehill, axe
NO 137 235   NO 12 SW 83
PMAG 16/1969; *DES 1970,* 37.

Cranley, axe
NO 145 413   NO 14 SW 25
STIGM 1976.

East Mill, Rattray, axe
NO 212 446   NO 24 SW 3
PMAG 12/1960;
Trans Proc Perths Soc Natur Sci,
11 (1963-65), 52.

Franklyden, axe
NO 188 296   NO 12 NE 57
PMAG 1989.336; *DES 1990,* 42.

Friarton, mace-head
NO *c.*14 30   NO 13 SW 76
PMAG 1980.438.

Glencarse, axe
NO 196 215   NO 12 SE 28
DUNMG 1964-63;
Coutts 1971, 38, no.40.

Hoolmyre, axe
NO 215 314   NO 23 SW 8
PMAG 2528;
Trans Proc Perths Soc Natur Sci,
8 (1923-29), 146.

Kinfauns Sand-Pit, axe
NO 1680 2200   NO 12 SE 26
DUNMG 1968-18; *DES 1968,* 29;
Coutts 1971, 41, no.47.

Megginch, axe
NO *c.*24 24   NO 22 SW 4
PMAG 77;
Trans Proc Perths Soc Natur Sci,
7 (1918-23), 143, pl.17, no.2.

Meikleour, axe
NO *c.*15 39   NO 13 NE 39
STIGM 3280.

Milton, axe
NO *c.*26 30   NO 23 SE 10
PMAG 72 & 1445;
Trans Proc Perths Soc Natur Sci,
7 (1918-23), 129, pl.17, no.3.

Murie, axe
NO *c.*23 21   NO 22 SW 11
STIGM 2886.

Nether Logie, axe
NO 3220 4686   NO 34 NW 13
PMAG 5/1970; *DES 1970,* 38.

Newton Gray, axe
NO 2595 3220   NO 23 SE 49
With finder; *DES 1992,* 78.

North Pitkindie, axe
NO 253 321   NO 23 SE 50
With finder; *DES 1992,* 78.

North Pitkindie, axe
NO 254 323   NO 23 SE 51
With finder; *DES 1992,* 78.

Rait, axes (2)
NO 225 267   NO 22 NW 17
NMS AF 374-5;
Proc Soc Antiq Scot,
24 (1889-90), 6.

River Ericht, axe
NO *c.*19 44   NO 14 SE 10
Jadeite axe; NMS AF 56;
Smith 1963, 167.

Skavins, axe
NO 181 314   NO 13 SE 16
NMS AF 373;
Proc Soc Antiq Scot,
24 (1889-90), 6.

Cargill Parish, perforated axe
Unlocated   NO 13 NE 23
NMS AF 408; Baxter 1892, 224.

Craigie, perforated axe
NO 118 436   NO 14 SW 24
Palace of History,
2 (1911), 839, no.16.

Meigle, perforated axe
NO *c.*28 44   NO 24 SE 74
NMS AM 114.

Ford of Pitcur, carved ball
NO 241 361   NO 23 NW 61
PMAG 1987.300; *DES 1987,* 55.

Franklyden, carved ball
NO 203 293   NO 22 NW 1
PMAG 17/1959; Marshall 1979, 67.

New Scone, carved balls (2)
NO *c.*14 26   NO 12 NW 18
PMAG 1290 & 1290b;
Marshall 1979, 65, 71.

Tarrylaw Farm, carved ball
NO 192 299   NO 12 NE 58
PMAG 1992.836.

Bronze Age metalwork

Baldowrie, flat axe
NO 268 399   NO 23 NE 11
PMAG 122 & 2842;
Coles 1971a, 80.

Blairgowrie, flat axe
NO *c.*17 45   NO 14 NE 57
PMAG 1983.337;
Cowie and Reid 1987, 69-72.

Cranley, flat axe
NO 144 413   NO 14 SW 12
GAGM LA 5737a;
Scott 1960, 178-9.

Glencarse, flat axe
NO *c.*19 21   NO 12 SE 61
PMAG 16/1967; Coles 1971a, 84.

Inchtuthil, flat axe
NO 125 397   NO 13 NW 5
NMS DA 125; Coles 1971a, 84.

Loan Farm, Errol, flat axe
NO 247 231   NO 22 SW 45
DUNMG 1964-17-3;
Coutts 1971, 60.

Newtyle Hill, flat axe
NO *c.*05 42   NO 04 SE 9
Blair Castle; Coles 1971a, 85.

Redford, flat axe
NO 147 330   NO 13 SW 8
PMAG 122a; Coles 1971a, 85.

Wolfhill, flat axe
NO 139 337   NO 13 SW 33
NMS DA 96;
Proc Soc Antiq Scot,
64 (1931-2), 25.

Haer Cairn, Rattray, 'dagger'
NO 1926 4551   NO 14 NE 4
Name Book, Perth, No.70, p.37.

Williamston, armlet
NO 1416 3074   NO 13 SW 16
PMAG 1473; Callander 1919.

River Tay, near Errol, sickle
Unlocated   NO 22 SE 3
PMAG 137 & 1294;
Smith 1870, 377-8;
Coles 1962, 88.

Blairgowrie, flanged axe
NO *c.*17 45   NO 14 NE 38
DUNMG 1964-19-2;
Coutts 1971, 60.

Bowhouse, Balbeggie, flanged axe
NO 190 293   NO 12 NE 1
PMAG 9/1956; Coles 1966, 137.

Hallroom, flanged axe
NO 1367 3267   NO 13 SW 35
With finder; *DES 1970*, 38.

Jordanstone, flanged axe
NO *c*.27 47   NO 24 NE 11
NMS DA 71;
Proc Soc Antiq Scot,
38 (1903-4), 12;
Coles 1971a, 84.

Kinnoull, flanged axe
NO *c*.12 23   NO 12 SW 157
Ulster Mus B.181B.1913;
Coles 1966, 137.

Marlee Loch, flanged axe
NO *c*.14 43   NO 14 SW 36
PMAG 1984.327;
Cowie and Reid 1987, 72-74.

Spittalfield, flanged axe
NO 1058 4073   NO 14 SW 27

Stobhall, flanged axe
NO 132 343   NO 13 SW 9
NMS DC 92; Coles 1966, 137.

Strelitz Wood, flanged axe
NO *c*.18 36   NO 13 NE 34
DUNMG 1958-467;
Coles 1966, 137.

Clockmaden, socketed axe, ferrule and armlets
NO 188 315   NO 13 SE 17
PMAG 1982.236.1-17;
Cowie and Reid 1987, 80-7.

Craigmakerran, flanged axe
NO 140 322   NO 13 SW 26
NMS DC 38; Coles 1962, 71.

Cronan, socketed axe
NO 247 435   NO 24 SW 7
NMS L.1926.12; Coles 1962, 72.

Delvine, socketed axe
NO *c*.12 40   NO 14 SW 11
PMAG 133; Coles 1962, 72.

Hoolmyre, socketed axe
NO 2119 3121   NO 23 SW 24
PMAG 1978.1061;
Cowie and Reid 1987, 78.

Murray Royal Hospital, socketed axe
NO 129 240   NO 12 SW 3
PMAG 131 & 2854;
Coles 1962, 71.

Rait, socketed axe
NO 229 271   NO 22 NW 63
PMAG 1992.108; *DES 1992*, 80.

River Tay, Delvine, socketed axe
NO *c*.13 39   NO 13 NW 1
PMAG 2406; Coles 1962, 71.

South Friarton, socketed axe
NO 146 299   NO 12 NW 7
NMS DE 75; Coles 1962, 72.

St Martin's Manse, socketed axe
NO 154 301   NO 13 SE 7
NMS DE 34; Coles 1962, 71.

Blairgowrie, sword
NO *c*.17 45   NO 14 NE 29
GAGM 55-96; Coles 1962, 85.

Dunsinane Hill, swords (2)
NO *c*.21 31   NO 23 SW 9
Present location unknown;
Coles 1962, 125.

Druidstone Park, Errol, swords (2)
Unlocated   NO 22 SE 6
ABDUA 19685;
Hunterian B 1951.3254;
Coles 1962, 124-5.

River Tay, Seggieden, sword
NO *c*.16 21   NO 12 SE 16
PMAG 136 & 1338;
Coles 1962, 85.

Stobcross, sword and socketed spearhead
NO 245 419   NO 24 SW 10
NMS DG 1 (spearhead);
Coles 1962, 101.

Blacklaw, socketed spearhead
NO *c*.22 45   NO 24 NW 16
NMS DG 43; Coles 1962, 79.

Craigie, socketed spearhead
NO *c*.11 43   NO 14 SW 8
NMS DG 57; Coles 1962, 80.

Meikleour, socketed spearhead
NO 150 399   NO 13 NE 38
DES 1975, 60; Close-Brooks 1978, 310-13.

Kinnoull Hill, socketed gouge
NO 132 228   NO 12 SW 214
PMAG 1990.137; *DES 1990*, 42.

Fingask, gold armlet
Unlocated   NO 22 NW 10
Present location unknown;
Taylor 1980, 94.

Prehistoric pottery

Inchtuthil, Neolithic sherd
NO 115 393   NO 13 NW 6
NMS FY 108;
Cowie forthcoming.

Beech Hill, Coupar Angus, Grooved Ware
NO 2202 4040   NO 24 SW 8
Beneath cairn; *DES 1989*, 63-4.

Franklyden, Beaker
NO 2187 2992   NO 22 NW 62
PMAG 1992.826 (single sherd).

Law Hill, Arnbathie, vessel
NO 1696 2580   NO 12 NE 3
NMS EQ 564;
Proc Soc Antiq Scot,
82 (1947-8), 317.

Later prehistoric small finds

Deuchny Hill, stone cup
NO 153 237   NO 12 SE 3
PMAG 111 & 2164;
Watson 1923, 307.

Fairygreen, stone cup
NO 207 333   NO 23 SW 5
ABDUA 15592;
Small 1964, 222.

Glencarse, stone cup
NO *c*.19 21   NO 12 SE 72
PMAG 1992.837.

Hill House, Stormontfield, stone cup
NO *c*.10 30   NO 13 SW 74
PMAG 2/1935.

Inchtuthil, stone cup
NO *c*.12 39   NO 13 NW 40
NMS AQ 83.

Jeanniebank, stone cup
NO 109 287   NO 12 NW 26
PMAG 113 & 2390.

Old Scone, stone cup
NO *c*.11 26   NO 12 NW 17
NMS AQ 80;
Proc Soc Antiq Scot,
42 (1907-08), 324.

Tarrylaw Farm, stone cup
NO *c*.18 29   NO 12 NE 59
PMAG 6/1972.

Cargill, stone lamp
NO 185 380   NO 13 NE 68
DUNMG 1971-189;
Coutts 1971, 67, no.142.

Coupar Angus, stone lamp
NO *c*.21 40   NO 24 SW 5
NMS BG 137;
Proc Soc Antiq Scot,
32 (1897-8), 239.

Inchmichael, stone lamp
NO *c*.24 25   NO 22 NW 35
Present location unknown
Melville 1935, 180.

Beech Hill, Coupar Angus, stone head
NO 2200 4035   NO 24 SW 77
PMAG 1992.503; *DES 1992*, 76.

Templelands, Meigle, armlet
NO 288 447   NO 24 SE 13
Iron Age bronze armlet;
Present location unknown;
Jervise 1859, 245.

Deuchny Hill, armlet
NO 1522 2367   NO 12 SE 3
Fragment of jet armlet;
now lost; Watson 1923, 307.

Law Hill, Arnbathie, tuyere
NO 1696 2580   NO 12 NE 3
NMS CM 40;
Proc Soc Antiq Scot,
82 (1947-8), 317.

Pitcur, bone bodkin
NO 2478 3657   NO 23 NW 9
NMS HD 4; MacRitchie 1900, 211.

Roman finds from non-Roman contexts

Barnhill, bronze figurine
NO 125 226   NO 12 SW 65
Mercury; PMAG 3106;
Proc Soc Antiq Scot,
71 (1936-7), 93-4, fig. 2.

Stormont Loch, patera
NO 188 423   NO 14 SE 21
PMAG 1295;
McPeake and Moore
1978, 333, no.10.

River Tay, Inchyra, brooch
NO 184 203   NO 12 SE 73
PMAG 1992.600;
Collingwood Class R (ii);
DES 1992, 77.

Dunkeld Cathedral, coins
NO 024 425   NO 14 SW 1.1
Hoard containing 'some' Roman
coins, now lost;
NSA, 10 (Perth), 978.

Greenbank Cottage, Blairgowrie, coin
NO 1742 4481   NO 14 SE 3
Bronze, Hadrianic; now lost
NSA, 10 (Perth), 914.

Pitcur Souterrain, coin
NO 2529 3738   NO 23 NE 1
Now lost; MacRitchie 1900.

Barton Hill, pottery
NO 243 285   NO 22 NW 25
Two sherds of Samian ware;
found in excavation of motte;
present location unknown.

Pitcur Souterrain, pottery
NO 2529 3738   NO 23 NE 1
ADM B 1977.295a;
Type D.37 Samian bowl;
MacRitchie 1900.

Pitcur, pottery
NO 247 365   NO 23 NW 9
NMS HD 1-2;
two sherds of Samian ware;
Wainwright 1963, 200-2.

South West Fullarton, pottery
NO 294 438   NO 24 SE 61
One sherd of Flavian coarse
pottery; present location
unknown; Strong 1987.

Wester Denhead, pottery
NO 2290 4100   NO 24 SW 46
Sherd of amphora; from outer
ditch of enclosure containing
square barrow; with finder.

Unenclosed settlements

Ardgaith, round-houses
NO 2206 2264   NO 22 SW 53

Baledgarno, maculae
NO 273 304   NO 23 SE 40

Baledgarno, round-houses
NO 2831 3007   NO 23 SE 41

Balgarvie, maculae
NO 147 262   NO 12 NW 51

Balgersho, round-house
NO 222 382   NO 23 NW 59

Bankhead of Kinloch, round-houses
NO 258 440   NO 24 SE 72

Blackhillock, round-house
NO 0981 4096   NO 04 SE 33

Bonhard Park, round-houses
NO 155 265   NO 12 NE 30

Boyne, round-houses
NO 2681 2867   NO 22 NE 33

Cairnie Mill, round-house
NO 1931 2084   NO 12 SE 54

Cambusmichael, round-house
NO 1156 3227   NO 13 SW 42

Clashbenny, round-houses
NO 2230 2132   NO 22 SW 38

Coin Hill, round-houses
NO 178 392   NO 13 NE 56

Craigie, round-houses
NO 119 440   NO 14 SW 49

Dalbeathie, macula
NO 0600 4027   NO 04 SE 37

Dunsinane Hill, ring-ditch house
NO 2104 3172   NO 23 SW 26

Easter Bendochy, round-houses
NO 220 417   NO 24 SW 69

Easter Essendy, round-houses
NO 150 425   NO 14 SE 67

Gallowflat, round-houses
NO 210 211   NO 22 SW 57

Gannochy, maculae
NO 1305 2496   NO 12 SW 190

Glencarse, round-house
NO 2026 2243   NO 22 SW 12
DES 1982, 33;
Maxwell 1987, 37-40.

Glendelvine, maculae
NO 0971 4132   NO 04 SE 38

Hatton, round-house
NO 1714 3777   NO 13 NE 79

Hill House, maculae
NO 1068 3057   NO 13 SW 65

Hill of Errol, round-houses
NO 2362 2147   NO 22 SW 20

Hill of Errol, macula
NO 2276 2133   NO 22 SW 42

Inchcoonans, maculae
NO 2353 2353   NO 22 SW 40

Inchtuthil, macula
NO 126 391   NO 13 NW 27

Isla Cottage, maculae
NO 166 376   NO 13 NE 80

Kemphill, round-houses
NO 2130 4009   NO 24 SW 14

Kilspindie, round-houses
NO 2210 2580   NO 22 NW 36

Kinloch, round-houses
NO 1365 4483   NO 14 SW 47

Kinloch, round-house
NO 1373 4478   NO 14 SW 47

Law Hill, Arnbathie, hut-circles
NO 171 262   NO 12 NE 14 & 38
Stewart 1950, 11;
NMRS, MS/591/1.

Leyston, maculae
NO 186 380   NO 13 NE 59

Leyston, macula
NO 1888 3846   NO 13 NE 60

Lintrose House, round-house
NO 2277 3812   NO 23 NW 58

Lornie Wood, maculae
NO 2222 2192   NO 22 SW 49

Mains of Errol, maculae
NO 2416 2138   NO 22 SW 16

Mains of Gourdie, maculae
NO 117 420   NO 14 SW 71

Mains of Murie, round-houses
NO 2315 2206   NO 22 SW 19

Mains of Murie, round-house
NO 2339 2198   NO 22 SW 41

Middlebank, round-houses
NO 2588 2747   NO 22 NE 14

Middlebank, round-houses
NO 2598 2754   NO 22 NE 14

Middlebank, round-houses
NO 2543 2752   NO 22 NE 35

Middlebank Holdings, round-house
NO 2562 2661   NO 22 NE 25

Middle Gourdie, round-houses
NO 1181 4186   NO 14 SW 38

Middle Gourdie, maculae
NO 114 416   NO 14 SW 70

Middle Gourdie, maculae
NO 113 417   NO 14 SW 80

Millbank, macula
NO 179 402   NO 14 SE 64

Mill of Bonhard, round-houses
NO 1517 2624   NO 12 NE 32

Ninetree Brae, round-house
NO 2548 2523   NO 22 NE 24

Paddockmuir Wood, round-houses
NO 216 204   NO 22 SW 13

Peattie, round-houses
NO 229 356   NO 23 NW 49

Peattie, round-houses
NO 232 358   NO 23 NW 64

Peattie, round-houses
NO 228 353   NO 23 NW 65

Pitroddie, round-houses
NO 2170 2522   NO 22 SW 44

Pitroddie, round-houses
NO 2169 2521   NO 22 SW 44

Pitroddie, round-houses
NO 2166 2500   NO 22 SW 44

Pitroddie, round-house
NO 2170 2496   NO 22 SW 44

Pitroddie, round-houses
NO 2162 2485   NO 22 SW 44

Pitroddie, round-houses
NO 2184 2480   NO 22 SW 44

Plaistow, maculae
NO 2462 2553   NO 22 NW 30

Pole Hill, ring-ditch house
NO 1976 2584   NO 12 NE 41

Priorland, round-house
NO 1906 2045   NO 12 SE 63

Rait, round-house
NO 222 269   NO 22 NW 66

Rossie, round-houses
NO 290 304   NO 23 SE 19

Rossie Priory, round-houses
NO 277 304 to   NO 23 SE 30
280 304

Sandyhall, round-houses
NO 2180 2328   NO 22 SW 37

Sherifftown, round-house
NO 1043 2777   NO 12 NW 42

Sherifftown, round-houses
NO 1037 2770   NO 12 NW 42

Spittalfield, round-house
NO 1089 4145   NO 14 SW 19

Spittalfield, round-house
NO 106 415   NO 14 SW 65
Maxwell and Wilson 1987, 27.

Tay Farm, macula
NO 150 404   NO 14 SE 48

Tofthill, round-houses
NO 1763 2138   NO 12 SE 37

Tofthill, maculae
NO 178 213   NO 12 SE 69

Warren Wood, maculae
NO 2450 3977   NO 23 NW 51

The Welton, round-houses
NO 1960 4393   NO 14 SE 29
DES 1981, 88;
Maxwell 1987, 40-1.

The Welton, round-houses
NO 190 440   NO 14 SE 71-5

The Welton, round-houses
NO 193 438   NO 14 SE 78-9

Wester Bonhard, round-houses
NO 1571 2676   NO 12 NE 31

Wester Denhead, round-houses
NO 229 410   NO 24 SW 46

Wester Denhead, round-houses
NO 2322 4103   NO 24 SW 47

Wester Drumatherty, round-houses
NO 1155 4119   NO 14 SW 20
DES 1982, 33; *DES 1984,* 38-9.

Whitemyre, hut-circle
NO 2078 2841   NO 22 NW 28

Whitemyre, hut-circle
NO 2022 2839   NO 22 NW 50

Ring-ditches

Ardgilzean, ring-ditch
NO 1244 2941   NO 12 NW 40

Cardean, ring-ditch
NO 2857 4564   NO 24 NE 51

Cargill, ring-ditches
NO 162 376   NO 13 NE 71

Cargill, ring-ditches
NO 167 379   NO 13 NE 57, 72

Dalbeathie, ring-ditch
NO 0600 4027   NO 04 SE 37

Grange of Aberbothrie, ring-ditch
NO 2351 4461   NO 24 SW 42

Grassy Walls, ring-ditch
NO 105 278   NO 12 NW

Hallhole, ring-ditch
NO 1862 3899   NO 13 NE 53

Inchcoonans, ring-ditch
NO 2361 2379   NO 22 SW 34

Inchture, ring-ditch
NO 2803 2928   NO 22 NE 10

Inchture, ring-ditch
NO 2799 2924   NO 22 NE 28

Inchtuthil, ring-ditch
NO 1235 3936   NO 13 NW 35

Islabank, ring-ditches
NO 200 415   NO 24 SW 57

Kemphill, ring-ditch
NO 2030 3994   NO 23 NW 48

Little Keithick, ring-ditches
NO 192 392   NO 13 NE 93

Loanfoot, ring-ditch
NO 2297 2266   NO 22 SW 36

Lochlands, ring-ditches
NO 2138 4536   NO 24 NW 60

Mains of Errol, ring-ditches
NO 2446 2177   NO 22 SW 15

Mains of Fullarton, ring-ditch
NO 2933 4390   NO 24 SE 73

Mains of Gourdie, ring-ditch
NO 1201 4189   NO 14 SW 18

Mains of Inchture, ring-ditch
NO 2823 2883   NO 22 NE 17

Mains of Keithick, ring-ditch
NO 2073 3868   NO 23 NW 10

Mains of Rattray, ring-ditch
NO 2042 4561   NO 24 NW 65

Millhorn, ring-ditch
NO 2219 4373   NO 24 SW 43

Mill of Bonhard, ring-ditch
NO 1517 2624   NO 12 NE 32

Mill of Bonhard, ring-ditches
NO 1523 2632   NO 12 NE 32

Myreside, ring-ditch
NO 169 443   NO 14 SE 54

North Grange, ring-ditches
NO 2676 2640   NO 22 NE 16

Pepperknowes, ring-ditch
NO 1925 2226   NO 12 SE 30

Pitroddie, ring-ditches
NO 217 248   NO 22 SW 44

Pow of Glencarse, ring-ditch
NO 1878 2245   NO 12 SE 52

Princeland, ring-ditches
NO 2241 4072   NO 24 SW 58

Rait, ring-ditch
NO 2272 2660   NO 22 NW 61

Ryehill, ring-ditch
NO 2266 4369   NO 24 SW 45

Ryehill, ring-ditch
NO 2275 4351   NO 24 SW 62

St Martins, ring-ditch
NO 1628 2972   NO 12 NE 20

Sandyhall, ring-ditches
NO 217 232   NO 22 SW 37

Sherifftown, ring-ditch
NO 1075 2802   NO 12 NW 31

Tofthill, ring-ditch
NO 1763 2138   NO 12 SE 37

Wester Denhead, ring-ditch
NO 2328 4105   NO 24 SW 47

Whiteloch, ring-ditch
NO 1676 4284   NO 14 SE 37

Woodhead, ring-ditches
NO 1438 3463   NO 13 SW 11, 71

Enclosed crescents

Cambusmichael, enclosed crescent
NO 1158 3229   NO 13 SW 42

Easter Bendochy, enclosed crescent
NO 220 417   NO 24 SW 69

Mains of Murie, enclosed crescent
NO 2315 2206   NO 22 SW 19

Middlebank, enclosed crescent
NO 2589 2749   NO 22 NE 14

Mudhall, enclosed crescent
NO 2265 4227   NO 24 SW 13

Sherifftown, enclosed crescent
NO 1043 2777   NO 12 NW 42

The Welton, enclosed crescent
NO 1960 4393   NO 14 SE 29

The Welton, enclosed crescent
NO 1933 4393   NO 14 SE 78

Wester Drumatherty, enclosed crescents (2)
NO 1155 4119   NO 14 SW 20

Palisaded sites

Inchtuthil, palisaded enclosure
NO 1152 3930   NO 13 NW 6
Abercromby, Ross and Anderson
1902, 230-4.

157

Leyston, palisaded enclosure
NO 1888 3846   NO 13 NE 60

Old Mains of Rattray, palisaded enclosure
NO 2039 4568   NO 24 NW 44

Spittalfield, palisaded enclosure
NO 109 414   NO 14 SW 19

Stralochy, palisaded enclosure
NO 086 409   NO 04 SE 18

Stralochy, palisaded enclosure
NO 086 408   NO 04 SE 34

Upper Gothens, palisaded enclosure
NO 1677 4152   NO 14 SE 43

The Welton, palisaded enclosure
NO 1895 4414   NO 14 SE 70

The Welton, palisaded enclosure
NO 1886 4406   NO 14 SE 76

The Welton, palisaded enclosure
NO 1963 4397   NO 14 SE 35

Fortifications

Little Dunsinane Hill, broch
NO 2225 3253   NO 23 SW 25
Stat. Acct., 9 (1793), 154;
NSA, 10 (Perth), 221.

Kilwhannie Den, Glenbran, ring-fort
NO 2440 3320   NO 23 SW 22
SRO, RHP 1005;
NSA, 10 (Perth), 221-2;
Melville 1939, 149.

Deuchny Hill, fort
NO 1526 2367   NO 12 SE 3
Watson 1923, 304-5, fig.1.

Dunsinane Hill, fort
NO 2137 3167   NO 23 SW 1.1
Robertson 1799; Playfair 1819;
Skene 1832; Wise 1859;
Brown 1873, 378-9;
Christison 1900, 88, fig.42;
Alcock 1981, 173-4.

Evelick, fort
NO 1995 2573   NO 12 NE 12
NSA, 10 (Perth), 1164;
Christison 1900, 56-8.

Hill of Dores, fort
NO 2573 3606   NO 23 NE 8
Stat. Acct., 17 (1796), 18;
Name Book, Perth, No.52, p.53.

Inchtuthil, fort
NO 1150 3928   NO 13 NW 6
Maitland 1757, 199;
Stobie 1783;
Roy 1793, pl.xviii;
Abercromby, Ross and Anderson
1902, 230-34.

Kemp's Hold, Stenton, fort
NO 0665 4068   NO 04 SE 11
Stat. Acct., 9 (1793), 504.

King's Seat, Dunkeld, fort
NO 0094 4399   NO 04 SW 19
Feachem 1966, 75.

Law Hill, Arnbathie, fort
NO 170 258   NO 12 NE 2
Watson 1930b, 270-2.

Mains of Hallyburton, fort
NO 2446 3916   NO 23 NW 43

Over Durdie, fort
NO 2096 2492   NO 22 SW 33

Rait, fort
NO 2298 2679   NO 22 NW 6
Stat. Acct., 4 (1792), 208;
Christison 1900, 57-9.

Rosemount, fort
NO 1619 3114   NO 13 SE 8

The Welton, fort
NO 1963 4397   NO 14 SE 35

Gold Castle, earthwork
NO 0966 2788   NO 02 NE 26
Maitland 1757, 199;
DES 1964, 38.

Tofthill, earthwork
NO 176 213   NO 12 SE 37

Crannogs

Keiter's Loch, Kinfauns, crannog
NO 1688 2191   NO 12 SE 19
Name Book, Perth, No.40, p.31.

Loch of Clunie, crannog
NO 1142 4445   NO 14 SW 26
Dixon and Andrian 1991.

Stormont Loch, crannog
NO 1930 4222   NO 14 SE 55

Enclosures

Ardblair, curvilinear enclosure
NO 1660 4451   NO 14 SE 2
NSA, 10 (Perth), 915;
OS 6-inch map, Perth,
1st ed. (1867), sheet 63.

Baledgarno, curvilinear enclosure
NO 284 300   NO 23 SE 41

Balhary, curvilinear enclosure
NO 2632 4621   NO 24 NE 46

Blackbank, curvilinear enclosure
NO 2131 2825   NO 22 NW 19

Burnside, curvilinear enclosure
NO 1522 4346   NO 14 SE 22

Commonbank, curvilinear enclosure
NO 1766 2483   NO 12 SE 41

Crathies Cottages, curvilinear enclosure
NO 282 453   NO 24 SE 71

East Myreriggs, curvilinear enclosure
NO 2143 4292   NO 24 SW 36

Hallhole, curvilinear enclosure
NO 1822 3954   NO 13 NE 32

Haughend, curvilinear enclosure
NO 2869 4644   NO 24 NE 44

Knowehead, curvilinear enclosure
NO 2154 4195   NO 24 SW 37

Links, curvilinear enclosure
NO 1793 3851   NO 13 NE 54

Meikleour, curvilinear enclosure
NO 161 396   NO 13 NE 94

Middlebank, curvilinear enclosure
NO 2543 2752   NO 22 NE 35

Peattie, curvilinear enclosure
NO 2293 3646   NO 23 NW 50

Plaistow, curvilinear enclosure
NO 2461 2554   NO 22 NW 30

Upper Muirhall, curvilinear enclosure
NO 1414 2341   NO 12 SW 187

Ardgaith, rectilinear enclosure
NO 219 225   NO 22 SW 62

Balgove, rectilinear enclosure
NO 2428 3778   NO 23 NW 42

Balgove, rectilinear enclosure
NO 2395 3755   NO 23 NW 47

Bankhead of Kinloch, rectilinear enclosure
NO 258 440   NO 24 SE 72

Bardmony, rectilinear enclosure
NO 246 457   NO 24 NW 69

Blackbank, rectilinear enclosure
NO 2131 2825   NO 22 NW 19

Bridgehaugh, rectilinear enclosure
NO 2266 4386   NO 24 SW 63

Brunty, rectilinear enclosure
NO 1994 3813   NO 13 NE 73

Chapelton, rectilinear enclosure
NO 2728 4406   NO 24 SE 30

Chapelton, rectilinear enclosure
NO 2711 4390   NO 24 SE 60

Cleaves, rectilinear enclosure
NO 160 430   NO 14 SE 36

Gannochy, rectilinear enclosures
NO 1305 2496   NO 12 SW 191

Haughend, rectilinear enclosure
NO 2871 4680   NO 24 NE 47

Hill of Gourdie, rectilinear enclosure
NO 109 423   NO 14 SW 33

Inchture, rectilinear enclosure
NO 2803 2928   NO 22 NE 10

Inchtuthil, rectilinear enclosure
NO 1223 3927   NO 13 NW 14

Kinloch, rectilinear enclosure
NO 1364 4488   NO 14 SW 47

Knowehead, rectilinear enclosure
NO 2158 4183   NO 24 SW 44

Mains of Inchture, rectilinear enclosure
NO 2824 2885   NO 22 NE 17

Mains of Murie, rectilinear enclosure
NO 2299 2196   NO 22 SW 18

Meikleour, rectilinear enclosure
NO 1618 3980   NO 13 NE 33

Mills of Keithick, rectilinear enclosure
NO 2019 3812   NO 23 NW 56

Nether Gothens, rectilinear enclosure
NO 1727 4054   NO 14 SE 28

Newmill, rectilinear enclosure
NO 323 458   NO 34 NW 32

Pleasance, rectilinear enclosure
NO 1353 3389   NO 13 SW 68

Rossie, rectilinear enclosure
NO 292 307   NO 23 SE 48

Sandyhall, rectilinear enclosure
NO 217 232   NO 22 SW 37

Scone Park, rectilinear enclosure
NO 0965 2762   NO 02 NE 27
Maitland 1757, 199.

The Welton, rectilinear enclosure
NO 1977 4396   NO 14 SE 34

Wester Denhead, rectilinear enclosure
NO 2292 4102   NO 24 SW 46

Whiteloch, rectilinear enclosure
NO 1684 4297   NO 14 SE 38

Woodside, rectilinear enclosure
NO 210 372   NO 23 NW 44

Interrupted ring-ditches

Byres, interrupted ring-ditch (possible)
NO 1327 3310   NO 13 SW 49

Cargill Church, interrupted ring-ditches
NO 1519 3677 &   NO 13 NE 44
1522 3676

Coin Hill, interrupted ring-ditches
NO 178 392   NO 13 NE 56

Gallowflat, interrupted ring-ditches
NO 210 211   NO 22 SW 57

Grangemount, interrupted ring-ditches
NO 238 452   NO 24 NW 40

Hallhole, interrupted ring-ditch (possible)
NO 183 397   NO 13 NE 97

Hatton, interrupted ring-ditch
NO 177 378   NO 13 NE 91

Jordanstone, interrupted ring-ditches
NO 2709 4721   NO 24 NE 53

Leyston, interrupted ring-ditches
NO 186 380   NO 13 NE 59

Leyston, interrupted ring-ditches
NO 1888 3846   NO 13 NE 60

Lintrose House, interrupted ring-ditch
NO 2271 3800   NO 23 NW 58

Millhorn, interrupted ring-ditch
NO 2200 4346   NO 24 SW 38

Mudhall, interrupted ring-ditches
NO 2265 4227   NO 24 SW 13

Newton of Glencarse,
interrupted ring-ditches (possible)
NO 1996 2192   NO 12 SE 38

Sherifftown, interrupted ring-ditch
NO 1037 2770   NO 12 NW 42

Woodhead, interrupted ring-ditches
NO 1431 3463   NO 13 SW 71

Souterrains

Balgersho, souterrain
NO 222 382   NO 23 NW 59

Barnhill, Perth, souterrain
NO 1248 2271   NO 12 SW 67
Hutcheson 1904, 541-7;
1908, 96-100;
Wainwright 1963, 172-3.

Blackhillock, souterrain
NO 0981 4096   NO 04 SE 33

Bonhard Park, souterrains
NO 155 265   NO 12 NE 30

Boyne, souterrain
NO 2681 2867   NO 22 NE 33

Cambusmichael, souterrain
NO 1159 3240   NO 13 SW 45

Cargill, souterrains
NO 166 379   NO 13 NE 74

Carsie Mains, souterrain
NO 178 414   NO 14 SE 61

Clashbenny, souterrains
NO 2230 2132   NO 22 SW 38

Clashbenny, souterrain
NO 218 214   NO 22 SW 63

Crathies Cottages, souterrain
NO 282 453   NO 24 NE 71

Culthill, souterrains
NO 0994 4180   NO 04 SE 31

Doo-cot Cottages, souterrain
NO 2121 2283   NO 22 SW 60

Easter Denhead, souterrain
NO 2391 4161   NO 24 SW 71

Easter Essendy, souterrain
NO 150 425   NO 14 SE 67

Gallowflat, souterrains
NO 210 211   NO 22 SW 57

Gasconhall, souterrain
NO 218 263   NO 22 NW 67

Glencarse, souterrain
NO 2026 2243   NO 22 SW 12
DES 1982, 33;
Maxwell 1987, 37-40.

Glencarse, souterrain
NO 2030 2259   NO 22 SW 39

Glencarse, souterrain
NO 2029 2248   NO 22 SW 56

Glencarse House, souterrains
NO 199 229   NO 12 SE 79

Glendelvine, souterrain
NO 0979 4115   NO 04 SE 36

Glendelvine, souterrain
NO 0971 4132   NO 04 SE 38

Goukton, souterrain
NO 174 221   NO 12 SE 80

Hatton, souterrain
NO 1714 3777   NO 13 NE 79

Hill House, souterrains
NO 1068 3057   NO 13 SW 65

Hill of Errol, souterrain
NO 2364 2105   NO 22 SW 17

Jordanstone, souterrains
NO 2709 4721   NO 24 NE 53

Kilspindie, souterrain
NO 2210 2580   NO 22 NW 36

Leyston, souterrains
NO 190 385   NO 13 NE 82

Lintrose House, souterrains
NO 2271 3800   NO 23 NW 3, 58
NSA, 9 (Forfar), 643-4.

Lornie Wood, souterrain
NO 2222 2192   NO 22 SW 49

Mains of Errol, souterrain
NO 244 217   NO 22 SW 15

Mains of Fordie, souterrain
NO 0925 4190   NO 04 SE 32

Mains of Murie, souterrain
NO 2315 2206   NO 22 SW 19

Meigle, souterrain
NO 2874 4447   NO 24 SE 23
MacRitchie 1900, 210;
Wainwright 1963, 196-7.

Middlebank, souterrain
NO 2585 2745   NO 22 NE 14

Middlebank, souterrain
NO 2543 2752   NO 22 NE 35

Middle Gourdie, souterrain
NO 1181 4186   NO 14 SW 38

Middle Gourdie, souterrain
NO 113 417   NO 14 SW 80

Millhorn, souterrain
NO 2242 4375   NO 24 SW 78

Mudhall, souterrains
NO 226 422   NO 24 SW 2, 13
Pennant 1776, 448-9;
Stat. Acct., 19 (1797), 359-60;
NSA, 10 (Perth), 1188-9;
Name Book, Perth, No.9, p.27;
Wainright 1963, 183.

New Mains, souterrain
NO 2783 2935   NO 22 NE 26

Ninetree Brae, souterrains
NO 2548 2523   NO 22 NE 24

Old Mains of Rattray, souterrains
NO 2041 4570   NO 24 NW 44

Pans Hill, souterrain
NO 188 217   NO 12 SE 78

Peattie, souterrains
NO 228 353   NO 23 NW 65

Pitcur, souterrain
NO 2529 3738   NO 23 NE 1
MacRitchie 1900.

Pitcur, souterrain
NO 2478 3657   NO 23 NW 9
Curle 1932, 387-8;
Proc Soc Antiq Scot,
5 (1862-4), 82;
Wainwright 1963, 200-2.

Pitcur, souterrain
NO 2476 3660   NO 23 NW 53
Mackenna 1972,18.

Pitroddie, souterrain
NO 2175 2517   NO 22 SW 44

Pitroddie, souterrains
NO 2171 2500   NO 22 SW 44

Pitroddie, souterrains
NO 2181 2479   NO 22 SW 44

Rait, souterrains
NO 2263 2666   NO 22 NW 61

Rossie Priory, souterrains
NO 277 304 to   NO 23 SE 30
280 304

Ryehill, souterrain
NO 2266 4369   NO 24 SW 45

South Inchmichael, souterrain
NO 2478 2529   NO 22 NW 29

South Inchmichael, souterrain
NO 2485 2540   NO 22 NW 29

Spittalfield, souterrains
NO 109 414   NO 14 SW 19
Pitts and St Joseph 1985, 261.

Spittalfield, souterrains
NO 106 415   NO 14 SW 65
Maxwell and Wilson 1987, 27.

Tofthill, souterrains
NO 1763 2138   NO 12 SE 37

The Welton, souterrains
NO 1960 4393   NO 14 SE 29
DES 1981, 88;
Maxwell 1987, 40-1.

The Welton, souterrain
NO 1919 4397   NO 14 SE 74

The Welton, souterrain
NO 1933 4393   NO 14 SE 78

West Buttergask, souterrains
NO 210 345   NO 23 SW 29

Wester Drumatherty, souterrain
NO 1155 4119   NO 14 SW 20.1
DES 1982, 33.

Woodside, souterrain
NO 212 375   NO 23 NW 46

Rectangular cropmarks, buildings and lobate enclosures

Bankhead of Kinloch, rectangular
building (possible)
NO 258 440   NO 24 SE

Berryhill, rectangular buildings
NO 1164 3198   NO 13 SW 48

Bonhard Park, rectangular cropmarks
NO 154 264   NO 12 NE 30

Clashbenny, rectangular cropmarks
NO 2230 2132   NO 22 SW 38

Glencarse, rectangular building
NO 196 219   NO 12 SE 29

Hill of Errol, rectangular cropmark
NO 2326 2163   NO 22 SW 65

Inchcoonans, rectangular cropmarks
NO 2353 2353   NO 22 SW 40

Inchture, lobate enclosure
NO 2816 2923   NO 22 NE 9

Inchtuthil, lobate enclosure
NO 1214 3945   NO 13 NW 24

Mains of Errol, rectangular building (possible)
NO 2416 2138   NO 22 SW 16

Mains of Inchture, rectangular cropmarks and
building
NO 2842 2871   NO 22 NE 17

Mains of Murie, rectangular cropmark
NO 2315 2206   NO 22 SW 19

Rossie Priory, rectangular cropmark
NO 2811 3029   NO 23 SE 31

Rossie, rectangular cropmark
NO 292 307   NO 23 SE 48

South Inchmichael, rectangular cropmarks and
building
NO 2480 2530   NO 22 NW 29

ROMAN MONUMENTS

Black Hill, Meikleour, watch-tower
NO 1760 3915   NO 13 NE 7
Abercromby 1904;
Richmond 1940, 37-40;
Robertson 1974;
Maxwell 1990, 353-5.

Cargill, fort
NO 1661 3790   NO 13 NE 27
Maxwell and Wilson 1987, 16;
Maxwell 1989, 108.

Coupar Angus, temporary camp (possible)
NO 223 397   NO 23 NW 12
Maitland 1757, 199-200;
Stat. Acct., 17 (1797), 10-11;
Crawford 1949, 82-5.

Grassy Walls, temporary camp
NO 1050 2800   NO 12 NW 8
Roy 1793, vii-viii, pl.xii;
Callander 1919b;
Crawford 1949, 64-7;
St Joseph 1951, 63; 1958, 91;
1977, 143.

Hill of Gourdie, quarry
NO 10 94   NO 14 SW 33
Pitts and St Joseph 1985, 61, 255-6.

Inchtuthil, legionary fortress, compounds,
temporary camps and linear earthworks
NO 12 39   NO 13 NW 5
Maitland 1757, 199;
Pennant 1776, 67-70, pl.vii;
Roy 1793, pl.xviii;
Abercromby, Ross and Anderson 1902;
Macdonald 1919;
Crawford 1949, 70-74;
Richmond 1943, 47;
Pitts and St Joseph 1985.

Lintrose, temporary camp
NO 2200 3760   NO 23 NW 5
Roy 1793, 67-8, pl.xiv;
Crawford 1949, 85-7;
St Joseph 1969, 116.

Mains of Cargill, fortlet
NO 1632 3766   NO 13 NE 26
Richmond 1943, 47;
DES 1965, 30.

Scone Park, temporary camp
NO 1044 2715   NO 12 NW 14
St Joseph 1955, 87; 1969, 111;
DES 1970, 38.

Steeds Stalls, temporary camp
NO 1151 4271   NO 14 SW 15
Richmond 1943, 47-9;
Crawford 1949, 75-6;
Maxwell 1981, 44.

St Madoes, temporary camp
NO 209 196   NO 21 NW 39
St Joseph 1969, 110-11.

Wester Drumatherty, road and linear ditch
NO 1075 4156 to   NO 14 SW 30 & 66
1151 4097
Pitts and St Joseph 1985, 47, 191, 256;
Maxwell and Wilson, 1987, 27.

EARLY HISTORIC

Pictish and Early Christian stone monuments

Balholmie House, Pictish symbol stone
NO 1477 3623   NO 13 SE 1
Formerly stood in a wall north-west of
West Whitefield Farm, Cargill;
Hutcheson 1884, 315-16;
Allen and Anderson 1903, iii, 283-4.

Dunkeld Cathedral, Early Christian stones (4)
NO 0237 4259   NO 04 SW 1
Stuart 1856, pl.l; 1867, pl.xvi;
Allen and Anderson 1903, iii, 284-5; 317-9.

Fairygreen, Collace, Pictish symbol stone
NO 2069 3319   NO 23 SW 4
Small 1964;
Ralston and Inglis 1984, 46-7.

Inchyra, Pictish symbol stone
NO 1904 2120   NO 12 SE 9
Stevenson 1961, 32-39;
Wainwright 1961;
Padel 1972, 100-7.

Keillor, Pictish symbol stone
NO 2733 3976   NO 23 NE 3
Chalmers 1848, 14, pl.xx;
Stuart 1856, 34-5, pl.cxii;
Allen and Anderson 1903, iii, 207-8.

Kettins, cross-slab
NO 2378 3906   NO 23 NW 1
Stuart 1867, pl.viii;
Allen and Anderson 1903, iii, 224-5.

Meigle Museum,
Pictish and Early Christian stones (33)
NO 2872 4459   NO 24 SE 25
Pennant 1776, ii, pl.xvii;
Chalmers 1848, pls.vii-ix, xvii-xx;
Stuart 1856, pls.lxxii-lxxvii, xciii,
cxxvii, cxxxi, cxxxii;
1867, pls.iii, v-vii;
Galloway 1878, 426-34;
Reid 1889;
Allen and Anderson
1903, iii, 296-305, 330-40;
Aglen 1923; Cruden 1964;
Henderson 1967, 145; 1982, 94-6;
Ross 1967, 140;
Stevenson 1971, 73;
Lang 1975, 229.

New Scone, cross-slab
NO 1382 2619   NO 12 NW 38
Lye and Fisher 1982.

Rossie Priory, cross-slab
NO 2915 3080   NO 23 SE 4
Stuart 1867, pl.xcviii;
Allen and Anderson 1903, iii, 306.

St Madoes, cross-slabs (2)
NO 1966 2119   NO 12 SE 15, 21
Stuart 1856, pl.iv; Allen 1883;
Allen and Anderson 1903, iii, 292-6, 328-9.

Tower of Lethendy, cross-slab
NO 1405 4170   NO 14 SW 13
Fisher and Greenhill 1974.

Stray finds

Clunie Castle, Pictish brooches
NO 110 440   NO 14 SW 69
NMS FC 176-7;
Anderson 1880, 449-52.

Coupar Angus, bronze pin
NO c.22 40   NO 24 SW 50
Projecting ring-headed pin;
in private possession;
Clarke 1971, 48, no.27.

Dunkeld, Viking pin
NO c.02 42   NO 04 SW 5
Bronze ring-headed pin;
NMS FC 235; Grieg 1940, 157;
Fanning 1983, 338, no.29.

Dunsinane Hill, bronze ring
NO 2137 3167   NO 23 SW 1
Spiral finger-ring; now lost;
Christison, 1900, 91.

Errol, Norse brooches (2)
NO c.25 22   NO 22 SE 1
Two tortoise brooches;
PMAG 1891-2; Grieg 1940, 100-1.

SETTLEMENT AND LANDSCAPE FROM THE TWELFTH TO THE EIGHTEENTH CENTURY

Early castles

Barton Hill, Kinnaird, motte
NO 2436 2864   NO 22 NW 25
Reg. Reg. Scot., ii, no.135;
Stewart and Tabraham 1974.

Cairnbeddie, earthwork
NO 1498 3082   NO 13 SW 1
NSA, 10 (Perth), 873-4;
Christison 1900, 46;
Scott 1911, 43-4.

Cargill, Castle Hill, ringwork
NO 1579 3743   NO 13 NE 22
Reg. Reg. Scot., ii, no.334, 377;
Stat. Acct., 13 (1794), 534.

Castle of Rattray, motte-and-bailey
NO 2098 4539   NO 24 NW 21
Stat Acct., 4 (1792), 149;
Douglas 1798, 274-6;
Disposition P Lawson, 1818;
NSA, 10 (Perth), 241;
Name Book, Perth, No.70, p.46;
Millar 1890, 104-6;
Paul 1983, 18-29.

Clunie Castle
NO 1107 4403   NO 14 SW 5
Dunkeld Rentale, 187;
Stat. Acct., 9 (1793), 265-7;
MacGibbon and Ross 1889, 589;
Lawrie 1905, no.136;
Anderson 1922, 288;
Reg. Reg. Scot., ii, no. 29;
Alcock 1981, 161.

Law Knowe, Murie, motte
NO 2315 2238   NO 22 SW 2
NSA, 10 (Perth), 386;
Melville 1935, 176-9;
Reg. Reg. Scot., ii, no.204;
Reg. Mag. Sig., 3, no.3221.

Meikleour, motte
NO 1536 3869   NO 13 NE 87
Reg. Reg. Scot., ii, no.399;
no.472; vi, no.287; v, no.130.

Moated sites

Friarton, moated site (possible)
NO 1409 3051   NO 13 SW 31

Gourdie, moated site (possible)
NO 1210 4195   NO 14 SW 7, 37

Hallyards, moated site
NO 2790 4642   NO 24 NE 9
Macfarlane 1906, 110;
Dunkeld Rentale, 76;
Meikle 1925, 100.

Links, moated site
NO 1825 3864   NO 13 NE 55

Moncur, moated site (possible)
NO 2835 2952   NO 22 NE 2, 11

Newhall, moated site (possible)
NO 1865 3192   NO 13 SE 14
Name Book, Perth, No.17, p.17;
Reg. Mag. Sig., 4, no.12.

Eclessiastical estate centres

Campsie, abbot's house and chapel
NO 1243 3394   NO 13 SW 10
Stat. Acct., 13 (1794), 534-5.
Coupar Angus Rental,
i, no.299; ii, no.66.

Cambusmichael, grange (possible)
NO 115 324   NO 13 SW 30

Cambusmichael, rectilinear enclosure
NO 1164 3240   NO 13 SW 41

Coupar Grange, grange
NO 2253 4313   NO 24 SW 52, 59, 74

Rural settlement

Abernyte, fermtoun
NO 2579 3115   NO 23 SE 45
Winter 1976;
Stat. Acct., 9 (1793), 142-3.

Abernyte, manse
NO 2674 3113   NO 23 SE 44
NSA, 10 (Perth), 224.

Arnbathie, fermtoun
NO 1748 2598   NO 12 NE 48
Reg. Mag. Sig., 4, no.1708.

Balthayock, building and enclosure
NO 1925 2390   NO 12 SE 57

Balthayock Wood, building
NO 1853 2397   NO 12 SE 56

Beal Hill, buildings
NO 201 276 to   NO 22 NW 49.2-4
202 276

Beal Hill, buildings
NO 2018 2751   NO 22 NW 49.1

Boghall, buildings
NO 1768 2743   NO 12 NE 45

Cargill, cruck-framed cottage
NO 1505 3693   NO 13 NE 88
SRO, RHP 3422.

Commonbank, farmstead
NO 1709 2486   NO 12 SE 17

Dunkeld, Bishop's Hill, windmill
NO 0211 4252   NO 04 SW 28
Donnachie and Stewart 1967, 296.

Franklyden, farmsteads
NO 2187 2982   NO 22 NW 48

Franklyden, farmstead
NO 2178 2966   NO 22 NW 57

Franklyden, farmstead
NO 2184 2960   NO 22 NW 56

Franklyden, shieling
NO 2233 2972   NO 22 NW 58

Goddens, farmstead
NO 1964 2545   NO 12 NE 34

Knowehead, huts
NO 1629 2454   NO 12 SE 58

Law Hill, Arnbathie, building
NO 1711 2584   NO 12 NE 4

Over Fingask, farmstead and enclosure
NO 226 288   NO 22 NW 53, 54

Over Fingask,
field-system, building and enclosures
NO 221 289   NO 22 NW 37-9

Pole Hill, buildings
NO 1972 2647   NO 12 NE 47

Pole Hill, shieling
NO 1950 2583   NO 12 NE 35

Pole Wood, building
NO 1879 2663   NO 12 NE 46

Rossie, village
NO 2921 3072   NO 23 SE 5
Stat. Acct., 4 (1792), 193;
NSA, 10 (Perth), 831;
Name Book, Perth, No.10, p.12;
Millar 1890, 33-4;
Melville 1939, 89;
Reg. Reg. Scot., i, no.194;
Scottish Countryside
Commission (SDD) 1987, 240-1.

Scone, village
NO 1170 2655   NO 12 NW 9, 9.5
Stat. Acct., 18 (1796), 69-88;
Scon Liber, 47;
NSA, 10 (Perth), 1062-4;
Skene 1870, 71;
Urquhart 1883, 20;
Dicks 1983, 39-40.

Shanry, buildings, huts
NO 196 271   NO 12 NE 40

Strelitz, fermtoun and planned village
NO 189 362   NO 13 NE 84-6
Lesslie 1763;
Stat. Acct., 13 (1794), 538.

West Cult, building
NO 0615 4178   NO 04 SE 40

Whitemyre, building
NO 1995 2842   NO 12 NE 39

Whitemyre, building
NO 2025 2839   NO 22 NW 51

ECCLESIASTICAL MONUMENTS

Abernyte, church and burial-ground
NO 2669 3114   NO 23 SE 43, 35
NSA, 10 (Perth), 222, 224;
Melville 1939, 155-9;
Cowan 1967, 4.

Arthurstone, architectural fragments
NO 2612 4310   NO 24 SE 20

Balhary, architectural fragments
NO 2630 4659   NO 24 NE 28

Bendochy, church and burial-ground
NO 2184 4145   NO 24 SW 1
Stat. Acct., 19 (1797), 358-9;
NSA, 10 (Perth), 1189, 1198-9;
Walker 1909, 391-2;
Cowan 1967, 16.

Cambusmichael, church and burial-ground
NO 1156 3258   NO 13 SW 17
Stat. Acct., 13 (1794), 505;
Cowan 1967, 25.

Caputh, church and burial-ground
NO 0832 4000   NO 04 SE 10, 30
Stat. Acct., 9 (1793), 485-6;
NSA, 10 (Perth), 682;
Hannay 1915, 312;
Cowan 1967, 26-7;
Willsher 1987, 83-91.

Caputh, chapel
Unlocated   NO 04 SE 28
Scott 1923, 147.

Cargill, church and burial-ground
NO 1501 3699   NO 13 NE 83
Stat. Acct., 13 (1794), 544;
NSA, 10 (Perth), 1171;
Reg. Reg. Scot., ii, no.377.

Carsegrange, chapel
NO 27 25   NO 22 NE 19
Melville 1935, 104;
Coupar Angus Charters,
i, xlv-xlvi; ii, 67-71.

Chapelton, chapel
NO 2725 4418   NO 24 SE 22,
                                    SW 55
Name Book, Perth, No.54, p.9;
Coupar Angus Rental,
i, no.207; ii, p.207.

Chapelton, Clunie Parish, chapels
Unlocated   NO 14 SW 46
Scott 1950, 348.

Charlestown, architectural fragment
NO 2450 2761   NO 22 NW 42

Clunie, church and burial-ground
NO 1095 4405   NO 14 SW 44
Stat. Acct., 9 (1793), 253;
NSA, 10 (Perth), 1026;
Cowan 1967, 32;
NMRS, PTR/18/1.

Clunie, chapel
NO 1092 4416   NO 14 SW 6
Name Book, Perth, No.16, pp.41, 47.

Collace, church and burial-ground
NO 1970 3198   NO 13 SE 13
Stat. Acct., 20 (1798), 240;
NSA, 10 (Perth), 216-17;
Cowan 1967, 33.

Coupar Angus, abbey
NO 2233 3980   NO 23 NW 12-14
Maitland 1757, 199-200;
Cardonnel 1788;
Roy 1793, 133;
Stat. Acct., 17 (1796), 10-11;
Hutcheson 1888, 146-8;
MacGibbon and Ross 1897, 491-7;
Greenhill 1944, 81-6;
Coupar Angus Charters;
Crawford 1949, 82-5;
Cowan 1967, 36;
Reg. Reg. Scot., ii, no.154;
Cowan and Easson 1976, 73-4.

Dunkeld Cathedral, cathedral
NO 0237 4259   NO 04 SW 1
Root 1950;
Cowan and Easson 1976, 47, 175.

Dunkeld, Bishop's Palace,
house and tower-house
NO 022 425   NO 04 SW 15
Slezer 1693, plate 24;
NSA, 10 (Perth), 972-3;
Dunkeld Rentale, 117, 315, 336.

Dunkeld, hospital
NO 0256 4262   NO 04 SW 2
Stat. Acct., 28 (1791), 428n;
NSA, 10 (Perth), 993;
Dunkeld Rentale, 80, 82, 242, 312;
Cowan and Easson 1976, 175.

Dunkeld, St Jerome's, chapel
NO 0319 4248   NO 04 SW 12
NSA, 10 (Perth), 985.

Easter Bendochy, architectural fragments
NO 2215 4198   NO 24 SW 67

Errol, church and burial-ground
NO 2520 2280   NO 22 SE 2
Reg. Reg. Scot., ii, no.562;
Stat. Acct., 4 (1792), 489;
NSA, 10 (Perth), 386;
Cowan 1967, 62.

Errol, 'Polkalk', chapel
NO *c*.247 213   NO 22 SW 47
Melville 1935, 104.

Fingask Castle,
architectural fragments and font
NO 2280 2745   NO 22 NW 7.3

Inchture, church and burial-ground
NO 2812 2878   NO 22 NE 30
Cowan 1967, 86.

Keithick, chapel
NO 20 38   NO 23 NW 41
Coupar Angus Rental, ii, p.207.

Kettins, church and burial-ground
NO 2379 3904   NO 23 NW 6
Stat. Acct., 17 (1796), 15;
Hutcheson 1894; Smart 1951;
Cowan 1967, 93-4.

Kettins Parish, chapels
Unlocated   NO 23 NW 4, 7, 19, 63;
                             23 NE 4;
                             24 SW 12
Stat. Acct., 17 (1796), 15.

Kilspindie, church and burial-ground
NO 2199 2575   NO 22 NW 43
Melville 1939, 127-32;
Cowan 1967, 109.

Kinfauns, church and burial-ground
NO 1666 2226   NO 12 SE 13
Stat. Acct., 14 (1795), 222, 225;
MacGibbon and Ross 1897, 513-17;
Melville 1939, 37-9;
Cowan 1967, 111-12.

Kinnaird, church and burial-ground
NO 2430 2864   NO 22 NW 55
Melville 1939, 144;
Cowan 1967, 114;
Stat. Acct., 6 (1793), 259.

Kinnaird, graveslab
NO 2430 2864   NO 22 NW 27.1

Kinnoull, church and burial-ground
NO 1229 2331   NO 12 SW 10
Stat. Acct., 18 (1796), 555;
NSA, 10 (Perth), 942;
MacGibbon and Ross 1897, 580-1;
Cowan 1967, 115-16.

Kirkton of Lethendy,
church and burial-ground
NO 1300 4180   NO 14 SW 40
Stat. Acct., 17 (1796), 526;
NSA, 10 (Perth), 1001;
Cowan 1967, 131; SDD HBC List.

Lethendy, graveslab
NO 1405 4170 NO 14 SW 13
Fisher and Greenhill 1974, 238-41.

Little Gourdie, chapel
Unlocated NO 14 SW 45
Scott 1950, 348.

Meigle, church and burial-ground
NO 2873 4460 NO 24 SE 33
Boethius 1526;
Stat. Acct., 1 (1791), 506-7;
NSA, 10 (Perth), 234-5;
Chalmers 1848, 9-10;
Jervise 1859, 242-5;
MacGibbon and Ross 1897, 517-18;
Allen and Anderson 1903, iii, 296-8;
Cowan 1967, 145.

Old Bridge of Dean,
architectural fragments
NO 2878 4587 NO 24 NE 13.1

Over Kincairney, chapel
NO 0834 4398 NO 04 SE 6
Allen 1881, 86-7.

Rait, church and burial-ground
NO 2274 2685 NO 22 NW 3
Stat. Acct., 4 (1792), 202;
Melville 1939, 127-8;
Cowan 1967, 167-8.

Ross, chapel
NO *c.*210 220 NO 22 SW 46
Melville 1935, 104.

Rossie, church and burial-ground
NO 2915 3080 NO 23 SE 4
Stat. Acct., 4 (1792), 191;
NSA, 10 (Perth), 831;
Name Book, Perth, No.36, p.11;
Millar 1890, 29-33;
Melville 1939, 98-9, pl.18;
Greenhill 1958, 232;
Reg. Reg. Scot., i, nos.120;
Cowan 1967, 173;
Cowan and Easson 1976, 236.

Rossie Priory, cross
NO 2821 3061 NO 23 SE 6

St Madoes, church and burial-ground
NO 1965 2120 NO 12 SE 51
Stat. Acct., 3 (1792), 573;
NSA, 10, Perth, 633;
Melville 1939, 53-4, 56;
Cowan 1967, 178.

St Martins, church and burial-ground
NO 1547 3036 NO 13 SE 26
Stat. Acct., 13 (1794), 503;
NSA, 10 (Perth), 874;
Cowan 1967, 145.

Scone, abbey
NO 1146 2654 NO 12 NW 9.3-4
Pennant 1776, 116-17;
Stat. Acct., 18 (1796), 83-6;
Scone Liber, ix-xx;
NSA, 10 (Perth), 1062-3;
Skene 1870, 70-1 and n;
Cowan and Easson, 1976, 77;
Stuart 1870b.

Scone, folk-moot
NO 1145 2665 NO 12 NW 9.2, 45-6
Pennant 1776, 115;
Stat. Acct., 18 (1796), 85-7;
NSA, 10 (Perth), 1064-5;
Name Book, Perth, No.72, p.43;
Paul 1911, 196.

Scone, hospital
NO 11 26 NO 12 NW 48
Cowan and Easson 1976, 191.

Westown, church and burial-ground
NO 2493 2746 NO 22 NW 21
NSA, 10 (Perth), 386;
MacGibbon and Ross 1897, 522-4;
Melville 1935, 104-5;
Cowan 1967, 86.

FORTIFIED AND DOMESTIC ARCHITECTURE

Ardblair Castle, tower-house
NO 1636 4453 NO 14 SE 1
MacGibbon and Ross 1892, 282-5;
Reg. Mag. Sig., 1, App.2, no.1867.

Arthurstone, dovecot
NO 2630 4313 NO 24 SE 29

Balthayock Castle, tower-house
NO 1741 2295 NO 12 SE 4
Stat Acct., 18 (1796), 559;
NSA, 10 (Perth), 938;
MacGibbon and Ross 1889, 132-4.

Bandirran, dovecot
NO 1976 3034 NO 13 SE 3

Belmont Castle, tower-house
NO 2861 4391 NO 24 SE 19
Stat. Acct., 1 (1791), 511;
NSA, 10 (Perth), 235;
Jervise 1859, 243;
Reg. Mag. Sig., 2, no.2608.

Bonhard, tower-house and dovecot
NO 1484 2573 NO 12 NW 16, 27
NSA, 10 (Perth), 1065.

Byres, house
NO *c.*129 329 NO 13 SW 56
Scott 1911, 16;
Retours, Perth, no.82.

Castlehill, Baledgarno, carved stones
NO 2760 3044 NO 23 SE 7
Boethius 1526;
NSA, 10 (Perth), 832;
Name Book, Perth, No.36, p.10.

Dunkeld, Dean's House, house
NO 0246 4260 NO 04 SW 14
NSA, 10 (Perth), 987.

Dunkeld House, house
NO 0242 4268 NO 04 SW 16, 29
Slezer 1693, plate 24;
Atholl Muniments, D3.34;
NSA, 10 (Perth), 963;
Pococke 1887, 226.

Errol Park, tower-house
NO 2475 2260 NO 22 SW 25
Melville 1935, 152-7.

Evelick Castle, tower-house
NO 2039 2595 NO 22 NW 4
NSA, 10 (Perth), 1164;
MacGibbon and Ross 1887, 89-90;
RCAHMS 1980, 25.

Fingask Castle, tower-house
NO 2280 2745 NO 22 NW 7.1-2, 44
Scone Liber, 2;
NSA, 10 (Perth), 1164;
Name Book, Perth, No.38, p.16;
Millar 1890, 181;
Melville 1939, 116-22;
Reg. Reg. Scot., i, no.243.

Fullarton Castle, house and policies
NO 292 439 NO 24 SE 58, 61
Mackay 1876, 54;
Jervise 1882, 362, 405;
Paul 1908, 108, 405;
Paul 1911, 108-9; Strong 1987;
Reg. Mag. Sig., 6, nos.800, 2135;
8, no.1697; 10, no.588.

Glencarse House, house
NO *c.*195 226 NO 12 SE 5
Retours, Perth, no.780;
Scon Liber, nos.1, 69;
Melville 1939, 33-4;
Reg. Mag. Sig., 4, no.1778.

Glendoick House, tower
NO 2075 2361 NO 22 SW 54
Melville 1939, 33-5;
Reg. Mag. Sig., 3, no.760;
Retours, Perth, no.780.

Gourdie, house and policies
NO 1210 4195 NO 14 SW 7, 37
Douglas 1798, 535; Kinloch 1888.

Inchmartine, house
NO 2638 2775 NO 22 NE 23
Melville 1939, 172;
Reg. Mag. Sig., 9, no.1909.

Keillor, tower-house and dovecot
NO 268 403 NO 24 SE 28, 63
Retours, Perth, no.579; Forfar, no.589;
Duncan 1979, 17-18.

Kilspindie, castle and dovecot
NO 2190 2577 NO 22 NW 11, 33
Melville 1939, 106-7, 130.

Kincarrathie, dovecot
NO 2475 1230 NO 12 SW 113

Kinfauns Castle, castle
NO 1505 2264 NO 12 SE 25
Stat. Acct., 14 (1795), 223-5;
Reg. Reg. Scot., vi, no.6.

Kinloch, house
NO 2675 4435 NO 24 SE 64
Stat. Acct., 1 (1791), 512.

Kinnaird Castle, tower-house and dovecot
NO 2412 2889 NO 22 NW 24, 27
Stat. Acct., 6 (1793), 233-4;
NSA, 10 (Perth), 228-9;
MacGibbon and Ross 1887, 270-5;
Melville 1939, 136-9;
Reg. Reg. Scot., ii, nos.470-1.

Kinnoull, castle
NO 1239 2286 NO 12 SW 69
Stat. Acct., 18 (1796), 557;
Cowan 1904, i, 75-6;
Reg. Reg. Scot., vi, no.239.

Lawton, sundial and architectural fragments
NO 20 34 NO 23 SW 28

Lethendy, tower-house
NO 1405 4170 NO 14 SW 13
NSA, 10 (Perth), 1002;
MacGibbon and Ross 1889, 590-1.

Loch of Clunie, tower-house
NO 1132 4402 NO 14 SW 4
Stat. Acct., 9 (1793), 242-3, 261-5;
NSA, 10 (Perth), 1024;
Name Book, Perth, No.16, pp.48-9;
MacGibbon and Ross 1889, 589-90;
Myln's *Vitae* 1915, 310, 312;
Dunkeld Rentale, 183-4;
Dixon and Andrian 1991.

Mains of Rattray, architectural fragment
NO 2120 4512 NO 24 NW 66

Marlee House, house
NO 1489 4450 NO 14 SW 63
Brown 1808;
Meacher 1905, 95; 1956, 82;
SRO, RHP 3547.

Megginch Castle, fortified house
NO 2418 2460 NO 22 SW 1, 9
MacGibbon and Ross 1887, 499-500;
Paul 1906, 314; 1908, 219, 223;
Melville 1935, 167-71;
Reg. Mag. Sig., 4, no.1894; 11, no.623.

Meigle, architectural fragments
NO 2972 4465 NO 24 SE 70

Meikleour House, tower-house
NO 1542 3870 NO 13 NE 4
Name Book, Perth, No.13, p.171;
Reg. Reg. Scot., vi, no.287.

Moncur Castle, fortified house
NO 2835 2952 NO 22 NE 2, 11
NSA, 10 (Perth), 408, 832-3;
MacGibbon and Ross 1887, 269-70;
Millar 1890, 12, 22, 36-7;
Melville 1939, 86-7.

Newbigging, dovecot
NO 2645 2518 NO 22 NE 8

Old Mains of Rattray, house
NO 2065 4525 NO 24 NW 48
Dunbar 1966, 82, 84; NMRS, PTR/10/11.

Panshill, house
NO *c.*180 222 NO 12 SE 60
Retours, Perth, no.780; Melville 1939, 33-4.

Pitcur Castle, tower-house
NO 2515 3699 NO 23 NE 2
Reg. Reg. Scot., v, no.56; Paul 1907, 334.

Pitfour, house
NO 19 20 NO 12 SE 50
Melville 1939, 48;
Reg. Mag. Sig., 6, no.1032.

Pitkindie, architectural fragments
NO 2488 3173 NO 23 SW 15
Stat. Acct., 9 (1793), 153;
NSA, 10 (Perth), 224;
Melville 1939, 149;
SRO, RHP 1005.

Pitroddie, carved fragments
NO 2148 2521 NO 22 NW 41
Retours, Perth, no.744.

Polcalk, dovecot
NO 2326 4638 NO 24 NW 23

Scone, palace
NO 1135 2655 NO 12 NW 9.1
Roy 1747-55, sheet 17/4;
Stat. Acct., 18 (1796), 83-5;
Scone Liber, xxi;
NSA, 10 (Perth), 1060;
Skene 1870, 70;
Urquhart 1883, 13-14;
Pococke 1887, 258;
Millar 1890, 17;
Defoe 1968, 803; Walker 1970;
Cowan and Easson 1976, 98;
Scottish Countryside
Commission (SDD), 1987, 246-54;
NMRS PTD/94.

South West Fullarton, architectural fragments
NO 2981 4376 NO 24 SE 71

Stobhall, tower-house and chapel
NO 1320 3435 NO 13 SW 6
Name Book, Perth, No.16, p.27;
MacGibbon and Ross 1887, 358-69;
Paul 1910, 28-62;
Patullo 1974, 90-6;
Scottish Countryside
Commission (SDD) 1987, 255-61;
NMRS, MS/232/Ta/Pe/5.

Viewbank, architectural fragment
NO 2484 4219 NO 24 SW 65

Waterybutts, dovecot
NO 2766 2592 NO 22 NE 7

MISCELLANEOUS

Kinnoull, medieval pottery kiln
NO 1236 2333 NO 12 SW 156
Stevenson and Henshall 1957;
Laing 1971; Brooks 1980, 395-401.

The Long Man's Grave, stone slab
NO 2218 3154 NO 23 SW 12
NSA, 10 (Perth), 221;
Hunter 1883, 89.

ABBREVIATIONS AND BIBLIOGRAPHY

ABDUA
—Anthropological Museum, University of Aberdeen

Abercromby, J 1904
—Excavations made on the Estate of Meikleour, Perthshire, in May 1903
Proc Soc Antiq Scot, 38 (1903-4), 82-96

Abercromby, J, Ross, T and Anderson, T 1902
—Account of the Excavation of the Roman Station at Inchtuthil, Perthshire,
undertaken by the Society of Antiquaries of Scotland in 1901
Proc Soc Antiq Scot, 36 (1901-2), 182-242

Adamson, H and Gallagher, D 1986
—Excavation at Cleaven Dyke, Perthshire, 1975
Glasgow Archaeol J, 13 (1986), 63-68

ADM
—Angus District Museum

Aglen, A S 1923
—*The Sculptured Stones at Meigle*
Dundee

Ainslie, 1794
—Map of the County of Forfar or Shire of Angus

Aitken, W G 1964
—Two Bronze Age Cist Burials. (i) Lochlands Farm, Rattray
Proc Soc Antiq Scot, 95 (1961-2), 126-31

Alcock, L 1981
—Early Historic Fortifications in Scotland
in Guilbert, G (ed.) 1981, 150-81

Alcock, L 1982
—Forteviot: a Pictish and Scottish royal church and palace
in Pearce, S M (ed.) 1982, 211-40

Alcock, L 1987
—Pictish studies: present and future
in Small, A (ed.), 1987, 80-92

Alcock, L, Alcock, E A and Foster, S M 1987
—Reconnaissance excavations on Early Historic fortifications and other royal
sites in Scotland, 1974-84: 1, excavations near St Abb's Head,
Berwickshire, 1980
Proc Soc Antiq Scot, 116 (1986), 255-80

Allen, J R 1881
—Notice of Three Cup-marked Stones, and the Discovery of an Urn,
in Perthshire
Proc Soc Antiq Scot, 15 (1880-1), 82-92

Allen, J R 1882
—Notes on some Undescribed Stones with Cup-Markings in Scotland
Proc Soc Antiq Scot, 16 (1881-2), 79-143

Allen, J R 1883
—On the Discovery of a Sculptured Stone at St Madoes,
with an Analysis of Interlaced Ornament
Proc Soc Antiq Scot, 17 (1882-3), 211-71

Allen, J R and Anderson, J 1903
—*The Early Christian Monuments of Scotland*
Edinburgh

Anderson, A O 1922
—*Early Sources of Scottish History AD 500 to 1286*
Edinburgh and London

Anderson, J 1880
—Notice of a fragment of a silver penannular brooch, ornamented with gold
filigree work and amber settings, found at Achavrole, Dunbeath, Caithness in
1860; and of two silver brooches, the property of Andrew Heiton, FSAScot,
said to have been found in the neighbourhood of Perth
Proc Soc Antiq Scot, 14 (1879-80), 445-452

Anderson, M O 1980
—*Kings and Kingship in Early Scotland*
Edinburgh and London

Anderson, M O 1982
—Dalriada and the creation of the kingdom of the Scots
in Whitelock, D, McKitterick, R and Dumville, D (eds.) 1982, 106-32.

Atholl Muniments
—Muniments of His Grace the Duke of Atholl, Blair Castle, Perthshire

Barber, J W 1983
—The investigation of some plough truncated features at Kinloch Farm,
Collessie in Fife
Proc Soc Antiq Scot, 112 (1982), 524-33

Barclay, G J 1981
—Newmill and the "Souterrains of Southern Pictland"
Proc Soc Antiq Scot, 110 (1978-80), 200-8

Barclay, G J 1984
—Sites of the third millennium bc to the first millennium ad
at North Mains, Strathallan, Perthshire
Proc Soc Antiq Scot, 113 (1983), 122-281

Barclay, G J 1990
—The cultivation remains beneath the North Mains, Strathallan, barrow
Proc Soc Antiq Scot, 119 (1989), 59-61

Barclay, G J, Brooks, M and Rideout, J 1983
—The cup and ring marked stone
at Newbigging Farm, Perth and Kinross District, Tayside Region
Proc Soc Antiq Scot, 112 (1982), 559-61

Barclay, G J and Maxwell, G S 1992
—Excavation of a Neolithic long mortuary enclosure within the
Roman legionary fortress at Inchtuthil, Perthshire
Proc Soc Antiq Scot, 121 (1991), 27-41

Barclay, G J and Russell-White, C (eds.) (forthcoming)
—Excavations in the ceremonial complex of the fourth to second millennium BC
at Balfarg/Balbirnie, Glenrothes, Fife

Barnatt, J 1989
—*Stone Circles of Britain*
Brit Archaeol Rep, Brit Ser 215
Oxford

Barrow, G W S 1983
—The childhood of Scottish Christianity: a note on some place-name evidence
Scottish Studies, 27 (1983), 1-15

Baxter, G C 1892
—Some Unrecorded Relics in the Parishes of Cargill,
Scone and St Martins
Proc Soc Antiq Scot, 26 (1891-2), 221-4

Baxter, G C 1897
—Notice of a Cup-marked Stone recently found at Gallow Hill,
Parish of Cargill
Proc Soc Antiq Scot, 31 (1896-7), 290-2

Boethius (Boece), H 1526
—*Scotorum Historia*
Paris

Brooks, C M 1980
—Medieval pottery from the kiln site at Colstoun, E. Lothian
Proc Soc Antiq Scot, 110 (1978-80), 364-403

Brown, T 1808
—Survey of the Invercauld Estate
SRO, RHP.3896

Brown, T 1873
—Notes Relating to Dunsinnane Hill
Proc Soc Antiq Scot, 9 (1870-2), 378-80

Burgess, C 1976
—Meldon Bridge: a Neolithic defended promontory complex near Peebles
in Burgess, C and Miket, R (eds.) 1976, 151-79

Burgess, C 1990
—The Chronology of Cup-and-Ring Marks in Britain and Ireland
Northern Archaeology, 10 (1989-90), 21-6

Burgess, C and Miket, R (eds.) 1976
—*Settlement and Economy in the third and second millennium B.C.*
Brit Archaeol Rep, Brit Ser 33
Oxford

Burl, H A W 1976
—*The Stone Circles of the British Isles*
Yale

Burl, H A W 1985
—Report on the excavation of a Neolithic mound at Boghead,
Speymouth Forest, Fochabers, Moray, 1972 and 1974
Proc Soc Antiq Scot, 114 (1984), 35-73

Caldwell, D H 1988
—The use and effect of weapons: the Scottish experience
Rec Scot Culture, 4 (1988), 53-62

Callander, J G 1918
—Three Food-Vessel Urns, a Cup-Marked Stone, and Other Objects
discovered at Sheriffton, near Perth
Proc Soc Antiq Scot, 52 (1917-18), 131-9

Callander, J G 1919a
—Discovery of (1) A Short Cist containing Human Remains and a Bronze
Armlet, and (2) a Cup-marked Stone, at Williamstone, St Martins, Perthshire
Proc Soc Antiq Scot, 53 (1918-19), 15-24

Callander, J G 1919b
—Notes on the Roman remains at Grassy Walls and Bertha near Perth
Proc Soc Antiq Scot, 53 (1918-19), 145-52

Cardonnel, Adam de 1788
—*Picturesque Antiquities of Scotland*
London

Caseldine, C 1979
—Early Land Clearance in South-east Perthshire
Scot Archaeol Forum, 9 (1977), 1-15

Caseldine, C 1983
—Palynological evidence for early cereal cultivation in Strathearn
Proc Soc Antiq Scot, 112 (1982), 39-47

Chalmers, G 1887
—*Caledonia,* I
Paisley

Chalmers, P 1848
—*The Ancient and Sculptured Monuments of the County of Angus*
Edinburgh

Childe, V G 1933
—Excavations at Castlelaw Fort, Midlothian
Proc Soc Antiq Scot, 67 (1932-3), 362-88

Christison, D 1898
—*Early Fortifications in Scotland*
Edinburgh

Christison, D 1900
—The Forts, 'Camps', and other Field-works of Perth, Forfar and Kincardine
Proc Soc Antiq Scot, 34 (1899-1900), 43-120

Chron. Melrose
—*The Chronicle of Melrose* (Facsimile Edition)
Anderson, A O and others (eds.) 1936
London

Clarke, D L 1970
—*Beaker Pottery of Great Britain and Ireland*
Cambridge

Clarke, D V 1971
—Small Finds in the Atlantic Province: Problems of Approach
Scot Archaeol Forum, 3 (1971), 22-54

Close-Brooks, J 1978
—New finds of late bronze-age spearheads from Scotland
Proc Soc Antiq Scot, 107 (1975-6), 310-13

Close-Brooks, J 1981
—Excavations in the Dairy Park, Dunrobin, Sutherland, 1977
Proc Soc Antiq Scot, 110 (1978-80), 328-345

Close-Brooks, J 1984
—Pictish and other burials
in Friell, J G P and Watson, W G (eds.) 1984, 145-50

Coates, H 1919
—Note on Stone Cists found at Flawcraig and Burnfoot, in the Carse of Gowrie
Trans Proc Perthshire Soc Natur Sci, 6 (1914-18), 149-50

Coles, F R 1908
—Report on Stone Circles surveyed in Perthshire — North Eastern Section;
with measured Plans and Drawings (obtained under the Gunner Fellowship)
Proc Soc Antiq Scot, 42 (1907-8), 95-162

Coles, F R 1909
—Report on Stone Circles surveyed in Perthshire (South-east District),
with measured Plans and Drawings; (obtained under the Gunning Fellowship)
Proc Soc Antiq Scot, 43 (1908-9), 93-130

Coles, J M 1962
—Scottish Late Bronze Age Metalwork: Typology, Distributions and Chronolgy
Proc Soc Antiq Scot, 93 (1959-60), 16-134

Coles, J M 1966
—Scottish Middle Bronze Age Metalwork
Proc Soc Antiq Scot, 97 (1963-4), 82-156

Coles, J M 1971a
—Scottish Early Bronze Age Metalwork
Proc Soc Antiq Scot, 101 (1968-9), 1-110

Coles, J M 1971b
—The early settlement of Scotland: excavations at Morton, Fife
Proc Prehist Soc, 37, part 2 (1971), 284-366

Coles, J M and Simpson, D D A 1965
—The Excavation of a Neolithic Round Barrow at Pitnacree, Perthshire
Proc Prehist Soc, 31 (1965), 34-57

Colvin, H and Harris, J (eds.) 1970
—*The Country Seat*
London

Coppock, J T 1976
—*An Agricultural Atlas of Scotland*
Edinburgh

Cottam, M B and Small, A 1974
—The distribution of settlement in southern Pictland
Medieval Archaeol, 18 (1974), 43-65

Coupar Angus Charters
—D E Easson (ed.) 1947
Scottish History Society
Edinburgh

Coupar Angus Rental
—*Rental Book of the Cistercian Abbey of Cupar-Angus*
C Rogers (ed.) 1879-80
Grampian Club
London

Coutts, H 1966
—Recent discoveries of Short Cists in Angus and East Perthshire
Proc Soc Antiq Scot, 97 (1963-4), 157-65

Coutts, H 1970
—*Ancient Monuments of Tayside*
Dundee

Coutts, H 1971
—*Tayside before History*
Dundee

Cowan, I B 1967
—*The Parishes of Medieval Scotland*
Scottish Record Society, 93
Edinburgh

Cowan, I B and Easson, D E 1976
—*Medieval Religious Houses; Scotland*
2nd ed., London

Cowan, S 1904
—*The Ancient Capital of Scotland*
London

Cowie, T G 1978
—*Bronze Age Food Vessel Urns*
Brit Archaeol Rep, Brit Ser 55
Oxford

Cowie, T G 1992
—Neolithic pottery from Barbush Quarry, Dunblane, Perthshire,
with notes on the Earlier Neolithic pottery of eastern and central Scotland
in Sharples, N and Sheridan, A (eds.) 1992, 272-85

Cowie, T G and Reid, A 1987
—Some recent finds of Bronze-Age metalwork from Perthshire
Proc Soc Antiq Scot, 116 (1986), 69-88

Crawford, O G S 1939
—Air Reconnaissance of Roman Scotland
Antiquity, 13 (1939), 280-92

Crawford, O G S 1949
—*Topography of Roman Scotland North of the Antonine Wall*
Cambridge

Cruden, S 1957
—*The Early Christian and Pictish Monuments of Scotland.*
An illustrated introduction, with an illustrated and descriptive catalogue of the
Meigle Collection in Perthshire
Edinburgh

Cruden, S 1964
—*The Early Christian and Pictish Monuments of Scotland.*
An illustrated introduction with illustrated and descriptive catalogues of the
Meigle and St Vigeans collections
2nd ed., Edinburgh

Curle, J 1932
—An Inventory of Objects of Roman and Provincial Origin found on Sites in
Scotland not definitely associated with Roman constructions
Proc Soc Antiq Scot, 66 (1931-2), 277-397

Davidson, J L and Henshall, A S 1984
—A Neolithic chambered long cairn at Edinchip, Perthshire
Proc Soc Antiq Scot, 113 (1983), 35-9

Davies, W 1982
—The Latin charter-tradition in western Britain, Brittany and Ireland in the early
medieval period
in Whitelock, D, McKitterick, R and Dumville, D (eds.) 1982, 258-80

Defoe, D 1968
—*A Tour thro' the Whole Island of Great Britain*
London (Reprint of 1724-26 ed.)

DES (date)
—*Discovery and Excavation in Scotland (date)*
Council for Scottish Archaeology

Dicks, B 1983
—The Scottish medieval town a search for origins
in Gordon, G and Dicks, B (eds.) 1983, 23-51

Disposition, P Lawson 1818
—Disposition Patrick Lawson to Thomas Chrichton
in Liferent and James Chrichton in fee, 1818
McCash and Hunter Solicitors, 25 Methven Street, Perth

Dixon, P J 1988
—*Springwood Park Excavation* Interim Report, March 1988
Border Architects Group

Dixon, T N and Andrian, B L 1991
—Underwater Survey: Loch of Clunie
The Scottish Trust for Underwater Archaeology
unpublished report in NMRS

Dodgshon, R A 1980
—Medieval Settlement and Colonisation
in Parry, M L and Slater, T R (eds.) 1980, 45-68

Dodgshon, R A 1981
—*Land and Society in Early Scotland*
Oxford

Donnachie, I L and Stuart, N K 1967
—Scottish windmills: an outline and inventory
Proc Soc Antiq Scot, 98 (1965-6), 276-99

Douglas, R 1798
—*The Baronage of Scotland*
Edinburgh

Driscoll, S T 1987
—The Early Historic Landscape of Strathearn:
the archaeology of a Pictish kingdom
unpublished PhD dissertation, University of Glasgow

Dunbar, J G 1966
—*The Historic Architecture of Scotland*
London

Dunbar, J G and Duncan, A A M 1971
—Tarbert Castle: a contribution to the history of Argyll
Scot Hist Rev, 50 (1971), 1-17

Duncan, W M 1979
—*Newtyle, a planned manufacturing village*
Coupar Angus

Dunkeld Rentale
—see Hannay, R K (ed.) 1915

DUNMG
—Dundee Art Galleries and Museums

Easson, D E (ed.) 1947
—*Charters of the Abbey of Coupar Angus*
Edinburgh

Edwards, K J and Ralston, I B M 1985
—Postglacial hunter-gatherers and vegetational history in Scotland
Proc Soc Antiq Scot, 114 (1984), 15-34

Eeles, F C 1915
—A note on the cathedral church
in Hannay, R K (ed.) 1915

Evans, J G, Limbrey, S and Cleere, H (eds.) 1975
—The Effect of Man on the Landscape: the Highland Zone
CBA Res Rep 11

Fanning, T 1983
—Some aspects of the bronze ringed pin in Scotland
in O'Connor, A and Clarke, D V (eds.) 1983, 324-42

Feachem, R W 1966
—The Hillforts of Northern Britain
in Rivet, A L F (ed.) 1966, 59-87

Feachem, R W 1977
—*Guide to Prehistoric Scotland*
2nd ed., London

Fisher, I and Greenhill, F A 1974
—Two unrecorded carved stones at Tower of Lethendy, Perthshire
Proc Soc Antiq Scot, 104 (1971-2), 238-41

Foster, S M and Stevenson, J B (forthcoming)
—Neolithic discoveries in Central Region, Scotland:
Britain's longest cairn and a close parallel to the house at Balbridie

Fraser, W 1878
—Notice of a Small Urn, of the so-called 'Incense Cup' type, found within a
large Urn at Blairgowrie in March last, and now presented to the Museum
Proc Soc Antiq Scot, 12 (1876-8), 624

Friell, J G P and Watson, W G (eds.) 1984
—*Pictish Studies: Settlement, Burial and Art in Dark*
Age Northern Britain
Brit Archaeol Rep, Brit Ser 125
Oxford

GAGM
—Glasgow Art Gallery and Museum, Kelvingrove

Galloway, W 1878
—Notice of several sculptured stones at Meigle,
Perthshire, still undescribed
Proc Soc Antiq Scot, 12 (1876-8), 425-34

Glasgow Art Gallery and Museum 1951
—*Scotland's Ancient Treasures. From the National Museum of*
Antiquities, Exhibited in Kelvingrove Museum, Glasgow, 1951

Gibson, A 1988
—*The Essendy Road Stones*
Blairgowrie

Gordon, A 1726
—*Itinerarium Septentrionale: or, a Journey through most of*
the Counties of Scotland and those in the North of England
London

Gordon, G and Dicks, B (eds.) 1983
—*Scottish Urban History*
Aberdeen

Graham, A 1973
—Records and Opinions: 1780-1930
Proc Soc Antiq Scot, 102 (1969-70), 241-285

Grant, F J 1952
—*The Manual of Heraldry*
Edinburgh

Greenhill, F A 1944
—Notes on Scottish Incised Slabs (I)
Proc Soc Antiq Scot, 78 (1943-4), 80-91

Greenhill, F A 1958
—*The Incised Slabs of Leicestershire and Rutland*
Leicester

Grieg, S 1940
—Viking Antiquities in Scotland
in H Shetelig (ed.) 1940, 1-206

Guilbert, G (ed.) 1981
—*Hill-fort Studies*
Leicester

Hannay, R K (ed.) 1915
—*Rentale Dunkeldense, being accounts of the bishopric (AD 1505-1517)*
with Myln's 'Lives of the Bishops' (AD 1483-1517).
And a note on the Cathedral Church by FC Eeles
Edinburgh

Hanson, W S 1987
—*Agricola and the Conquest of the North*
London

Hanson, W and Maxwell, G S 1983
—*Rome's North-west Frontier*
Edinburgh

Harbison, P 1971
—Wooden and Stone *Chevaux-de-frise* in Central and Western Europe
Proc Prehist Soc, 37, part 1 (1971), 195-225

Harding, D W (ed.) 1982
—*Later Prehistoric Settlement in South-east Scotland*
University of Edinburgh Occasional Paper No. 8
Edinburgh

Headrick, J 1813
—*General View of the Agriculture of the County of*
Angus, or Forfarshire
Edinburgh

Henderson, I 1967
—*The Picts*
London

Henderson, I 1975
—Pictish Territorial Divisions
in McNeill, P and Nicholson, R (eds.) 1975, 9-10

Henderson, I 1978
—Sculpture north of the Forth
in Lang, J (ed.) 1978, 47-74

Henderson, I 1982
—Pictish Art and the Book of Kells
in Whitelock, D, McKitterick, R and Dumville, D (eds.) 1982, 79-105

Henderson, I 1986
—The 'David Cycle' in Pictish Art
in Higgitt, J (ed.) 1986, 87-124

Henderson, I 1990
—*The Art and Function of Rosemarkie's Pictish Monuments*
Groam House Museum Trust
Rosemarkie

Higgitt, J (ed.) 1986
—*Early Medieval Sculpture in Britain and Ireland*
Brit Archaeol Rep, Brit Ser 152
Oxford

Hill, P H 1982
—Settlement and chronology
in Harding, D W (ed.) 1982, 4-43

Hind, J G F 1984
—Caledonia and its occupation under the Flavians
Proc Soc Antiq Scot, 113 (1983), 373-8

Hume Brown, P 1891
—*Early Travellers in Scotland*
Edinburgh

Hunter, T 1883
—*Woods, Forests, and Estates of Perthshire*
Perth

Hutcheson, A 1884
—Notice of a Cup and Ring-Marked Stone, and of Incised Stones recently
discovered at Cargill, and of an Incised Boulder at Fowlis Wester
Proc Soc Antiq Scot, 18 (1883-4), 313-18

Hutcheson, A 1886
—Notice of the discovery of a stratum containing worked flints
at Broughty Ferry
Proc Soc Antiq Scot, 20 (1885-6), 166-9

Hutcheson, A 1888
—Notes of the Recent Discovery of Pavement and Flooring Tiles at the Abbey of
Coupar-Angus and the Cathedral of St Andrews
Proc Soc Antiq Scot, 22 (1887-8), 146-8

Hutcheson, A 1889
—Notice of Cup-Marked Stone found at Williamston, in the Parish of St Martins,
Perthshire
Proc Soc Antiq Scot, 23 (1888-9), 142-3

Hutcheson, A 1894
—Notice of the Bell and other Antiquities at the Church of Kettins, Forfarshire
Proc Soc Antiq Scot, 28 (1893-4), 90-100

Hutcheson, A 1904
—Notice of the Discovery of the Remains of an Earth-house at Barnhill, Perth
Proc Soc Antiq Scot, 38 (1903-4), 541-47

Hutcheson, A 1908
—Notes on the Discovery of the Remains of an Earth-house at Barnhill, Perth
Trans Proc Perthshire Soc Natur Sci, 4 (1904-8), 96-100

Jackson, A 1984
—*The Symbol Stones of Scotland*
Stromness

Jackson, K H 1954
—Two early Scottish names
Scot Hist Rev, 33 (1954), 14-18

Jackson, KH 1955
—The Pictish Language
in Wainwright, F T (ed.) 1955, 129-66

Jervise, A 1853
—*The History and Traditions of the Land of the Lindsays in Angus and Mearns,*
with Notices of Alyth and Meigle
Edinburgh

Jervise, A 1859
—Notices Descriptive of the Localities of Certain Sculptured
Stone Monuments in Forfarshire, etc., — Meigle, Essie, Glamis,
Thornton, and Cossins. Part II
Proc Soc Antiq Scot, 2 (1854-7), 242-51

Jervise, A 1861
—*Memorials of Angus and the Mearns*
Edinburgh

Jervise, A 1882
—*The History and Traditions of the Land of the Lindsays in Angus and Mearns with Notices of Alyth and Meigle*
2nd ed., Edinburgh

Jones, R J A and Evans, R 1975
—Soil and crop marks in the recognition of archaeological sites by air photography
in Wilson, D R (ed.) 1975, 1-11

Kendrick, J 1980
—Douglasmuir: the excavations of an early iron age settlement and a neolithic enclosure 1979-1980
unpublished preliminary report

Kendrick, J 1982
—Excavations at Douglasmuir
in Harding, D W (ed.) 1982, 136-40

Kinloch, K M 1888
—Notes concerning the family of Kinloch of Gourdie
unpublished typescript in NMRS
NMRS, DS/PT[P]

Kinnes, I 1979
—*Round Barrows and Ring-ditches in the British Neolithic*
British Museum Occasional Paper 7
London

Kinnes, I 1987
—Circumstance not context: the Neolithic of Scotland as seen from the outside
Proc Soc Antiq Scot, 115 (1985), 15-57

Knox, J 1831
—*The Topography of the Basin of the Tay*
Edinburgh

Laing, L R 1971
—Pottery from Kinnoull, Perth, and the distribution of tubular spouts in Scotland
Proc Soc Antiq Scot, 103 (1970-1), 236-9

Lang, J T 1975
—Hogback monuments in Scotland
Proc Soc Antiq Scot, 105 (1972-4), 206-35

Lang, L (ed.) 1978
—*Anglo-Saxon and Viking Age Sculpture*
Brit Archaeol Rep, Brit Ser 49
Oxford

Lawrie, A C 1905
—*Early Scottish Charters Prior to 1153*
Glasgow

Lesslie, J 1763
—A Plan of the Farm of Whiteley in the Barony of Stobhall
SRO, RHP.3410

Longworth, I H 1984
—*Collared Urns of the Bronze Age in Great Britain and Ireland*
Cambridge

Loveday, R 1985
—Cursuses and Related Monuments of the British Neolithic
unpublished PhD thesis, University of Leicester

Lye, D M and Fisher, I 1982
—A cross-slab from New Scone, Perthshire
Proc Soc Antiq Scot, 111 (1981), 521-3

Macdonald, G 1919
—The Agricolan occupation of North Britain
J Roman Stud, 9 (1919), 113-22

MacDonald, A 1973
—Annat in Scotland: a provisional review
Scot Stud, 17 (1973), 135-46

Macfarlane, W 1906
—*Geographical Collections Relating to Scotland,* 1
Mitchell, A (ed.)
Edinburgh

MacGibbon, D and Ross, T 1887
—*The Castellated and Domestic Architecture of Scotland from the Twelfth to the Eighteenth Century,* 2
Edinburgh

MacGibbon, D and Ross, T 1889
—*The Castellated and Domestic Architecture of Scotland from the Twelfth to the Eighteenth Century,* 3
Edinburgh

MacGibbon, D and Ross, T 1892
—*The Castellated and Domestic Architecture of Scotland from the Twelfth to the Eighteenth Century,* 4
Edinburgh

MacGibbon, D and Ross, T 1897
—*The Ecclesiastical Architecture of Scotland,* 3
Edinburgh

Mackay, A 1876
—*Meigle: past and present*
Arbroath

Mackenna, F S 1972
—Recovery of an Earth House
The Kist, 4 (1972), 16-20

MacKie, E W 1969
—Radiocarbon dates and the Scottish Iron Age
Antiquity, 43 (1969), 15-26

MacKie, E W 1973
—Duntreath
Curr Archaeol, 36 (1973), 6-7

MacRitchie, D 1900
—Description of an Earth-House at Pitcur, Forfarshire
Proc Soc Antiq Scot, 34 (1899-1900), 202-14

Maitland, W 1757
—*The History and Antiquities of Scotland*
London

Mann, J C and Breeze, D J 1988
—Ptolemy, Tacitus and the tribes of north Britain
Proc Soc Antiq Scot, 117 (1987), 85-92

Manning, W H 1975
—Roman military timber granaries in Britain
Saalburg Jahrbuch, 32 (1975), 105-29

Marshall, D N 1979
—Carved Stone Balls
Proc Soc Antiq Scot, 108 (1976-7), 40-72

Mathewson, A 1879
—Notes on Stone Cists and an Ancient Kitchen Midden near Dundee
Proc Soc Antiq Scot, 13 (1878-9), 303-7

Maxwell, G S 1969
—Excavations at Drumcarrow, Fife: an Iron Age Unenclosed Settlement
Proc Soc Antiq Scot, 100 (1967-8), 100-8

Maxwell, G S 1981
—Agricola's campaigns: the evidence of the temporary camps
Scot Archaeol Forum, 12 (1980), 25-54

Maxwell, G S 1983
—Recent Aerial Survey in Scotland
in Maxwell, G S (ed.) 1983, 27-40

Maxwell, G S (ed.) 1983
—*The Impact of Aerial Reconnaissance on Archaeology*
CBA Res Rep 49
London

Maxwell, G S 1987
—Settlement in Southern Pictland — A New Overview
in Small, A (ed.) 1987, 31-44

Maxwell, G S 1989
—*The Romans in Scotland*
Edinburgh

Maxwell, G S 1990
—*A Battle Lost: Romans and Caledonians at Mons Graupius*
Edinburgh

Maxwell, G S and Wilson, D R 1987
—Air Reconnaissance in Roman Britain, 1977-84
Britannia, 18 (1987), 1-48

McNeill, P and Nicholson, R (eds.) 1975
—*An Historical Atlas of Scotland c.400 - c.1600*
St Andrews

McOmie, J 1784
—Plan of the Roman Wall and Camp near Mickleour
Manuscript copy in Perth Museum

McPeake, J C M and Moore, C N 1978
—A bronze skillet-handle from Chester and other vessels from the British Isles
Britannia, 9 (1978), 331-4

Meacher, A J 1905
—'Inventory of Titles belonging to the estate of Marlee',
inventoried by A J Meacher in the year 1905
Marlee Muniments

Meacher, A J 1956
—*History of the Lands of Kinloch*
Edinburgh

Megaw, J V S and Simpson, D D A (eds.) 1979
—*Introduction to British Prehistory*
Leicester

Meikle, J 1925
—*Place Names around Alyth*

Melville, L 1935
—*Errol: its Legends, Lands and People*
Perth

Melville, L 1939
—*The Fair Land of Gowrie*
Coupar Angus

Mercer, R J 1988
—Sketewan, Balnaguard, Perthshire
University of Edinburgh, Department of Archaeology,
34th Annual Report, 26-27

Millar, A H 1890
—*The Historical Castle and Mansions of Scotland, Perthshire and Forfarshire*
Paisley and London

Mowat, R J C (forthcoming)
—The Logboats of Scotland with notes on related artefact types

Murray, D 1991
—Square-ditched Barrows and Enclosures
in Forays into Fife, 35-9
Privately circulated papers. NMRS

Myln's *Vitae*
—*Vitae Episcoporum Dunkeldensium*
in Hannay, R K (ed.) 1915, 302-34

NMRS
—National Monuments Record of Scotland

NMS
—National Museum of Scotland, Queen Street, Edinburgh

NSA
—*The New Statistical Account of Scotland*
1845, Edinburgh

Name Book (County)
—Original Name Books of the Ordnance Survey

Nicolaisen, W F H 1979
—*Scottish Place-names, their study and significance*
London

O'Connor, A and Clarke, D V (eds.) 1983
—*From the Stone Age to the 'Forty-Five*
Edinburgh

Omand, D (ed.) 1987
—*The Grampian Book*
Golspie

OS
—Ordnance Survey

Padel, O 1972
—Inscriptions of Pictland
unpublished M.Litt. thesis, University of Edinburgh

***Palace of History* 1911**
—Catalogue of exhibits for the Scottish exhibition of national history, art
and industry

Parry, M L and Slater, T R (eds.) 1980
—*The Making of the Scottish Countryside*
London

Patullo, N 1974
—*Castles, Houses and Gardens of Scotland,* 2
Edinburgh

Paul, B 1983
—Old Mains of Rattray, a study of an independent Scottish farmhouse
unpublished dissertation, Department of Architecture, University of Dundee

Paul, J B (ed.) 1906
—*The Scots Peerage*
Founded on Wood's Edition of Sir Robert Douglas's Peerage of Scotland
Containing an Historical and Genealogical Account of the Nobility of that
Kingdom, 3
Edinburgh

Paul, J B (ed.) 1907
—*The Scots Peerage,* 4
Edinburgh

Paul, J B (ed.) 1908
—*The Scots Peerage,* 5
Edinburgh

Paul, J B (ed.) 1910
—*The Scots Peerage,* 7
Edinburgh

Paul, J B (ed.) 1911
—*The Scots Peerage,* 8
Edinburgh

Pearce, S M (ed.) 1982
—The Early Church in Western Britain and Ireland.
Studies Presented to C A Ralegh Radford
Brit Archaeol Rep, Brit Ser 102
Oxford

Pennant, T 1776
—*A Tour in Scotland 1772,* 2
London

Perry, D R 1988
—*Pitmiddle Village and Elcho Nunnery*
Perthshire Soc Natur Sci
Perth

PMAG
—Perth Museum and Art Gallery

Piggott, S 1974
—Excavation of the Dalladies long barrow, Fettercairn, Kincardineshire
Proc Soc Antiq Scot, 104 (1971-2), 23-47

Pitts, L F and St Joseph, J K S 1985
—*Inchtuthil: the Roman Legionary Fortress: excavations 1952-65*
Britannia Monograph Series No. 6
London

Platt, C P S 1969
—*The Monastic Grange in Medieval England*
London

Playfair, J 1819
—*Description of Scotland*
Edinburgh

Pococke, R 1887
—*Tours in Scotland 1747, 1750, 1760*
D W Kemp (ed.), Scot Hist Soc, i
Edinburgh

Pollock, D 1987
—The Lunan Valley Project: medieval rural settlement in Angus
Proc Soc Antiq Scot, 115 (1985), 357-400

Pryde, G S 1965
—*The Burghs of Scotland: a Critical List*
Oxford

Ralston, I B M 1982
—A timber hall at Balbridie farm: the Neolithic settlement of
North East Scotland
Aberdeen University Review, 49 (1981-2), 238-49

Ralston, I and Inglis, J 1984
—*Foul Hordes: the Picts in the North-East and their background*
Anthropological Museum, University of Aberdeen

RCAHMS
—Royal Commission on the Ancient and Historical Monuments of Scotland

RCAHMS 1956
—*An Inventory of the Ancient and Historical Monuments of Roxburghshire*
Edinburgh

RCAHMS 1980
—*Catalogue of Air Photographs Taken by the
Royal Commission on the Ancient and Historical Monuments of Scotland
in 1980*
Edinburgh

RCAHMS 1982
—*South Kincardineshire*
The Archaeological Sites and Monuments Series, 15
Edinburgh

RCAHMS 1983
—*Central Angus*
The Archaeological Sites and Monuments Series, 18
Edinburgh

RCAHMS 1990
—*North-east Perth: an archaeological landscape*
Edinburgh

RCAHMS 1992
—*Dundee on Record: Images of the Past*
Edinburgh

Reg. Mag. Sig.
—*Registrum Magni Sigilli Regum Scotorum*
J M Thomson and others (eds.) 1882-1914
Edinburgh

Reg. Reg. Scot.
—*Regesta Regum Scotorum*
G W S Barrow and others (eds.) 1960-1988
Edinburgh

Reid, J J 1889
—Notice of a Fragment of a Monumental Sculptured
Stone Found at Meigle, 1888
Proc Soc Antiq Scot, 23 (1888-9), 232-4

Reid, A G, Shepherd, I A G and Lunt, D A 1987
—A beaker cist from Upper Muirhall, Perth
Proc Soc Antiq Scot, 116 (1986), 63-7

Retours 1811-16
—*Retours Inquisitionum ad Capellam Domini Regis Retornatarum quae
in Publicis Archivis Scotiae adhuc servantur, Abbreviatio*

Richmond, I A 1940
—Excavations on the Estate of Meikleour, Perthshire
Proc Soc Antiq Scot, 74 (1939-40), 37-48

Richmond, I A 1943
—Recent discoveries in Roman Britain from the air and in the field
J Roman Stud, 33 (1943), 45-54

Richmond, I A 1960
—Roman Britain in 1959
J Roman Stud, 50 (1960), 210-42

Ritchie, A 1989
—*Picts, an introduction to the life of the Picts and the carved
stones in the care of the Secretary of State for Scotland*
Historic Buildings and Monuments Directorate
Edinburgh

Ritchie, J 1935
—A short cist found at Bridge Farm, near Meikleour, Perthshire
Proc Soc Antiq Scot, 69 (1934-5), 401-15

Rivet, A L F (ed.) 1966
—*The Iron Age in Northern Britain*
Edinburgh

Robertson, A S 1974
—Roman 'signal stations' on the Gask Ridge
Trans Perthshire Soc Natur Sci
Special Issue, 14-29

Robertson, J 1799
—*General View of the Agriculture in the County of Perth with
Observations on the Means of its improvement*
Perth

Root, M E 1950
—*Dunkeld Cathedral*
Edinburgh

Ross, A 1967
—*Pagan Celtic Britain*
London

Roy, G 1763
—A Plan of Whitely farm
SRO, RHP.3411

Roy, W 1747-55
—Military Survey of Scotland
Photocopy in NMRS

Roy, W 1793
—*The Military Antiquities of the Romans in Britain*
London

Russell-White, C 1988
—Excavation of a Cropmark site at Balneaves, Friockheim, Angus District
*Central Excavation Unit and Ancient Monuments Laboratory
Annual Report 1988,* 14-16

St Joseph, J K S 1951
—Air reconnaissance of north Britain
J Roman Stud, 41 (1951), 52-65

St Joseph, J K S 1955
—Air reconnaissance in Britain, 1951-5
J Roman Stud, 45 (1955), 82-91

St Joseph, J K S 1958
—Air reconnaissance in Britain, 1955-7
J Roman Stud, 48 (1958), 86-101

St Joseph, J K S 1969
—Air reconnaissance in Britain, 1965-68
J Roman Stud, 59 (1969), 104-28

St Joseph, J K S 1973
—Air reconnaisance in Roman Britain, 1969-72
J Roman Stud, 63 (1973), 214-46

St Joseph, J K S 1977
—Air reconnaissance in Roman Britain
J Roman Stud, 67 (1977), 125-61

St Joseph, J K S 1987
—Air reconnaissance: recent results, 44
Antiquity, 52 (1978), 47-50

Sanderson, M H B 1982
—*Scottish Rural Society in the Sixteenth Century*
Edinburgh

Sanderson, D C W, Placido, F and Tate, J O 1988
—Scottish vitrified forts: TL results from six study sites
Int J Radiat Appl Instrum, Part D
Nucl Tracks Radiat Meas, 14, Nos.1/2 (1988), 307-16

Schrickel, W (ed.) 1971
—*Kolloquium uber spatantike und fruhmittelalterliche Skulptur,* 2
Mainz

Scone Liber
—*Liber Ecclesie de Scon, munimenta vetustiora monasterii Sancte Trinitatis et Sancti Michaelis de Scon*
Maitland Club, 1843
Edinburgh

Scott, A 1911
—*St Martins and Cambusmichael: A Parochial Retrospective*
Perth

Scott, H et al. (eds.) 1923
—*Fasti Ecclesiae Scoticanae:*
the Succession of the Ministers in the Church of Scotland
from the Reformation, 4
Edinburgh

Scott, H et al. (eds.) 1950
—*Fasti Ecclesiae Scoticanae:*
the Succession of the Ministers in the Church of Scotland
from the Reformation, 8
Edinburgh

Scott, J G 1960
—A Decorated Bronze Axehead from Perthshire
Proc Soc Antiq Scot, 91 (1957-8), 178-9

**Scottish Countryside Commission and Historic Buildings and Monuments —
Directorate, Scottish Development Department 1987**
—*An Inventory of Gardens and Designed Landscapes in Scotland,* 4
Glasgow

SRO
—Scottish Record Office

Seymour, W A (ed.) 1980
—*A History of the Ordnance Survey*
Folkestone

Sharples, N and Sheridan, A (eds.) 1992
—*Vessels for the Ancestors*
Edinburgh

Shepherd, I 1987
—The early peoples
in Omand, D (ed.) 1987, 119-30

Shetelig, H (ed.) 1940
—*Viking Antiquities in Great Britain and Ireland,* 2
Oslo

Simpson, J Y 1868
—On Ancient Sculpturings of Cups and Concentric Rings, etc
Proc Soc Antiq Scot, 6 (1864-6), Appendix, 1-147

Skene, J 1832
—Sketch plan in pencil of Dunsinane hillfort
NMRS, SAS 465, PTD/323/2

Skene, W F 1870
—The coronation stone
Proc Soc Antiq Scot, 8 (1868-70), 68-99

Slezer, J 1693
—*Theatrum Scotiae*
London

Small, A 1964
—Two Pictish Symbol Stones. (ii) Fairygreen, Collace, Perthshire
Proc Soc Antiq Scot, 95 (1961-2), 221-2

Small, A (ed.), 1987
—*The Picts: a new look at old problems*
Dundee

Smart, A T 1951
—*The Parish Church of Kettins*
Kettins

Smith, J A 1870
—Note on bronze sickles; with special reference to those found in Scotland
Proc Soc Antiq Scot, 7 (1866-8), 375-81

Smith, W C 1963
—Jade Axes from Sites in the British Isles
Proc Prehist Soc, 29 (1963), 133-72

Soil Survey of Scotland 1982
—*Soil and Land Capability for Agriculture: Eastern Scotland*
The Macaulay Institute for Soil Research, Aberdeen

Stat. Acct.
—*Statistical Account of Scotland*
1791-9, Edinburgh

Steer, K A 1958
—The Early Iron Age homestead at West Plean
Proc Soc Antiq Scot, 89 (1955-6), 227-51

Stevenson, J B 1973
—Survival and destruction
in Evans, J G, Limbrey, S and Cleere, H (eds.) 1975, 104-8

Stevenson, J B 1984
—Garbeg and Whitebridge: Two Square-Barrow Cemeteries in Inverness-shire
in Freill, J G P and Watson, W G (eds.) 1984, 145-50

Stevenson, R B K 1955
—Pictish Art
in Wainwright, F T (ed.) 1955, 97-128

Stevenson, R B K 1961
—The Inchyra Stone and other Unpublished Early Christian Monuments
Proc Soc Antiq Scot, 92 (1958-9), 33-55

Stevenson, R B K 1971
—Sculpture in Scotland in the 6th-9th centuries AD
in Schrickel, W (ed.) 1971, 65-75

Stevenson, R B K and Henshall, A S 1957
—Probable 13th-century Kiln-site at Perth
Proc Soc Antiq Scot, 90 (1956-7), 250-2

Stevenson, S J 1989
—A Kerb Cairn at Beech Hill House, Coupar Angus, Perth and Kinross
Archaeological Operations and Conservation
Annual Report 1989, 10-13

Stewart, M E C 1950
—CBA (Scottish Regional Group), Fifth Report

Stewart, M E C 1966
—Excavation of a Circle of Standing Stones at Sandy Road, Scone, Perthshire
Trans Proc Perthshire Soc Natur Sci, 11 (1963-5), 7-23

Stewart, M E C 1967
—The Excavation of a Setting of Standing Stones
at Lundin Farm near Aberfeldy, Perthshire
Proc Soc Antiq Scot, 98 (1964-6), 126-149

Stewart, M E C 1987
—The excavation of a henge, stone circles and metal-working area
at Moncrieffe, Perthshire
Proc Soc Antiq Scot, 115 (1985), 125-50

Stewart, M E C and Tabraham, C J 1974
—Excavations at Barton Hill, Kinnaird, Perthshire
Scot Archaeol Forum, 6 (1974), 58-65

STIGM
—Smith Art Gallery and Museum, Stirling

Stobie, J 1783
—*The Counties of Perth and Clackmannan*
Surveyed and Published by James Stobie
Engraved by Thomas Conder
London

Stringer, K J (ed.) 1985
—*Essays on the Nobility of Medieval Scotland*
Edinburgh

Stuart, J 1856
—*Sculptured Stones of Scotland,* 1
Aberdeen

Stuart, J 1867
—*Sculptured Stones of Scotland,* 2
Edinburgh

Stuart, J 1870a
—Notice of Letters addressed to Captain Shand, R A, by
Professor Thorkelin and General Robert Melvill, on
Roman Antiquities in the North of Scotland, 1788-1790
Proc Soc Antiq Scot, 7 (1866-68), 26-34

Stuart, J 1870b
—Note on the coronation stone
Proc Soc Antiq Scot, 8 (1868-70), 99-105

Strong, P 1987
—Investigation of plough-truncated features at South-west Fullarton Farm,
Meigle, Perthshire
Proc Soc Antiq Scot, 115 (1985), 211-21

Tavener, N 1987
—Bannockburn: The pit and post alignments excavated in 1984 and 1985
*Central Excavation Unit and Ancient Monuments Laboratory
Annual Report 1987,* 71-5

Taylor, D B 1983
—Excavation of a promontory fort, broch and souterrain at
Hurley Hawkin, Angus
Proc Soc Antiq Scot, 112 (1982), 215-253

Taylor, D B 1990
—*Circular Homesteads in North West Perthshire*
Abertay Historical Society, publication no.29
Dundee

Taylor, J J 1980
—*Bronze Age Goldwork of the British Isles*
Cambridge

Thom, A, Thom, A S and Burl, A 1980
—*Megalithic Rings*
Brit Archaeol Rep, Brit Ser 81
Oxford

Thomas, A C 1964
—The interpretation of the Pictish symbols
Archaeol J, 120 (1963), 30-97

Thoms, L M 1980
—*Some Short Cist Burials from Tayside*
Dundee Museum and Art Gallery Occas Paper, 2
Dundee

Tolan, M 1988
—Pit Circles in Scotland; Some Possible Interpretations
undergraduate dissertation, University of Newcastle

Urquhart, J D 1883
—*Historical Sketches of Scone*
Perth

Wainwright, F T (ed.) 1955
—*The Problem of the Picts*
Edinburgh

Wainwright, F T 1961
—*The Inchyra Stone*
Dundee Museum and Art Gallery
(a reprint of *Ogam,* 11 (1959), 269-78)

Wainwright, F T 1963
—*The Souterrains of Southern Pictland*
London

Walker, B 1981
—Rait, Perthshire, Scotland: An exploration in architectural archaeology.
*Permanent European Conference for the study of the rural landscape:
Collected Papers: Denmark Session, 1979,* 201-11
Geographisk Centralinstitut, Kobenhavns Universitet,
Copenhagen

Walker, B 1983
—The Agricultural Buildings of Greater Strathmore, 1770-1920
unpublished PhD dissertation, University of Dundee

Walker, B and Ritchie, G 1987
—*Exploring Scotlands' Heritage, Fife and Tayside*
Edinburgh

Walker, D 1970
—Scone Palace, Perthshire
in Colvin, H and Harris, J (eds.) 1970, 210-14

Walker, R C 1909
—Sacramount house at Bendochy
Trans Scot Ecclesiol Soc, 2 (1906-9), 391-2

Warden, A J 1880
—*Angus or Forfarshire, the Land and People,
Descriptive and Historical,* 1
Dundee

Warden, A J 1884
—*Angus or Forfarshire, the Land and People,
Descriptive and Historical,* 4
Dundee

Watkins, T 1981a
—Excavation of an Iron Age open settlement at Dalladies, Kincardineshire
Proc Soc Antiq Scot, 110 (1978-80), 122-64

Watkins, T 1981b
—Excavation of a settlement and souterrain at Newmill, near Bankfoot,
Perthshire
Proc Soc Antiq Scot, 110 (1978-80), 165-208

Watkins, T and Freeman, P 1991
—Settlement and land-use in NE Fife:
Leuchars project, Craigie Hill, North-east Fife
*University of Edinburgh, Department of Archaeology,
37th Annual Report,* 31-2

Watson, R R B 1923
—The Deuchny Hill Fort
Proc Soc Antiq Scot, 57 (1922-3), 303-7

Watson, R R B 1930a
—The Deuchny Hill Fort
Trans Proc Perthshire Soc Natur Sci
8, pt 4 (1928-9), 3-7

Watson, R R B 1930b
—Fortification or Hillfort at Arnbathie
Trans Proc Perthshire Soc Natur Sci
8, pt 6 (1928-9), 270-2

Wedderburn, L M 1973
—*Excavations at Greencairn, Cairnton of Balbegno, Fettercairn, Angus:
a preliminary report*
Dundee Museum and Art Gallery Occas Paper, 1
Dundee

Wedderburn, L M and Grime, D M 1984
—The Cairn Cemetery at Garbeg, Drumnadrochit
in Freill, J G P and Watson, W G (eds.) 1984, 151-67

Whitelock, D, McKitterick, R and Dumville, D (eds.) 1982
—*Ireland in Medieval Europe*
Cambridge

Whittington, G 1977
—Placenames and the settlement pattern of dark-age Scotland
Proc Soc Antiq Scot, 106 (1974-5), 99-110

Whittington, G and Soulsby, J A 1968
—A preliminary report on an investigation into *pit-* place-names
Scot Geogr Mag, 34 (1968), 117-25

Willsher, B 1987
—Scottish Gravestones, Perthshire
unpublished manuscript in NMRS

Wilson, D 1851
—*The Archaeology and Prehistoric Annals of Scotland*
Edinburgh

Wilson, D 1863
—*Prehistoric Annals of Scotland,* 1 and 2
London

Wilson, D R (ed.) 1975
—*Aerial Reconnaissance in Archaeology*
CBA Research Report 12

Wilson, D R 1982
—*Air Photo Interpretation for Archaeologists*
London

Winter, T 1756
—A Plan of Abernyte, the Property of James Morray of Abercairny
SRO, RHP.1005

Wise, T A 1859
Notice of Recent Excavations in the Hill Fort of Dunsinane, Perthshire
Proc Soc Antiq Scot, 2 (1854-7), 93-9

Young, A 1938
—Cup and Ring-markings on Craig Ruenshin, with some Comparative Notes
Proc Soc Antiq Scot, 72 (1937-8), 143-9

Youngs, S (ed.) 1990
—*'The work of Angels': masterpieces of Celtic Metalwork, 6th-9th centuries AD*
London

INDEX

Printed in Scotland for HMSO by (22926) Dd287452 C7 2/94